Land Squandering and Social Crisis in the Spanish City

Land Squandering and Social Crisis in the Spanish City

Special Issue Editors

Jesús M. González-Pérez
Francisco Cebrián-Abellán
María José Piñeira-Mantiñán

MDPI • Basel • Beijing • Wuhan • Barcelona • Belgrade

MDPI

Special Issue Editors

Jesús M. González-Pérez
University of the Balearic Islands
Spain

Francisco Cebrián-Abellán
Castilla-La Mancha University
Spain

María José Piñeira-Mantiñán
University of Santiago de Compostela
Spain

Editorial Office
MDPI
St. Alban-Anlage 66
4052 Basel, Switzerland

This is a reprint of articles from the Special Issue published online in the open access journal *Urban Science* (ISSN 2413-8851) from 2018 to 2019 (available at: https://www.mdpi.com/journal/urbansci/special_issues/land_squandering_social_crisis).

For citation purposes, cite each article independently as indicated on the article page online and as indicated below:

LastName, A.A.; LastName, B.B.; LastName, C.C. Article Title. *Journal Name* **Year**, *Article Number, Page Range.*

ISBN 978-3-03897-946-3 (Pbk)
ISBN 978-3-03897-947-0 (PDF)

Contents

About the Special Issue Editors vii

Francisco Cebrián-Abellán, María José Piñeira-Mantiñán and Jesús M. González-Pérez
Readings of the Post-Crisis Spanish City: Between Social Inequity and Territorial Destruction
Reprinted from: *Urban Science* **2019**, 3, 43, doi:10.3390/urbansci3020043 1

Francisco Cebrián Abellán and Irene Sánchez Ondoño
Urban Sprawl in Inner Medium-Sized Cities: The Behaviour in Some Spanish Cases Since the
Beginning of the 21st Century
Reprinted from: *Urban Science* **2019**, 3, 10, doi:10.3390/urbansci3010010 8

Irene Sánchez Ondoño and Luis Alfonso Escudero Gómez
Land Squandering in the Spanish Medium Sized Cities: The Case of Toledo
Reprinted from: *Urban Science* **2019**, 3, 16, doi:10.3390/urbansci3010016 25

Arlinda García-Coll and Cristina López-Villanueva
The Impact of Economic Crisis in Areas of Sprawl in Spanish Cities
Reprinted from: *Urban Science* **2018**, 2, 113, doi:10.3390/urbansci2040113 42

Joan Checa and Oriol Nel·lo
Urban Intensities. The Urbanization of the Iberian Mediterranean Coast in the Light of
Nighttime Satellite Images of the Earth
Reprinted from: *Urban Science* **2018**, 2, 115, doi:10.3390/urbansci2040115 61

Álvaro-Francisco Morote, Jorge Olcina, Antonio-Manuel Rico and María Hernández
Water Management in Urban Sprawl Typologies in the City of Alicante (Southern Spain):
New Trends and Perception after the Economic Crisis?
Reprinted from: *Urban Science* **2019**, 3, 7, doi:10.3390/urbansci3010007 78

Elia Canosa Zamora and Ángela García Carballo
The Failure of Eco-Neighborhood Projects in the City of Madrid (Spain)
Reprinted from: *Urban Science* **2018**, 2, 111, doi:10.3390/urbansci2040111 96

Roxana-Diana Ilisei and Julia Salom-Carrasco
Urban Projects and Residential Segregation: A Case Study of the Cabanyal Neighborhood in
Valencia (Spain)
Reprinted from: *Urban Science* **2018**, 2, 119, doi:10.3390/urbansci2040119 120

Juan M. Parreño-Castellano, Josefina Domínguez-Mujica, Maite Armengol-Martín,
Tanausú Pérez García and Jordi Boldú Hernández
Foreclosures and Evictions in Las Palmas de Gran Canaria during the Economic Crisis and
Post-Crisis Period in Spain
Reprinted from: *Urban Science* **2018**, 2, 109, doi:10.3390/urbansci2040109 139

Antonio Palacios, Ana Mellado and Yazmín León
Qualitative Methodologies for the Analysis of Intra-Urban Socio-Environmental Vulnerability
in Barcelona (Spain): Case Studies
Reprinted from: *Urban Science* **2018**, 2, 116, doi:10.3390/urbansci2040116 154

Aina Gomà Garcia and Joel Muñoz Aranda
Segregated in the City, Separated in the School. The Reproduction of Social Inequality through
the School System
Reprinted from: *Urban Science* **2018**, 2, 112, doi:10.3390/urbansci2040112 . . . . **168**

Luis del Romero Renau
Touristification, Sharing Economies and the New Geography of Urban Conflicts
Reprinted from: *Urban Science* **2018**, 2, 104, doi:10.3390/urbansci2040104 . . . . **181**

Víctor Jiménez and Antonio-José Campesino
The Clandestine Transition towards an Unsustainable Urban Model in Extremadura, Spain
Reprinted from: *Urban Science* **2018**, 2, 103, doi:10.3390/urbansci2040103 . . . . **198**

About the Special Issue Editors

Jesús M. González-Pérez has a Ph.D. in Geography and has been an Associate Professor at the University of the Balearic Islands (Spain), Assistant Professor in the Master of Spatial Planning and Environmental Management of the University of Barcelona (Spain), and Visiting Scholar (2015) and Visiting Professor (2016) at Stanford University. He has also been a visiting researcher at thirteen European and American universities. He has contributed as author to more than 150 national and international publications. He was a member of a research team that has undertaken a total of 30 funded research projects. Dr. González is currently Chairman of the Urban Geography Group of the Association of Spanish Geographers and a member of the Urban Geography Commission of the International Geographical Union. Professor González is an expert evaluator for different Spanish scientific agencies. He is also a member of the scientific or editorial committees of seven international journals and a reviewer for another 30.

Francisco Cebrián Abellán has a Ph.D. in Geography. He has been an Associate Professor and Director of the Master Degree in Rural Tourism and Local Development at the Castilla–La Mancha University. He has been a visiting scholar, visiting researcher, and visiting professor at different European, North American, and Latin American universities. He has contributed as an author to more than 50 book chapters and more than 60 congress contributions, and he has written 23 articles in specialized journals. He has taken part as a researcher in 15 national and international research projects. At the moment, he leads one that pays attention to urban sprawl in medium-sized Spanish cities. He is currently Chairman of the Latin American Group of the Association of Spanish Geographers. He is an expert for different Spanish scientific agencies, and he is a reviewer and member of the editorial board of different geographic journals.

María José Piñeira-Mantiñán has a Ph.D. in Geography. She is Lecturer Professor at the Department of Geography, in the University of Santiago de Compostela. She has experience teaching in Spanish and foreign universities, both in undergraduate courses, as in the third cycle in Galicia, Portugal, Brazil and Barcelona. She has participated in 35 projects and contracts under public funding which. At the moment, she leads one that pays attention to rehabilitation processes in historic cities, the impact of housing bubble in Spain, smart cities, poverty and social exclusion in the cities. She has stayed as researcher in foreign research institutes (Norway, Ecuador, Italy, France-Paris1, Brazil) and has published numerous books and articles in international Journals. Currently she is the vice president of Geographers Professional Association, vice president of the Urban Geography Group of the Association of Spanish Geographer and member of the Steering Committee of the IGU Urban Geography Commission. She is an expert for different Spanish scientific agencies, and she is a reviewer of several international journals.

urban science

MDPI

Editorial

Readings of the Post-Crisis Spanish City: Between Social Inequity and Territorial Destruction

Francisco Cebrián-Abellán [1], María José Piñeira-Mantiñán [2] and Jesús M. González-Pérez [3,*]

[1] Department of Geography and Land Planning, Faculty of Humanities, Campus Universitario s/n, Benjamín Palencia Building, University of Castilla-La Mancha, 02071 Albacete, Castilla-La Mancha, Spain; Francisco.Cebrian@uclm.es

[2] Department of Geography, Faculty of Geography and History, University of Santiago de Compostela, Praza da Universidade, 1, 15782 Santiago de Compostela, A Coruña, Spain; mariajose.pineira@usc.es

[3] Department of Geography, Guillem Colom building, University of the Balearic Islands, Cra. de Valldemossa km 7.5, 07122 Palma, Balearic Islands, Spain

* Correspondence: jesus.gonzalez@uib.es; Tel.: +34-971-172380

Received: 10 April 2019; Accepted: 11 April 2019; Published: 16 April 2019

Abstract: The 2008 crisis entailed a turning point in the process of creating and managing cities and territories. There has been a change from a city model, based on expansive growth, which was also speculative and deregulated, had provoked an unprecedented expansion of the outskirts of towns and cities, and the artificialization of thousands of hectares of land, to a model based on the reconstruction of the original city, before the impact of the crisis. Gone are the days of urban mega-projects—source of indebtedness for local administrations- and big urbanizations, which, in many occasions, have not been inhabited. The financial, social, and residential reality requires a better thinking of the city models, as well as recuperating the neighborhoods and recomposing the social gap and conflicts, which had become affected by unemployment, evictions, and austerity policies. In this paper, two models of understanding and managing cities have been presented, as a way of identifying strengths, weaknesses, and impacts on the modern city. Several case studies have been collected at a regional level (Extremadura and Valencian Community), and at an urban level (Las Palmas, Madrid, Barcelona, Valencia, and Toledo), and even at a sub-urban level (via the study of certain neighborhoods).

Keywords: urbanization process; real estate bubble; urban sprawl; urban vulnerability; residential segregation; urban inequality; Spain

Over the last decades, the dynamics and characters of urbanization in the developed areas have been conditioned by three big change scenarios that were very closely intertwined—in the economy, due to the logics of globalization; in demography, due to the deceleration of dynamics; and in governance, due to the appearance of new actors and local policies [1]. This has not been a homogeneous process, as different contexts, space, and time responses have occurred, which have become accelerated since the end of the last century. All things considered, the biggest impacts and effects were a consequence of the finance capital strategies [2,3], which have influenced the relocation of industrial activities, the progressive switch to a service economy, the appearance of the Information Society, and the effects of modern communication infrastructures. To this, we can add the evolution of behavior, preferences, and the perception of the society regarding environmental and social problems [4,5]. The transformations that have taken place in Spanish cities must be understood in the frame of the aforementioned global rationales. However, these can also be explained by certain distinguishing features, which have given them personality, apart from singular contexts and rhythms, and which have differentiated them in their behavior, in comparison to other neighboring countries. This has meant that there has been a change in the systems and urban hierarchies, in city morphology, in the organization processes, and social relations, but it has all occurred with differentiated temporalities and socio-territorial effects.

In terms of time, the urbanization context has been marked by two different periods. The first involved a strong economic and demographic expansion since the end of the twentieth century, until 2008. During this time, the world economy became invigorated, supported by the accelerated transnationalization of capital (in the context of the speculative bubble) [6]. There was free access to cheap credit, favored by bank convenient terms to lend money to governments, companies, and households. People's incomes grew significantly. The capacity of generating incomes and administration investments, increased. This had intense consequences, especially in the real-estate sector, since there was a considerable public and private investment in the elaboration of cities. The most visible result was the creation of new housing, infrastructures, and services, greatly above the real needs of society. In the case of Spain, there were some factors which contributed to feed such trends. On the one hand, the adoption of legal policies aimed at favoring urban land (Ley del suelo de 7/1997 de 14 de abril de medidas liberalizadoras en materia de suelo y de colegios profesionales). On the other hand, the adoption of the Euro in 2002, permitted money-laundering related to urban development. Also worth mentioning is the arrival of more than six million immigrants in a relatively short period of time, as well as the strong investment in communication infrastructures, by the public sector. New commercial centers proliferated around the urban areas. All this took place in a context where the average income kept increasing, which also favored home purchases. Finally, we could also to add the fact that banks gained entry into the building industry by providing easy credits for urban developers and final buyers. The building industry was acknowledged as the stabilizer of the economy, and small and big investors turned their attention to households, due to their capacity of generating capital gains [7–9]. All these factors worked together, until 2008.

The effects were visible in the different tiers of the urban hierarchy, mainly in the big and medium-sized cities, where there was a significant increase in population, and in urbanized land and housing. There is data available which illustrates what occurred during this decade, something that certain authors have rightly labelled as "the prodigious decade of Spanish urbanism" [8], although others have been more critical and have presented it as the "brick economy" or the "urbanizing tsunami" [9,10]. Between 2002 and 2008, the most intensive years, nearly 3.7 million homes were built, and in 2006, which was the greatest exponent of the urbanizing years in the model, almost seven hundred and fifty thousand households were constructed (number of homes according to work license, Ministerio de Fomento, 2017 [11]). Likewise, it was a period of strong demographic dynamism, in which the Spanish population increased by 4.3 million people, mainly as a consequence of international immigration (the population grew from 41.8 to 46.1 million people, according to the Spanish National Statistics Institute).

The effects of this process, on the territory, have been highly intense, as most of the urban expansion was made in the form of big developments of collective housing, or as single-family houses on the outskirts of well-connected areas. The data supplied by the Corine Land Cover, show that in Spain, on average, there was an increase from 6700 km^2 to 10,170 km^2 of developed areas, between 1987 and 2006 (3470 km^2, equivalent to 34%; the highest ever growth in Spanish history). In fact, the increase in housing was higher than the actual needs of the population, although this affirmation could be different in certain territories, especially in those where the dynamics have been affected by tourism related to second dwellings, mainly on the islands (Baleares and Canary Islands) and the Mediterranean coast (Andalucia, Murcia, the Valencian Community, and Catalonia).

From 2008, the effects of the high level of financialization of the economy and the debt of the governments, the administration, and households, triggered a structural crisis which dramatically affected the Spanish economic model. The bubble burst resulted in the collapse of the markets, the failure of financial institutions caused by the non-payment of debt, or by high risk (mainly savings banks), and provoked a sharp decline in real-estate and financial activity, as a side effect. Furthermore, in urban areas, regional, urban, and social issues were uncovered. There was a paralysis of the financial activities, capital gains, and transactions. The construction market decelerated significantly, so in 2013, the least active year during the crisis cycle, only 31,000 new houses were created (5% of the houses built in 2007). Meanwhile, the behavior of the population had also changed reflecting a drop, in housing sales since 2012. The average price of housing dropped by 30%, between 2007, when the highest prices of built m^2 were reached and 2014 that is, when the lowest prices appeared. Wages were lowered and unemployment indices increased (1.7 million in 2007 to 6.2 million in 2013). In addition to this, there were social effects derived from poverty (according to different criteria), which were very clear in the processes of eviction, as many of them were in the hands of financial entities [12]. The territorial and urban consequences have left many developed areas without buildings, and provided many examples of failed constructions. There has remained a considerable suplie of houses and vacant urban land.

As a result of these processes, different issues and social realities have emerged. The academic field has approached them in a new reflective scenario, where the analyses are contributing to help us understand the nature of conflicts and their resulting situations. Tis work, *Readings of the Post-Crisis Spanish City: Between Social Inequity and Territorial Destruction* is meant to contribute to such debates. We pay attention to different urban scales (big cities, metropolitan areas, towns, and urban areas) and space (inland Spanish towns, coastal cities, and main cities, such as Madrid, Barcelona, and Valencia). In terms of topics, other aspects related to morphological transformations are addressed, in order to present the negative effects caused by geographic dispersion and territorial overflow that have taken place in metropolitan areas and the environment, associated with daily mobility and sustainability. There is a clear need of revising the strategies linked to services and public infrastructure (water management not only in touristic areas, but in cultural spaces, sports areas, transports, hospitals, and communication centers, as well), in order to solve the growing territorial fragmentation in urban, industrial, commercial, and leisure areas. We present some issues that have taken place in the traditional historical or functional centers, which have happened to become affected by segregation, dispossession, vulnerability, gentrification, and social inequalities. The relation between the city and the nearby rural environments or the new sustainable responses, is also present. Another aspect that should be noted is governance, which is understood as the management of different political and administrative fragmented spaces that encompass the same territorial reality—issues of conurbation and how democratization of decision making affects communities, by incorporating citizen engagement is also analysed. These works were initially presented in the 14th Congress of Urban Geography from the Society of Spanish Geographers (XIV Congreso de Geografía Urbana de la Asociación de Geógrafos Españoles). The authors have performed a revision of the texts, in order to transform the initial ideas into twelve book chapters, which combine a scientific analysis with a profound critical view of a whole series of processes that played a crucial role in the interpretation of Spanish cities in the 21st century, as seen from a development point of view and an intra-urban characterization.

Not only did urban sprawl processes affect big Spanish cities, but also towns, where these processes have paradoxically been greater than in the nearby cities. This is a phenomenon which Luis A. Escudero, Irene Sánchez, and Francisco Cebrián (University of Castile-La Mancha) present in two chapters (*Land Squandering in the Spanish Medium Sized Cities: The Case of Toledo; Urban Sprawl in Inner Medium-Sized Cities: The Behaviour in Some Spanish Cases Since the Beginning of the 21st Century*), Toledo being the case study in one of them. In another chapter, a group of 23 different Spanish cities are presented, where the relation between population, urbanized surface, and built surface is analyzed. Their conclusions indicate that even though the dispersion dynamics have been bigger in the inserted medium-sized cities, with a polynuclear metropolitan area, the areas that are further away from the big cities tend to maintain trends that are closely associated with demand for growth. The consequences of this situation can be observed through disjointed and morphologically impersonal spaces, as well as the abundance of unfinished spaces and uninhabited urbanizations, whose future is quite uncertain.

In any case, authors like Arlinda García y Cristina López (University of Barcelona) (*The Impact of Economic Crisis in Areas of Sprawl in Spanish Cities*), who analyzed the case of Barcelona, consider that dispersed areas still retain their appeal for people in the life stages of the creation and expansion of households. They accept that, for this reason, an effective economic recovery and a renewed rise in the price of housing in denser cities, might contribute to an upturn in the popularity of the dispersed residential model, which nowadays could be considered to be in a "lethargic" phase, waiting for certain factors to concur and reactivate its expansion.

There is solid scientific evidence of the impact of urban sprawl on the growth of big cities, and medium-sized cities and towns, resulting in a web that Joan Checa y Oriol Nel·lo (Autonomous University of Barcelona) (*Urban Intensities. The Urbanization of the Iberian Mediterranean Coast in the Light of Nighttime Satellite Images of the Earth*) have studied through night-time light. They have analyzed urban development not only from the point of view of the physical occupation of land, but have also considered the changes in the intensity of the deployment of space. Through a complex procedure of image interpretation of satellite images of the Earth, they have proved how light intensity can serve as an indicator of efficiency, with regards to the use of territory and resources, the population distribution, and the production of goods and services; so the best lit areas do not always correspond to the areas with the highest populated areas, and the absence of urban brightness does not automatically indicate an absence of urban use.

Álvaro Morote (University of Valencia), Jorge Olcina, Antonio M. Rico, and María Hernández (University of Alicante) (*Water Management in Urban Sprawl Typologies in the City of Alicante (Southern Spain): New Trends and Perception after the Economic Crisis?*) introduced the impacts of territorial transformations which have occurred on the Spanish Mediterranean coast, due to the increase of urbanized and built lands, which have generated contradictions and internal conflicts that are linked to the overconsumption of resources (land, energy, water) and pollution (air, water, heat island effect, urban solid waste). Taking the city of Alicante as a reference, they are able to demonstrate how certain urban sectors that are characterized by low-density urban development, are not very sustainable, particularly, in terms of water management. They have successfully confirmed that water use per single family detached house amounted to 712 L per day, due to the high water demand, such as watering the garden or filling the swimming pool. These are alarming figures, more importantly so if we take the dynamics of the Mediterranean climate into account and how water scarcity might aggravate in the future.

In contrast to overbuilding, urban sprawl, and urban expansion, different initiatives emerge as a way of pursuing environmental sustainability in the city. This is the case of Eco-Neighborhood Projects in the city of Madrid, which are presented by Elia Canosa and Ángela García (Autonomous University of Madrid) (*The Failure of Eco-Neighborhood Projects in the City of Madrid (Spain)*). This is a project that could mean the arrival of innovative initiatives to the neighborhood of Vallecas (South Madrid), which might provide centralized heating and hot water for all buildings, as well as the installation of an underground solid waste collection system. With this project, the three basic dimensions of sustainability could be tackled—the environment, the society, and the economy. However, according to the authors, the result might not be as expected. The cause could be the existing gap between the projects and their achievements, between official statements and urban practices, and finally, between the wishes of politicians and technicians, and the aspirations of citizens. In this sense, the lack of the residents' participation, burdened the entire process, even the start-up of the built elements.

Roxana-Diana Ilisei and Julia Salom (University of Valencia) (*Urban Projects and Residential Segregation: A Case Study of the Cabanyal Neighborhood in Valencia (Spain)*) study the residential mobility processes that are associated with the urban sprawl in the historical neighborhood of Cabanyal (Valencia). The authors identified the territorial pattern of the socio-demographic changes that have affected the neighborhood during the last decade. They linked such changes to the cycle of urban degradation that the neighborhood is familiar with, and also to the renovation plans. The authors present an exhaustive research backed by abundant graphic and cartographical material, where they proved that, due to the neoliberal policies in the Special Plan for Protection and Interior Reform (PEPRI), there was a progressive loss of the Spanish population and non-EU immigrants (who were mostly Colombians and Equadtorians, until that point) by other EU immigrants (mostly Romanians). To conclude, Ilisei and Salom claimed that the dynamics of the residential changes in Cabanyal, during the recent years, indicated that the processes of residential segregation, have created a strong social inertia and resistance towards urban revitalization policies implemented by the new municipal government.

Foreclosures and evictions were the main social impacts of the 2007 crisis, but are also a cause of a society based on social inequality. In recent years, many documents about evictions in Spain have been published. This can not only be explained by a rise in the number of evictions in the last decades, but can also be accounted for by the necessity of expanding the city beyond its physical territory as well, as a social product of a constant revision. As shown by Juan M. Parreño, Josefina Domínguez, Maite Armengol, Tanausú Pérez, and Jordi Boldú (University of Las Palmas de Gran Canaria) (*Foreclosures and Evictions in Las Palmas de Gran Canaria during the Economic Crisis and Post-Crisis Period in Spain*), evictions increased significantly during the crisis, but these have not ceased to show an upward tendency, thus, causing a complex situation. Dispossession and loss of use are two structural occurrences that are coherent with the capitalist model of secondary accumulation developed in the world, in the last 20 years. The authors focused on the study of the territorial impact and the trend of mortgage foreclosures and evictions in the urban space of Las Palmas de Gran Canaria, from 2009 to 2017, and it contributed to understanding the causes and delved into this debate with solid scientific evidence. Working with disaggregated data (street names and gate number) from judicial statistics, provides a highly detailed spatial dimension. The city that was studied was very interesting, due to the fact that it was located in the outermost European region, in an important tourist destination where the international property demand is quite high. Between 2009 and 2017, a total of 4138 case files aimed at the forcible deprivation of use and ownership, were executed in the judicial district for Las Palmas de Gran Canaria, 460 case files per year and 1.2 per thousand inhabitants. In conclusion, two main results must be emphasized. On the one hand, as proved by other researchers [12], the territorial distribution of the legal actions adopted was generally concentrated in the city's central spaces, nonetheless, the incidence of dispossession and rental-related evictions, overflowed these spaces, and also intensely affected the urban periphery. On the other hand, dispossession in Las Palmas was concentrated in the early years of the crisis, whereas the loss of use had affected the more recent period, when the incipient post-crisis was taking place.

Barcelona was the case study in the next two chapters, where there was a coincidence in the use of innovative methodology for the study of the indicators of social inequality in urban areas, such as vulnerability and social segregation. Antonio Palacios, Ana Mellado (Autonomous University of Madrid), and Yazmín León (University of Costa Rica) (*Qualitative Methodologies for the Analysis of Intra-Urban Socio-Environmental Vulnerability in Barcelona (Spain): Case Studies*) present an interesting work about the socio-environmental vulnerability in the municipality of Barcelona, thanks to the use of qualitative methodologies. Focused on the social approach to vulnerability, they showed how socio-spatial structures and processes are indeed dynamic and might determine the daily lives of the disadvantaged people and groups. Thus, the objective was to show that qualitative methodologies can play a major part in the studies on urban socio-environmental vulnerability, when detecting deficiencies or non-quantifiable social and urban problems. The authors introduced a synthetic indicator of the relative socio-spatial vulnerability. Although this was calculated for all neighborhoods in Barcelona, the chapter was centered, as a case study, in the most vulnerable ones—Trinitat Nova, El Raval, La Marina del Prat Vermell, and La Barceloneta. They worked with seventeen variables related to education, age, and demographic mortality indicators; income and professional status, immigration status, and size of household. On the one hand, at the neighborhood level, the research crystallized in a synthetic index of relative socio-spatial vulnerability (ISVuSAR), which was represented by a map. An interesting table with qualitative indicators was presented for the four neighborhoods. The results revealed the multidimensionality of vulnerability in the neighborhoods analyzed, as well as the validity of qualitative methodology, to detect and support public policies that were destined to reducing intra-urban inequalities.

Additionally, Aina Gomà and Joel Muñoz (Autonomous University of Barcelona) (*Segregated in the City, Separated in the School. The Reproduction of Social Inequality through the School System*) showed a study on urban sprawl, from the analysis of the education level of the population, an education which could replicate and spread social inequality in the city. Gomà and Muñoz contributed to this debate by producing a combined analysis of three variables—knowledge of the dynamics of urban segregation; educational levels achieved by the population aged between 15 and 34; and enrolment strategies and scholar performance, according to the place of residence. The last section was especially interesting, as it associates the socio-economic variables, the complexity of the schools' situation, and the academic results of the students. Albeit the information was presented with an introductory section about residential segregation and school segregation in Catalonia, the scale of the study was intra-urban—neighborhoods and school districts in Barcelona. To conclude, the authors affirmed that school segregation, as well as residential segregation, are directly intertwined and, therefore, education affects in the spread of inequality. On the one hand, the residential origin is of key importance in the professional career and expectations of the young population. On the other, spatial differences in the schools' conditions, act as enhancer elements for school segregation, due to, above all, the stigmatization of schools in the vulnerable neighborhoods, and the enrolment procedure.

The new companies of the so-called sharing economy were very important urban factors, for the transformation of the current cities, especially those that were related to tourism and gentrification. As a consequence, there is an important opportunity for research in urban studies. Luis del Romero (University of Valencia) (*Touristification, Sharing Economies and the New Geography of Urban Conflicts*) addressed this issue mainly from the point of view of tourism, in the third most populated city in Spain, Valencia. The new types of holiday rentals dominated by online marketplaces (such as Airbnb), Uber, and Cabify, which formed the center of the analyses. The most notable novelty in this chapter could be the relation between the outbreak of social conflicts in an urban area, which was measured by el Romero, from the location in the city map, with four factors in two different stages (real-estate bubble and crisis)—family evictions for tourist apartments, protests against touristification, protests against noise and public space privatization, and taxi driver protests. According to del Romero, the conflicts could be divided into three categories—land-use conflicts, land revenue conflicts, and mobility conflicts, which, like the studied sharing economy companies they face, have adopted a new organization scheme and renewed fight. Social networks are not only promoting digital platforms but also social resistances.

Another chapter is centered in the study of urban processes that take place in regions and beyond. In "The Clandestine Transition towards an Unsustainable Urban Model in Extremadura, Spain", Víctor Jiménez and José A. Campesino (University of Extremadura) (*The Clandestine Transition towards an Unsustainable Urban Model in Extremadura, Spain*) showed the unsustainability of the urban model in Extremadura, an autonomous community characterized by its weak urban system and the lowest (49.07%) Average Urbanization Rate (AUR) in Spain. Nevertheless, Extremadura has seen an important development of rural areas, near cities and towns, mainly from a residential growth outside the limits of the urban and developable land. This has been an intense process in recent years which, according to the authors, is eminently clandestine. The methodologies and analyses from urban planning are predominant and they could be extrapolated to other territories. Among other results, the number and density of houses in the Undevelopable Land (UL) in the municipalities, are mapped. The authors detected almost 40,000 houses on the UL of Extremadura, with a very unbalanced distribution in the quantitative level but very distributed in spatial terms. Only two municipalities of the 388 that comprise Extremadura, are free of housing on the UL. As a conclusion, we highlighted, on one hand, that the atypical 'rururban' expansion is the main urban and territorial problem of the region. On the other hand, it is clear that Extremadura needs a new territorial scheme that conditions urban regulation. Extremadura must face the creation and application of a Regional Plan for Management and Control of Rurban Development.

As a result of this revision set, we presented a reality marked by the end of unregulated expansive growth, the re-involvement of administrations in the process of planning and management of cities, the change in the territorial priorities of towns and cities, which have shifted their focus from metropolitan

Urban Sci. **2019**, *3*, 43

areas to more central neighborhoods; and the concern for those communities that were greatly affected by the crisis, which are still very present. It remains to be seen how the administrations will react to certain challenges, such as the overexploitation of lands, the energy transition, the need for services, the governance or the democratization of the decision-making process, among others.

Funding: This research has been funded by three research projects (Ministry of Science, Innovation and Universities/ FEDER): CSO2015-63970-R; CSO2016-75236-C2-1-R; CSO2015-68738-P.

Conflicts of Interest: The authors declare no conflict of interest.

References

1. Uhaldeborde, J.M. Las ciudades europeas: Nuevos paradigmas, nuevas estrategias. *Pap. Econ. Española* **2017**, *153*, 2–22.
2. Harvey, D. *A Brief History of Neoliberalism*; Oxford University Press: New York, NY, USA, 2005; p. 247.
3. Lois, R.C.; Piñeira, M.J.; Vives, S. El proceso urbanizador en España (1990–2014): Una interpretación desde la Geografía y la teoría de los circuitos del capital. *Rev. Scr. Nova* **2016**, *20*, 539.
4. Herce, M. *El Negocio del Territorio. Evolución y Perspectivas de la Ciudad Moderna*; Alianza: Madrid, Spain, 2013.
5. Valenzuela, M. Tendencias y desafíos de la planificación urbana y del gobierno del territorio. La perspectiva de los geógrafos españoles (2005-15). In *Crisis, globalization and social and regional imbalances in Spain, Spanish Contribution to 33rd IGC Beijing*; Asociación de Geógrafos Españoles: Madrid, Spain, 2016; pp. 211–229.
6. Baraona, M.; Herra, E. *Danzando en la Bruma Junto al Abismo. Las Cuatro Crisis y el Futuro de la Humanidad*; Lom Ediciones: Santiago, Chile, 2018.
7. Romero, J. Construcción residencial y gobierno del territorio en España. De la burbuja especulativa a la recesión. Causas y consecuencias. *Rev. Cuad. Geogr.* **2010**, *47*, 17–46.
8. Burriel, E. *La Década Prodigiosa del Urbanismo Español (1997–2006)*; Scripta Nova, XII, 270 (64); Universidad de Barcelona: Barcelona, Spain, 2008.
9. Gaja, F. *El "Tsunami Urbanizador" en el Litoral Mediterráneo. El Ciclo de Hiperproducción Inmobiliaria 1996–2006*; X Coloquio Internacional de Geocrítica. Diez Años de Cambio en el Mundo, en la Geografía y en las Ciencias Sociales, *1999–2008*; Universidad de Barcelona: Barcelona, Spain, 2008.
10. Naredo, J.M. Un Episodio Relevante: La Burbuja Especulativa y la Crisis Inmobiliaria en Perspectiva. *Cuad. Investig. Urbanística* **2015**, *100*, 77–82. [CrossRef]
11. De Fomento, M. *Observatorio de la Vivienda y Suelo, Boletín Anual 2017*; Ministerio de Fomento. Gobierno de España: Madrid, Spain, 2017.
12. Vives, S.; Rullan, O.; González, J.M. *Understanding Geographies of Home Dispossession through the Crisis: Evictions Palma Style*; Icaria: Barcelona, Spain, 2018.

urban science

MDPI

Article

Urban Sprawl in Inner Medium-Sized Cities: The Behaviour in Some Spanish Cases Since the Beginning of the 21st Century

Francisco Cebrián Abellán * and **Irene Sánchez Ondoño**

Department of Geography, University of Castilla-La Mancha, 02071 Albacete, Spain; irene.sanchezzondono@uclm.es
* Correspondence: francisco.cebrian@uclm.es; Tel.: +34-967599200-2788

Received: 12 November 2018; Accepted: 15 January 2019; Published: 21 January 2019

Abstract: The processes of urban sprawl that have been present over the past two decades in the different strata of the urban hierarchy have also affected, as a whole, medium-sized cities. The urban sprawl has been particularly pronounced during the period of expansive Spanish urbanism, in which many of the municipalities situated in the vicinities of large cities have been affected by major demographic dynamics and (sub)urbanisation development outside the traditional city limits. Sometimes, these processes have been greater than the nearby cities in the urban area where they are inserted. In this study, we examine the general mechanisms identified within an urban crown size (within a radius of 30 km) and at the scale of the municipality, based on an analysis of two distinct periods: one linked to a strong growth dynamic (2000–2008), and another related to subsequent crisis (2009–2016). A group of 23 inner medium-sized Spanish cities has been analysed, taking into account the trends of the population, the surface of unbuilt plots, the built surface, and the amount of housing. We have identified the typologies of their respective urban areas over the two periods considered.

Keywords: urban sprawl; medium-size cities; expansive city planning

1. Introduction

From the beginning of the new millennium, Spain has been affected by an economic context that has had a major impact on the dynamics and ways of building Spanish cities [1,2]. There has been an explosive urban growth up to the year 2008, which produced a spectacular impact on the real estate sector. Before this time, there had been a considerable territorial expansion of land suitable for development, which substantially modified the urban sprawl and the constructive typologies, incorporating modalities of low-density alternatives to those traditionally used in Spain. However, since 2008, the Global Financial Crisis has opened a period marked by a different scenario, causing an abrupt slowdown in social and economic dynamics.

In this context, there are factors throughout the periods (2000–2008 and 2009–2016) that can be understood as structural, and that have widely affected different European societies [3]. Other factors are typical of the present Spanish reality, which has contributed to accentuate and single out the effects of the economic boom and the subsequent crisis of those years. These local and structural factors have marked differences, singularities, and sometimes specific responses, and have been supplemented elsewhere. Thus, there are cities that have dominated the processes of regeneration and the reform of traditional consolidated urban spaces; in other cities, dispersal strategies have taken over landscapes, but situations of decline and deterioration of intra-urban system elements have also appeared.

However, less attention has been paid to the dynamics of medium-size Spanish cities, where the intensity and time frame has not always coincided with the those mentioned before. From the demographic point of view, these medium-sized cities have been more dynamic than larger Spanish ones, reinforcing their role as the backbone of the territory and as sites of intercommunication.

This report pays attention to a group of inner medium-sized cities, away from the influence of coastal residential tourism. Here, the processes of urban sprawl are associated with factors of a different nature, but they have acted jointly, in some cases favoring urban dynamics in areas that have traditionally been agricultural being rapidly turned into forms of dispersion from the city. This process is part of a theoretical context that has been defined by a lack of agreement in relation to the concept of what a medium-sized city is from the point of view of statistical thresholds. Unfortunately, there are no criteria that could provide precise clarification on what is behind the idea of urban sprawl. To address this, this report deals with the behaviour of the peripheries of 24 cities, analysing the evolution of the population, the urban land, and the built-up land over two distinct periods. The first one coincides with the great dynamics of the construction (2000–2008). The second one focusses its attention on the subsequent crisis and the beginning of the recovery (2009–2016).

The main focus of this report examines the territorial point of view and the processes of urban sprawl in the surroundings of inner medium-sized cities in Spain. These are framed in a context of urban growth from the end of the last century up to the year 2008, which was an especially intense period for big cities; the dynamics that have affected their metropolitan areas have been much studied by the scientific community. The report also investigates the behaviour patterns of the city model, the logic behind territorial management, and adaptations to the requirements for sustainable development, social inclusion, and governance, which have changed [4]. These changes have also been observed along the Mediterranean coast and among its islands, where sun and beach tourism have generated a strong demand for second homes [5].

2. The Medium-Sized Cities and Urban Sprawl

Through studying what has happened during the periods 2000–2008 and 2009–2016, it can be said that these have been characterised by different dynamics. This report pays attention to what has happened in city outskirts, with the complexity associated with the conceptualisation of medium-sized cities and urban sprawl. The very idea of what a city is requires considerable effort by administrations and academics to define it. In Spain, it is associated with the statistical threshold of 10,000 inhabitants [6]; the European Union sets the population limit at 50,000 inhabitants residing in the urban center, with densities higher than 1500 inhabitants per km^2 [7]. There is not a shared definition of a compact city either, although some authors present it as a multidimensional reality including complex interactions that are more like an interpretative image of a spatial framework than a model developed from accurate data, which shows a certain functional mixture and a greater environmental sustainability [8] (p. 24). The truth is that their morphology appears to be associated with cities that are consolidated with a certain building and demographic density.

Together with the complexity of the definition of the traditional, compact, intense, and dense city, there is a definition of urban sprawl shared by the academic community (territorial scope, building density, functional specialisation, constructive types, etc.). This originated in the United States, joining in a progressive movement after World War II, and marking some of the guidelines of progressive territorial integration, which has moved to define the different steps of the American urban hierarchy [9] (p. 26). Subsequently, this has been reproduced in the European countries [10–14]. Different authors, with different visions and approaches, have tried to provide terms in order to establish a reality that has gradually deterritorialised and reterritorialised the city [15]. Some of these are: diffused city [16], scattered city [17], dispersed city [18], or inefficient city [19] (p. 72).

There are different reasons and different factors involved in the process. Some are of a general nature, and which highlight the close relationship between the way of building the city and globalisation. Technological innovations are the most important, particularly those related to the Global Information System [20]. Along with this, close relationships with neoliberalism, capitalism, and financial sector strategies arise in relation to the real estate sector [21–23]. In connection with these processes, normative frameworks that drive the forms of dispersed cities and enticing business opportunities have emerged; these have also occurred in a context of economic growth, which has provided significant amounts of money to the residential sector. We also have to add the reduction in travel costs; transport improvements and new communications infrastructure; the support of the public sector in favour of housing and property; the emergence of large companies engaged in the construction sector; the generalisation of large supermarkets within urban peripheries; the deterioration of the quality of life in some central urban areas; the progressive delegation of urban policies to private actors; and social changes (increase of rent, new housing preferences, and lack of affordable inner city housing) [15,24].

Apart from these structural factors, we must add others that are typical of the Spanish situation, from the beginning of the century until 2008, where unusual urban activity and a housing boom have occurred. These can be explained to some extent by the diverse nature and demographic constraints as Spain increased its population by six million people in just one decade as a result of intense international migratory flows [25]. We must add the rise in the average incomes of the population in a context of economic prosperity; the presence of favourable policies for the acquisition of housing; the emergence of legislation turning from a rigid model of administrative control in the supply of land into another one based on flexibility and deregulation, converting virtually all of the developable land (Law of the Soil 7/1997 of 14 April measuring soil and the liberalisation of professional associations), and incorporating the figure of the urbanisation agent, who with no property but with authorisations and credit can initiate urban developer proceedings [1,2,24,26]. However, it has been mainly the effect of a financial sector that has set eyes on building as a window of opportunity, in the context of low interest rates, lending money to developers, construction companies, and end-buyers [22,27].

The result of this process has been threefold. On the one hand, traditional urban morphologies, with increased decentralisation and the dispersion of the population, housing, and activities in space areas that transcend the traditional city limits have changed. A second effect highlights that the reterritorialisation of the city towards its periphery has left monofunctional spaces in the outskirts (residential areas, mostly, but also commercial, leisure, or industrial areas), which are sometimes very far away, but remain well-connected, are dependent on cars, and have intense daily traffic flows between home and the workplace or leisure centers. Its impact is so strong that it has become one of the greatest problems for the 21st century [28]. Finally, the construction typologies, which are associated with new social patterns of consumption but also the interests of local governments and real estate agents and preferences, have caused roads and transport logistics to change and improve.

A very different situation has been felt from the year 2008. The Global Financial Crisis meant an almost total halt to the economy in general, and specifically for the real estate sector. At the same time, a reflection in the political and administrative scope occurred in order to try to stop and correct some dysfunctions inherited from the period of "expansive urbanism" or "urban tsunami" [1,2].

On the other hand, a process of progressive return to the traditional city model has started to consolidate, to the detriment of the forms of urban sprawl. In the Spanish case, the emergence of new laws stand out; these have looked towards the consolidated city (identify the 2007 and 2014 laws), and which have opened the door to a new stage in urban spaces, now with less attention to the dispersed city and a growing interest in returning to a city model that is more sustainable in the social, environmental, and economic scope.

This set of situations has occurred over different stages of the urban system. They are located in two different territorial and functional areas: some are part of the polynuclear metropolitan areas, which affects their demographic and urban dynamics (in the case of Madrid, Barcelona, or Valencia), while in others, the dynamics are justified by internal logic (cities relatively far from large national capitals). In medium inner cities, these processes have also taken place, and have played out, with different intensities, in contrast to the dynamics and processes of the larger ones and their respective metropolitan areas.

3. Methodology and Sources

From the methodological point of view, a temporary framework that aims to focus attention on what happened in the 21st century has been used, differentiating between two well-marked periods. The first covers 2000 to 2008 and, as pointed out in previous pages, forms part of a context of an accelerated growth of the economy and the construction sector. The second corresponds to what happened between 2009–2016, which in this case is the reflection of an intense crisis felt until 2013 that had effects of a different nature, but which had among its causes and consequences construction that has left numerous social problems and failed examples of buildings, PAUs (Urban Planning Plans), or large projects related to urban marketing [29,30].

From the territorial point of view, we have selected 24 cities. See Figure 1.

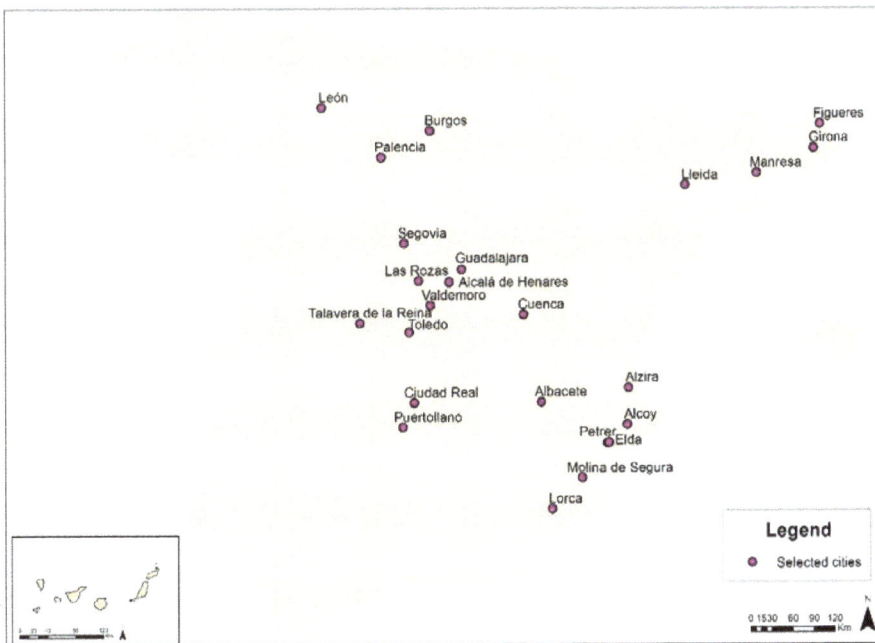

Figure 1. Selected cities.

In order to analyse the behavior of the city outside its limits, a space of analysis consisting of a crown with a radius of 30 kilometers from each of the central cities has been generated, including the municipalities that have their own town council and local government within this radius (those whose council is outside this limit have been excluded from the analysis). This implies extending the idea of an urban area beyond municipalities adjacent to the city (the last criteria has been used in the preparation of the Urban Audit, Eurostat, and the Atlas of the Spanish Metropolitan Areas by the Ministry of Development) [31,32]. For cases in which urban areas (UAs) overlap with other cities (they appear as cutting circles), the surface has been divided into two equal parts starting from the intersection points (Figure 2). This situation occurs in: (1) Ciudad Real and Puertollano; (2) Guadalajara and Alcalá de Henares; (3) Alcoy and Alzira; (4) Alcoy and Elda-Petrer; (5) las Rozas and Segovia; (6) las Rozas de Madrid, Valdemoro, and Alcalá de Henares; (7) Toledo and Valdemoro; and (8) Figueras and Gerona.

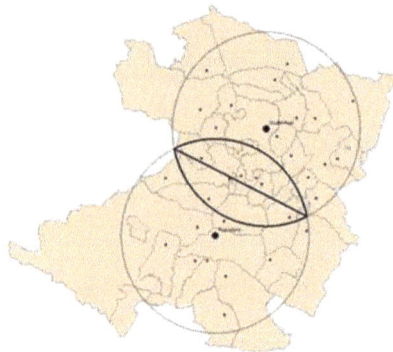

Figure 2. Territorial redefinition of urban areas.

On the other hand, when these analysed urban areas are in close proximity to other larger areas not included in the medium-city category, and their respective areas of influence overlap, the municipalities forming part of the greater city have been excluded, meaning that they depend functionally on them. Once the areas of distribution are identified, tables with the information added have been generated, differentiating between the core 'city', on the one hand, and the respective urban areas, on the other.

We have used two types of variables in order to analyse the changes operated in the respective urban crowns: population and residential plots (built and not built). In the case of the demography, the municipal register of inhabitants has been used (2000, 2008, and 2016, on 1 January each year, INE -Instituto Nacional de Estadística-). To understand the production process of the city, the Real Estate Register of the Ministry of Finance and Public Service (Cadastre) has been used as a source of information, from which several variables have been extracted, including the surface of urban plots built and urban plots surface not built for the three years considered (2000, 2008, and 2016). Similarly, from the files of the catalogue type in plain text format, which was provided by the Register's electronic site, we have obtained information concerning the number of properties by municipality. These were established with the key of the property "urban" and the key of the group "housing", which respond to the following types: 1.1. Collective housing of urban character (1.1.1. Open buildings and 1.1.2. Building in closed blocks), 1.2. Single-family houses of urban character (1.2.1. detached or semi-detached buildings and 1.2.2. terraced or closed blocks) and 1.3.1. Rural construction: exclusive use for housing.

A relative variation has been calculated. The municipality has been used as the unit of analysis.

An appropriate scale has been designated, assuming that it can cover certain realities, such as unequal territorial, demographic dimensions, or the presence of different settlement models, which can cover the presence of separated urban developments, and sometimes remote, municipal capitals. An example of this would be the case of Seseña, which has had much media coverage, where many of the new developments have been generated outside of the traditional city limits [33]. Nevertheless, for the purposes of this report, this unit of calculation is valid to identify what has happened.

The final data has been worked on using a double scale: the city and urban areas (UA). The results have been mapped with ArcMap at the municipal scale when it has fallen to this level of detail, while the aggregate urban areas are presented in tabular form and using panel data, showing absolute values of the population within unbuilt and built surfaces.

4. Development of the Methodology

4.1. Demographic Transformations

The first issue that draws our attention while analysing the demographic dynamics [6] is that urban areas (UAs) provide positive dynamics in the first stage, while facing a situation of stagnation and even recession in the years after 2009 (Figure 3). Another aspect to be highlighted is that the overall trend between 2000–2016: UAs has left variation rates higher than those of the cities. Only in six of the 23 cases considered (Ciudad Real, Cuenca, Molina de Segura, Puertollano, Las Rozas, and Valdemoro) has there been a greater dynamic of central urban spaces facing a more leisurely situation in their respective crowns. Considering the behaviour of the different UAs (excluding the central cities) on the basis of the values obtained for periods, four categories have been established from the resulting quartiles (Figure 4).

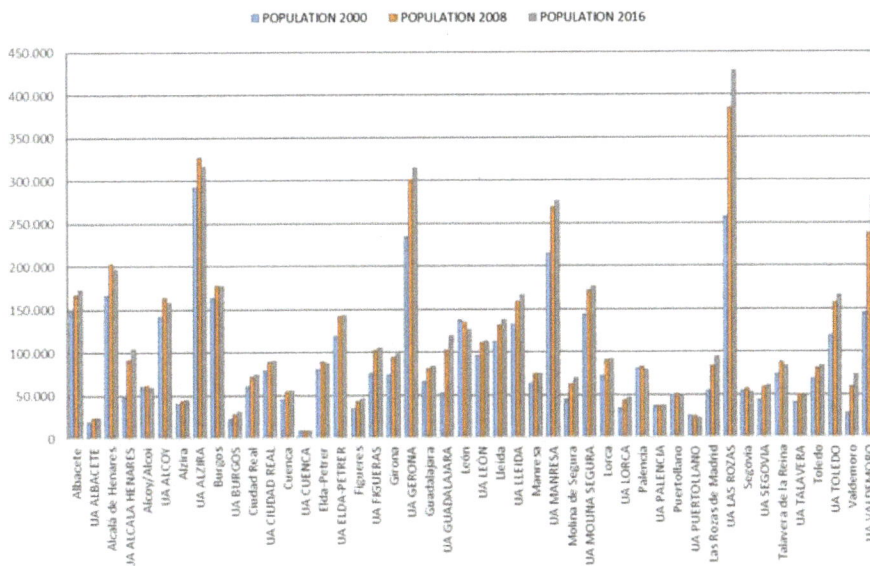

Figure 3. Population in cities and urban areas (UAs) [2]. Own elaboration.

Within the first category (first quartile), there are five UAs that have experienced a very positive and sharp increase—above 40%–along the two cycles considered. This suggests that the trends that were initiated at the beginning of the century as a result of the crisis have not slowed down. The ones in Guadalajara are located at this first level (population increased by 225% from 2000 to 2016); Alcalá de Henares (increased by 213%); Valdemoro, which almost reached these thresholds (191%); Las Rozas (166%); and Figueras (138%). In most cases, they are nearby cities integrated in the metropolitan area of Madrid (the first four).

Within the category II (second quartile), there are six cities, with more moderate increases, since they are all located between 28.3% for Manresa and 138.6% for Toledo. Lleida holds a medium position, with 124.75%.

The third category (third quartile) is made up of six urban areas with increase rates ranging from 112.5% (Ciudad) to 122% (Molina de Segura) between 2000–2016. Finally, the fourth category is made up of the UAs, with very contained and regressive dynamics, and with rates averaging around 110.9% for Alcoy and Puertollano, which experienced a population decrease (it lost 12% between 2000–2016).

Obviously, this first view, as pointed out before, is partial, because it captures the behaviour of UAs in an aggregate manner. In the scale below, there are considerable imbalances in the dynamics of the different municipalities that are part of each one of them. Figure 5 shows the rates of growth at the municipal level. It can be seen how higher behaviours usually appear in spaces adjacent to the central cities. However, they are mostly present in the environment of the large metropolitan areas. This is the case of the integrated or close to polynuclear organisation of Madrid, Barcelona, Alicante, or Valencia, although the phenomenon occurs with uneven intensity and variable geometry, and is conditioned by the position of the areas in relation to the communication networks and the economic dynamics of different areas. There is no doubt that the most pronounced growth situations have occurred between Guadalajara and Alcalá de Henares. More than 500% of superior dynamics occurred in the period 2000–2016, such as in the case of Yebes, with a 4706% of increase; Cañizar, which grew by 2233%; Quer (2157%); Chiloeches (1361%); Tórtola de Henares (1533%); Loranca de Tajuña (904%); Torija (722%); Pioz (705%); or Fuentelviejo (572%).

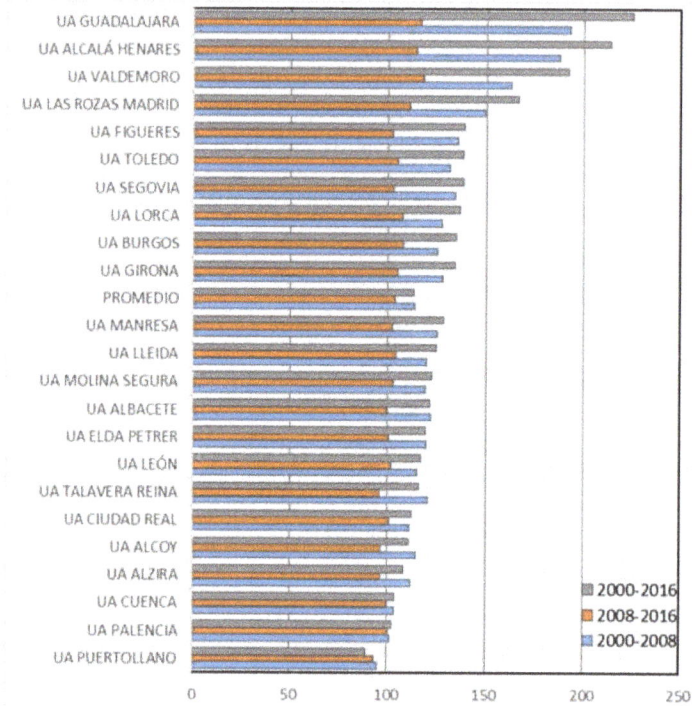

Figure 4. Rate of population change in urban areas (UAs) [2]. Own elaboration.

The municipalities that have grown between 100–500% are located in the geographical urban area of Las Rozas, Alcalá, and Valdemoro, and thus have become transitional between them and the cities of Toledo and Madrid, which articulates a polynuclear metropolitan system that includes Toledo and Guadalajara. A similar situation occurs in the municipalities located in the surroundings of Manresa and Gerona, which are linked with the urban area of Barcelona. These dynamics are lessening as the distance to each of the respective central cities increases. On the opposite extreme, with regressive taxes, we have the cases of Puertollano, Castilla-La Mancha, and Palencia in Castilla y León.

4.2. Changes in the Surface of Unbuilt Urban Plots

The processes of transformation of the surfaces of urban unbuilt plots (reserve flooring) leave variation rates pointing in two directions. In the cities, it can be seen, on the one hand, that a small group has left especially significant growth (Lorca, Valdemoro, and Toledo). From the temporal point of view, it is striking that the process has been mainly focused on the period 2000–2008, which is when the surface increased most (Figure 6). However, in some cases, the trend is maintained, and it is even increasing over the long term (2000–2016), which indicates that urban land has continually been created in the UA after the onset of the crisis (Albacete, Ciudad Real, Cuenca, Molina del Segura, and Puertollano).

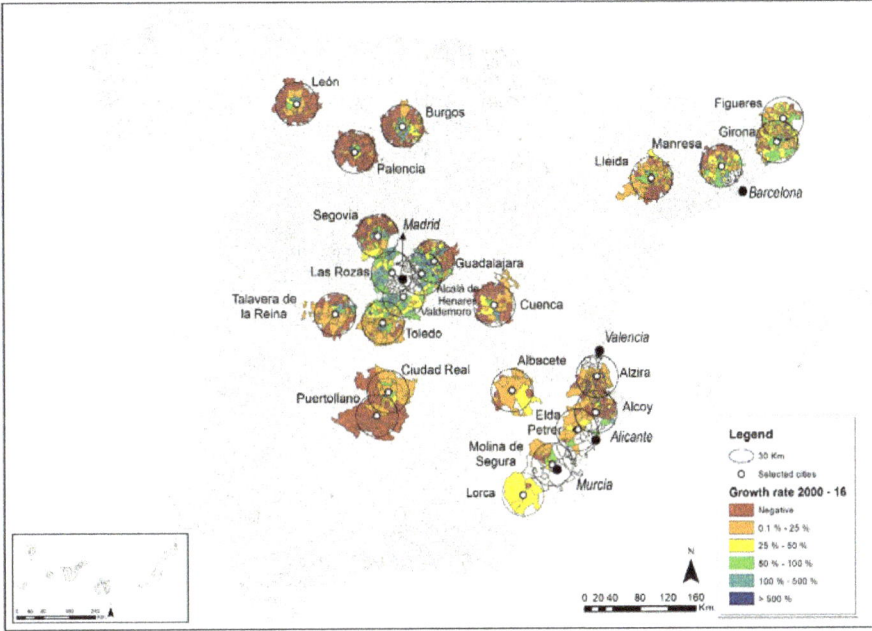

Figure 5. Rate of population change for the period 2000–2016 [2]. Own elaboration.

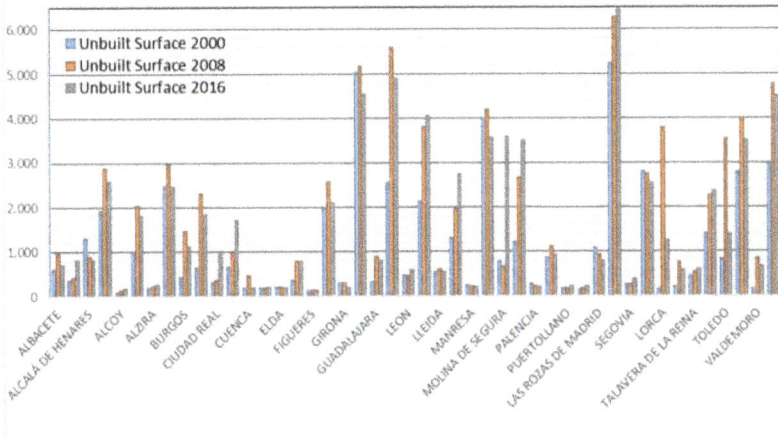

Figure 6. Unbuilt surface. Source: Register, several years. Own elaboration.

The momentum experienced by some of them, which sometimes has been greater than the main city (this situation has been given in 15 of the 23 areas), is highlighted. During the whole analysed period (2000–2016), we highlight the response of Burgos, where urban plots have grown by 285%; in Albacete, where urban plots have grown by 223%; in Alcoy, where urban plots have grown by 182%; León, where urban plots have grown by 190%; in Lleida, where urban plots have grown by 109%;

and in Talavera, where urban plots have grown by 165%. We have to especially indicate the case of Lorca, which between 2000–2008 multiplied its land surface by a factor of 10.

Organising the dynamics of the UAs by quartiles is a situation that differs substantially from the one presented in the demographic behaviour (Figure 7). In the first category (first quartile), the cases of Molina del Segura (286%), Burgos (285%), Lorca (275%), Ciudad Real (269%), and Albacete (223%) have been included. If you set a comparison with the demographic behaviour, none of them are included among those that have left major variation in population rates. In the second category (second quartile), the cases of Elda-Petrer, Lleida, Guadalajara, León, Alcoy, and Talavera de la Reina have been included. These have growth rates ranging from 211% for the first to 165% in Talavera de la Reina. In this case, Valdemoro appears in the medium position. The third category includes the urban areas of Puertollano, Alcalá, Toledo, Las Rozas, Cuenca, and Palencia, with rates of variation ranging from 141% for the growth in first case to 106% in the last. The fourth category is the least dynamic example; it includes the cases of Figueras, Gerona, Segovia, Alzira, and Manresa, with variation rates between 105% and the first negative changes in the other four, which reached a minimum of 89.4% in the case of Manresa.

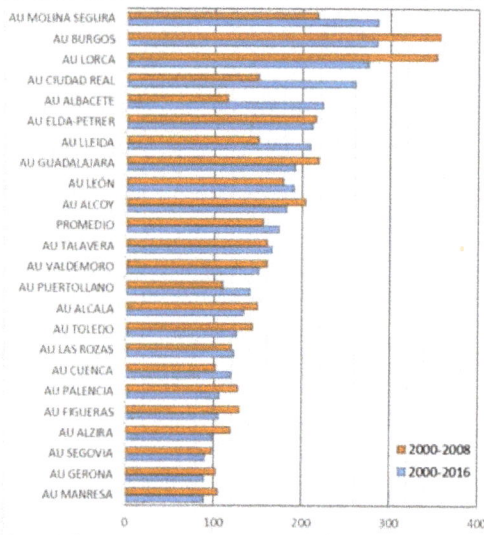

Figure 7. Rate of change in unbuilt surfaces in urban areas. Source: Register, several years. Own elaboration.

4.3. Variations in Urbanised Areas

For the built-up area, there are also distinct territorial and temporal realities. From a spatial point of view, the most relevant absolute values appear in the UAs of Las Rozas, Gerona (above 8000 hectares); Valdemoro, Manresa, Alzira, or Toledo (over 4000 hectares). On the other hand, it is the largest area in almost all of the urban areas by comparison with the central cities. Only in three cases (Albacete, Cuenca, and Lorca) do the cities have a greater size than the crowns in the built areas (it must be taken into account that these municipalities have large surface areas) (Figure 8).

In terms of the timescale of operated changes, the significant thing to notice is that in practically all of them, a much more dynamic behaviour between 2000–08 (Lorca, Guadalajara, Molina, and Albacete) was produced compared to what happened between 2009–2016, where at a general level, substantially lower dynamics are observed, and nuances have appeared because of improved behaviour over the first period analysed (Talavera, Royal Toledo, Lleida, or Puertollano) in the UAs.

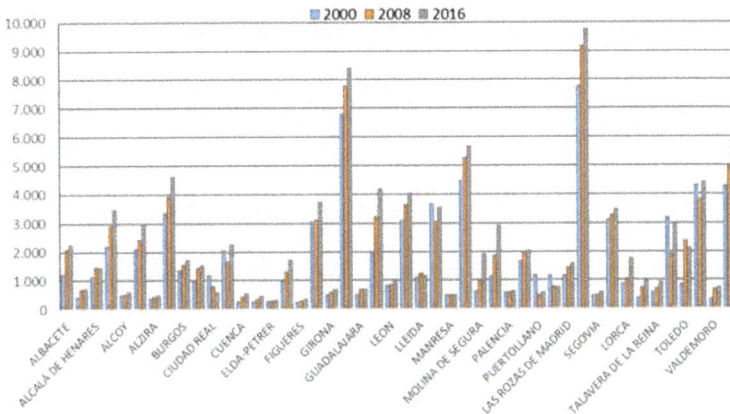

Figure 8. Variation rate of the built-up area. Source: Register, several years. Own elaboration.

When ordering urban areas by quartiles, different situations also appeared to those previously considered (Figure 9). In Category I (quartile I), we can see growths of 168–257% between 2000–2016, and hence we include Molina del Segura, Lorca, Guadalajara, Elda-Petrer, and Cuenca in this category. In Category II (second quartile), with rates ranging between 136–164%, we have Albacete, Alcalá, Burgos, Alcoy, Alzira, and Valdemoro. In Category III (quartile III), growth rates were between 131–111%, including Leon (medium-sized), Manresa, Las Rozas, Gerona, Palencia, Figueras, and Segovia. Finally, the last group (with growth rates ranging between 134–97%) included Ciudad Real, Toledo, Lleida, Talavera, and Puertollano.

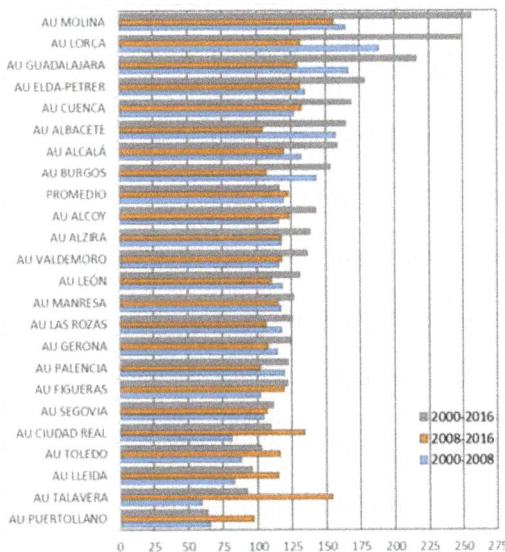

Figure 9. Variation rate of built-up area. Source: Register, several years. Own elaboration.

4.4. Evolution in the Number of Housing

The number of housing presents diverse situations between the cities and respective metropolitan areas. The urban areas of 23 cases, except in seven (Albacete, Alcalá, Burgos, Cuenca, Puertollano,

Palencia, and Lorca), have more homes than their central cities. They had greater relevance in the UAs of Alzira, Las Rozas, Gerona, Valdemoro, and Manresa (Figure 10).

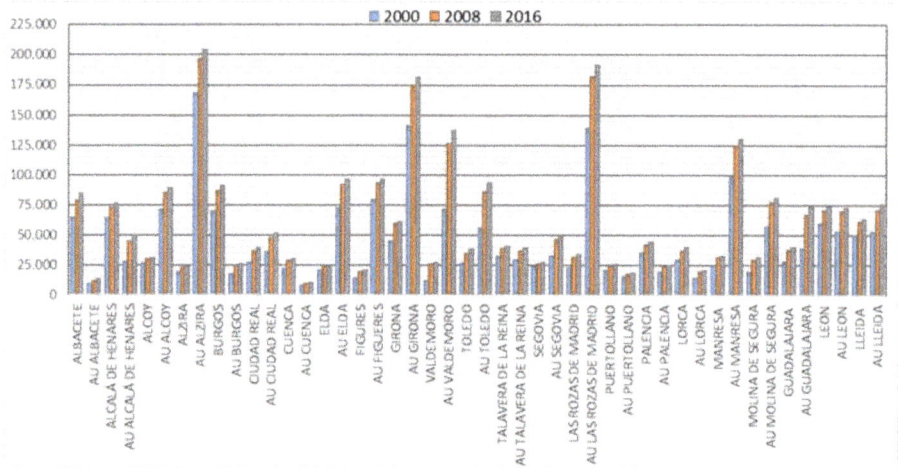

Figure 10. Evolution of the number of houses. Source: Register, several years. Own elaboration.

From an evolutionary point of view, it is clear how the widespread behaviour has been intense between 2000–2008; in most of the cases, the urban areas have remained, with superior trends over the city (Figure 11).

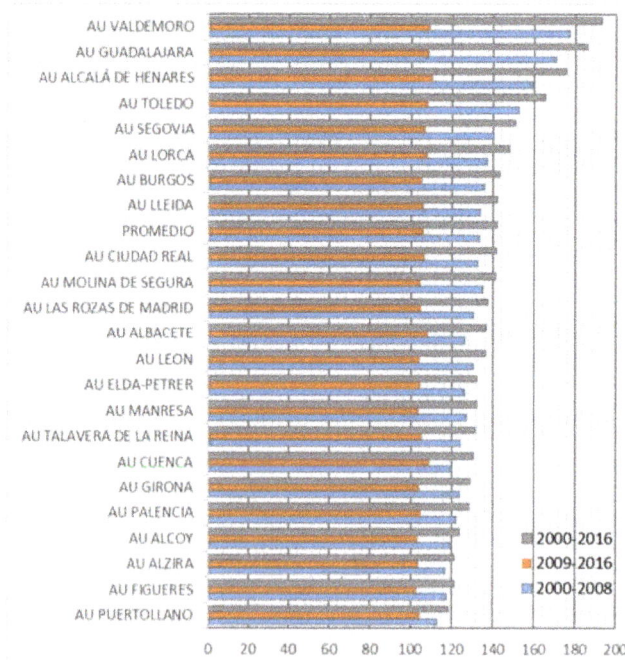

Figure 11. Rate of variation of the number of dwellings in urban areas. Source: Register, several years. Own elaboration.

Especially striking are the dynamics of the UAs of Valdemoro, Guadalajara, Alcalá de Henares, Toledo, or Segovia. These five urban areas appear in the first category (first quartile), where there has been a growth of more than 50% within those years. The second group (second quartile) includes Lorca, Burgos, Lleida, Ciudad Real, Molina, and Las Rozas (between 137–150% increase). Within the third category, we have Albacete, León, Elda-Petrer, Manresa, Talavera de la Reina, and Cuenca (with percentages of increase ranging from 136–148%). Finally, in the last group, we have those with less than 128% dynamics. The really remarkable thing here is that there was particularly intense behaviour between 2000–2008; in contrast, the dynamics were very contained between 2009–2016.

Possibly the best illustration of the process is the relationship, in absolute values, between the variations of population and housing. In some cases, this highlights the situation of housing deficit (when there is an increase of more than two inhabitants per built housing), as it happens in the cities located in the surroundings of Madrid, Barcelona, or some especially dynamic nuclei in which the trend has not slowed since 2000. Compared to these cases, we can see how the proportion decreases substantially in most of the analysed urban areas such as in León, Palencia, Segovia, Toledo, Figueras, Elda, Cuenca, Ciudad Real, Burgos, Alzira, Alcoy, and Albacete (where the ratio is one housing per capita). In these cases, it is reasonable to think that there has been a considerable stock of housing, inherited from the expansive cycle, that has not been absorbed by the market or that has been built under some unrealistic expectations of population growth and real need for housing (Figure 12).

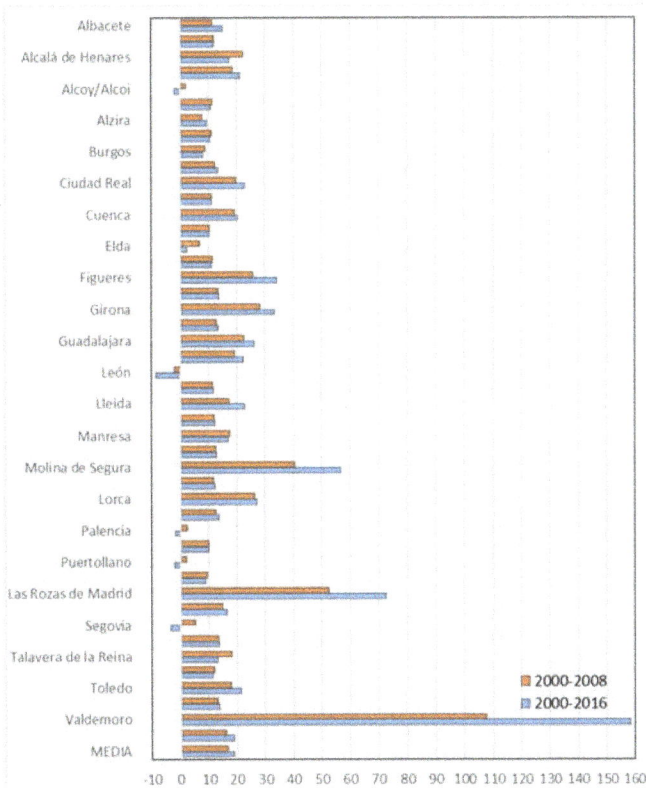

Figure 12. Relationship between the increase of population and housing. Source: Register, INE several years. Own elaboration.

5. Classification of Urban Areas Based on Its Dynamics

Grouping the behaviour of the UAs depending on the quartiles (to produce the grouping, values between one and four have been assigned to the Figure 13), six categories have been established (Table 1):

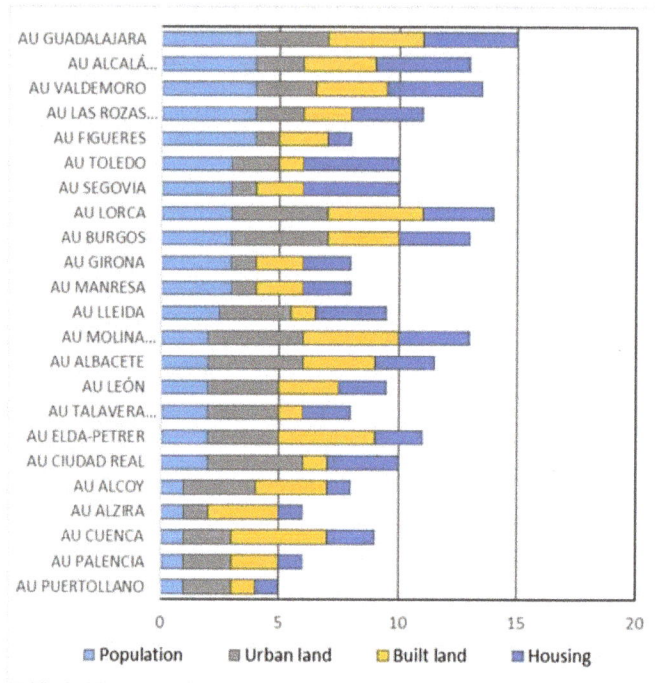

Figure 13. Score added by quartiles. Source: Register, Own elaboration.

Table 1. Classification of Urban Areas.

Category	Cities
Strong and balanced dynamics [1]	Guadalajara, Alcalá, Valdemoro, Las Rozas
Balanced dynamics [2]	Gerona, Manresa, Figueras
Accentuated dynamics of urban land creation	Ciudad Real, Albacete, León, Talavera, Lérida, Alcoy
Accentuated dynamics of land and built-up surface	Lorca, Burgos, Elda-Petrer, Cuenca, Molina del Segura
Pronounced dynamics in housing production	Toledo, Segovia
Contained dynamics	Alzira, Palencia, Puertollano

[1] In population, urban land, and housing. [2] The population has marked the trend of land and housing growth.

To establish the relationship (using regression) between the population and surface urbanised on the one hand, and the population and surface built on the other, the situation in which each urban area in relation to the rest is shown, as well as the changes that have operated over the time considered. The figures supplied (Figures 14 and 15) show how widespread an increase there has been in the three criteria (population, urban land, and built-up area), but with unequal intensity.

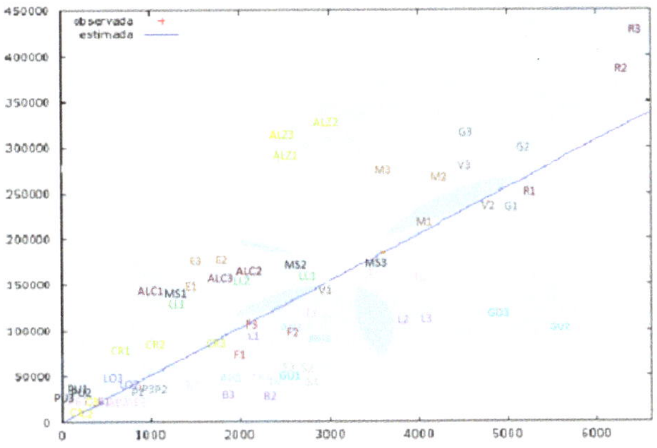

Figure 14. Regression: population and surface urbanised. X axis: Surface urbanised, Y axis: Population.

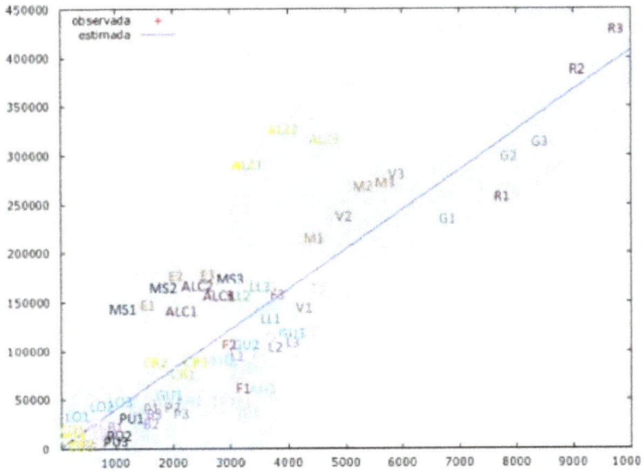

Figure 15. Regression: population and surface built. X axis: Surface built, Y axis: Population.

If we compare the population and built-up area, the regression from the values used leaves on balance an increase in all the crowns, which has been especially pointed between 2000–2008. This evolution is perceived especially in Las Rozas, Guadalajara, Valdemoro, Toledo, or León. It can also be seen that between 2008–2016 (a temporary cycle marked by crisis), there was a considerable brake on construction and new building sites. Despite this, there have been changes at lower intensity, although in some cases, these have been barely perceptible.

The graphic showing the ratio of site surface and population allows us to identify five categories of urban areas: (1) Las Rozas, Girona, Manresa, Valdemoro, and Alzira, which are urban areas with a high level of population and site surface; (2) Guadalajara, León, Toledo, and Manresa, which have average population levels, but high site surface; (3) average and moderate population weight areas such as Alcoy, Elda, Lérida, and Molina del Segura; (4) low and moderate population areas such as Figueras, Alcalá de Henares, Ciudad Real, and Burgos; and lastly, (5) cases with low dynamics in both criteria, such as Palencia, Lorca, Puertollano, and Albacete.

If we take into consideration the relationship between population and built-up area (i.e., what has been actually built until 2016), we can see how significant the changes appear. If we apply the same criteria of classification, we would have (1) a group of areas with a high presence of population and built-up areas, consisting of Las Rozas, Manresa, and Alzira; these cases could be added to that of

Gerona; (2) areas with an average and low weight of population in housing, including Alcoy, Lerida, Molina del Segura, and Elda; (3) a third category including areas with an average weight in housing areas and low weight in population, as we can see in León, Guadalajara, Toledo, Figueras, or Alcalá de Henares; and finally, we have (4) the areas with a low presence of population and building, such as the cases of Puertollano, Lorca, Burgos, Palencia, and Albacete.

The integration of the three criteria, through the use of variation rates for the period 2000–2016, from the geometric averages weighted (2016 population) (Figure 16) leaves an illustrative situation of the differential behavior among them, with urban areas in which the population has increased above the urbanised and built ground (Alcalá de Henares, Las Rozas, Valdemoro, or Segovia). Others have done so with a predominance of urbanised population area (Ciudad Real, Puertollano, Albacete, Leon, Lerida, Burgos, Lorca, or Molina del Segura). In other cases, there has been a clear dominance of the built-up surface area over the population (such as Cuenca, Ciudad Real and Elda, and cases added such as Albacete). In Guadalajara in contrast, there have been strong dynamics, which have simultaneously affected the population, built-up area, and land.

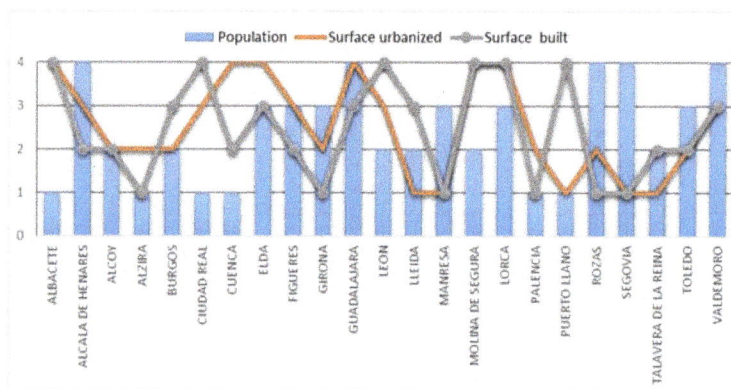

Figure 16. Relation between population, surface urbanised, and surface built.

6. Conclusions

In conclusion, it can be pointed out that the process of urban sprawl, in the cases and in the analysed periods, has been marked by very different territorial and temporal behaviours. On the one hand, we highlight the increase in dispersion that is associated with the context of economic growth in the first decade of the century. In those years, strong dynamics with different territorial intensities have appeared in the periphery. This can be seen in the significant increase of the population, the surface of unbuilt plots (where the change has been most intense), the surface of built-up plots, and the number of homes in some nearby towns, especially the border with the central city.

Dispersion dynamics have been bigger in the inserted medium-size cities with polynuclear metropolitan areas, such as is the case of Madrid. Meanwhile, the areas that are farther away from big cities tend to keep the trends that are more associated with the will of growth than a real need for it. In the latter, the demographic dynamics have been soft, while the processes of reclassification of land and house construction have been well above the real needs.

Subsequently, from 2009, the trend has slowed down sharply. The dynamics of population growth, along with the processes of urbanisation and the morphological and functional transformation of the peripheries, have stalled.

This growth has created changes in the location of the residential units and the type of housing, sometimes due to the interests of the peripheral municipalities, to join the dynamics of urban areas. What remains is a process of change for the city model that is associated with an economic context of growth. As a result, we also have a considerable reserve of land for future actions in urban peripheries.

Finally, a stock of built-up areas and very important housing appears for which there is a clear solution, since the expectations of growth from 2009 have stalled in peri-urban areas. There is an open debate on the future strategies of many urban areas regarding a change of look, which now is mainly focussed on the consolidated city.

Author Contributions: Both authors have jointly participated in the entire elaboration process of the article.

Funding: This article is part of the research project Dinámicas de urbanización y políticas urbanísticas en ciudades medias interiores. De expansión y dispersión a reformulación: ¿Hacia un urbanismo más ¿urbano? (Dynamics of urbanisation and urban planning policies in inner medium-sized cities. From expansion and dispersion to reformulation: towards a more urban urbanism?) subsidised by the State Research Programme of Development and Innovation Aimed to the challenges of society, 2015 Summon, Mode 1: 'R &D Projects» of the Ministry of Economy and Competitiveness with reference CSO2015-63970-R (MINECO/FEDER).

Conflicts of Interest: The authors declare no conflict of interest.

References

1. Burriel, E. La década prodigiosa del urbanismo español 1997–2006. *X Coloquio Internacional de Geocrítica: Diez años de Cambios en el Mundo, en la Geografía y en las Ciencias Sociales, 1999–2008.* Available online: http://www.ub.edu/geocrit/sn/sn-270/sn-270-64.htm (accessed on 15 September 2018).
2. Gaja, F. El "tsunami urbanizador" en el litoral mediterráneo. El ciclo de hiperproduccion inmobiliaria 1996–2006. *X Coloquio Internacional de Geocrítica. Diez años de cambio en el mundo, en la Geografía y en las Ciencias Sociales, 1999–2008.* Arroyo, M., Bonastra, Q., Casals, V., Jori, G., Sunyer, P., Hermi Zaar, M., Eds. Available online: http://www.ub.edu/geocrit/-xcol/189.htm (accessed on 15 September 2018).
3. Brenner, N. Restructuring, rescaling and the urban question. *Crit. Plan.* **2009**, *16*, 61–79.
4. Uhaldeborde, J.M. Las ciudades europeas: Nuevos paradigmas, nuevas estrategias. *Pap. Econ. Española* **2017**, *153*, 2–22.
5. Gonzalez, J.M. Urbanización turística. Reconversión y rehabilitación de destinos turísticos consolidados en Mallorca. In *Ciudades y Paisajes Urbanos en el Siglo XXI*; Delgado, C., Juaristi, J., Tomé, S., Eds.; ESTVDIO: Santander, España, 2012; ISBN 978-84-9320236.
6. Instituto Nacional de Estadística (INE). Padrón Municipal de Habitantes. Available online: http://www.ine.es (accessed on 16 April 2018).
7. U.E. *Methodological Manual on City Statistics*; Publications Office of the European Union: Luxembourg, 2017; ISBN 978-92-79-68736-5.
8. Navarro, J.R.; Ortuño, A. Aproximación a la génesis de la contribución de la densidad en la noción de ciudad compacta. *EURE* **2011**, *37*, 23–41. [CrossRef]
9. Garreau, J. *Edge City: Life on the New Frontier*; Anchor Books: New York, NY, USA, 1992.
10. Phelps, N.A.; Parsons, N.; Ballas, D.; Dowling, A. *Post-Suburban Europe. Planning and Politics at the Margins of Europe's Capital Cities*; Palgrave Macmillan: Basingstoke, UK, 2006; ISBN 978-0-230-62538-9.
11. EEA (Agencia Europea de Medio Ambiente). Urban Sprawl, the Ignored Challenge. Available online: https://www.eea.europa.eu/publications/eea_report_2006_10 (accessed on 9 March 2018).
12. Dematteis, G. Contraurbanizaçao, periurbanizaçao, cidade dispersa e rede de cidade na Italia. *Rev. Ciudad.* **2015**, *12*, 14–34.
13. Salvati, L.; Gargiulo, V. Unveiling Urban Sprawl in the Medierranean Region: Towards a Latent Urban Transformation? *Int. J. Urban Reg. Res.* **2014**, *6*, 1935–1953. [CrossRef]
14. Ekers, M.; Hamel, P.; Keil, R. Governing Suburbia: Modalities and Mechanisms of Suburban Governace. *Reg. Stud.* **2012**, *46*, 405–422. [CrossRef]
15. Soja, E.W. *Postmetrópolis. Estudios Críticos Sobre las Ciudades y las Regions*; Traficantes de Sueños: Madrid, España, 2008; ISBN 978-84-96453-32-6.
16. Indovina, F. *La Citta Diffusa*; Daest: Venecia, Italia, 1990.
17. Pumain, D.; Gyerois, M.; Pulus, F. L'etalement urbain en France. *GeoInnova* **2003**, *8*, 81–102.
18. Monclús, F. *La Ciudad Dispersa: Suburbanización y Nuevas Periferias*; Centre de Cultura Contemporània, D.L.: Barcelona, España, 1998; ISBN 84-88811-35-7.
19. Fariña, J. Cambiar el modelo urbano. *Rev. Ciudad.* **2015**, *18*, 69–78. [CrossRef]
20. Castells, M. *Sociedad Red*; Alianza Editorial: Madrid, España, 2006; ISBN 9788420647845.

21. Harvey, D. *Ciudades Rebeldes. Del Derecho de la Ciudad a la Revolución Urbana*; Akal: Madrid, España, 2013; ISBN 978-84-460-3799-6.
22. Lois, R.C.; Piñeira, M.J.; Vives, S. El proceso urbanizador en España (1990–2014): Una interpretación desde la Geografía y la teoría de los circuitos del capital. *Scr. Nova* **2016**, *20*, 539.
23. Rossi, U. *Cities in Global Capitalism*; Polity Press: Cambridge, UK, 2017; ISBN 9780745689678.
24. Herce, M. *El Negocio del Territorio. Evolución y Perspectivas de la Ciudad Moderna*; Alianza Editorial: Madrid, España, 2013; ISBN 978-84-206-7449-0.
25. Miyar, M.; Muñiz, J. Inmigrantes sucesivos en el mercado de trabajo español. Trayectorias migratorias y capital de movilidad. *Rev. Int. Sociol.* **2018**, *76*, 088. [CrossRef]
26. Romero, J. Construcción residencial y gobierno del territorio en España. De la burbuja especulativa a la recesión. Causas y consecuencias. *Rev. Cuad. Geogr.* **2010**, *47*, 17–46.
27. Pezzi, C.H. De la ciudad caótica a la ciudad sostenible ¿hay respuestas urbanísticas para la ciudad sostenible? In *Ciudades Resistentes, Ciudades Posibles*; Borja, J., Carrión, F., Corti, M., Eds.; UOC: Barcelona, España, 2017; ISBN 9788491168706.
28. Arellano, B.; Roca, J. El urban Sparwl ¿un fenómeno de alcance plantario? Los ejemplos de España y México. *Arquit. Ciudad Entono* **2010**, *12*, 115–147.
29. Brandis, D.; Del Río, I.; Morales, G. *Estudios de Geografía Urbana en Tiempos de Crisis. Territorios Inconclusos y Sociedades Rotas*; Biblioteca Nueva: Madrid, España, 2016; ISBN 978-84-16647-72-9.
30. Nación Rotonda. Available online: http://www.nacionrotonda.com (accessed on 7 September 2018).
31. EUROSTAT: Urban Audit. Available online: http://ec.europa.eu/eurostat/web/cities/data/database (accessed on 25 September 2018).
32. Ministerio de Fomento. Las Áreas Urbanas (Atlas Estadístico Áreas Urbanas). Available online: https://www.fomento.gob.es/MFOM/LANG_CASTELLANO/_ESPECIALES/SIU/ATLAS/ (accessed on 25 September 2018).
33. Pozo Rivera, E.; Cebrián Abellán, F. Residencial Francisco Hernando. Una urbanización desmedida e inconclusa en Seseña (Toledo). In *Estudios de Geografía Urbana en Tiempos de Crisis. Territorios Inconclusos y Sociedades Rotas*; Brandis, D., Del Río, I., Morales, G., Eds.; Biblioteca Nueva: Madrid, España, 2016; ISBN 978-84-16647-72-9.

urban science

MDPI

Article

Land Squandering in the Spanish Medium Sized Cities: The Case of Toledo

Irene Sánchez Ondoño [1] and Luis Alfonso Escudero Gómez [2],*

[1] Department of Geography, University of Castilla-La Mancha, 02071 Albacete, Spain;
    irene.sanchezondono@uclm.es
[2] Department of Geography, University of Castilla-La Mancha, 45071 Toledo, Spain
*   Correspondence: luisalfonso.escudero@uclm.es; Tel.: +34-925268800-5312

Received: 31 December 2018; Accepted: 24 January 2019; Published: 27 January 2019

Abstract: A process of land squandering began in Spain in the mid 1990s until the great crisis of 2008. The intensive production of urban land affected the Spanish medium-sized towns. They were characterized by their compact nature and then they underwent an intense diffuse urbanization. However, in some cases there had been previous examples of urban sprawl. In this article, we study one of them, the unique and historic city of Toledo, in the Centre of the Iberian Peninsula. We will show how the city has experienced the land squandering and has been extensively widespread throughout the hinterland, consisting of their peripheral municipalities. We will also check how Toledo has had a previous internal dispersion process in the last quarter of the 20th Century through the called *Ensanche* (widening). We will use the urban estate cadaster as a fundamental source for evolutionary and present analysis of the city and its hinterland. The field and bibliographic work complete the methodology. The final conclusion is that there have been remarkable urban increments in Spanish medium-sized cities such as Toledo, in external and peripheral districts, under the logic of speculation and profit, resulting in a disjointed space.

Keywords: urban geography; urbanism; urban growth; medium-sized city; suburbanization; Spain

---

1. Introduction

The processes of urban growth have been usually associated with large cities and coastal towns with great influence in the sector of tourism. However, the interior medium-sized cities have also taken part of morphological and territorial transformation processes. These urban entities have been of undoubted scientific interest, however, there is not absolute consensus with its definition. Roger Brunet, given such complexity, came to define them as UGO, standing for Unidentified Geographic Object [1].

The term of medium-sized city has its origins in France [2]. In the Spanish context, early work on medium-sized cities dates back to the 1980s [3–5]. They tried to clarify some of the most significant features of these cities in Spain and, although no definition is required, it can be noted how the size of the population was the best exponent for the definition of this urban reality.

Also, the problems arising around Barcelona and Madrid and the complex territorial articulation of their metropolitan areas will lead to a reflection that places medium-sized cities as elements of territorial cohesion [6]. Over the years, they are associated with positions of urban equilibrium and conceived as more urban spaces, having more apprehensible scales for their citizens [7,8].

With the turn of the century, the term intermediate city was almost generally accepted. Then, a new door of debate on the problems of conceptualization was open, medium-sized cities had been affected by intense processes of change that inevitably forced to study the urban hierarchy within the international context influenced by the complex logic derived from globalization. Thus, intermediate cities are characterized by the role played in the territory not only regarding the capacity to articulate their environment but also regarding the influence that they generate and the relationships that they are able to establish with other spaces. In short, it must be highlighted their role as carriers of goods and services to those cities and/ or rural municipalities on which they exert influence. In addition, their ability to connect different levels of networks (at a local, national, and even international level) is remarkable [9].

The definition of intermediate cities with their clear vocation of intermediation, left the quantitative criteria behind to conceptualize from the explanation of qualitative, economic, functional and territorial factors, where the capacity to organize more balanced urban systems with a higher quality of life is essential [10].

The most recent studies on medium-sized cities have been approached from different perspectives (scattered and oversized growths-in most cases-which leave the traditional compact city model aside) that share one thing in common: the model of diffuse city. However, the term is not subject to a concise definition. On the contrary, and it is the same as with the concept of medium-sized cities, this reality associated with urban sprawl does not have a clear definition since their building density, the morphological typologies, the intensity of use and/or the possible territorial effects to which urban dispersion refers are unknown [11].

This phenomenon has been characterized from different terms that come to represent a similar reality: city-region [12], urbanized field [13], diffuse city model [14], city sprawl [15], no city [16], inefficient city [17]. The explanatory processes that derive in this situation are also complex and are hidden under vague terminologies: Urban Sprawl [18], Counter-urbanization [19], and Suburbanization [20].

Defining and specifying its characterization is complex. However, it is a structural process that reorganizes the urban form from the displacement of population and activities to the periphery of the cities. In Spain, it has been strengthened, among other factors, by the modernization of the production system, the use of new technologies, the continuous increase of accessibility, the availability of land with more competitive prices, the widespread use of private vehicles, and the change in demand preferences [21].

Thus, it can be corroborated how the urban growth has spread to the periphery of the medium-sized cities in the last decades [1]. An intensive process of urbanization at the expense of neighboring rural municipalities [22] has taken place in most of them. The trend in these nuclei and areas is the progressive occupation of the territory, which takes part of the residential function, until recently reserved to the central city [23]. Large urban areas that have substantially modified the structure and the characteristics of the medium-sized cities and their peripheries have been formed.

The new logic of urbanization that appeared in recent decades in these cities has altered its traditional, compact, intense, and dense structure. They have given way to new forms, extensive territorial and more scattered structures, accompanied by morphological, functional and social transformations [24].

Chronologically the existence of two very distinct stages can be emphatically stated: an initially exaggerated growth that begins to be noticed in the middle of the 1990s and the first years of the 21st century, called by some authors "the prodigious decade of urbanism" [25] or "urban tsunami" [26]; and a second phase where the model that had been raised years ago comes to an end by its own unsustainability, leading to a deep economic crisis that eventually burst in 2008 [27].

Since the 1980s, and primarily between 1990 and up to the 2008 crisis, an intense process of dispersed urbanization affecting medium-sized cities occurred in Spain [28]. There are recent dynamics related to the real estate boom and the increasing artificialization of soil in 2000 [29]. In fact, the nearby municipalities now play a residential function that is associated with the increase in daily movements between home and place of work [23]. We must also add urban planning that encouraged the expansive growth based on considering large tracts of land as urban and thus encouraging urbanization [30].

The result has been that these cities have gone from more or less continuous, and compact structures, especially in the interior and provincial capitals, to others more dispersed and discontinuous that extend over their respective urban areas [31]. It is a new model of residential production that has resulted in a dispersed urban territory [32]. The model of suburbanization has deeply permeated with the growth of cities towards its peripheries. In medium sized cities we can see urban decentralization, peri-urbanization, and the formation of low density frames, analogous to the processes of soil expansion and consumption [23]. Thus, a supra-municipal city is created, generated by the sum of fragments without continuity in its urban fabric [33]. This recent growth in diffuse medium urban areas has meant a strong intake of soil and considerable environmental consequences [34].

This process of speculative urban growth related to neoliberal capitalism is of great interest for the above-mentioned scholars focused on urban studies [35–38]. Spain is a good example of it within the urban sciences in recent years and the phenomenon has been analyzed as a whole. There have been studies since the end of the 20th century [39], which already had a concern about urbanism that would be applied in the 21st century and some recommendations were given but they were not applied [40]. On the other hand, there was a process of appropriation of the incomes of the soil in the neo-liberal Spanish city, which resulted in land squandering [41] and, after the crisis, there was a profit topography characterized by its modern ruins [42] and serious social and territorial consequences [43]. Lois, Piñeira and Vives deeply, synthetically and completely describe this urbanization process that has taken place in Spain in the last decade of the 20th century until the great recession that began in 2008 [44]. Today, scholars proclaimed the necessity of overcoming this model of building [45].

More specifically, they also tried to understand the expansion of the urban peripheries and new spatial forms that are generated in the Spanish cities [46] and the challenge of sustainability that has been generated [47]. In a concrete way, the dynamics of the area of concern to this research, the *Ensanches* (widenings) are studied by Coudroy de Lille [48]. In Spanish urbanism *Ensanche* is an extension of the first comprehensive planned development outside of the historic centre and its proximity in each city, although chronologically the first and authentic *Ensanches* are of the 19th century and beginning of the 20th century, in cities like Toledo, characterized by its atony, become much more contemporary phenomena.

In addition, case studies have been spread in order to understand the process of a more extensive and specific way. A case study is a research approach that facilitates the exploration of a phenomenon within a specific context using a variety of sources of data [49]. These studies are mainly focused on the large metropolitan areas of Spain, with a great interest in those of Barcelona [50,51] and Madrid [52,53]. There are also essays based on large cities within the Spanish urban system. Thus, Díaz Parra [54] discusses the growth of Seville as a production of a commodity for the logic of neo-liberal capitalism and Escolano, López, and Pueyo study the case of Zaragoza [55] in the first fifteen years of the 21st century as an example of neo-liberal urbanism and urban fragmentation. Case studies of medium-sized cities as Albacete [56] or Burgos [57] have also been published.

In this article we study the medium sized city of Toledo, with a population of 83,741 inhabitants in 2017 [58], and a diffuse growth that has spread to the municipalities that surround it. How has the land squandering taken place in the medium-sized cities of Spain, as in the case of Toledo? This is the first research question. The first objective of the research is to analyze this process. But, immediately, a question about its novelty came out. Before the recent process of diffuse city we referred to a model that characterized the medium sized cities as compact [31]. Was it always this way? In other words, did the Spanish medium-sized cities have examples of urban dispersion before the recent diffuse urbanization process towards the peripheral municipalities? Did compact but, at the same time, equally unconnected growth occur? These are the second and third research questions. These research questions are answered in the second part of the article: a case study of the so-called *Ensanche* of Toledo. Through this example, it can be observed that a speculative urban growth had already resulted in Toledo in fragmented spaces.

Toledo is located at latitude 39°51′24″ North and longitude 4°1′28″ West, in the center of the Iberian Peninsula, in the so-called South Plateau and about 70 km south of Madrid, capital of Spain. It is inserted within the autonomous community of Castilla-La Mancha, an inner region characterized by low demographic density and relatively stable population dynamics in recent decades. One of its most notable features is that the distribution and size of cities have not allowed the establishment of a regional capital capable of organizing the rest of the urban nuclei [59]. This derives its status as a acephalous region and the great influence of Madrid on the territory of Castilla-La Mancha, especially striking in the case of Guadalajara and Toledo (autonomic capital) [60].

In such a way, Toledo, standing as a medium-sized city with a status of regional administrative center, belongs to an urban agglomeration of higher level (Madrid), has a high tourist attraction derived from its declaration as a World heritage City by UNESCO and organizes a wide rural area [61].

To understand the dynamics of urban growth in Toledo, it is necessary to take into account different peculiarities of geographic type, historical type-related to the multiple archaeological finds [61], and legislative type. Regarding the first, the Tagus river is the main key to understand the actual configuration of the current space. Around it, you can notice up to four types of landscapes: historic center, the peri-urban area called "Los Cigarrales", Las Vegas del Tajo, and the northern spaces [58].

Legislative-type reasons are directly linked to the absence of territorial planning that allows an orderly connection to the city of Toledo. In this sense, it is worth highlighting the disarticulation in the urban development of the city by the lack of a model of growth coherently managed from the different urban planning plans that they have had in Toledo" [62].

The structure of the article fits the presented speech: an introductory part, a second part analyzing the dispersion of Toledo towards their peripheral municipalities, and a third part studying the *Ensanche*.

The article is located in the current research on the medium-sized cities and in the processes observed in their central core and respective urban areas.

The inclusion of the paper in the special issue "Land Squandering and Social Crisis in the Spanish City" is perfectly justified by observing the changes that have taken place as well in the urban area of Toledo as in the central city. These morphological transformations have been derived from the different economic, social and political processes that have been developing in the Spanish context in the 21st century.

In addition, the tendencies appreciated in the city of Toledo and its hinterland coincide with the dynamics given throughout the national territory, observing a period of growth that ends in 2008. Currently, there is an open discussion around the problems caused by a model that has been unsustainable in most cities in Spain.

2. Methodology

The research starts from the study of the growth of the city of Toledo in relation to the urban morphology. For the analysis of the urban sprawl of Toledo and the municipalities that are in their area of influence has been proceeded to the analysis of indicators that allow to study the evolution of the soil that has been urbanized and/or constructed. The importance is not exclusively confined to the main city (Toledo) but it is intended to observe the dynamics, derived from the processes of suburbanization, given in the municipalities that make up the suburbs. This has established a 30-km hinterland around the central city that allows us to know the area of urban sprawl. The analysis unit of the study has been the municipality, as long as it is considered as the basic local entity of the National Territorial Organization. The use of this unit allows us to study the added behavior of the city suburbs of Toledo. However, there are also some difficulties arising from the great variety in terms of area and population existing between municipalities.

Other factors that can determine the study are also highlighted. In this case we refer to the importance of the situation of the elements studied with respect to the main routes of communication, the proximity to Madrid and/or Toledo. From the temporal point of view, the period 2000–2016 has been selected, which has been analyzed from different perspectives. In order to establish similarities or differences, the variables have been analyzed separately around two completely distinguished moments: a first cycle originating from the beginning of the 21st century and culminating in the year

2008 with the crash of the economic crisis that same year and a later period until the year 2016. In these two phases, very adverse behaviors can be distinguished in the real-estate sector and in the construction of cities. The particularly abrupt recess caused by the crisis of the year 2008 led to a huge change from the predecessor period, giving way to a new cycle defined by completely inverse features, that is, a time of absence of dynamics in contrast with a growth excessive in most cases. The methodology allows us to analyze what happened throughout the period according to the unequal behavior of two periods that have the same number of years but are incomparable in turn by the logics carried out.

The objective of studying the whole period (2000–2016) around the built surface and surface not built is to verify the differences between the hectares of land that have been urbanized and those that were urbanized and materialized in the practice, that is to say, those that were actually built.

Thus, the variables used have been population, surface of built urban areas and surface of urban area without building. The first one has been obtained from the data provided by the National Institute of Statistics, while the remaining ones have been downloaded from the website of the land registry.

The cartography of the first part of the work shows a series of intervals that aim to reflect the different behavior of the municipalities. This always establishes a negative value and an increase ranging from: moderate growth rates 0–50, high growth 50–100 and very high growth more than 100). Summary-tables have also been used to introduce the data that have been believed to be most significant.

The analysis around the *Ensanche* of Toledo allows us to analyze the temporal evolution of the shaping of the widening over the period from 1950 to the present, as well as the structuring and uses of its use. To show such results, cartographic representation has been proceeding. Taking for granted, the methodology has been completed with fieldwork and a bibliographical review.

The article is located in the current research on the medium-sized cities and on the processes observed both in its central areas and in their respective urban areas.

3. Results

3.1. The Urban Area of Toledo: An External Dispersion

Toledo is located at latitude 39°51′24″ North and longitude 4°1′28″ West, in the center of the Iberian Peninsula, in the so-called South Plateau and about 70 km south of Madrid, capital of Spain. It is inserted within the autonomous community of Castilla-La Mancha. The city of Toledo has actively participated in the process of urban growth that has spread to the outskirts of Spanish medium-sized cities in recent decades [63]. Thus, there has been an intense urbanization in their neighboring municipalities. This section discusses this aspect through demographic data and the evolution of the surface built between 2000 and 2016 by the land registry. To study the outskirts of the central city we choose to establish a hinterland of 30 km and we take into consideration all its municipalities.

From the demographic point of view, and in response to Figure 1, the most populous municipalities of the province of Toledo in the year 2016 correspond to the capital city and Talavera de la Reina, with a population of 83,459 and 84,119 inhabitants respectively. This is a reality that does not represent the vast majority of the municipalities of Toledo, which do not exceed the number of 5000 inhabitants (175 of a total 204). Immediately thereafter, the major municipalities are concentrated in the hinterland of the 30 km of Toledo and in the North area with respect to the capital city, adjoining with the province of Madrid.

Table 1 shows the municipalities 30 km away fromToledo that have acquired rates of population variation over 50% between 2000 and 2016. Up to 18 of them meet this premise with percentages ranging from 65% of Recas to 605% of Barcience. In fact, a total of 9 municipalities have seen their population doubled or more in the last 15 years. The demographic dispersion in the urban area of the medium-sized city and capital of Castilla-La Mancha, Toledo, is evident.

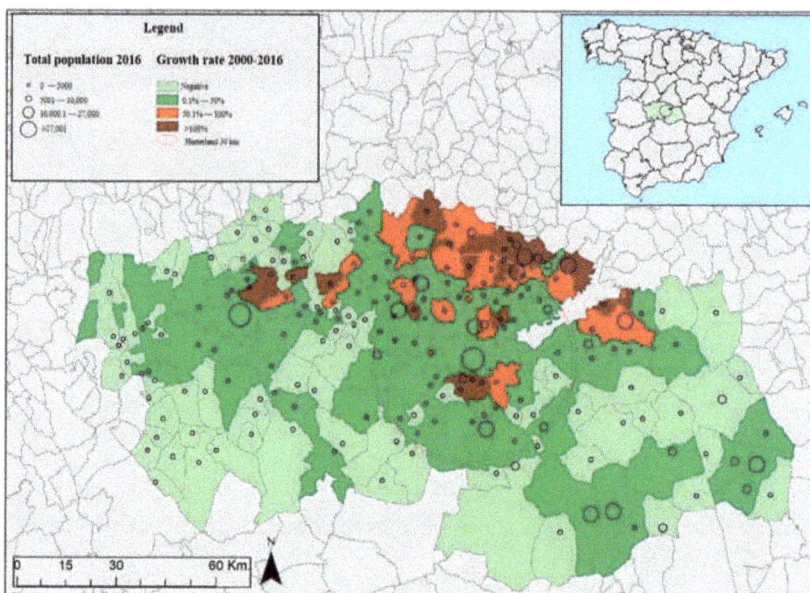

Figure 1. Total population in 2016 and growth rate in the province of Toledo by municipalities for the period 2000–2016. Source: INE [58] and self-elaboration.

Table 1. Municipalities of the urban area of Toledo with a growth rate exceeding 50% between 2000 and 2016 Source: INE [58].

Municipality	Population 2000	Population 2008	Population 2016	Variation Rate 2000–2016 (%)
Barcience	111	481	783	605
Chozas de Canales	1002	3485	3710	270
Burguillos de Toledo	965	2399	3092	220
Magán	1137	2738	3225	184
Yuncos	3760	8623	10,613	182
Cobisa	1618	3645	4186	159
Argés	2477	5178	6093	146
Cedillo del Condado	1542	2520	3680	139
Layos	268	444	625	133
Lominchar	1198	1735	2365	97
Yuncler	1855	3161	3648	97
Numancia de la Sagra	2555	4448	4734	85
Palomeque	483	878	876	81
Villamiel de Toledo	477	812	857	80
Novés	1545	2500	2707	75
Nambroca	2603	3415	4524	74
Olías del Rey	4287	6413	7357	72
Recas	2614	3498	4309	65

One of the variables that can help to realize the effects of urban sprawl is the surface of built and unbuilt urban plots. The used information has been extracted from the cadaster [64]. So, it has been selected for Toledo and its area of influence, 30 km, the area of urban plots, both built and unbuilt, for the years 2000, 2008 and 2016 in order to identify the dynamics occurred before (2000–2008) and after the crisis (2009–2016). In Figure 2 the results are mapped. You can see how the surface of urban plots has varied considerably in the two periods mentioned. Between 2000 and 2008 a strong growth of the surface built in the central core of Toledo and its Northern and Southern peripheral municipalities takes place. With respect to the period, 2009–2016, the dynamic presents different features. There are many more municipalities with negative rates, a direct result of the effects of the crisis, although some still keep growth rates, although they are lower.

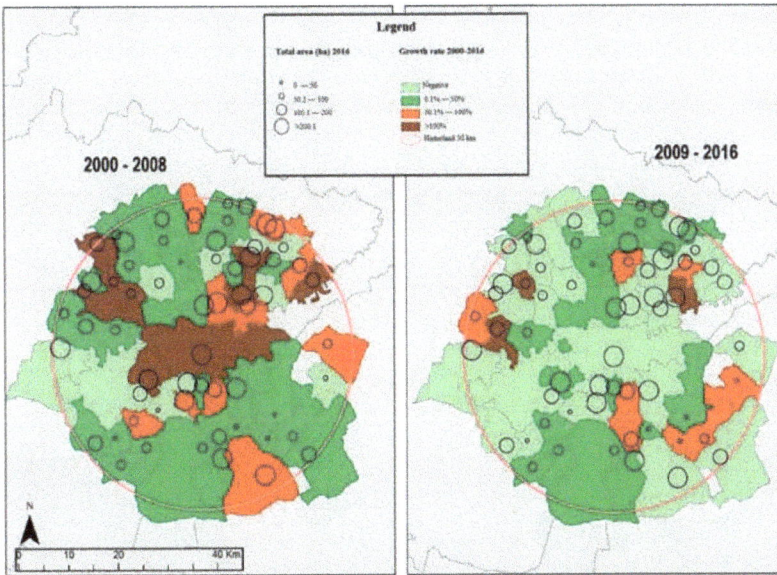

Figure 2. Growth rate of the built surface in the municipalities of the urban area of Toledo between 2000–08, and 2008-16. Source: Land Registry [64] and self-elaboration.

From Table 2 we can see the importance that the hinterland acquires as a whole with respect to the city of Toledo. The group of municipalities located within thirty kilometers, both in built-up areas and unbuilt surface for the three years analyzed represent a clear superiority to the central city. As for temporal evolution, in the year 2000 we can see the overall trends associated to the time with the greatest growth, thus grouping a total of 7900 hectares between built and unbuilt areas. Of course, the role of the urban area is much more significant with respect to the city of Toledo (15% hectares of built-up area and 21.3% hectares of unbuilt surface compared to 85% and 78.7%). Indeed, the percentages of the hinterland always exceed, in greater or lesser extent, the central city. However, in 2008 Toledo managed to increase 19.7% of hectares of built-up area and 22.2% of hectares of unbuilt areas with respect to the previous year. In 2016, the capital shows back descendant dynamics, losing 5.8% of the built-up area, but tripling the corresponding hectares with the plots (17.4%). The analysis of the data shows one of the symptoms of the change in the model of compact city to the sparse urban area.

Table 2. Evolution of the built-up and unbuilt areas between 2000 and 2016 in Toledo and in its hinterland of 30 km. Source: Land Registry [64].

	Built-up Surface (Ha)						Unbuilt Surface (Ha)					
	2000	%	2008	%	2016	%	2000	%	2008	%	2016	%
Toledo	853	15	2376.6	34.7	2106.0	28.9	834.1	21.3	3553.3	43.5	1388.4	26.1
Hinterland	4827.4	85	4471.2	65.3	5191.4	71.1	3072.6	78.7	4613.3	56.5	3934.0	73.9
Total	5680.4	100	6847.8	100	7297.4	100	3906.6	100	8166.6	100	5322.5	100

Another important issue is related to the amount of built-up and unbuilt areas shown in Figure 3. One of the conclusions that can be extracted having a look to the map is that the amount of developable surface generated in the period has been really excessive. If we look at the rate of variation of the built-up area for the period 2000–2016, we appreciate how five municipalities obtain values greater than 100%, this is the case of Burguillos de Toledo (106.27%), Toledo (146.90%), Novés (153.49%), Villaluenga de la Sagra (156.58%), and Barcience (404.14%), a municipality that obtains a rate of 572.99% of the total area of urban plots (built and unbuilt) throughout the cycle.

But perhaps the unbuilt surface is really significant. Many municipalities have exceeded 100% of the rate of growth, but still the most striking are Layos 3,270% and Burujón 1,105%. Both greatly exceed 1000%! Barcience (753%), Magan (642%), Guadamur (609%), and Villaseca de la Sagra (607%) are between 500 and 1000%. Below, but also with very high values, are Villaminaya (430.76%) Ajofrín (363.19%), Toledo (327.11%), Camarenilla (264.31%), and Escalonilla (228.85%). As a reference, Toledo has a growth rate of 66.5% of unbuilt surface and 146.90% of built-up area.

Ultimately, approximately half of the municipalities of the hinterland in Toledo within a radius of thirty kilometers exceeds growth rates of urban parcels higher than 50%, reaching really striking levels in some cases.

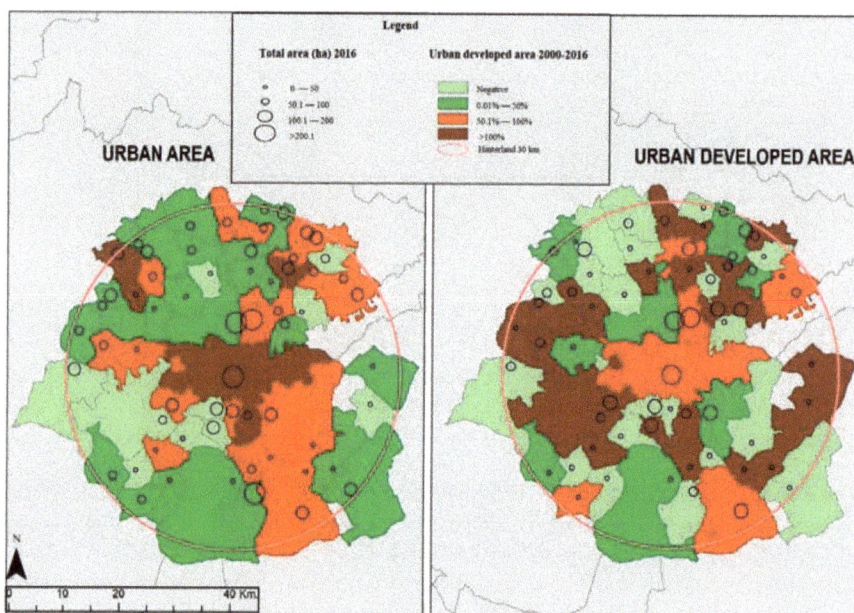

Figure 3. Total of urban area and urban developed area in 2016 and growth rates between 2000 and 2016 in the hinterland within a radius of 30 km in Toledo. Source: Land Registry [64] and self-elaboration.

This way of showing the urban sprawl from the indicators that have been analyzed (built-up and unbuilt areas) helps us to understand how the "urbanizing tsunami", continuing with the metaphor of Gaja [27], has reached the heart of the Iberian Peninsula and has resulted in dramatic increases in the built surface of the urban area of Toledo, at the same time that it entirely applied the rule that everything is buildable [65] in a lot of their municipalities.

3.2. Ensanche (Widening) of Toledo: An Internal Dispersion.

The urban sprawl of Spanish medium-sized cities towards its periphery has resulted in a dispersed city in Toledo, both within the central municipality and in the peripheral municipalities. Changing from a central compact city to a scattered and fragmented urban area. However, Toledo already had a clear dislocation before the real estate boom and the intense urbanization process in the last years. Since the 1960s and up to the most contemporary transformation beginning in the 1990s, the city, through two general plans of urban development, in 1964 and 1986, had already experienced an internal scattering process through the so-called *Ensanche* [66].

The emergence of a number of peripheral districts in the outskirts of Toledo takes place during this urban growth, and they completely lack the urban agenda typical of the Spanish *Ensanches* of the nineteenth-century. An urban planning was applied in a minority of cities [48] among which Toledo is not included. In fact, the Laws for *Ensanches* of the 19th-century responded to the needs of growth of the industrial city [48]. This requirement did not exist in Toledo. For this reason, the widening was not proposed. And the one which would be eventually created, many decades later, responds to the model of capitalist post-industrial town, and the speculative designs on the market.

The *Ensanche* of Toledo takes place in the northern part of the municipality, it started in the decade of 1960–1970, but it is mainly developed from the General Plan of 1986 (see Figure 4) and reaches its most extreme location, the neighborhood of Buenavista in 2008. It mainly covers Palomarejos, Santa Teresa, Avenida de Europa and Buenavista. It is located in the area known as Vega Baja, alluvial plain of the river Tajo downstream from the historic centre, until the slope that closes the Valley in the North. This is not a compact urban development, but a space built in different eras and interstitial spaces (see Figure 5). The expansion does not form a single planned set. On the contrary, it results from the sum of sectors situated in the Northern part of Toledo, built in a long temporal process and with a clear dispersion and fragmentation.

Figure 4. The *Ensanche* of Toledo in the 1986 PGOU. Source: City Council of Toledo [67] and self- elaboration.

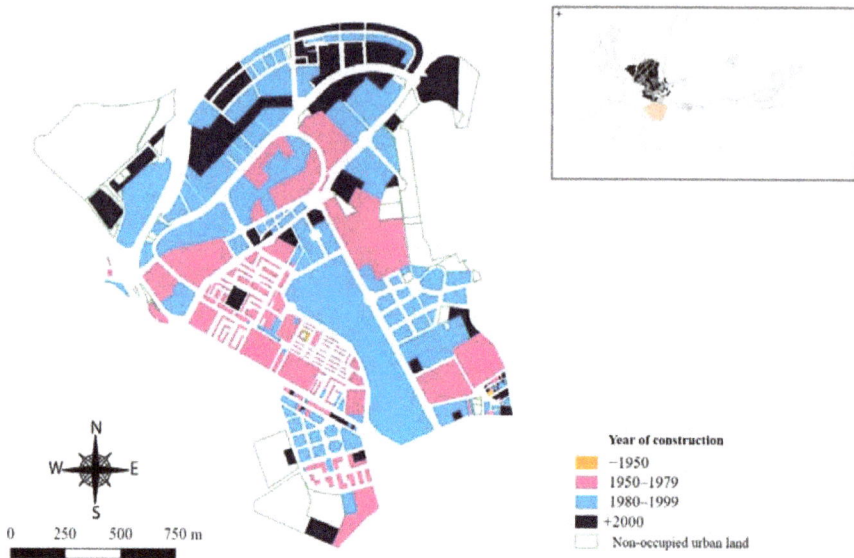

Figure 5. Year of construction of the real estate of the *Ensanche* of Toledo. Source: own elaboration based on CartoCiudad [68] and the land registry [64].

In this way, the *Ensanche* does not form a unit, but it is a mosaic of different neighborhoods. Chronologically, the first one is Palomarejos. It was created in the decade of 1960 with public housing in order to absorb the population living in substandard housing settlements in the municipality. Its volume of rectangular blocks, and small-sized households differs from the rest of the sectors of the *Ensanche*. Despite being a public performance, it was not executed as it was planned. Thus, Palomarejos is abruptly cut on its western side. It's a neighborhood locked up in itself by its own architecture.

Santa Teresa and Avenida de Europa, on the other hand, are sectors of towers of middle and upper-middle class, of mainly private housing constructions. They are expensive and speculative real estate products. However, urban problems appear again. Santa Teresa is also an incomplete neighborhood radically cut by the West. Here we find a wide interstitial space, today used as free parking outdoor. The aim was to make a great urban performance which included the presence of a department store. The autonomous Government stopped this process due to the emergence of important archaeological sites and social pressure [69]. The area known as *Avenida de Europa* presented a regular map, but with sloping topography. Despite the quality of the buildings, it is a clearly fragmented and unattractive neighborhood for passers-by from the rest of the city. Their volumes and forms gave rise to another differential unit in the contemporary landscape of Toledo, in the East of the *Ensanche* (see Figure 6).

Finally, the distant district of Buenavista is located in the North of the *Ensanche*. The duration of the process of urbanization has been extended (see Figure 5). It still possesses large empty building spaces. The interests of its builders and promoters have marked the times and the irrational urban fabric of this sector is out of all urban logic. A wide variety of building types and volumes are mixed together. The public spaces are disconnected and a great part of the built areas consists of common private spaces. It is also very common to find the typology of closed blocks of buildings. The sloping topography also contributes to the unstructured nature of this industry.

The fragmentation and disconnection of sectors forming the *Ensanche* lead to a variety of uses (see Figure 7). The dispersion, together with the residential character of well-off people of all sectors, except Palomarejos (just the opposite, a clear popular district), has resulted in the emergence of facilities, services and economic activities. Thus, urban substructures were formed, according to

Mierzejewska [70]. Santa Teresa, Avenida de Europa, and Buenavista are respectively structural and functional areas relatively uniform and autonomous, isolated and scattered fragments within the compact city of Toledo. Private investors, most of them promoters, led to the appearance of these substructures as multifunctional properties.

Figure 6. Panoramic view of the *Ensanche* of Toledo.

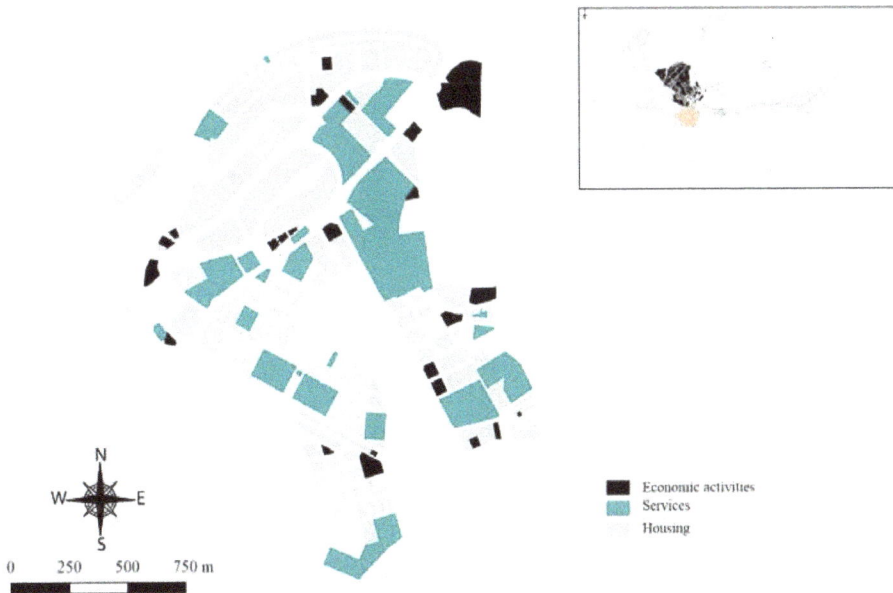

Figure 7. Main uses of the soil of the *Ensanche* of Toledo. Source: self- elaboration from Cartociudad [68] and the Land Registry [64].

4. Discussion

The urban landscapes of the 21st century have been the subject of intense scientific debate due to the deep morphological and structural modifications that have taken place throughout the national territory. This article is a case study through the urban area of Toledo and, in particular, a fragment of its urban structure: the *Ensanche*. For this reason, it presents the limitations derived from this fact. However, this is a significant case of this process in the medium-sized cities of Spain. Spanish cities have adopted the typical forms of urban sprawl by building the city based on certain parameters that have nothing to do with the precepts of the compact model where the limits of the city are well defined. The resulting space presents discontinuous and fragmented traits that, however, are related [25].

From the case studies, you can see the different manifestations of this mode in Spain. It is worth highlighting the studies on Spanish medium cities that have been analyzed around this debate, in different territorial areas, giving rise to a rich scientific literature: Castilla y León [71,72], Castilla-La Mancha [73–77], Catalonia and the provinces of Girona [78], Lerida [79,80], and Manresa [81], Santiago de Compostela [82], and Andalusia [83,84].

This profound change resulted in the transformation of the national territory, with greater or lesser intensity according to the different zones that have been questioned from multiple perspectives. The criticisms are related to a model that derives in territorial incoherence because there is no scheduled planning, together with a high consumption of urban land, an excessive mobility in terms of environmental pollution and higher consumption, and the increase in public spending by the scattered city [14,85].

Regarding the *Ensanche* of Toledo, it is noteworthy to point out its dispersed form because the buildings are separated from each other and with intermediate interstitial spaces. In addition, some of these fragments have not been finished and do not correspond to the previous planning. Its limits are incomplete and have unoccupied soil in its internal morphology. For this reason, the *Ensanche* of Toledo does not respond to the idea of a continuous urban development that characterizes the construction of the suburbs areas close to the historic city centre of most of the Spanish cities, in which there are no free spaces and a compact form of the buildings built. The *Ensanche* of Toledo gives rise to a dispersed area, with small urban sectors separated from each other, and fragmented, with incomplete sectors with disarticulated fragments and free spaces not occupied. It is a reality of dispersion and fragmentation different from that of the urbanization of the Anglo-Saxon cities [86] in the shape, since they are not single-family houses with garden but blocks of flats.

Thus, the alternatives follow the trend proposed by Oriol Nel.lo: "A Sprawl, specialization and banality must be opposed compactness, diversity and complexity, ie urban intensity. Against dispersion, intensity: this must be the first guide of the new policy." [87] (p. 282).

5. Conclusions

A process of artificialization of land and extension of built-up areas qualified as a real estate boom took place in Spain from the decade of 1990 and until 2008. In the last decade, the economic crisis, just worsened by the outbreak of the called "real estate bubble", has paralyzed the urban growth. Even so, the medium sized cities had already accumulated an urban sprawl that collides head-on with a past of compact central core. This dispersed urbanization, in fact, overflowed the central municipality in order to extend itself through the peripheral municipalities of their urban areas. It happened in the capital of Castilla-La Mancha, Toledo. With the case study we can answer the first question of the investigation: How has the land squandering taken place in the medium-sized cities of Spain, as in the case of Toledo? It has mainly taken place through a demographic growth and the construction of the suburbs areas in the peripheral municipalities in the period 2000–08. After the crisis, this dispersed urbanization of the central municipality to the peripherals has been paralyzed.

However, it has been shown, through the case study of Toledo, that in the peripheral districts of Spanish medium-sized towns, under the logic of speculation and profit, it occasionally resulted in a disjointed and morphologically impersonal space. This responds to the second main research question of the paper: Did the Spanish medium-sized cities have examples of urban dispersion before the recent diffuse urbanization process towards the peripheral municipalities? Yes, they had it. The so-called *Ensanche* of Toledo is a clear example of this inner dispersion. This name has its origin in the figure of the Spanish urbanism of the nineteenth century, very far away from the nineteenth-century paradigms, it is mainly a private and speculative growth. It does not fit a planned unit: the urban management plans of the city gave rise to a dispersed construction process lengthened in time and with a hodgepodge of architecture and volumetry. After discovering this fact, the third question of the investigation can be answered: Did compact growth but, at the same time, equally unconnected growth occur? Yes, that happened in medium-sized Spanish cities like Toledo. The final result has been a fragmented urban fabric, sectors disconnected with respect to the rest of the city. Some of them remain unfinished. They have finally caused substructures within Toledo.

We have focused the debate on the scope of study of the article: Spain. The methodology can be implemented in other Spanish medium-sized cities. In other different international contexts, it would be necessary to find a source similar to the Spanish urban estate cadaster. The study provides an interesting case study within the urban studies of Spain and it can serve as a comparative example for other medium-sized cities in other national contexts. However, the particularities of the spatial planning framework have an important influence on the urban areas development mode. The differences of the compactness of European medium-sized cities are evident [88], as well as the way of expanding cities and the urban sprawl [89]. These differences make it necessary to analyze more cases to obtain a general understanding of the process. In this regard, this article provides a significant case study for the understanding of the dynamics of European medium-sized cities.

Author Contributions: Both authors have jointly participated in the entire process of elaboration of the article.

Funding: This article is part of the research project Dinámicas de urbanización y políticas urbanísticas en ciudades medias interiores. De expansión y dispersión a reformulación: ¿Hacia un urbanismo más ¿urbano? (Dynamics of urbanization and urban planning policies in inner medium-sized cities. From expansion and dispersion to reformulation: Towards a more urban urbanism?) subsidized by the State Research Programme of Development and Innovation Aimed to the challenges of society, 2015 Summon, Mode 1: 'R &D Projects» of the Ministry of Economy and Competitiveness with reference CSO2015-63970-R (MINECO/FEDER).

Acknowledgments: We would like to thank the *Urban Science* journal editors and reviewers for careful reading, and constructive suggestions for our manuscript.

Conflicts of Interest: The authors declare no conflict of interest.

References

1. Brunet, R. Des villes comme Lleida. Place et perspectives des villes moyennes en Europe. In *Ciudades Intermedias. Urbanización y Sostenibilidad*; Bellet, A., Llop, J.M., Eds.; Editorial Milenio: Lérida, Espana, 2000; pp. 109–124, ISBN 84-89790-85-X.
2. Marques Da Costa, E. Cidades médias. Contributos para sua definição. *Finisterra* **2002**, *37*, 101–128.
3. Abellán García, A.; Moreno Jiménez, A.; Vinuesa Angulo, J. Propuesta de tipología para ciudades españolas de tipo medio. *Es. Geo.* **1978**, *39*, 285–306.
4. Esteban, A.; López, A. El papel de las ciudades medias en España. Presente y futuro. *Urbanismo* **1989**, *6*, 6–16.
5. Vinuesa, J. La población de las ciudades medias españolas. *Urbanismo* **1989**, *6*, 17–27.
6. Enguita Puebla, A. Alrededor de Madrid. Una red fuerte de ciudades medianas. Buscando un nuevo modelo descentralizador. *Urbanismo* **1995**, *26*, 6–25.
7. Busquets, J. La escala intermedia. Nueve planes catalanes. *Urbanismo* **1985**, *2*, 24–48.
8. Solá-Morales, M. La Identitat del Territorio Català. Les Comarques. *Quad. D'Arq. I Urb.* **1981**, 3–12.
9. Llop, J.M.; Bellet, C. *Ciudades Intermedias y Urbanización Mundial. Resultados de la Primera fase del Programa UIA-CIMES*; Ayuntamiento de Lleida: Lérida, Spain, 1999; ISBN 84-89790-85-X.
10. Andrés, G. Geografía y ciudades medias en España: ¿A la búsqueda de una definición innecesaria? *Scr. Nova* **2008**, *12*, 49.
11. Cebrián Abellán, F. Ciudades con límites y ciudades sin límites. Manifestaciones de la ciudad difusa en Castilla-La Mancha. *Bol. AGE* **2007**, *43*, 221–240.
12. Storper, M. *The Regional World: Territorial Development in a Global Economy*; Guilfords Press: New York, NY, USA, 1997; ISBN 9781572303157.
13. Samoná, G. *La città in Estensione*; STASS: Palermo, Italy, 1976.
14. Indovina, F. La ciudad difusa. In *Lo Urbano en 20 Autores Contemporáneos*; Monclús, F., Ed.; Centre de Cultura Contemporània: Barcelona, Spain, 2004; pp. 49–59, ISBN 9788483017524.
15. Monclús, F. *La Ciudad Dispersa: Suburbanización y Nuevas Periferias*; Centre de Cultura Contemporània: Barcelona, Spain, 1998; ISBN 84-88811-35-7.
16. Delgado, M. La no ciudad como ciudad absoluta. *Sileno* **2003**, *14–15*, 123–138.

17. Fariña, J. Cambiar el modelo urbano. *Re. Ciu.* **2015**, *18*, 69–78. [CrossRef]
18. Garreau, J. *Edge City. Life on the New Urban Frontier*; Doubleday: New York, NY, USA, 1991; ISBN 385262493.
19. Berry, B. *Urbanization and Counter-Urbanization*; Arnold: New York, NY, USA, 1976; ISBN 0803904991.
20. Stanback, T.J.R. *The New Suburbanization: Challenge to the Central City*; Westview Press: Boulder, CO, USA, 1991; ISBN 0-8133-8051-0.
21. Cebrián Abellán, F. Las trasformaciones recientes operadas en las periferias de las ciudades medias. El contexto de la ciudad difusa en la realidad española. In *Ciudades Medias: Formas de Expansión Urbana*; Cebrián, F., Panadero, M., Eds.; Biblioteca Nueva: Madrid, Spain, 2013; pp. 25–38, ISBN 978-84-9940-594-0.
22. Mallarach Isern, J.; Vilagrasa Ibarz, J. Los procesos de descentralización urbana en las ciudades medias españolas. *Rev. Ería.* **2002**, *57*, 57–70.
23. Ganau Casas, J.; Vilagrasa Ibarz, J. Ciudades medias en España: Posición en la red urbana y procesos urbanos recientes. In *Mediterráneo Económico: Ciudades, Arquitectura y Espacio Urbano*; Capel, H., Ed.; Cajamar Caja Rural: Bareslona, Spain, 2003; pp. 37–73, ISBN 8495531127.
24. Cebrián Abellán, F.; García González, J.A.; Panadero Moya, M. Los territorios de la suburbanización en Castilla-La Mancha. Análisis a escala municipal. In *Ciudades, Culturas y Fronteras en un Mundo en Cambio*; Junta de Andalucía: Sevilla, Spain, 2009; pp. 114–126, ISBN 9788480955553.
25. Burriel de Orueta, E.L. La década prodigiosa del urbanismo español (1997–2006). *Scr. Nova* **2008**, *12*, 270.
26. Gaja, I.; Díaz, F. El "Tsunami urbanizador" en el litoral mediterráneo. El ciclo de hiperproducción inmobiliaria, 1996–2006. *Scr. Nova* **2008**, *12*, 270.
27. Gaja, I.; Díaz, F. Reparar los impactos de la burbuja constructora. *Scr. Nova* **2015**, *19*, 517.
28. Bellet Sanfeliu, C. Las ciudades intermedias en los tiempos de la globalización. In *Ciudades Intermedias. Dimensiones y Definiciones*; Llop Torné, J.M., Usón Guadiola, E., Eds.; Milenio: Lérida, Spain, 2012; pp. 222–251, ISBN 9788497434935.
29. Bellet Sanfeliu, C.; Olazábal Salgado, E. Las ciudades intermedias en España: Dinámicas y procesos de urbanización recientes. In *Sistemas Urbanos y Ciudades Medias en Iberoamérica*; Maturana, F., Beltrão, M.E., Bellet, C., Henriquez, C., Arenas, F., Eds.; GEOLibros: Santiago de Chile, Chile, 2017; pp. 146–185, ISBN 9789561421103.
30. Bellet Sanfeliu, C.; Gutierrez, A. Los efectos territoriales del crecimiento y la producción inmobiliaria en ciudades medias españolas. El caso de Lleida (1990–2012). In *Urbanización, Producción y Consumo en Ciudades Medias/Intermedias*; Bellet, C., Melazzo, E.S., Sposito, M.E.B., Llop, J.M., Eds.; Universitat de Lleida: Lérida, Spain, 2015; pp. 297–314, ISBN 9788484097525.
31. Bellet Sanfeliu, C. Los nuevos espacios residenciales. Estructura y paisaje. In *Espacios Públicos, Espacios Privados: Un Debate Sobre el Territorio*; Delgado, C., Frochoso, M., González, R., González, E., Meer, A., de Puente, L., de la Reques, P., Eds.; Asociación de Geógrafos Españoles: Santander, Spain, 2007; pp. 93–130, ISBN 9788481024500.
32. Artigues, A.A.; Rullán, O. Nuevo modelo de producción residencial y territorio urbano disperso (Mallorca, 1998-2006). *Scr. Nova* **2007**, *11*, 245.
33. Zúñiga Sagredo, I. La forma del límite en las ciudades medias españolas. *Cuad. Investg. Urban.* **2016**, *105*, 3450. [CrossRef]
34. Harvey, D. *Ciudades Rebeldes. Del Derecho de la Ciudad a la Revolución Urbana*; Akal: Madrid, Spain, 2013; ISBN 9788446037996.
35. Romano, B.; Zullo, F. Half a century of urbanization in southern European lowlands: A study on the Po Valley (Northern Italy). *Urban Res. Prac.* **2015**, *9*, 109–130. [CrossRef]
36. Romano, B.; Zullo, F.; Fiorini, L.; Marucci, A.; Ciabò, S. Land transformation of Italy due to half a century of urbanization. *Land Use Policy* **2017**, *67*, 387–400. [CrossRef]
37. Saganeiti, L.; Favale, A.; Pilogallo, A.; Scorza, F.; Murgante, B. Assessing Urban Fragmentation at Regional Scale Using Sprinkling Indexes. *Sustainability* **2018**, *10*, 3274. [CrossRef]
38. Romano, B.; Zullo, F.; Fiorini, L.; Ciabò, S.; Marucci, A. Sprinkling: An Approach to Describe Urbanization Dynamics in Italy. *Sustainability* **2017**, *9*, 97. [CrossRef]
39. López de Lucio, R. *Ciudad y Urbanismo a Finales del Siglo XX*; Universitat de Valencia: Valencia, Spain, 1993; ISBN 84-370-1439-5.
40. Serrano Rodríguez, A. El urbanismo del siglo XXI: Problemas previsibles y líneas de actuación recomendables. *Ciu. Te.* **1993**, *95–96*, 15–40.

41. Vives, S.; Rullán, O. La apropiación de las rentas del suelo en la ciudad neoliberal española. *Bo. AGE* **2014**, *65*, 387–408. [CrossRef]

42. Schulz-Dornburg, J. *Ruinas Modernas. Una Topografía del Lucro*; Ámbit: Barcelona, Spain, 2012; ISBN 978-8496645141.

43. García Cabeza, M. The breakdown of the Spanish urban growth model: Social and territorial effects of the global crisis. *Int. J. Reg. Res.* **2010**, *34*, 967–980. [CrossRef]

44. Lois González, R.C.; Piñeira Mantiñán, M.J.; Vives Miró, S. El proceso urbanizador en España (1990–2014): Una interpretación desde la geografía y la teoría de los circuitos de capital (2016). *Scr Nova* **2016**, *20*, 539.

45. Gaja, I.; Díaz, F. Al salir del túnel. Superar el modelo hiperconstructor. In *Estudios de Geografía Urbana en Tiempos de Crisis*; Brandis, D., Del Río, I., Morales, G., Eds.; Biblioteca Nueva: Madrid, Spain, 2016; pp. 49–62, ISBN 978-8416647729.

46. Mas Hernández, R. Periferias urbanas y nuevas formas espaciales. In *La Ciudad. Tamaño y Crecimiento*; Domínguez, R., Ed.; Universidad de Málaga: Málaga, Spain, 1999; pp. 201–241, ISBN 84-922182-4-X.

47. Sorribes, J.; Perelló, S.; Izquierdo, V. *Las Ciudades del Siglo XXI: El Reto de la Sostenibilidad*; UNED: Valencia, Spain, 2000; ISBN 84-95484-06-4.

48. Coudroy De Lille, L. Los ensanches españoles vistos desde fuera: Aspectos ideológicos de su urbanismo. *Ciu. Te.* **1999**, *119–120*, 239–255.

49. Baxter, P.; Jack, S. Qualitative case study methodology: Study design and implementation for novice researchers. *Qual. Rep.* **2008**, *13*, 544–559.

50. Montaner, J.M. La evolución del modelo Barcelona (1979–2002). In *Urbanismo en el Siglo XXI*; Borja, J., Muzí, Z., Eds.; Universitat Politècnica de Catalunya: Barcelona, Spain, 2004; pp. 202–220, ISBN 84-8301-740-7.

51. Nel·Lo, O. Desigualdad social y segregación urbana en la región metropolitana de Barcelona. In *Estudios de Geografía Urbana en Tiempos de Crisis*; Brandis, D., Del Río, I., Morales, G., Eds.; Biblioteca Nueva: Madrid, Spain, 2016; pp. 95–120, ISBN 978-8416647729.

52. Naredo, J.M. Naturaleza de la conurbación madrileña y sus tendencias actuales. Segunda parte. Anatomía y fisiología de la conurbación madrileña: Gigantismo e ineficiencia crecientes. In *Urbanismo en el Siglo XXI*; Borja, J., Muzí, Z., Eds.; Universitat Politècnica de Catalunya: Barcelona, Spain, 2004; pp. 101–119, ISBN 84-8301-740-7.

53. Morcillo Álvarez, D. Producción de espacio en la expansión neoliberal de Madrid. *Scr. Nova* **2017**, *XX*, 574.

54. Díaz Parra, I. Sevilla 1929–1992. La producción de una mercancía. In *Cartografía de la Ciudad Capitalista. Transformación Urbana y Conflicto Social en el Estado Español*; Rodríguez, J., Salguero, O., Eds.; Traficantes de Sueños: Madrid, Spain, 2016; pp. 219–248, ISBN 978-84-945978-0-0.

55. Escolano Utrilla, A.; López Escolano, X.; Pueyo Campos, A. Urbanismo neoliberal y fragmentación urbana: El caso de Zaragoza (España) en los primeros quince años del siglo XXI. *EURE* **2018**, *44*, 183–210. [CrossRef]

56. Cebrián Abellán, F. y García González. La ciudad de Albacete y el incipiente proceso de conformación de ciudad difusa. In *Ciudades Medias: Formas de Expansión Urbana*; Cebrián, F., Panadero, M., Eds.; Biblioteca Nueva: Madrid, Spain, 2013; pp. 67–98, ISBN 978-84-9940-594-0.

57. Andrés López, G. *La Estructura Urbana de Burgos en los Siglos XIX y XX. El Crecimiento y la Forma de la Ciudad*; Cajacírculo: Burgos, Spain, 2004; ISBN 84-89805-14-8.

58. Instituto Nacional de Estadística (INE). Padrón Municipal de Habitantes. Available online: http://www.ine.es (accessed on 16 April 2018).

59. Cebrián Abellán, F. La red urbana. In *Geografía de Castilla-La Mancha*; Pillet Capdepón, F., Ed.; Biblioteca añil: Real, Spain, 2007; pp. 177–194, ISBN 978-84-935656-0-2.

60. Tamames, R.; Heras, R. *Enciclopedia de Castilla-La Mancha*; Ediciones Corporativas: Madrid, Spain, 1999; ISBN 84-95343-00-2.

61. García Martínez, C. Las ciudades. In *Geografía de Castilla-La Mancha*; Pillet Capdepón, F., Ed.; Biblioteca añil: Ciudad Real, Spain, 2007; pp. 159–176, ISBN 978-84-935656-0-2.

62. Campos Romero, M.L.; Escudero Gomez, L.A.; Rodríguez Domenech, M.A. Los nuevos desarrollos urbanos en la capital de Castilla-La Mancha. In *Las Escalas de la Geografía, del Mundo al Lugar*; Cebrián, F., Pillet, F., Carpio, J., Eds.; Ediciones de la Universidad de Castilla-La Mancha: Cuenca, Spain, 2010; pp. 329–356, ISBN 978-84-8427-753-8.

63. Álvarez Ahedo, I. *El Urbanismo del Término Municipal de Toledo en el Siglo XX*; Colegio de Arquitectos de Castilla-La Mancha: Toledo, Spain, 2004; ISBN 9788492322633.

64. Ministerio de Hacienda y Función Pública. Sede Electrónica del Catastro. Available online: http://www.sedecatastro.gob.es/ (accessed on 16 April 2018).
65. Calderón Calderón, B. La ciudad del todo urbanizable: Estrategias del sector inmobiliario y nuevas e insostenibles formas de urbanización. *Ciudades* **2004**, *8*, 135–155. [CrossRef]
66. Gómez Mendoza, J. Ecología urbana y paisaje de la ciudad. In *La Ciudad del Futuro*; Bonet, A., Ed.; Instituto de España: Madrid, Spain, 2009; pp. 177–217, ISBN 9788485559657.
67. Ayuntamiento de Toledo. Modificación Puntual Número 28 del PGMOU de Toledo. Available online: http://www.toledo.es/modificacion-puntual-numero-28-del-pgmou-de-toledo/ (accessed on 3 April 2018).
68. Centro Nacional de Información Geográfica (CNIG). Centro de Descargas: CartoCiudad. Available online: http://centrodedescargas.cnig.es/CentroDescargas/index.jsp (accessed on 9 January 2017).
69. Campos Romero, M.L.; Escudero Gómez, L.A. Planificación urbana de Toledo y el crecimiento en áreas de protección. Las Vegas del Tajo. In *Homenaje al Profesor José Manuel Casas Torres*; Gutiérrez, S., Sanz, J.J., Eds.; Universidad Complutense: Madrid, Spain, 2007; pp. 397–414, ISBN 9788496702189.
70. Mierzejewska, L. Urban structures and substructures. *Bul. Geo. Soc. Eco. Ser.* **2017**, *36*, 117–125.
71. Andrés López, G. Sobre el crecimiento y la estructura de las ciudades medias: El estudio de Burgos como aportación al conocimiento geográfico de la historia urbana. In *Historiografía Sobre Tipos y Características Históricas, Artísticas y Geográficas de las Ciudades y Pueblos de España*; Delgado Viñas, C., Sazatornil Ruiz, L., Rueda Hernanz, G., Eds.; Ediciones TGD: Santander, Spain, 2009; pp. 63–68, ISBN 978-84-96926-31-8.
72. Álvarez Perla, J.M.; Carda Abella, A.; Pinillos Mora, S. El papel de las ciudades medias en Castilla y León. In *Proceedings of the III Congreso de Economía Regional de Castilla y León*, Segovia, Spain, 26–28 November 1992; pp. 864–878.
73. Cebrián Abellán, F.; García González, J.A.; Panadero Moya, M. Dinámicas y transformaciones recientes en los procesos de expansión territorial de las ciudades medias de Castilla-La Mancha. In *Ciudades y Paisajes Urbanos en el Siglo XXI*; Delgado Viñas, C., Juaristi Linacero, J., Tomé Fernández, S., Eds.; Ediciones de Librería Estudio: Santander, Spain, 2012; pp. 263–278, ISBN 9788493202361.
74. Rodriguez Domenech, M.A. Paisajes urbanos de crisis, paisajes para la reflexión. El caso de Ciudad Real. *Cua. Ma.* **2014**, *39*, 147–190.
75. Pillet Capdepón, F.; Cañizares Ruiz, M.C.; Ruiz Pulpón, A.R.; Martínez Sánchez-Mateos, H.S.; Plaza Tabasco, J. Dinámicas demográficas y su relación con la cohesión territorial en las áreas funcionales urbanas de Castilla-La Mancha (España). *Bol. AGE* **2018**, *76*, 153–182. [CrossRef]
76. Sánchez Ondoño, I.; Cebrián Abellán, F. Las transformaciones urbanas en las periferias de las ciudades medias. Cambios y dinámicas desde comienzos de siglo a la actualidad en el entorno de la ciudad de Albacete (España). In *Forma Urbana: Pasado, Presente y Perspectivas. Actas del I Congreso ISUF-H*; Ruiz-Apilánez, B., Solís, E., Romero de Ávila, V., Eds.; Ediciones de la Universidad de Castilla-La Mancha: Cuenca, Spain, 2017; pp. 268–277.
77. Vázquez Varela, C.; Martínez Navarro, J.M. Caracterización de los tejidos residenciales urbanos producto del boom inmobiliario en la ciudad de Cuenca. In *Forma Urbana: Pasado, Presente y Perspectivas. Actas del I Congreso ISUF-H*; Ruiz-Apilánez, B., Solís, E., Romero de Ávila, V., Eds.; Ediciones de la Universidad de Castilla-La Mancha: Cuenca, Spain, 2017; pp. 347–358.
78. Castañer, M.; Vicente, J.; Boix, G. Assaig de definició de l'area urbana de Girona. *Do. Geo.* **1998**, *33*, 81–90.
79. Ganau, J. El sistema urbà de Lleida: Definició, estructura i dinámiques recents. *Do. Geo.* **1998**, *33*, 91–106.
80. Olazábal, E.; Bellet, C. estudio. In *XIV Coloquio de Geografía Urbana. Ciudades Medias y Áreas Metropolitanas*; Cebrián Abellán, F., Ed.; Ediciones de la Universidad de Castilla-La Mancha: Cuenca, Spain, 2018; pp. 117–138, ISBN 978-84-9044-315-6.
81. Llussá Torra, R. Dinámiques detropolitanes i la Cataluña central, o la creixent integració de l'espai caralá a finals del sigle XX. In *L'Estructuració Territorial de Catalunya. Els Eixos Cohesionadors de L'espai. V Congres Internacional d'Historia Local de Catalunya*; Sabaté, F., Ed.; L'Avenç: Barcelona, Spain, 2001; pp. 574–582, ISBN 84-88839-12-X.
82. Ferras Sexto, C. *Cambio Rural na Europa Atlántica. Os Casos de Irlanda e Galicia (1970–1990)*; Universidad de Santiago de Compostela y Xunta de Galicia: Santiago de Compostela, Spain, 1996; ISBN 84-8121-466-3.
83. Acosta, G. El caso de Andalucía. In *VII Semana de Estudios Urbanos. Ciudades Intermedias: Urbanización y Sostenibilidad*; Bellet, C., Llop, J.M., Eds.; Editorial Milenio: Lérida, Spain, 1998; pp. 189–208, ISBN 84-89790-85-X.

84. Caravaca, I.; González, G.; Mendoza, A. Indicadores de dinamismo, innovación y desarrollo. Su aplicación en ciudades pequeñas y medias de Andalucía. *Bol. AGE* **2007**, *43*, 131–154.
85. Serrano, J.M. Expansión del parque inmobiliario en España. Algunas reflexiones desde la perspectiva territorial. *Bol. Int. Com. Esp.* **2004**, *2798*, 11–30.
86. Hayden, D. *A field Guide to Sprawl*; Norton & Co.: New York, NY, USA, 2006; ISBN 978-0-393-73198-9.
87. Nel·lo, O. Contra la dispersión intensidad. Contra la segregación, ciudad. In *Ordenación del Territorio y Desarrollo Territorial. El Gobierno del Territorio en España: Tradiciones, Contextos, Culturas y Nuevas Visions*; Romero, J., Farinós, J., Eds.; Ediciones Trea: Gijón, Spain, 2004; pp. 261–285, ISBN 84-9704-133-X.
88. Stathakis, D.; Tsilimigkas, G. Measuring the compactness of European medium-sized. *Int. J. Image Data* **2015**, *6*, 42–64. [CrossRef]
89. Couch, C.; Petschel-Held, G.; Leontidou, L. *Urban. Sprawl in Europe: Landscapes, Land-Use Change and Policy*; Blackwell: London, UK, 2007; ISBN 978-1405139175.

urban science

MDPI

Article

The Impact of Economic Crisis in Areas of Sprawl in Spanish Cities

Arlinda García-Coll [1,*] and Cristina López-Villanueva [2]

[1] Department of Geography, University of Barcelona, 08001 Barcelona, Spain
[2] Department of Sociology, University of Barcelona, 08034 Barcelona, Spain; clopez@ub.edu
* Correspondence: arlindagarcia@ub.edu; Tel.: +34-934-037-852

Received: 21 October 2018; Accepted: 23 November 2018; Published: 28 November 2018

Abstract: The development of dispersed urbanism in Spain ran parallel to the real estate boom and consolidated a new model of city sprawl based on the expansion of suburban areas. This process, which started in the mid 1980s, came to a halt with the onset of the economic crisis in 2007. With it, construction stopped, mobility fell, and urban growth came to a standstill. The purpose of this article is, firstly, to analyse the recent evolution and chronology of the expansion of dispersed urbanism in the Barcelona Metropolitan Region (BMR) in order to gain an insight into some of its explanatory factors, and secondly, to look into the future middle-term prospects of dispersed urbanism in the BMR and Spain. To this end, we examine trends in the housing market and residential mobility and take stock of the impact of business cycles on them. The conclusion is that dispersed areas still retain their appeal for people in the life stages of the creation and expansion of households. For this reason, an effective economic recovery and a renewed rise in the price of housing in denser cities may contribute to an upturn in the popularity of the dispersed residential model, which nowadays could be considered to be in a 'lethargic' phase, waiting for certain factors to concur and reactivate its expansion.

Keywords: dispersed urbanism; residential strategies; residential mobility; economic crisis; Barcelona Metropolitan Region; social crisis; land squandering

---

1. Introduction: Dispersed Urbanism in the Reconfiguration of Spanish Urban Regions; Evidence and Questions

On 23 June 2015, *The Washington Post* [1] published a news item on the evolution of European cities as derived from the analysis of their growth in population between the censuses of 2001 and 2011. The main conclusion highlighted by the article could be summarised, in the authors' own words, as "European cities are becoming more American". It is significant that an American newspaper echoed the demographic decline of European urban centres and the increase in population of their respective metropolitan areas, comparing these with American cities, where these processes have been commonplace. Even if a comparison like this should be qualified by means of theoretical tools and empirical evidence [2,3]—especially in the case of the Mediterranean countries—it is clear that the boom of dispersed urbanism in Europe has not gone unnoticed.

Català et al. [4] point out the existence of common elements in the processes of urban dispersion undergone by the European Mediterranean countries. They specifically identify the following shared features: very late occurrence of the sprawl phenomenon; extreme urban densification in previous stages; great vitality of the central cities; and a high presence of small and medium-sized cities in the country's urban system. They also point to the existence of three overlapping urban models: the traditional compact model, the dispersed model of the new residential areas, and the mixed land uses exemplified by industrial and commercial activities that tend to occupy large land containers. Salvati [5] describes this last model as "hybrid", underscoring its importance in order to understand the particularities of Mediterranean Europe.

Despite all these shared aspects, Carlutti et al. [6] have recently centred on the differences between individual Mediterranean countries to reach the conclusion that it is not possible to speak of a single model of urban dispersion in Mediterranean Europe and it is necessary to take into account both regional and local factors to understand the specific evolution of each one of the countries in the area.

Spanish urban regions are a good example of the situation described by the *Washington Post* article, as well as of the Mediterranean model of urban dispersion. On comparing the sprawling processes in twenty-six European countries in the 1990s and the first half of the 2000s, Siedentop and Fina [7] concluded that Ireland, Portugal, and Spain were the European countries which had experienced the the greatest sprawl. After several decades of urban growth based on a model of compact urban development, at the turn of the century, Spanish cities began to change their patterns of urban expansion. On the one hand, they experienced an accelerated tendency towards suburbanisation, characterised by a loss of both population and compactness in the largest municipalities and the growth of their peripheral areas, which became more extensive [8,9]. On the other hand, a new model of dispersed city was established, a model which had been rarely seen before and which was scarcely relevant among Spanish urban territorial trends, besides being mostly associated with second homes. It is this last fact that constitutes a distinctive factor of the Spanish process of urban dispersion [10]. Thus, in the 1960s, Spain saw the development of areas of residential expansion at a short distance from the cities, areas which were mostly devoted to second homes and which in more recent stages would act as the germ of subsequent dispersed urban development. According to Burriel [11], this was a phenomenon unmatched in the rest of Europe, and it turned out to be a crucial factor to be taken into account if we wish to understand the expansion of dispersed urbanism in Spain at the end of the 20th century.

Initially, and in this context of mainly vacational use and reduced population and territorial extension, the pressure that dispersed urban areas exerted on their territories—and on the services offered there—was rather low, and so the relevance of such areas was minimal. However, the situation changed from the 1980s onwards. Then, a strong growth of dispersed urbanism took place in parallel with the real estate boom, and there was a rapid increase in the number of people that chose to live permanently in such locations, that is, to live '*dispersedly*'. Proof of this transformation can be seen, for example, in the Barcelona Metropolitan Region (BMR), where it is estimated that almost one-third of the urban land subjected to development between 1993 and 2000 was allocated to dispersed residential use [12], and where the annual population growth of low-density municipalities exceeded 4% between 1999 and 2006 [13].

The increase of dispersed urbanism in Spanish urban areas was a consequence of a series of factors. In the first place, the real estate bubble was responsible for an extraordinary rise in the price of homes in the city centres, causing an increase in the demand for affordable housing with better price-to-perfomance ratios. Additionally, among the several reasons for residential mobility, there was the demand for housing in places of greater environmental quality and closer to nature, which just added up to the demand for certain specific housing conditions which were difficult to find in city centres—larger, single-family houses, with a private garden, and so forth. The phase of economic growth prior to 2008 also contributed to this whole process by bringing about lower unemployment rates, rising salaries, and above all, increased facilities to obtain a mortgage loan. All these factors have been brought up by numerous studies dealing with such residential transformations from different outlooks: the demographic perspective [12], the economic one [14,15], the social point of view [16], and the perspective of environmental impact [17].

The bursting of the real estate bubble and the beginning of the economic recession from 2007 onwards brought this phase to an end and led into a new situation characterised by the minimising of new-house building in low-density areas as well as demographic stagnation. Thus, the process of residential dispersion came to a sudden halt. This new stage has posed several short and medium-term questions concerning the role of dispersed urbanism in the socio-residential dynamics of Spanish urban areas previously affected by processes of suburbanisation. First of all, the debates have focused on whether it is possible to speak of land squandering, or otherwise, the model of dispersed urban growth that can continue and proceed in an orderly, sustainable way. The way that the expansion of the dispersed model took place in the past—characterised by dubiously administered extremely fast growth, with an abrupt stop when the crisis set in—calls into question the viability and continuity of dispersed urbanism in cities that, apart from periods of intense property speculation, had traditionally displayed a compact type of urban growth. Moreover, the sudden decline of dispersed urban expansion brought about by the economic crisis has made students wonder whether we have just witnessed the end of a process, or rather the beginning of an impasse that will come to an end as soon as the economic situation improves. The economic crisis brought urban dispersion to a halt, but will the economic recovery trigger an upturn in the demand of housing in dispersed areas?

A second set of questions concerns the social impact of the economic crisis on the population that moved to live in dispersed areas. The higher cost of living in dispersed quarters [17], the difficulties derived from the breaking-up of neighbourhood solidarity networks as a consequence of moving to a new area [16], and the high rate of indebtedness of the families that changed their place of residence in a time of rising housing prices all make the residents in dispersed areas bound to suffer the social consequences of the crisis in a most severe way.

To answer all these questions, two different lines of enquiry are needed. First, it is necessary to undertake a revision of the past, since an analysis of past processes will certainly give us interesting clues about future possibilities. Also, it will be necessary to examine the most recent trends, especially those from 2014 on, when the Spanish government officially declared the end of the economic crisis in the country—despite the views of many microeconomics and social researchers.

The BMR is a good example of a metropolitan region where dispersed urban developement set in late and grew at an accelerated pace. Inititally, the territories were not prepared to respond to the new situations generated by the dispersed model, and thus, their adaptation to their new changing realities could only take place simultaneously to the implementation of the new urban model. By studying these features of the BMR case, the present article attempts to contribute some empirical evidence to the debates about the specificities of the establishment of dispersed urbanism outside the Anglo-Saxon regions, in line with the works of Couch et al. [18] or Richardson and Bae [2]. More particularly, it is our aim to help devise a framework which is useful in specifying the role of the economic crisis in processes of urban dispersion, according to the findings of Salvati [5] and Cho et al. [19], whose research discloses the undeniable effects of the economic crisis, which not only puts an end to construction, but also to trends of suburban development in a territory.

Also, the present article argues for the need of incorporating the perspective of demographic studies into morphological and urbanisation studies, with demographic studies focusing on specifying the elements responsible for residential dispersion, such as residential mobility or the different directions of this mobility, depending on people's stages in life. To this end, our research combines information coming from official statistics on residential mobility in Spain, with data coming from two surveys of people who moved to live in a dispersed setting. These surveys do not only inform us of the causes behind people's migration, but they also provide us with the interviewees' assessment of their change of residence and information about their future migration projects. Often, as Champion [20], Tyrell and Kraftl [21], or Coulter et al. [22] suggest, lack of data leads to analyses of the socioeconomic factors determining urban sprawl which only take into consideration the moment when people's migration take place (e.g., the analyses of Weilemmann et al. [23] for Switzerland, or Salvati [5] for Athens), without taking into account people's whole migratory course of life. This renders such analyses unable to tell us anything about future migration prospects. As Coulter et al. [22] state, the point here is to rethink residential mobility as "linking lives through time and space".

Our article deals with two main issues: On the one hand, it describes and explains the evolution of dispersed urbanism in the Barcelona Metropolitan Region (BMR) and establishes the chronology of its recent evolution based on the analysis of intrametropolitan residential mobility data (intensity, direction of flows, and characteristics of the moving persons), the observation of trends in the housing market (new constructions) at the metropolitan level, and the impact of business cycles. Based on these analyses, it will be possible to describe in greater depth the sociodemographic challenges facing dispersed areas in the recent past and at the present moment. On the other hand, the article deals with the future middle-term prospects of dispersed urbanism in the BMR and Spain. All in all, our study seeks to improve our knowledge of the present functioning of Spanish metropolitan dynamics based on their past and most recent developments, with the ultimate goal of contributing to the administering of low-density urbanism in Spain. Nowadays, low-density urbanism occupies a prominent place in territorial planning, since the changes in land use that it entails make it a relevant factor to be considered when planning both the present of urban development and, above all, its future prospects, as it is aptly observed by Ramankutty and Coomes [24].

2. Materials and Methods

In this section, we shall deal with three basic issues that constitute the departing point of our research. In the first place, we will centre on methodological questions to reflect about both the theoretical and the empirical difficulties when it comes to defining dispersed urbanism. As we shall see, although it is true that dispersed urbanism has been the subject of a good number of both theoretical and applied studies, its definition and measurement have important limitations, independent of whether we consider the Spanish case or that of other countries. Secondly, we shall introduce the methodology employed in our research, which was based on a classification of municipalities specifically designed to identify those with a strong presence of dispersed urbanism. Finally, we shall proceed to the description of the sources used in our empirical analysis.

2.1. Methodological Approach: Defining Dispersed Urbanism

To begin with, there is no consensus definition of dispersed urbanism, which often makes it difficult to establish the necessary criteria to demarcate the spatial extent of the phenomenon. Generally, studies have used extensive land occupation [25,26]—closely related to low-density areas [27,28]—as the most common criterion for demarcating dispersed urban areas. Sometimes, besides taking into account population density, the definition of dispersed urbanism additionally involves the presence of morphologically and functionally isolated urban elements, with the prevailing type of dwelling consisting of single-family, detached, or semidetached houses [29]. After all, population density is one of the most widely used criteria for measuring residential dispersion [30]. Several recent works have used net density to study dispersed urbanism, sometimes in combination with measures of distance and/or discontinuity from the city centre based on observations using CORINE Land Cover [31]. Multidimensional measurements of urban sprawl are frequent too, generally using Geographic Information System (GIS) tools. Jaeger and Schwick [32] proposed the use of weighted urban proliferation (WUP) to consider the area built over in a given landscape (amount of built-up area), the dispersion of the built-up area, and the land uptake of the built-up area per inhabitant or job. Weillenmann et al. [23] consider that built-up areas may spill across administrative borders, with neighbouring municipalities sharing a similar employment market and mobility infrastructure and requiring coordination when it comes to spatial planning. All these sophisticated methodologies undoubtedly feed an interesting debate; however, the most important thing to do before making a decision regarding the definition of dispersed urbanism to be used in a particular study is to establish the research objectives and to evaluate if the statistical data needed are available.

In our case, the main objective revolved around demographic trends rather than spatial structures. Moreover, in the Spanish case, we came across a serious limitation concerning the potential sources of information available to researchers, namely: there exists no exact correspondence between the various administrative and statistical divisions and dispersed residential areas, especially when it comes to suburban residential complexes. Thus, it was not always feasible for us to reconstruct the sociodemographic traits of such areas simply via the aggregation of census sections or the inspection of the municipal registers of inhabitants or other sources of intramunicipality information. In actual fact, only in the case of a few municipalities was it possible for us to gather statistical information regarding dispersed residential areas. Finally, we had to resource to fieldwork in order to complete our territorial analysis, something which proved also useful in order to put to the test the municipal typology we were using and to select the urban residential complexes where our interviews would subsequently be carried out. The combination of these three strategies produced a methodological approach properly adjusted to the objectives of our research.

2.2. Methods: A Municipality Typology Based on Dispersed Urbanism

In the face of all the aformentioned obstacles, our study used a methodological strategy of its own in order to define and characterise dispersed urbanism in the BMR; one which was developed in the context of the Program Research, Development and Innovation (R+ D+ i) projects entitled "Mobility, Family Solidarity, and Citizenship in the BMR" (2003–2006) and "Social Change and Urban Transformation Processes in a Context of Crisis in the Urban Peripheries of Large Metropolitan Areas in Spain. The Case of the BMR" (2014–2017). On the one hand, we used an indirect approach based on information about the municipalities taken as a whole, and on the other hand, we used two ad hoc surveys with interviews carried out in 2005 and 2017 in a sample of suburban residential areas.

First of all, to identify the phenomenon of dispersed urbanism at the municipal level, we considered the surface of urban land allocated for residential use and calculated its net density. Analysing the Swiss case, Weilenmann et al. [23] have shown that the municipality is a meaningful unit of analysis for the examination of sprawl because it is the political entity that makes decisions about urban spatial development and because it has sufficient data available. In our case, we also had information about the municipal surface allocated to "extensive, low-density patterns of land use, with single-family or two-family (semidetached) houses surrounded by a plot of land with a garden", from the Urban Planning Map of Catalonia (MUC) [33] prepared by the General Office for Country Planning and Urbanism of the Catalan Government. This allowed us to calculate the proportion of residential land surface allocated to this type of dwelling. By combining both indicators (net density and percentage of land allocated to detached/semidetached houses), we were able to group the different municipalities in the BMR in several categories according to their degree of compactness or dispersion (Figure 1). We identified five types of municipalities, categorising as 'dispersed' those situated in the first and second quintiles of the net-density distribution, i.e., with less than 140 inhabitants/hectare in 2015. The percentage of land allocated to detached/semidetached houses was used to distinguish between dispersed and highly dispersed areas as internal categories of urban dispersion (Table 1). According to 2015 data, in the BMR, there are 106 municipalities (64.7% of all municipalities) which satisfy the criteria for dispersed areas, amounting to 14.2% of the BMR population.

Table 1. Classification of Barcelona Metropolitan Region (BMR) municipalities by urban typology.

Typology	Municipalities		Population		Net Density	Isolated Houses
	Number	%	Number	%	Inhab/ha (*)	% Land (**)
Highly Compact	12	7.3	2,506,046	49.8	>501	<6.0
Compact	10	6.1	737,568	14.7	351–500	6.0–20.0
Medium	36	22.0	1,070,608	21.3	141–350	20.0–40.0
Dispersed	57	34.8	447,419	8.9	<140	40.0–80.0
Highly Dispersed	49	29.9	266,617	5.3	<140	>80.0
Total	164	100.0	5,028,258	100.0	204.8	58.0
Aggregated data						
Compact	22	13.4	3,243,614	64.5	576.7	10.2
Dispersed	106	64.6	714,036	14.2	50.5	82.3

(*) Computed using the surface area of urban soil allocated for residential use. (**) Percentage of land area allocated to detached/semidetached houses. Source: Compiled by the authors based on *Censo de población* (Population Census) 1991, *Padrón Municipal de habitantes* [Municipal Register of Inhabitants] 1996, and *Padrón continuo* (Continuous Register) 1998–2016, by the National Institute of Statistics (INE).

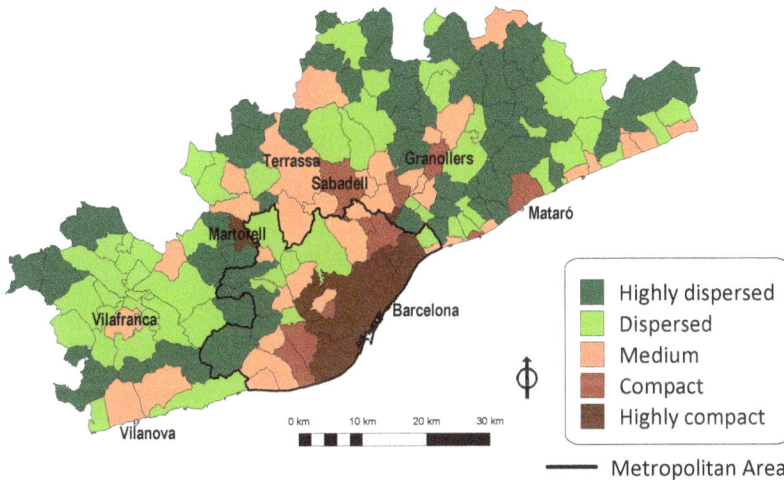

Figure 1. Classification of BMR municipalities by urban typology. Source: Compiled by the authors based on *Censo de población* (Population Census) 1991, *Padrón Municipal de habitantes* (Municipal Register of Inhabitants) 1996, and *Padrón continuo* (Continuous Register) 1998–2016, by the National Institute of Statistics (INE).

Once we had identified those municipalities with a strong presence of dispersed urbanism—which we termed as 'dispersed municipalities'—our analysis of their evolution was carried out based on statistical sources which provided us with individual data for each municipality. For this stage of the analysis, we grouped together the categories of 'dispersed' and 'highly dispersed' areas, since both of them satisfy the criteria established to identify municipalities with a sprawling residential pattern as an essential part of their urban morphology.

2.3. Data Sources

The sources used in this particular phase of the study were the microdata provided by the *Statistics of Residential Variation* (EVR) and the *Continuous Register* (Padrón continuo). The EVR allowed us to study intrametropolitan residential mobility in the period 1996–2016, and therefore, the migration flows displayed by the different types of municipality. The *Continuous Register*, on the other hand, made it possible to describe the characteristics of the populations in the different municipalities meeting the criteria for dispersed areas. Even though this was an indirect characterisation, because it included the totality of the population in the different municipalities, the trends identified provided us with a robust framework in order to delimit the existing processes.

Additionally, as a complement to this preliminary observation of our object of study, we used the results of two surveys that we ourselves carried out in 2005 and 2017. Both of them had been designed to gather information about the living standards of people residing in dispersed areas in the BMR. One section of the questionnaire was aimed at getting information about people's migratory experiences. Here, it must be taken into account that in 2005, all the interviewees had changed their municipality of residence at least once in their lifetime. More than 90% of them had lived in a compact area at some point and thus were able to compare both lifestyles. Also, all the interviewees had been living in a sprawl area for over 12 years, and so they had experienced the effects of the economic crisis while living in this type of residential area. Contrary to the basic general information provided by the Municipal Register or the EVR (which only include data about sex, age, place of birth, and nationality), our surveys allowed us to complete the sociodemographic profiles of the interviewees (profession, employment status, household income, etc.) and gave us information about their motives, assessment of their residential area, and future migratory projects, all of which was highly valuable to achieve the goals of our research.

The first survey, called "Mobility, Family Solidarity, and Citizenship in Metropolitan Regions", included a total of 600 households (1024 individuals) from a sample of 24 suburban residential complexes in 17 municipalities. This first survey was implemented by using quotas for different socioeconomic, age, and sex categories; this way, the results were representative of the totality of the population living in suburban residential complexes in the BMR. The second survey, entitled "Social Change and Urban Transformation Processes in a Context of Crisis in the Periphery of the BMR", was a replica of the one carried out in 2005. This time, information was gathered about 1759 individuals who had been living in the selected surburban residential complexes since at least 2005. Both surveys provided us with information about the living conditions of people residing in this kind of suburban setting: their family structure, labour conditions, spaces of life, family and social relationships, reasons for moving into a suburban residential complex, and reasons for choosing the place of residence. To this, other highly significant information must be added, such as: the residents' assessment of issues related to the house they lived in and the suburban residential complex they inhabited, or to municipal policies, as well as information concerning their future residential projects. The 2017 survey was complemented with questions aimed at comparing the situations in 2005 and 2017, apart from questions concerning the interviewees' assessment of the changes in their employment status or their family income during that period, all of which was helpful for evaluating the impact on them of the economic crisis.

3. Results

The process of residential expansion and increase of dispersed urbanism in the Barcelona Metropolitan Region took off in the second half of the 1980s, transforming the territory in a radical way [34]. This section deals with the recent chronology of dispersed urbanism based on an analysis of the growth and evolution of its population, intrametropolitan residential mobility rates, and rates of new property construction.

3.1. Business Cycles, Real Estate Market, and Residential Mobility: Stages in the Recent Evolution of Dispersed Urbanism in the BMR and its Explanatory Factors

In 1991, dispersed municipalities in the BMR contained 351,340 inhabitants. In 2016, their population was 717,832 (Table 2 and Figure 2), which means that their population had doubled in that period. Besides this steep rise in population, these municipalities had drastically changed their demographic structure and composition over that same period of time.

Table 2. Population evolution (1991–2016) in BMR municipalities by typology.

Typology	1991	2002	2008	2016	1991–2001	2002–2007	2008–2016
Highly Compact	2,540,899	2,395,323	2,511,575	2,514,324	−0.5	0.8	0.0
Compact	634,037	672,045	722,827	739,658	0.5	1.2	0.3
Medium	738,146	888,204	1,028,087	1,074,929	1.7	2.5	0.6
Dispersed	234,852	337,546	418,273	450,410	3.4	3.6	0.9
Highly Dispersed	116,488	189,505	248,090	267,422	4.5	4.6	0.9
Aggregate data							
Compact	3,174,936	3,067,368	3,234,402	3,253,982	−0.3	0.9	0.1
Medium	738,146	888,204	1,028,087	1,072,929	1.7	2.5	0.6
Dispersed	351,340	527,051	666,363	717,832	3.8	4.0	0.9
Total	4,264,422	4,482,623	4,928,852	5,046,743	0.5	1.6	0.3

Source: Compiled by the authors based on the *Censo de población* (Population Census) 1991, *Padrón Municipal de habitantes* (Municipal Register of Inhabitants) 1996, and *Padrón continuo* (Continuous Register) 1998–2016, by Instituto Nacional de Estadística (National Institute of Statistics) (INE).

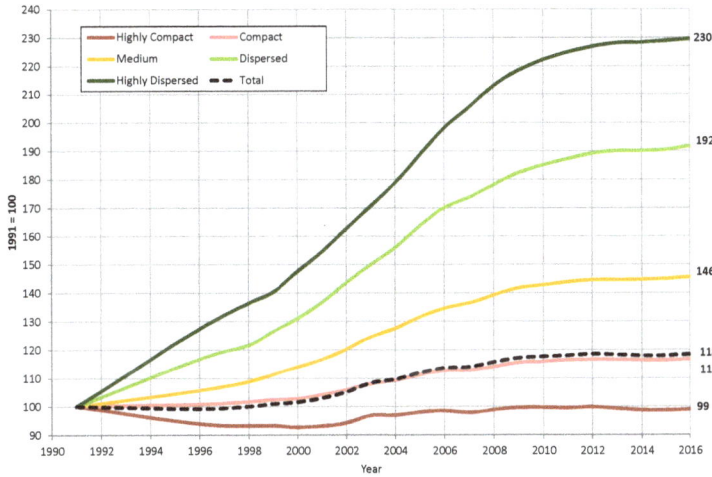

Figure 2. Population evolution in BMR municipalities classified by typology. Indexed annual data. Population in 1991 = 100. Source: Compiled by the authors based on the *Censo de población* (Population Census) 1991, *Padrón municipal de habitantes* (Municipal Register of Inhabitants) 1996, and *Padrón continuo* (Continuous Register) 1998–2016, by Instituto Nacional de Estadística (National Institute of Statistics) (INE).

However, this transformation process did not take place in a homogeneous way over the period, and it is possible to distinguish four stages of evolution:

(a) First, there is the stage from 1991 to 1999, when the population grew at an annual rate of slightly over 3%. At this point, we witness the consolidation of this form of residence, which had started to develop in a previous period, and the start of the boom of dispersed residential areas.

(b) A second stage comprises the period 2000–2006, when the great boom of dispersed urbanism took place in the BMR. In this phase, we see the effects of five factors. In the first place, we have a real estate market in which higher density areas were saturated, with rising prices and lack of diversity of the residential offer in the city. In that context, lower density areas offered unprecedented possibilities of population absorbtion and expansion [35]. Secondly, the type of property which was built was adressed to families with young children, fond of living in a quiet environment close to nature, with high environmental standards. Thirdly, this stage marked the beginning of an expansive business cycle which generated better economic prospects for households and created a climate of economic confidence that had an upward effect on the residential market. Fourthly, in view of the economic prosperity, banks focused their mortgage policy on the provision of credit facilities to buy a home [36]. Finally, the existence of a previous offer of suburban housing developments well-established in the territory made it easier for dispersed urbanism to expand. Although in the past, these had been of rather limited size and were mainly used for vacation purposes [35], they provided embryonic spaces for building projects.

As a result of this combination of elements, we witnessed a boom of dispersed urbanism, characterised by a very intense growth of population, with annual rates of over 4% that coincided with rates of initiation of new-property construction nearing 45% [37], and net migration rates higher than 33 per thousand persons (Figure 3 and Table 3).

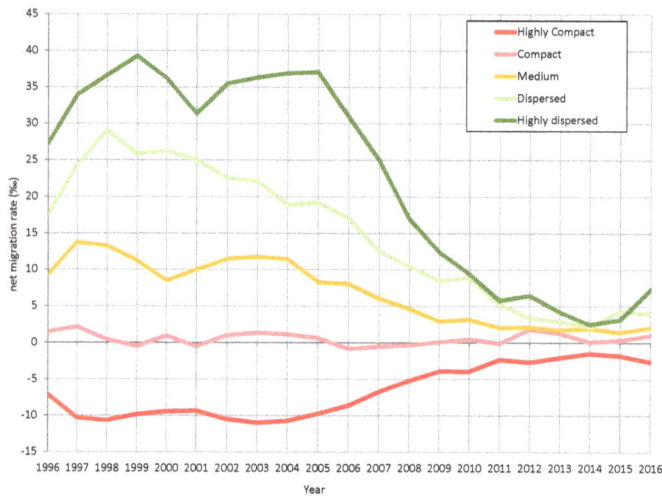

Figure 3. Net intrametropolitan migration rate by types of municipality in the BMR, 1996–2016. Source: Compiled by the authors based on *Padrón continuo* (Constinuous Register) 1996–2017 and *Estadística de Variaciones Residenciales* (Residential Change Statistics) 1996–2016, microdata file, INE.

(c) The third stage was marked by a profound turn away from the previous trajectory. It began with the sudden onset of the economic crisis, whose effects were gradually felt. Some authors [38,39], when dealing with the changes that took place in this period, have highlighted the advance in the metropolitanisation of the BMR.

First of all, there was a drop in the rates of new-property construction in dispersed municipalities, rates that, from 2006, went abruptly down to values of less than 5 per thousand in 2009 and thereafter.

Table 3. New-property construction rate by types of municipality in the BMR, 1999–2017.

	New-Property Construction Rate (‰)					Single Family New-Property Construction Rate (‰)				
Year	Highly Compact	Compact	Medium	Dispersed	Highly Dispersed	Highly Compact	Compact	Medium	Dispersed	Highly Dispersed
1999	9.17	20.43	27.54	37.40	36.58	1.04	3.26	6.72	16.68	27.07
2000	8.32	21.32	29.79	36.51	38.01	0.49	1.72	4.56	11.88	27.78
2001	7.10	16.80	24.11	30.98	31.00	0.31	1.37	2.86	8.32	18.55
2002	7.55	17.52	26.03	29.44	31.79	0.36	1.11	2.94	8.10	17.96
2003	7.68	21.05	28.37	31.69	35.79	0.33	1.14	3.06	9.82	21.61
2004	8.23	23.15	32.89	34.58	47.76	0.18	0.83	2.96	9.33	24.74
2005	8.15	21.26	34.07	47.07	49.21	0.16	0.79	2.82	9.40	25.07
2006	9.73	27.17	40.75	44.48	52.62	0.15	0.86	3.17	7.48	23.13
2007	7.67	16.58	25.41	31.67	34.75	0.11	0.59	1.99	4.89	13.07
2008	4.31	5.57	6.97	7.74	10.05	0.07	0.21	0.69	1.56	4.77
2009	2.12	2.67	3.47	2.45	5.09	0.04	0.15	0.35	0.94	2.00
2010	2.85	4.28	3.29	6.74	6.63	0.04	0.21	0.51	1.20	2.50
2011	1.83	3.14	1.75	5.71	2.71	0.03	0.16	0.30	0.86	2.02
2012	1.26	1.46	1.44	1.53	1.91	0.03	0.19	0.28	0.64	1.47
2013	0.84	0.33	0.70	1.36	1.80	0.03	0.08	0.27	0.54	0.99
2014	1.19	1.60	0.92	0.97	1.08	0.03	0.11	0.33	0.61	0.91
2015	1.95	1.60	1.71	3.42	2.00	0.04	0.27	0.37	0.88	1.40
2016	2.56	2.31	2.44	5.05	2.65	0.05	0.27	0.82	1.27	2.09
2017	3.40	4.55	4.45	7.17	3.22	0.05	0.45	0.72	1.75	2.36

Source: Compiled by the authors based on Generalitat de Catalunya Departament de Territori i Sostenibilitat (Department of Territory and Sustainability) *Licencias viviendas iniciadas y acabadas* (Building Licenses for Started and Finished Houses) and *INE Censos de viviendas* (Housing census), 2001 and 2011.

Secondly, in-migration came to a sudden standstill (Figure 4), with the subsequent effects on net migration rates, which fell to values of under 10 per thousand from 2009 onwards. A certain degree of saturation in the housing supply accounts for the fact that the first sector to experience the economic downturn was the construction sector, whose downfall preceded the drop in sales. The rise in the value of land once it was put to use increased the price of housing, and this slowed down the pace of new construction. Next, the effects of the economic crisis pulled down the rates of migration of people motivated by the search for a better dwelling due to an increase in the requirements to obtain a mortgage [36] and the readjustment of family budgets in the context of rising unemployment and wage settlements in the case of employed individuals [40]. Overall, property sales became stagnant due to the fall in arrivals of new residents, and this dragged the construction of new houses down to a minimum level.

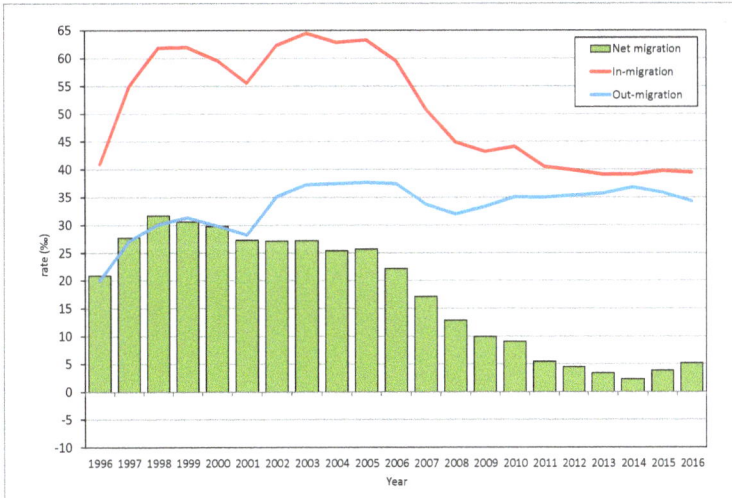

Figure 4. Component elements of the intrametropolitan migration dynamics of dispersed municipalities (1996–2016). Source: Compiled by the authors based on the *Padrón continuo* (Continuous Register) 1996–2017 and the *Estadística de Variaciones Residenciales* (Residential Change Statistics) 1996–2016, microdata file, INE.

Despite the gradual shrinking of the real estate market and the drop in the arrival of in-migrants, there was a certain inertia in the evolution of the growth of dispersed municipalities, which remained high until 2012 (Figure 4). This dynamic was a consequence of natural population growth in the context of a high birth rate due to the inflow of young adults. For this reason, it was not until 2012 that a phase of demographic stagnation set in.

(d) The fourth stage started in 2012 and was characterised by demographic stagnation in connection with reduced migration inflows. This situation of slow population growth tends to be associated with the end of the process of urban dispersion. However, only after some time shall we be able to assess if such a process has really come to an end, while some of the latest trends have reopened the debate about the future prospects of urban dispersion in the BMR.

3.2. The Choice of Living in a Suburban Residential Complex: Portraying the Actors of Residential Dispersion in the BMR

An analysis of the information gathered by the survey "Mobility, Family Solidarity, and Citizenship in Metropolitan Regions 2005" allowed us to establish the characteristics of the population who had moved to suburban residential complexes. These were people who had changed their residence mostly after 1996; 34% of them coming from the city of Barcelona, and 40% coming from the rest of the BMR. Their profile was that of young people with a great potential for growth (between 25 and 45 years of age); 20.39% were aged under 15, and only 10% were older than 65 years. Predominantly, they were in active employment, with both members of the couple working. Forty-five percent of those in work belonged to the categories of technicians, professionals, and managerial staff, and 56.8% were in medium–high socio-occupational groups. The prevalent family structure was that of a couple with underaged children (51.78%) living in a single-family house which was large (mean surface was 176 m^2), new (one-third of them had been built after 1985), and owned by the residents, but pending full payment (48.2%).

The appeal of dispersed areas was apparent in the reasons stated by the interviewees for moving to a suburban residential complex, which mostly had to do with the characteristics of the dwelling, the quality of life, nature, and the environment, and of lesser importance, with factors related to the actors' life trajectories, such as the creation or the extension of a family (Table 4).

Table 4. Reasons for moving to a surburban residential complex.

Reason	%
Residential reasons (home and environment)	54.1
Reasons related to the dwelling	31.6
Desire to own one's home	4.2
Quality of life, environment, nature	14.8
Moving out of the city	3.4
Changes in the life cycle	26.2
Marriage or stable union	10.9
Family growth	8.7
Family reduction	1.2
Break-up of sentimental union	2.1
Retirement	2.1
Retirement of one's partner	1.2
Work-related reasons	9.3
Change of jobs	3.9
Partner's change of jobs	1.6
Closeness to (own/partner's) place of work	3.7
Health	5.4
Taking care of an elderly person	1.8
Health-related reasons	3.6
Other	6.6
Financial reasons	1.3
Total	100

Source: Compiled by the authors based on the surveys "Mobility, Family Solidarity, and Citizenship in Metropolitan Regions 2005" and "Social Change and Urban Transformation Processes in a Context of Crisis in the Periphery of the BMR 2017".

The most significant reasons were those connected to residential factors (54.1%) and, in particular, the conditions of the house (31.6%): its price, the fact of being a single-family house or a newly built one, its surface area, its location in a natural environment and the quality of life (14.8%), or the desire to become the owner of one's residence (4.2%). Changes in people's life trajectories also affected the decision to live in a dispersed area (26.2%). In this respect, getting established as a couple (10.9%) or expanding the family (8.7%) were the most frequently stated reasons in this category. On the contrary, work-related motives did not play a very significant role, amounting to only 9.3% of the stated reasons. It must be noted that the interviewees prioritised reasons related to the appeal of low-density suburban areas over the rejection of denser areas. Thus, contrary to the North-American case [41], there is no mention of criminality, greater dangers, or higher pollution rates as reasons for migration.

This pattern of migratory behaviour produces a sex and age structure which both contrasts with and complements that of compact municipalities (Figure 5), which are actually the places feeding the migration flows towards dispersed municipalities. Thus, we find a population which is quite rejuvenated, with a strong presence of residents between the ages of 40 and 59 and little pressure from elderly groups.

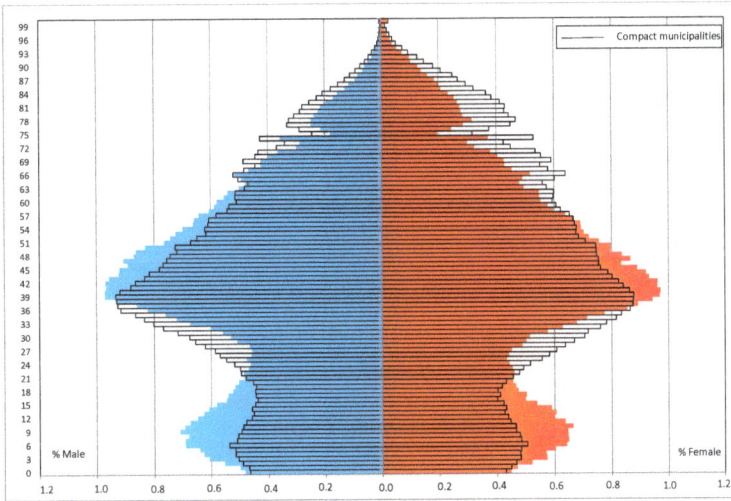

Figure 5. Sex and age structure in BMR dispersed municipalities, 2015. Source: Compiled by the authors based on *Padrón Continuo* (Continuous Register), 1 January 2015, INE.

When we consider the intrametropolitan migration profiles of different age groups, we appreciate the key role played by the strong appeal of dispersed residential areas to those between 25 and 44 years old, ages at which net migrations rates are the highest (Figure 6).

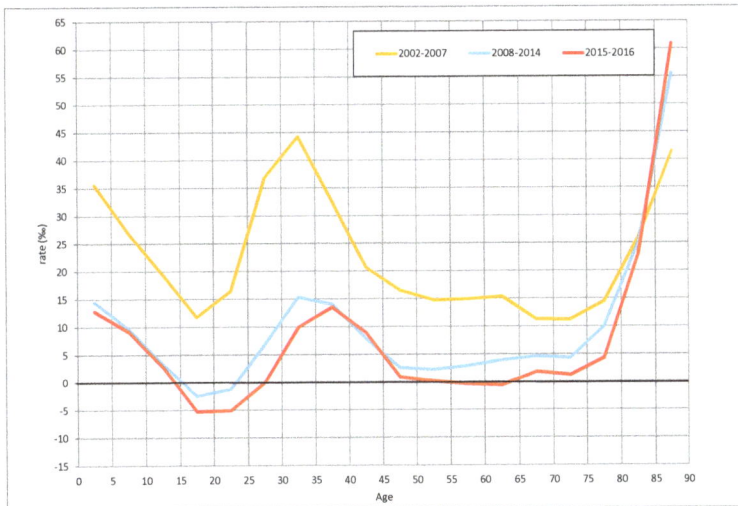

Figure 6. Net intrametropolitan migration rates by age in BMR dispersed municipalities (2002–2016). Source: Compiled by the authors based on data from the *Padrón continuo* (Continuous Register) 1996–2017 and the *Estadística de Variaciones Residenciales* (Residential Change Statistics) 1996–2016, microdata file, INE.

In this case, we must highlight the fact that this age pattern repeats itself over time, even when the effects of the economic crisis pull down the rates of migration towards dispersed destinations. Therefore, it is obvious that dispersed municipalities retain their appeal as places of residence for a specific target population, an appeal that may be boosted or curbed by the economic situation, but remains in place throughout our period of observation. Parallel to this, the mobility of adults has a pull on the mobility of both underaged young people, who migrated with their parents, and elderly people, who migrated in order to live closer to their children, who moved earlier in time, and thus moved in order to receive care from or provide care to them.

On the other hand, what we see is a pattern of residential appeal clearly segmented by age and socioeconomic category. This is a phenomenon which has been well described in the literature about migration focusing on the analysis of changes in residential preferences in relation with life stages [42,43].

3.3. Twelve Years Living in a Suburban Residential Complex: The Actors' Assessment

The last point we should like to stress in this study is the residents' assessment of, and satisfaction with, the suburban residential complex and housing, as revealed by our 2005 and 2017 surveys.

The answers to the questions regarding the level of residential satisfaction in our surveys display high values in relation to both the place of residence and the dwelling. In fact, the results obtained by the 2017 survey are even better than those of the 2005 one (Tables 5 and 6). Forty-five percent of the interviewees declared that the suburban residential complex where they lived had improved since 2005. Altogether, the average score obtained by the residential place of living in the survey was 4.2 out of 5, while people's satisfaction with their homes reached an average score of 4.5 out of 5. The interviewees were more critical about the town council administration of their residential areas, which they valued at 5.4 points out of 10.

Table 5. Evaluation of the residential area and the dwelling, 2017.

Score	Suburban Residential Complex	Dwelling
1	2.0	0.0
2	2.8	0.7
3	13.8	5.2
4	26.3	26.7
5	44.8	67.5
Total	100.0	100.0
Average Score	4.2	4.6

Source: Compiled by the authors based on the survey "Social Change and Urban Transformation Processes in a Context of Crisis in the Periphery of the BMR 2017".

Table 6. Perception of the town council actions in the residential area, 2005–2017.

Score	2005	2017	Diference
0	13.3	7.5	−5.8
1	4.0	2.2	−1.8
2	6.0	4.2	−1.8
3	7.7	7.0	−0.7
4	10.3	7.7	−2.6
5	19.8	19.3	−0.5
6	13.0	13.7	0.7
7	9.0	17.8	8.8
8	10.3	12.8	2.5
9	1.0	2.8	1.8
10	2.3	4.0	1.7
Total	100.0	100.0	0.0

Source: Compiled by the authors based on the surveys "Mobility, Family Solidarity, and Citizenship in Metropolitan Regions 2005" and "Social Change and Urban Transformation Processes in a Context of Crisis in the Periphery of the BMR 2017".

This information is especially significant for our investigation for two reasons: Firstly, because it tells us about the impact that the economic crisis had on the families that chose to move to this type of residential area. Thus, a drop in household income or in the funds allocated for the provision of services by public administrations—as a consequence of budget cuts imposed by the economic crisis—might give rise to a less positive evaluation of a residential choice that was made years before, in the context of economic welfare. Secondly, because the existence of high levels of dissatisfaction would point to the possible failure or rejection of life in dispersed residential areas, and this might lead to a new change of residence.

4. Discussion

The results presented in the previous section take us to the discussion of the future of dispersed residential areas as derived from their recent trajectory and the information gathered by our research up to this point.

First of all, it must be highlighted that despite the slowing down of the development of dispersed urbanism imposed by the economic crisis, the available intrametropolitan mobility data reveal that dispersed municipalities have not completely lost their appeal. They still display net migration rates higher than the rest of the urban typologies considered for the BMR. For this reason, it seems that its present situation is more of a phase of lethargy, while waiting for the evolution of the economy and the credit market, than one of disappearance of the residential model. This is the key to understanding the increase of net migration rates in 2015 and 2016, when the economic recovery started to be timidly revealed in some economic sectors. As can be seen in Figure 4, in those two years, the previous trends pointing to a sustained reduction of net migration rates were reversed. It is significant that this recent increase in net migration in dispersed municipalities coincided with a rise in the loss of population of more compact areas in the BMR due to intrametropolitan out-migration. This change of trend did not only coincide with the beginning of the economic recovery, but also with another phenomenon that took place at the same time, namely, the renewed increase in the price of housing in large metropolitan cities—both in the sale and rental markets. In the city of Barcelona, as it happened in other cities [44], the purchasing price of a newly built home rose by 20.05% between 2015 and 2017 (Table 7). As for rent prices, they increased by 19.36% [45]. This situation, which some commentators consider as a new real estate bubble, intensifies the process of population expulsion from the denser cities and stands in the way of the arrival or the return of potential residents to them.

Table 7. Evolution of the sale price of housing in Barcelona (2004–2017).

	New Housing		Used Housing		Total Housing	
Year	Value (€/m^2)	Change (%)	Value (€/m^2)	Change (%)	Value (€/m^2)	Change (%)
2004	3336	-	2986	-	3079	-
2005	3708	11.1	3782	26.7	3758	22.1
2006	4452	20.1	4296	13.6	4349	15.7
2007	5009	12.5	4505	4.9	4622	6.3
2008	5144	2.7	4235	−6.0	4464	−3.4
2009	4264	−17.1	3643	−14.0	3773	−15.5
2010	4259	−0.1	3577	−1.8	3745	−0.8
2011	4276	0.4	3327	−7.0	3559	-5.0
2012	3109	−27.3	2904	−12.7	2946	−17.2
2013	3197	2.9	2628	−9.5	2719	−7.7
2014	3116	−2.5	2705	3.0	2754	1.3
2015	3237	3.9	2934	8.4	2971	7.8
2016	3850	18.9	3167	7.9	3238	9.0
2017	4048	5.2	3714	17.3	3746	15.7

Source: Generalitat de Catalunya Departament de Territori i Sostenibilitat (Department of Territory and Sustainability) (2018). *Informe sobre el sector de l'habitatge a Catalunya* (Report on the Housing Sector in Catalonia) 2017 [44]

Given this state of affairs, the supply of housing in dispersed municipalities may gain prominence once more and provide a choice for intrametropolitan in-migration again. It will be necessary to stay attentive to the evolution of the metropolitan supply of housing, knowing that it is a type of market that generates dynamics which put different urban areas in relation to one another, as has happened before. Once again, the general evolution of the country's economy and the credit policies of its financial institutions will play a key role, as Lomax and Stillwell pointed out for the case of the United Kingdom [46].

The renewed increase in the price of housing in larger cities might produce a renewed dynamisation of the real estate market by encouraging the sale or renting out of homes; at the same time, this could reactivate migration flows towards dispersed municipalities, which boast a large supply of housing and a great potential for growth. In the same way, an exorbitant rise in the price of housing—both in rents and purchasing prices—might give rise to new family strategies such as the transference of second homes to their children (or the moving of parents to such second residences) in order to make it possible for the younger members of the family—victims of the recent skyrocketing of housing prices—to become emancipated.

On the other hand, it is obvious that the overrepresentation of some age groups will determine the municipal agenda for the planning of services and infrastructure. Besides this, the movement of these age groups up the population pyramid will also reshape the demands that the different administrations—especially the local ones—will have to satisfy (Figure 5). Moreover, if we examine the behaviour of migratory trends for the eldest age groups, we still observe net gains during all the periods under consideration and with similar intensity across time. This is another factor that could sensibly modify the demand for services. The residential strategies of the elderly display certain features of their own, due to the fact that mobility is here associated with preparation for old age. Thus, to the appeal for residential quality we must add other factors, such as proximity to family or friends and to services, and the rejection of excessive dependence on private vehicles for transportation [47]. Therefore, prima facie, the appeal of dispersed municipalities for elderly people that is evident in the case of the BMR would hardly agree with the behaviour stipulated by some theoretical frameworks.

The prevalent theoretical models often point to people's aging and entering an empty-nest life stage as factors leading to the relocation of populations. In our case, however, the results of the surveys show little intention of people to change places of residence, move again, and/or return to their previous areas of residence. Thus, there is a determination to become old in the same suburban residential complex: only 16% of the interviewees seemed to have taken into consideration a change of residence, and paradoxically, individuals aged between 40 and 54 years seemed more likely than elderly people to embark on a new migration process. Only a small minority declared their will to change homes in search of a dwelling with different characteristics: smaller, requiring less maintenance, and located in an area where there is not so much dependence on private means of transport. What our information reveals is a will to get old in areas of dispersed urbanism.

If one of the dimensions exposed by previous research was the weakness and shortage of family and support networks in environments of dispersed urbanism [48], the information gathered in our 2017 survey makes it clear that with the passing of time, people have managed to weave social networks that act as fixing factors and make residents stay in the suburban areas where they have spent their latest years. Even though emancipated children do not reproduce their parents' residential model (only 23% of them stay in the same municipality where their parents' suburban area of residence is located), our study reveals the beginning of the formation of the so-called family 'entourage' [49], which would reinforce people's attachment to their place of residence. This strategy of residential relocation in search of closer proximity to other family members does not only take the form of staying near the parents' home, but also accounts for the high in-migration rates of elderly people, who look for their children's vicinity in order to develop strategies of intergenerational solidarity.

On the whole, the worsening of economic indicators does not affect people living in dispersed areas in a more acute manner, despite the special features associated to this style of living: relative isolation, distant services, extra costs, and greater weakness of support networks. In this respect, the significant presence of middle- and upper-class households may account for the less dramatic impact of the economic crisis and the absence of situations of serious social degradation, situations that were feared at some point in time. Due to the lack of a tradition of living in dispered areas in Spain, the gradual evolution of the residential choices of families is observed with even greater interest, as those who moved to low-density areas in the 1980s were pioneers in displaying the effects of changes in life circumstances and in the business cycle on residential strategies involving migratory exchanges between dispersed and compact areas.

5. Conclusions: A Look into the Future

Nowadays, the key question concerning dispersed urbanism is what its future propects are in the middle and long term. As we have seen in the previous sections, residential sprawl occurred in Spain in the context of economic growth, accompanied by a series of other factors which facilitated its swift expansion. The setting in of the economic crisis brought such rapid expansion to a sudden halt, which was interpreted as the end of a process. This verdict was founded on the extra costs of living in dispersed areas, which would act as a deterrent for new residents and would favour a retreat to compact residential areas, and on the hardening of the requirements to access a mortgage loan, which would be the cause of putting off or giving up the purchase of a home. However, such views were not completely right in their predictions.

Despite the time already elapsed after their arrival in a dispersed residential area—all the interviewees had been living in a suburban area for at least 10 years—the hard impact of the economic crisis, and the expenses associated with living in such an environment, the level of satisfaction of the people who took part in our surveys was in 2005, and was still in 2017, very high. Thus, the crisis did not alter the residents' assessment of the option of living in a dispersed residential area.

As we have verified, the economic crisis curbed in-migration and limited the age range in which net migration took a positive value. Nevertheless, out-migration did not increase, and it even went down in the reported years. The conclusion is that dispersed areas retained their appeal in the stages of creation and expansion of households, as theoretical models point out. For this reason, an effective economic recovery and a renewed rise in the price of housing in denser cities—with Barcelona as an outstanding exponent of such an evolution—may contribute to an upturn in the popularity of the dispersed residential model, which nowadays could be considered to be in a 'lethargic' stage, waiting for certain factors to concur and reactivate it. Such reactivation would mostly involve the most affluent socioeconomic groups, being the only ones fulfilling the requirements to gain access to a mortgage loan or who might not even need one, unless we witness an easing of the conditions to obtain a mortgage. As a consequence, this type of residential mobility could be restricted to high-income households, which would result in the concurrence of processes of residential dispersion and social segregation.

Finally, neither the economic crisis nor the passing of time or the change of life-cycle stage have altered the indexes of residential satisfaction of our interviewees. There is a sustained highly positive appraisal of both the dwelling and the suburban areas of residence, while the presence of projects of relocation and of families waiting to sell their houses to move out of the area is scarce.

In conclusion, there is a demand for the lifestyle that dispersed urbanism represents, and in parallel, there does not appear to be a process of out-migration or strong rejection of such a residential type. Everything seems to suggest that dispersed urbanism is here to stay.

Author Contributions: A.G.-C. is a geographer specialising in residential mobility and has been in charge of drafting the sections concerning migration processes. C.L.-V. is a Sociology PhD and so her contribution has focused mainly on the social aspects dealt with in the article. Both authors have conducted joint studies of the processes of urban dispersion since 2004, with a special focus on the definition and measurement of dispersion and its demographic impact.

Funding: This piece of research has been carried out in the framework of the R + D + i project entitled "Social Change and Processes of Urban Transformation in a Context of Crisis in the Barcelona Metropolitan

Region", reference number CSO2013-48075-C2-1-R, funded by the Spanish Ministry of Economy, Industry and Competitiveness, State Research Agency, Spain.

Acknowledgments: The authors are grateful to the members of the collaborating team in the project "Social Change and Processes of Urban Transformation in a Context of Crisis in the Barcelona Metropolitan Region".

Conflicts of Interest: The authors declare no conflict of interest.

References

1. Noak, R.; Gamio, L. Map: Europe Is Growing and Where It Is Shrinking. *The Washington Post*, 23 June 2015.
2. Richardson, H.W.; Bae, C.H.H. *Urban Sprawl in Western Europe and the United States*; Ashgate: London, UK, 2004; ISBN 0754637891.
3. Leal, J. El diferente modelo residencial de los países del Sur de Europa: El Mercado, las viviendas, la familia y el Estado. *Arxius* **2004**, *10*, 11–37.
4. Catalán, B.; Saurí, D.; Serra, P. Urban sprawl in the Mediterranean? Patterns of growth and change in the Barcelona Metropolitan Region 1993–2000. *Landsc. Urban Plan.* **2008**, *85*, 174–184.
5. Salvati, L. Urban dispersion and economic crisis: Empirical evidence from a Mediterranean region. *J. Environ. Plan. Manag.* **2018**. [CrossRef]
6. Carlutti, M.; Grigoriadis, E.; Pontos, K.; Salvati, L. Revisiting a Hegemonic Concept: Long-term Mediterranean Urbanization. In Between City Re-polarization and Metropolitan Decline. *Appl. Spat. Anal. Policy* **2017**, *10*, 347–362.
7. Siedentop, S.; Fina, S. Who sprawls most? Exploring the paterns of urban growth across 26 European countries. *Environ. Plan. A Econ. Space* **2012**, *1*, 2765–2784. [CrossRef]
8. Susino, J.; Duque, R. Veinte años de suburbanización en España (1981–2001): El perfil de sus protagonistas. *Doc. Anàl. Geogr.* **2013**, *59*, 265–290. [CrossRef]
9. García Coll, A.; López Villanueva, C.; Pujadas, I. Movilidad residencial en tiempos de crisis. El caso de la Región Metropolitana de Barcelona. *Scr. Nova* **2016**, *XX*, 1–36.
10. Nel·Lo, O. Estrategias para la contención y gestión de las urbanizaciones de baja densidad en Catalunya. *Ciudad Territ. Estud. Territ.* **2011**, *43*, 81–98.
11. Burriel, E. Las viviendas secundarias ilegales de la etapa del desarrollismos. El ejemplo de Gilet (Valencia). *Cuad. Geogr.* **2018**, *100*, 23–58.
12. Garcia Coll, A. The process of residential sprawl in Spain: Is it really a problem? In *Urban Challenges in Spain and Portugal*; Benach, N., Walliser, A., Eds.; Routledge: London, UK, 2014; pp. 250–263, ISBN 978-0415705554.
13. López Villanueva, C.; Garcia Coll, A.; Bretones, M.T.; Crespi, M. Los efectos de la crisis económica en el urbanismo disperso de la Región Metropolitana de Barcelona. *Clivatge* **2017**, *5*, 290–331.
14. Hortas-Rico, M. Urban Sprawl and municipal budgets in Spain: A dynamic panel data analysis. *Pap. Reg. Sci.* **2014**, *93*, 843–864. [CrossRef]
15. Gielen, E. Costes del Urban Sprawl Para la Administración Local: El Caso Valenciano. Ph.D. Thesis, Department Urbanisme, Universitat Politècnica de València, Valencia, Spain, 2 February 2016.
16. Vilà, G.; Gavaldà, J. Efectos del urbanismo disperso y consecuencias para la sostenibilidad social: Análisis de la Región Metropolitana de Barcelona. *Cad. Metrop.* **2013**, *29*, 15–39.
17. Henry, G. Análisis de costes de la baja densidad: Una lectura desde la sostenibilidad. In *La Ciudad de Baja Densidad: Lógicas, Gestión y Contención*; Indovina, F., Ed.; Diputación de Barcelona: Barcelona, Spain, 2007; pp. 203–242.
18. Couch, C.G.; Petschel-Held, G.; Leontidou, L. (Eds.) *Urban Sprawl in Europe: Landscapes, Land-Use Change and Policy*; John Wiley and Sons: Hoboken, NJ, USA, 2008.
19. Cho, S.H.; Kim, S.G.; Roberts, D.M.; Lambert, D.M.; Kim, T. Effects of Land-related Policies and Land Development During a Real Estate Boom and a Recession. *Growth Chang.* **2014**, *46*, 218–232. [CrossRef]
20. Champion, A. A changing demographic regime and evolving poly centric urban regions: Consequences for the size, composition and distribution of city populations. *Urban Stud.* **2001**, *38*, 657–677. [CrossRef]
21. Tyrrell, N.; Kraftl, P. Lifecourse and Internal Migration. In *Internal Migration. Geographical Perspectives and Processes*; Smith, D.P., Finney, N., Walford, N., Eds.; Routledge: Abingdon, UK, 2015; pp. 16–29.
22. Coulter, R. Re-thinking residential mobility: Linking lives through time and space. *Prog. Hum. Geogr.* **2016**, *4*, 352–374. [CrossRef] [PubMed]

23. Weilenmann, B.; Seidl, I.; Shulz, T. The socio-economic determinants of urban sprawl between 1980 and 2010 in Switzerland. *Landsc. Urban Plan.* **2016**, *157*, 468–482. [CrossRef]

24. Ramankutty, N.; Coomes, O.T. Land-useregimeshifts: Ananalyticalframeworkand agenda for futureland-useresearch. *Ecol. Soc.* **2016**, *21*. [CrossRef]

25. López de Lucio, R. La incipiente configuración de una región urbana dispersa: El caso de la Comunidad Autónoma de Madrid (1960–1993). In *La Ciudad Dispersa*; Monclús, F.J., Ed.; Centre de Cultura Contemporània: Barcelona, Spain, 1998; pp. 169–196, ISBN 978-84-88811-35-6.

26. Luxána, M.V.; Matesanza, D.C.; Fernández, A.F.; Lázaro, F.J.; Cañasa, C.M.; Preciadoa, J.M. El proceso de urbanización dispersa de las metrópolis españolas, en el contexto del desarrollo urbano europeo. *Espac. Tiempo Forma Ser. VI Geogr.* **2010**, 13–26. [CrossRef]

27. Font, A. Morfologías metropolitanas contemporáneas de baja densidad. In *La Ciudad de Baja Densidad. Lógicas, Gestión y Contención*; Indovina, F., Ed.; Diputació de Barcelona: Barcelona, Spain, 2007; pp. 97–107, ISBN 978 84-9803-237-6.

28. Indovina, F. Introducción. In *La Ciudad de Baja Densidad. Lógicas, Gestión y Contención*; Diputació de Barcelona: Barcelona, Spain, 2007; pp. 13–24, ISBN 978-84-9803-237-6.

29. Muñoz, F. De la urbanització dispersa a la ciutat de baixa densitat: Un repte ignorat. In *Estratègies vers la Ciutat de Baixa Densitat: De la Contenció a la Gestió*; Muñoz, F., Ed.; Diputació de Barcelona: Barcelona, Spain, 2011; pp. 11–64, ISBN 978-84-9803-414-1.

30. Ewing, R.; Pendall, R.; Chen, D. *Measuring Sprawl and Its Impact: The Character and Consequences of Metropolitan Expansion*; Smart Growth America: Washington, DC, USA, 2002; ISBN 978-1138-645-51-6.

31. Díaz-Pacheco, J.; García-Palomares, J.C. Urban sprawls in the Mediterranean urban regions in Europe and the crisis effect on the urban land development: Madrid as study case. *Urban Stud. Res.* **2014**. [CrossRef]

32. Jaeger, A.G.; Schwick, C.H. Improving the measurement of urban sprawl: Weigthed Urban Proliferation (WUP) and its application to Switzerland. *Ecol. Indic.* **2014**, *38*, 294–308. [CrossRef]

33. Generalitat de Catalunya. *Mapa Urbanístic de Catalunya. Dades Bàsiques Municipals i Comarcals*; Direcció General d'Ordenació del Territori i Urbanisme: Barcelona, Spain, 2015.

34. Pujadas, I. Movilidad residencial y expansión urbana en la Región Metropolitana de Barcelona. *Scr. Nova* **2009**, *XIII*, 290.

35. Barba, J.; Mercadé, M. *Les urbanitzacions a la provincia de Barcelona: Localització i Característiques dels Sistemes de Baixa Densitat Residencial*; Diputació de Barcelona: Barcelona, Spain, 2016; ISBN 84-9803-111-7.

36. García Montalvo, J. *De la Quimera Inmobiliaria al Colapso Financiero. Crónica de un Desenlace Anunciado*; Antoni Bosch: Barcelona, Spain, 2008; ISBN 978-84-95348-44-9.

37. García Coll, A.; López Villanueva, C. El fenómeno del Sprawl residencial en la Región Metropolitana de Barcelona. Espacios, actores y tendencias. *Pap. Rev. Sociol.* **2017**, *102*, 727–760. [CrossRef]

38. Domínguez, M. Dinàmiques de metropolitanització: Ús i integració del territory. In *Crisi Econòmica, Creixement de les Desigualtats i Transformacions Socials. Informe General de l'Enquesta de Condicions de vida i Hàbits de la Població*; Trullén, J., Ed.; Institut d'Estudis Regionals i Metropolitans de Barcelona, Diputació de Barcelona, Àrea Metropolitana de Barcelona i Institut d'Estadística de Catalunya: Barcelona, Spain, 2014; pp. 248–290, ISBN 978-84-92940-18-9.

39. Feria, J.M. La movilidad residencial y los procesos de urbanización metropolitanos en España. In *La Ciudad Metropolitana en España: Procesos Urbanos en los Inicios del Siglo XXI*; Feria, J.M., Albertos, J.M., Eds.; Thomson Reuters: Pamplona, Spain, 2010; pp. 23–45, ISBN 978-84-470-3079-8.

40. Etxezarreta, A.; Hoekstra, J.; Dol, K.; Cano, G. De la burbuja inmobiliaria a las ejecuciones hipotecarias. *Ciud. Territ. Estud. Territ.* **2012**, *XIV*, 597–613.

41. Nelson, A.C. Urban containment American Style: A preliminary Asessment. In *Urban Sprawl in Western Europe and United States*; Richardson, H.W., Bae, C.H., Eds.; Ashgate: Aldershot, UK, 2004; pp. 237–253, ISBN 0 75463789.

42. Champion, A. Urbanization, Suburbanization, Counterurbanization and Reurbanization. In *Handbook of Urban Studies*; Paddison, R., Ed.; SAGE: London, UK, 2001; pp. 143–161, ISBN 9780803976955.

43. Smith, D.P.; Finney, N.; Halfacree, K.; Walford, H. Understanding of Internal Migration Process Using Integrated Geographical Perspectives. In *Internal Migration: Geographical Perspectives and Processes*; Smith, D.P., Finney, N., Walford, N., Eds.; Ashgate: London, UK, 2015; pp. 165–178, ISBN 978-1472452467.

44. Petsimeris, P. Out of squalor and towards another urban renaissance? Gentrification and neighbourhood transformations in Southern Europe. In *Gentrification in a Global Context: The New Urban Colonialism*; Atkinson, R., Bridge, G., Eds.; Routledge Taylor & Francis Group: Abingdon, UK, 2004; pp. 245–260, ISBN 978-020-3392-08-9.

45. Generalitat de Catalunya. Departament de Territori i Sostenibilitat (2018). *Informe Sobre el Sector de L'habitatge a Catalunya 2017*. July 2018. Available online: http://habitatge.gencat.cat/ (accessed on 25 September 2018).

46. Lomax, N.; Stillwell, J. United Kingdom: Temporal change in internal migration. In *Internal Migration in the Developed World: Are We Becoming Less Mobile?* Champion, T., Cooke, T., Shuttleworth, I., Eds.; Taylor and Francis: Abingdon, UK, 2016; pp. 120–146, ISBN 978-131711449-9.

47. Champion, A. The changing nature of urban and rural areas in the United Kingdom and other European countries. In *Population Distribution, Urbanization, Internal Migration and Development: An International Perspective*; Population Division; United Nations Department of Economic and Social Affairs: New York, NY, USA, 2011; pp. 144–160.

48. Alabart, A. Mobilitat residencial, solidaritat familiar i ciutadania a les regions metropolitanes. *Rev. Catal. Sociol.* **2007**, *10*, 23–39.

49. Bonvalet, C.; Lelièvre, E. *De la Famille à L'entourage. L'enquête Biographies et Entourage*; INED: Paris, France, 2012; ISBN 978-2733280034.

urban science

MDPI

Article

Urban Intensities. The Urbanization of the Iberian Mediterranean Coast in the Light of Nighttime Satellite Images of the Earth

Joan Checa * and Oriol Nel· lo

Research Group on Energy, Territory and Society, Department of Geography,
Autonomous University of Barcelona, Cerdanyola del Vallès, 08193 Bellaterra, Spain; oriol.nello@uab.cat
* Correspondence: joan.checa@uab.cat; Tel.: +34-93-581-1751

Received: 19 October 2018; Accepted: 24 November 2018; Published: 29 November 2018

Abstract: The contribution shares the approach of critical urban studies that have conceptualized urbanization more as a process than as a sum of spatial forms. Thus, the contribution studies the urbanization process not only from the point of view of the physical occupation of land but also considers changes in the intensity of the uses of space. To fulfill this aim, the new sources of nocturnal satellite images are particularly useful. These allow us to observe the intensity of urban uses both in terms of their distribution over space and their recurrence over time. The research focuses on the Iberian Mediterranean coast and permits the verification of the intensity of the urban uses of the space for the whole of this area and their seasonal variations throughout the year. The source of the study are the nighttime satellite images of the Earth for the 2012–2017 period from the NASA SNPP satellite equipped with the VIIRS-DNB instrument. By establishing a threshold of urban light the research shows that those districts with the greatest extensions of urban light do not necessarily correspond with the most densely populated areas. Similarly the absence of urban light does not necessarily indicate the absence of urban uses. Finally, the variations of intensity of light prove to be a good indicator of seasonal variations of activity in tourist areas.

Keywords: urbanization; night lights; remote sensing; land uses; seasonality; Suomi NPP VIIRS

---

1. Introduction

The traditional starting point of studies of urbanization processes has been a dual vision of space with a clear differentiation between urban and non- urban spaces. Accordingly, the basic premises of urban studies consider a city as an object characterized by particular attributes of form and function that clearly set it apart from the non-city—hence the configuration of the oppositions of country–city and rural–urban that have governed the conceptual development of this branch of the social sciences for decades [1,2].

This conceptual approach has given rise to countless studies seeking to establish the limits of urban and metropolitan settings on the basis of criteria related to administration, morphology, function, hierarchy of services, economic structures, and lifestyles [3,4]. These approaches have produced extremely interesting results that have often proved useful for the management and governance of a territory but have done nothing to refute the reality that nowadays a strict definition of urban limits is highly problematic in scientific terms.

This reality has led, in recent years, to a growing awareness that any understanding of spatial dynamics requires an analysis of urbanization as a process, rather than attempts to define a city, metropolis or region as circumscribed artifacts or areas. This process is made up of activities and social relationships in space that give rise to a complex and constantly changing network of settlements and flows of energy, resources, people, capital, goods, and information [4–6]. This approach therefore goes beyond the analysis and demarcation of spaces characterized by features traditionally ascribed to the city—compactness, complexity, and incessant continuity—to argue that urbanization should be studied as a process that, in its present phase, has led to the overall integration of planetary space as interdependent networks and a growing subjection of resources and goods to trading relationships [1,5,7–10].

However, the urbanization of space in terms of integration and interrelationships does not in any way imply its homogenization. On the contrary: just as urban macroregions present significant social and economic differences, they also display an extremely marked diversity in the intensity of uses in their territories. This diversity is not derived so much from the percentage of surface area that is artificialized, or even from the predominance of primary, secondary or tertiary uses of the space—as suggested by the old urban/rural duality—but by the fact that, in a territory entirely dominated by uses that could be described as urban, activities and flows present various levels of density and intensity. Thus, some areas experience intensive use as both flow and permanent installation of activities and population, while others present less intensity of use, but this absolutely does not mean that they are not also integrated into—and transformed by—the process of urbanization [10,11].

This article seeks to explore the dynamics of urbanization within a particular area: the eastern coast of the Iberian Peninsula and the Balearic archipelago. The territories of Catalonia, Valencian Community and the Balearic Islands form an urban macro-region with a population of almost 14 million residents, as well as 40 million international visitors per year. In fact, the Iberian Mediterranean coast constitutes an extensive urban region, which encompasses several regional metropolises—Barcelona, Tarragona, València, and Alacant-Elx—along with some of the most developed tourist areas of the Mediterranean—Costa Brava, Costa Daurada, Costa del Sol, and Mallorca—it is similar in size to the macro-regions of the Po Valley in Italy and the Randstad in the Netherlands and it is to be considered one of the main economic axes of Southern Europe. As various authors have pointed out this type of geographic areas are a particularly appropriate setting for a discussion of the intensity of urbanization, due to both the density of its urban uses and its striking seasonal variations [12,13].

In order to explore this subject, our research takes advantage of a relatively new source that is particularly suited to a study of the intensity of the urbanization process: the nighttime satellite images of the Earth issued by the USA's National Oceanic and Atmospheric Administration (NOAA). Various authors have pointed out the potential of this source [14–19]. Starting from the assumption that the nighttime brightness revealed by these means is an anthropogenic phenomenon, then its analysis makes it possible to detect the presence of settlements and human activities (urban areas, communication routes and bridges, traces of fishing boats and ships, and other) and establish the relationships between the intensity of nighttime light, land use and a wide range of socioeconomic variables [14–19].

The article is divided into four sections: the first focuses on methodological questions; the second shows the particularities of spatial urbanization on the Iberian Mediterranean coast in terms of extension and intensity, via the data derived from nighttime satellite images; there follows an exploration, by way of example, of the variations over time in these intensities on the Balearic Islands that establishes relationships with various economic indicators; finally, a few brief conclusions close the article.

2. Materials and Methods

2.1. Basic Information

As explained, the spatial scope of this study includes the most urbanized regions of the eastern seaboard of Iberian Peninsula and the Balearic Islands. It extends over approximately 600 km of coastal line and is made up of the regions of Catalonia, Valencia, and the Balearic Islands. This macro-region, which has been named Arc Mediterrani, has population that exceeds 13 million inhabitants and generates 31.1% of Spanish GDP, with total volume—361 thousand million euro—which doubles the output of countries like Greece or Portugal, and approaches that of medium-sized European nations such as Norway and Austria. The Mediterranean macro-region also originates 40% of Spanish exports and has two large metropolises—the metropolitan areas of Barcelona and València—the tourist island of

Mallorca, and a series of urban areas and medium-sizes cities: Girona-Costa Brava, Camps de Tarragona, Castelló-la Plana Alta, and Alacant-Elx.

Therefore, it can be said that Mediterranean coast, together with the metropolis of Madrid and the Atlantic coastal axis from Galicia to Lisbon, is one of the macro-regions with the highest demographic and economic potential of the Iberian Peninsula [20,21].

To treat the data we have used the subdivision of the study area in 86 "comarcas" or districts (Figure 1). The "comarca" is an administrative division of a political and statistical nature, somewhere between the local and regional levels, i.e., it is larger than municipality but smaller than a province.

Figure 1. Study area, and the boundaries of the districts.

The main source of basic information for this study is the nighttime satellite images of the Earth Observation Group (EOG), which belongs to the National Geophysical Data Center (NGDC) in the USA's National Oceanic and Atmospheric Administration (NOAA). More particularly, these images form part of the NOAA's teledetection products derived from satellite sensors with a capacity to capture light sensitivity in situations of little or no natural light and thus demonstrate the artificial lighting resulting from human activities. The EOG produces and makes available satellite images whose pixels contain values related to permanent nighttime lighting on the surface of the Earth.

The specific images used as a source herein only very recently became available to the researchers and they therefore provide new and exciting possibilities for analysis. They come from the Suomi National Polar-Orbital Partnership (SNPP) satellite, which supplies data via its VIIRS (Visible Infrared Imaging Radiometer Suite) and DNB (Day/Night Band) sensor. This sensor makes it possible to obtain calibrated global data on nighttime radiance within a spectral bandwidth of 500 to 900 nm, close to the bandwidth visible to humans [22].

This information is available in the form of monthly composites or the years 2012–2017, with periodic updates. The composites produced by the EOG are georeferenced rasters in a GeoTIFF format, with a pixel resolution of 15 arc-seconds, which makes it possible to work on the selected area with pixels of approximately 350 × 350 m (Table 1). Obviously this involves the limitation of not being able to observe the type of artifact or focus emitting the radiance inside each pixel, but in general terms it can be considered that the resolution level of the images is useful for our purposes and, in any case, it represents a great advance with regard to the quality of the images available until very recently [23].

The images basic information lies in each of their pixels, where the mean value of the radiance emitted by that area on the Earth's surface is presented in units of $nW/cm^2/sr$. The values of the radiometric detection range (degrees of light intensity) lie between 0 and 300 $nW/cm^2/sr$, with 0 as the value corresponding to absolute darkness and around 300 as maximum light (with some extreme values going beyond this range). This range of values makes it possible to distinguish small settlements and also differentiate values of radiance (intra-urban variations) without saturations in areas with the most light [24] (Figure 2). It is important to take into account that the treatment applied by the NOAA does not exclude relatively ephemeral incidents such as forest fires and gas ignition. Moreover, the monthly schedule of images prejudices the quality of the data, as some months might be very cloudy while others have an inordinate amount of sunlight, particularly in those latitudes far from the Equator around the time of the summer solstice. These circumstances can partially invalidate the satellite findings or prejudice the quality of the monthly composites. However, a raster file indicates the number of valid observations recorded for each month, and on this basis the NOAA has created the corresponding monthly composite of nighttime light. In the latitude of our study area, the surfeit of atmospheric light in the months of May, June, and July invalidate the satellite observations for that period, making it impossible to create the corresponding monthly composite. There are other effects that also have to be taken into account, such as that of the albedo of the land cover, although, according to [25], these have little influence.

Table 1. Main characteristics of the data, VIIRS-DNB (Visible Infrared Imaging Radiometer Suite Day/Night Band).

Characteristic	Description
Temporary series	April 2012–present (monthly)
Area coverage	Between the latitudes −65° to 75°
Quantization	14 bits/16.384 DN
Pixel brightness values	0 to 300 range of normals values (nanoWatts/(cm²·sr)
Saturation	Without saturation
Pixel size	15 s of arc (350 × 350 m our latitude)
Radiometric calibration	On board
Low light imaging bandpass	Pancromatic 500–900 nm
Nighttime overpass	~01:30
Low light imaging detection limit	~2 × 10^{-11} Watts/cm²/sr
Swath	3000 km

Source: Based on [23,26].

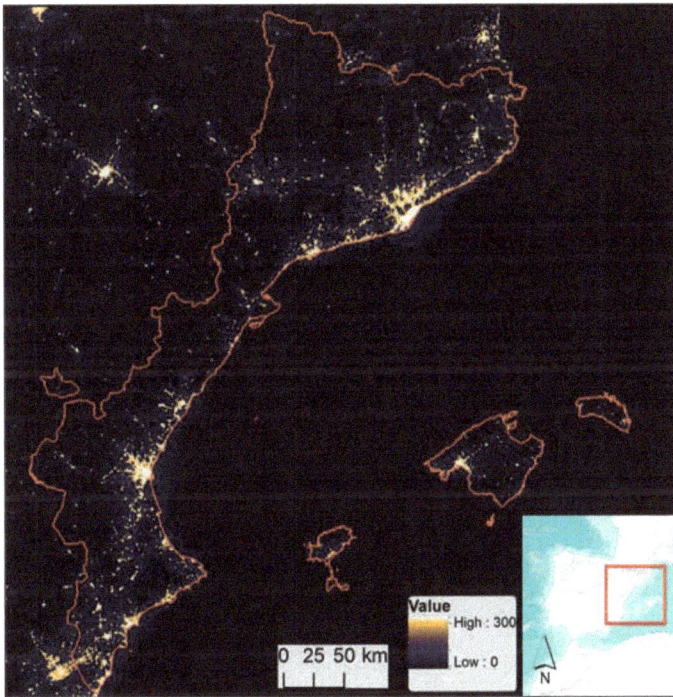

Figure 2. VIIRS/DNB image April 2012, study area.

2.2. Treatment of the Images

The procedure for the observation and treatment of the nighttime images involved, firstly, downloading the amount of the monthly satellite images available in the NOAA repository for the period from April 2012 to October 2017, and then the extraction (cropping) of the images corresponding to the study area. The period of time considered corresponds to the availability of the images at the initial moment of our research.

The images were subsequently converted to a vectorial format that permits the quantitative analysis of the data on light intensity in relation to other statistical and cartographic variables. This vectorization process required a previous conversion to whole numbers, due to the decimal format of the values of the cells. Whole numbers running from 0 to 300 (plus extreme values) were therefore used, with the original values from the NOAA raster images (which comprise up to fourteen digits) approximated to the nearest round number. In order to be able to work with other sources of information, all the cartographic bases were unified in a single cartographic space with the same projection and reference system (Datum: ETRS89, European Terrestrial Reference System 1989. Projection: UTM31N, Universal Transverse Mercator, spindle 31 north), all within a GIS work setting.

Furthermore, as evident from the above description of the characteristics of the source, measures had to be taken to compensate for any possible distortions resulting from accidental light emissions. Accordingly, when areas presented abnormal values in certain months—attributable to fires or other isolated incidents—these were corrected by calculating the mean value calculated for these months in undisrupted previous and subsequent years and then assigning it to the affected pixels. This allowed us to counteract the influence of large-scale fires detected by the images. Similarly, any undue influence of cloudiness on the monthly composites was ruled out by always having available at least two valid monthly observations per pixel.

Finally, in order to minimize any other possible effects on the images, new composites of mean monthly and annual light were generated on the basis of the available images. To obtain the annual means, the values for each pixel for all the months of each year were superimposed and added up to arrive at the annual arithmetic mean of the light emitted by each pixel (portion of surface area). In our case, the annual means for 2013–2016 were obtained on the basis of the nine months available to us, for, as explained above, we lack information about the months around the summer solstice. Only six months were available for 2012 (from April onwards, excluding the summer months) and only those up to October were available for 2017 (also excluding the months around the summer solstice). In order to study the seasonality of the urban uses of land without any of the sporadic effects that may occur in a specific year, the process was repeated, but this time adding up the data for each month of the six available years. This gave us the yearly mean of light for each month (January, February, etc.) for the entire study period.

This methodology allowed us to minimize any possible undue effects, while the use of annual and seasonal means for the whole study period reduced the impact of the possible effects of measures applied against light pollution and of changes in light sources over this time. Some studies have shown that a change of lighting system aimed at greater energy efficiency and/or reduction in light pollution can affect the amount of light captured by the satellite, as part of the wavelength of LEDs falls under the sensor's detection limits of 500 nm. Such changes could explain why light emissions fail to increase in some countries, or even decrease [27]. However, the rebound effect defined by the Jevons paradox is also well known [28]. Furthermore, it must be taken into account that transitions towards LED lighting can intensify the "skyglow" halo due to shortened wavelengths [29]. In short, the effects of saving energy with outdoor LED lighting may not necessarily suppose a reduction in the total light emitted and recorded.

2.3. Methodology to Establish the Threshold of Urban Light

In view of both our intention to study the intensity of urban land uses and the common practice in research involving this type of image [18,30], we considered it appropriate to determine the threshold value at which the brightness of a lit surface area most accurately reflects the artificialization of the land. The images show that not all the pixels with light values above zero correspond to an area with uses that involve a permanent artificialization of the land. A definition of the minimum value of light (from 0 to 300) at which a lit surface area most closely corresponds to the presence of constructions, infrastructures and other artifacts is therefore of great benefit.

The main purpose of this definition is to provide a reference threshold when it comes to measuring the intensity of the urban uses of the territory, without pretending to imply, in any way, that urban uses do not extend to areas with lower levels of light. In contrast, as indicated above, this research starts from the premise that urbanization nowadays is a process that tends to integrate and transform the uses of a territory in its entirety. The concept of nighttime urban light must therefore be understood in terms of intensity rather than exclusion.

The methodology established in [18,30] was used to define this threshold. This procedure contrasts the light values of the satellite images with information about land cover derived from a reliable source. More specifically, the data on light values were contrasted with information on the physical extension of urban settlements on the map of land cover in Catalonia drawn up by the Centre de Recerca Ecològica i Aplicacions Forestals (CREAF) in 2009, the available source that was considered most preferable. The equivalent of the CREAF map for the Spanish territory as a whole would be the Land Cover Map (SIOSE) of the Instituto Geográfico Nacional. The reference scale of the SIOSE is 1:25,000, as against the greater detail (1:2500) and greater specificity of the classifications of land cover of the CREAF map. Time difference between the two sources (2009 CREAF map and 2012 NOAA images) may entail some distortion. In any case it should be taken into account that between 2009 and 2012 the surface area of developed land in Spanish was very small due to the situation of economic crisis.

In order to make the calculations that adjusted light levels to the reference source for land cover (which establishes 411 categories for this parameter), 50 types of land cover were selected, all falling under the category of artificialized land. These include all types of residential, industrial and tertiary land and facilities but rule out any type of land with uses that are agricultural, woodland, aquatic, etc. The areas corresponding to the various levels of light intensity were superimposed on to selected areas of the reference map in order to establish the correlation between the two. The data were crossed by using an image of nighttime brightness corresponding to the annual mean obtained via the monthly composites from April to December 2012, thereby correcting any possible seasonal variations. It was therefore possible to statistically evaluate the light level at which there was the greatest coincidence (intersection) of artificialized land and light intensity.

The results of this intersection (Table 2, Figure 3) showed the value of 11 (out of 300) to be the reference threshold at which there was the greatest coincidence of light intensity and artificialization of the land. This threshold enabled us to quantitatively analyze surface area in terms of the level of light intensity, which we refer to as "nighttime urban brightness", i.e., light that emits radiance equal to or greater than 11 $nW/cm^2/sr$.

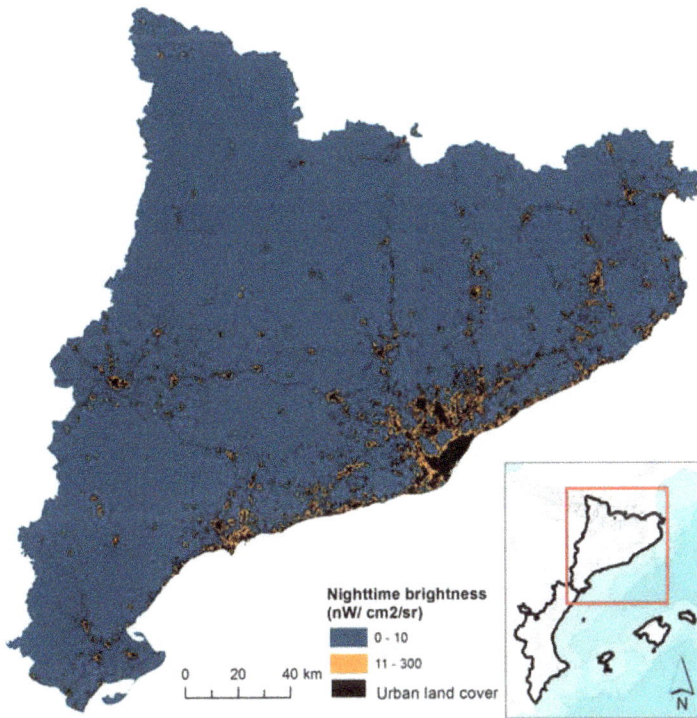

Figure 3. Light level ($nW/cm^2/sr$) 2012 and urban land cover in Catalonia (Centre de Recerca Ecològica i Aplicacions Forestals (CREAF)) 2009.

Table 2. Determination of the reference threshold between the luminosity and the urban land cover of CREAF (2009) for the whole of Catalonia.

Radiance (nW/cm²/sr) Starting from	Brightness	Urban Uses CREAF	Area (km²)					% Considered	
			Intersection	CREAF No Intersection	Brightness Not Intersected	Total Area	Intersection/Total Area × 100	Urban Uses	of Brightness
0	32,102.7	1914.8	1914.8	0.0	30,187.9	32,102.7	5.96	100	5.96
1	9089.8	1914.8	1741.8	173.0	7348.0	9262.8	18.80	90.97	19.16
2	5614.6	1914.8	1589.3	325.5	4025.3	5940.1	26.76	83.00	28.31
3	4495.8	1914.8	1496.7	418.1	2999.1	4913.9	30.46	78.16	33.29
4	3834.5	1914.8	1423.5	491.3	2411.0	4325.9	32.91	74.34	37.12
5	3355.6	1914.8	1358.2	556.7	1997.4	3912.3	34.72	70.93	40.47
6	2998.1	1914.8	1298.4	616.4	1699.7	3614.5	35.92	67.81	43.31
7	2711.1	1914.8	1245.1	669.7	1466.0	3380.8	36.83	65.03	45.93
8	2470.0	1914.8	1192.5	722.3	1277.5	3192.3	37.36	62.28	48.28
9	2273.1	1914.8	1148.0	766.8	1125.1	3040.0	37.76	59.95	50.50
10	2108.8	1914.8	1105.8	809.0	1003.0	2917.8	37.90	57.75	52.44
11	1957.6	1914.8	1066.0	848.9	891.6	2806.4	37.98	55.67	54.45
12	1838.7	1914.8	1031.4	883.4	807.3	2722.1	37.89	53.86	56.09
13	1732.1	1914.8	998.1	916.7	734.0	2648.8	37.68	52.13	57.62

3. Results and Discussion: Two Intensities of Urbanization

The results obtained allow us to calculate the extension of urban light intensity in terms of both space and time. With respect to space, the first result presented below is a general overview of the surface area that presented light levels, in all the 86 districts that comprise the studied territory. This is complemented by an analysis of the mean light levels displayed by each district. There follows an examination of light intensity in terms of time, with a special focus, as mentioned above, on the Balearic Islands, one of the regions with the most notable seasonal variations in this respect.

3.1. Light Intensity in Terms of Space

3.1.1. The Extension of Urban Light Intensity

The study and comparison of the nighttime urban light (from value 11 upwards) in the 86 districts provides information about the intensity of urbanization in each one, as well as information about the uses of land therein (Figure 4). The analysis was static and took in the means of all the available light values corresponding to the months of October within the study period. October is especially suited to synchronic studies and comparisons between territories within our study area because, on the one hand, atmospheric light does not affect nighttime observation and, on the other, there is less probability of any effects from the albedo of snow [27].

On the basis of the calculations of the light in the various districts, we can state that 6.7% of the territory in the study area presents light levels over the threshold of what we refer to as "nighttime urban brightness". In absolute terms, this represents 4037 km^2, somewhat bigger than the island of Mallorca.

Figure 5 shows the areas above his threshold, with 290.6 km^2 corresponding to the Balearic Islands (5.8% of the overall territory), 1938.8 to Catalonia (6%) and 1807 to Valencian Community (7.8%), which was the community that proportionally had the largest extension of urban intensity. It should be noted, however, that the area with the greatest urban intensity is not spread uniformly over the territory but traces a highly urbanized corridor along the coastline, most particularly around the two largest metropolitan regions—Barcelona and València—, as well as around Girona and the Costa Brava, the Camp de Tarragona, the Plana de Castelló, Alacant-Elx, and the Badia de Palma. Comparison with the surface area of artificialized land derived from other sources shows a close fit between the two values: in the case of Catalonia, for example, 1.02 km^2 of urban brightness was detected for every km^2 identified by the CREAF as urban land cover.

However, the results of some areas compensate those of others with respect to the relationship between artificialized land and urban brightness, so that a correlation as close as this may be somewhat deceptive. We have studied the relationship between the artificialization of land and brightness in [30]. In that work we showed that the use of data from the period 1992–2012 for the largest Spanish cities produced a ratio between artificialized land and urban light of 1 to 1.83. The very marked contrast with the results of the data from 2017 is due to the capacity to make much more accurate calculations with the Suomi NPP VIIRS images.

It would be wrong to suppose, however, that the largest areas of urban brightness in absolute terms are to be found in the most heavily populated districts: in fact, two of the most populated districts, Barcelonès and València, occupy the sixth and seventeenth positions, respectively, in the ranking of districts by surface area of urban brightness. In contrast, the districts with the largest extensions of land with urban brightness are characterized by more dispersed urbanization: the Baix Segura, on the southern border of València, with 348,622 inhabitants (INE 2017 [31]), has three times more surface area with urban brightness than València, with a population of 787,808. Similarly, the Vallès Occidental, with 910,031 inhabitants, has double the surface area with urban brightness in Barcelonès, with a population of 2,248,227. Urban brightness therefore clearly shows that the extension of urbanization does not necessarily correspond to a high density of population in much of the study area. This is because much of coastal developments related to tourism and second homes, covering a very large area, are of relatively low population density. Other factors such as the location of communication corridors, industrial plants and intensive agriculture along the coastline can also contribute to this effect.

The other side of the coin is represented by those districts with only a very small area above the threshold of urban light. Paradoxically, some of these districts devote a substantial part of their territory to producing energy via dams (as in the Alta Ribagorça and Pallars Jussà). Others are characterized by wine production (El Priorat and the Terra Alta), and others by tourism (the Serra de Tramuntana and the Pla de Mallorca and Formentera). In all these cases, these uses are highly urban and directly linked to the needs and dynamics of the urbanization process. An examination of urban light therefore reveals the presence, in more shaded areas, of what Neil Brenner [11] has called the "operational spaces" of the urbanization process: areas articulated by the provision of all kinds of resources and products essential to this process. Once again, it would be wrong to suppose that the evolution of these areas is not indissolubly linked to urbanization.

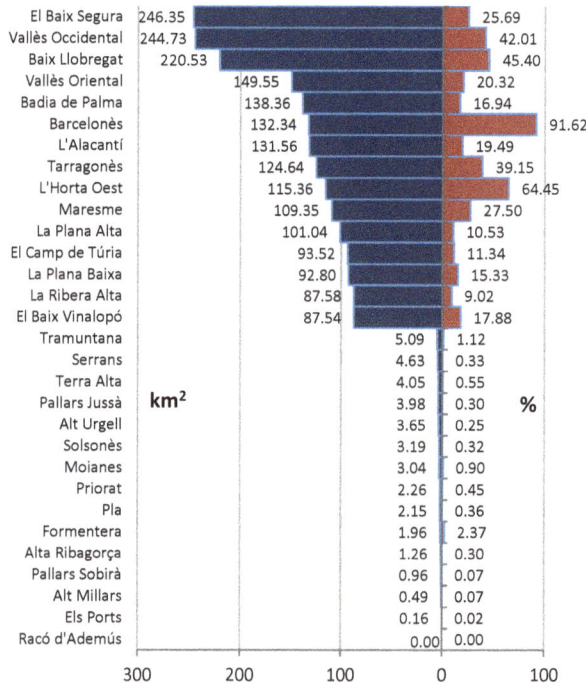

Figure 4. Absolute (km^2) and relative (%) values of the surface areas with levels of urban brightness per district for the mean of the months of October 2012–2017. Data for the 15 districts with the highest and lowest values of lit surface area.

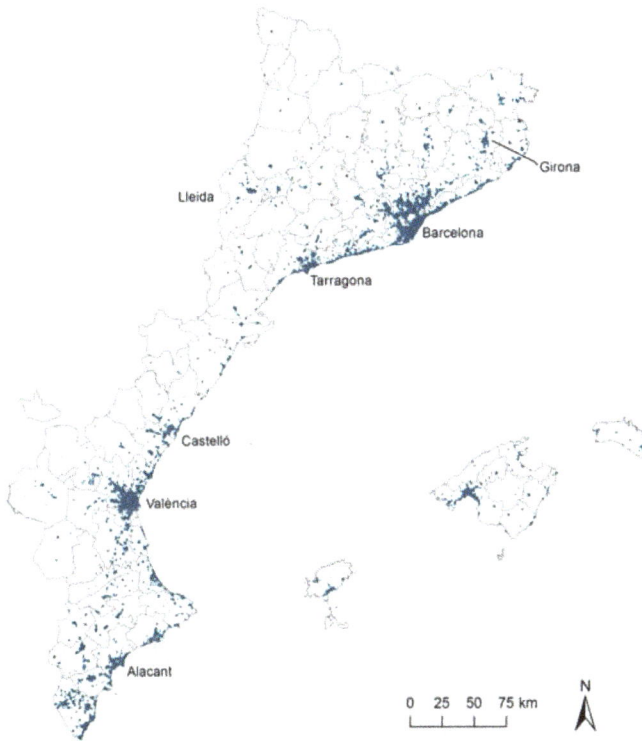

Figure 5. Surface area of urban brightness (>10), mean for the months of October.

3.1.2. The Intensity of Urban Brightness

The calculation of the mean brightness per district allows us to fine-tune still further the relationship between the level of brightness and the intensity of urbanization. The first step involves obtaining the weighted mean brightness of each territory. The weighted mean brightness value corresponds to the total of the brightness values for each pixel multiplied by its surface area and divided by the total surface area of the area under consideration. In the study area as a whole the weighted mean is 2.94 nW/cm^2/sr, with some differences between communities, with Valencian at the top with 3.43, followed by Catalonia with 2.66, and the Balearic Islands with 2.46. These figures broaden the picture of the relationship between brightness, population and GDP by suggesting that the territory that is relatively the most efficient in terms of light emitted per inhabitant or per unit of product would be Catalonia. This statement undoubtedly needs to be qualified by other factors (such as data on the transient population), but these fall beyond our present remit.

Secondly, the quality of the images and the range of the values allow us to move beyond a study of the brightness of a city to one of brightness in the city. In other words, we can evaluate the mean brightness of those areas that fall within the threshold for urban brightness and thus compare the intensities of use inside these areas.

The overall mean brightness of the areas above the threshold of urban brightness is 33.76 nW/cm^2/sr. As can be seen in Figure 6, this mean intensity is not uniform in all the districts. The districts containing the two most heavily populated cities stand out: València with an intensity of 89.7 and Barcelonès with 82.5. The intensity of the next highest urban areas in other districts is around half these figures. In Catalonia, Baix Llobregat presents a value of 43.6, followed by Tarragonès, Vallès Ocidental, and Gironès. In València, the brightness of Horta Oest and Baix Vinalopó is particularly noteworthy, although it should be pointed out that almost all the coastline and the land to the south of the Comarques

Centrals present very high levels of brightness. On the Balearic Islands, the light from the Bahia de Palma is particularly outstanding.

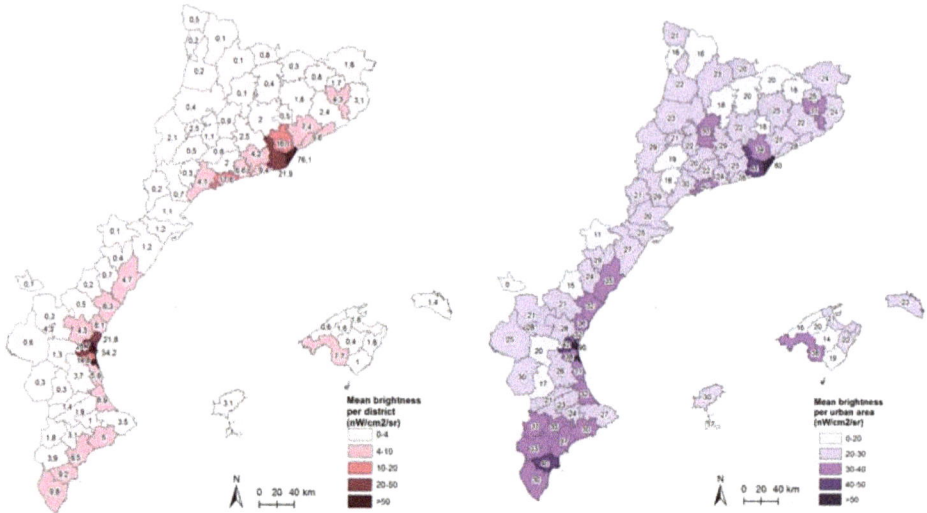

Figure 6. Weighted mean brightness, mean for the months of October (2012–2017).

3.2. Light Intensity in Terms of Time

One of the main features of the contemporary urbanization process is the fact that its dynamics tend not only to embrace an entire region, to a greater or lesser extent, but also reflect notable variations in time of the uses that characterize it. Thus, the intensity of the urbanization process varies not only in space but also in time. Despite their limitations, nighttime satellite images of the Earth offer an innovative means of observing this phenomenon, as demonstrated below by an examination of the seasonal evolution of light on the Balearic Islands and the Pitiüses.

Any analysis of seasonal variations in brightness obviously requires an indicator that measures the amounts of light emitted by each territory at various times of the year, thereby providing a basis for intra- and inter-territorial seasonal comparisons. In our case, this indicator is provided by the images of the mean monthly composites for each of the nine months available, and the variable used will be what is known as the total emitted light, also used by authors like [27,29]. This is the sum of the light values (radiant intensity) for each area/territory multiplied by its surface area and thus covers both the lit surface area and the light level, making it possible to compare a single territory on a seasonal basis, as the result obtained indicates the total light total emitted per district. In order to facilitate comparisons between different seasons and between different territories, the mean value of the light emitted by each of the latter will be correlated via an index of 100 (Figures 7 and 8). In this case we have considered brightness values above 2 $nW/cm^2/sr$ in order to obviate any noise from the instrument itself, as explained in, for example, [27,32,33]. Although the threshold of urban intensity enables us to differentiate intensities as regards land use, it does not take into account any settlements with lower intensity. In this exercise our concern is to use light to measure the activity of the human presence in the territory as a whole.

The usefulness of this exercise is particularly well demonstrated by its application to a territory such as the Balearic Islands. It is well known that, in territorial terms, these islands are characterized by both the vigor of by their urbanization process [34–37] and their striking seasonal variations in activity and population as a result of tourism [38–40]. An analysis of the total emitted light clearly reveals the intensity and variability of both these phenomena, although it must be stressed once again that the lack of data for the months of May, June and July, as explained above, represents a significant obstacle to a seasonal analysis of light using our source.

The results show that the average total light emitted in the various months of the year falls below the mean in the period from October to March but is well above it from April to September. This pattern obviously reflects the seasonal nature of the economic activities connected to the islands' tourism. Nevertheless, the contrasts in light emission are not as marked as in other variables, as we shall see in more detail below. This suggests, in the first instance, a possibility that the seasonal increases recorded in some territories are compensated by greater stability in others.

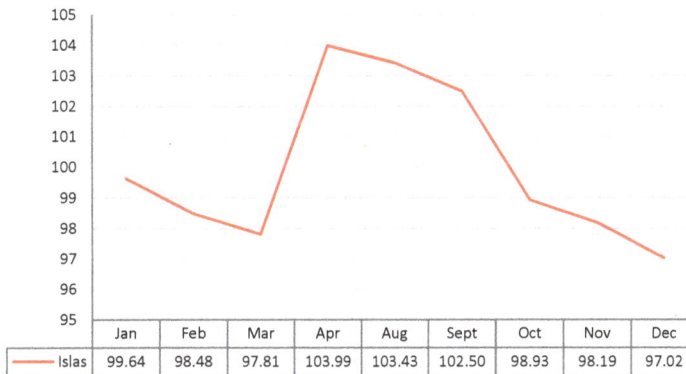

	Jan	Feb	Mar	Apr	Aug	Sept	Oct	Nov	Dec
——— Islas	99.64	98.48	97.81	103.99	103.43	102.50	98.93	98.19	97.02

Figure 7. Total light emitted/radiant intensity (>2 nW/sr). Monthy means 2012–2017. Balearic Islands. In indexed numbers (annual mean = 100).

It is useful to verify these results by analyzing the differentiated behavior of the various areas of the Balearic territory (islands and districts) with respect to the whole. Thus, the ten areas under consideration can be divided into three groups, according to their seasonal behavior. First, the most numerous group would comprise the islands of Formentera, Eivissa and Menorca, as well as the areas of Nord, Llevant, and Sud in Mallorca. These areas, with behavior that would most closely reflect seasonal tourism, are characterized by very high values on the 100 index from April to September and lower ones from October to December. Overall, we could classify them as districts marked by tourism. This seasonal behavior contrasts with the relative stability of the Badia de Palma, the biggest urban hub in Mallorca. Finally, a third group, comprising mountains and the interior of Mallorca—Raiguer, Tramuntana, and Pla—present a more erratic behavior. The following figure shows three examples of this contrasting seasonal behavior.

The tendency of certain territories to give off more light in the summer months of tourist activity is thus verified, as it has been in other Mediterranean islands, but it would also be interesting to establish the sensitivity of the fluctuations in brightness to the seasonal nature of the activity, for a similar case on some Greek islands, see [33]. This involves contrasting the evolution of the data obtained from the nighttime satellite images with specific socioeconomic indicators.

To do this, we have collated the variations in the number of workers affiliated to the Social Security, as these are registered on a monthly basis on a municipal scale. On the basis of data supplied by the Ministry of Labor and Social Security on workers signed up with the Social Security on the final days of each month in 2017. It should be noted, however, that although the data on Social Security affiliation cover all workers on a monthly basis, the municipalities in which they are recorded correspond to their employers' contribution center, which in many cases does not physically coincide with the location of their workplace. This would be the case, for example, when a hotel chain has a single provincial contribution center in which all its workers are registered, even though they are spread over hotels in various municipalities within a province. Despite this limitation, a comparison between this variable and nighttime brightness proves to be of value, as we shall see.

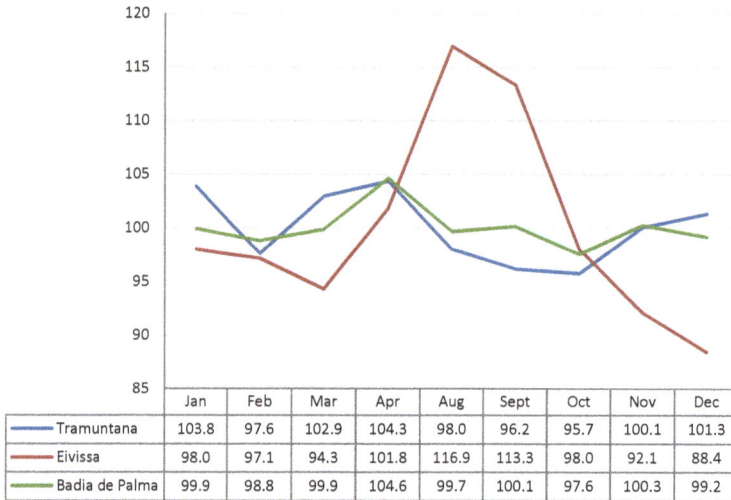

	Jan	Feb	Mar	Apr	Aug	Sept	Oct	Nov	Dec
Tramuntana	103.8	97.6	102.9	104.3	98.0	96.2	95.7	100.1	101.3
Eivissa	98.0	97.1	94.3	101.8	116.9	113.3	98.0	92.1	88.4
Badia de Palma	99.9	98.8	99.9	104.6	99.7	100.1	97.6	100.3	99.2

Figure 8. Total monthly emitted light (>2 nW/cm^2/sr). Monthly means 2012–2017. Serra de Tramuntana, Eivissa, and Badia de Palma. In indexed numbers (annual mean for each territory = 100).

To make this comparison, we first grouped together all the affiliated workers from all the municipalities in each of the areas (islands and districts) used in the brightness analysis for all the months of 2017 for which data on nighttime brightness were available. We then calculated the differences in the 100 index in each district with respect to the mean number of workers in these 9 months. An examination of the districts and their relationship with the affiliated workers shows that for the islands as a whole this is 0.689. A more detailed analysis, in line with the typology of the areas studied above, shows that areas with the most intense tourist activity present an even more significant relationship (0.8507) (Table 3).

Despite this clear relationship, however, the variations in brightness are considerably less marked than changes in occupation (Figure 9). Whilst there are only 16 points (in indexed numbers) separating the months with the most and least brightness, the monthly difference in terms of affiliated workers is 60 points. Brightness is therefore sensitive to seasonal variations but it is also subject to great inertia over the course of the year. This lack of precise correlation between the intensities of light and activity is, we believe, a very significant finding, with respect to both analytical procedures and energy and environmental policies.

Table 3. Relationship between monthly variations in total emitted light and variations in the number of total workers affiliated per month per district.

District	r^2	Pearson
Eivissa	0.889	0.943
Menorca	0.815	0.903
Formentera	0.785	0.886
Nord	0.670	0.819
Llevant	0.317	0.563
Sud	0.303	0.550
Badia de Palma	0.068	0.260
Raiguer	0.116	−0.340
Tramuntana	0.132	−0.363
Pla	0.316	−0.562

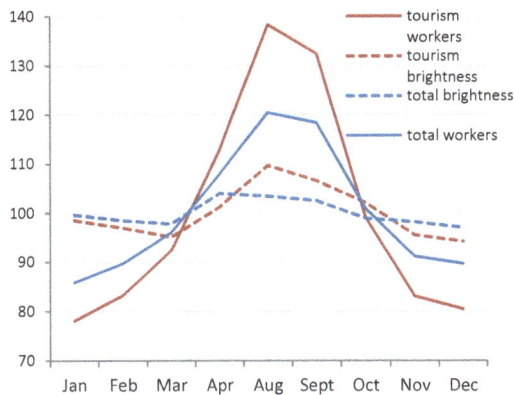

Figure 9. Annual evolution of workers affiliated to the Social Security and total emitted light with respect to its annual mean on the 100 index for the Balearic Islands and their tourist districts. Source: Based on VIIRS images and affiliated workers, according to the Ministry of Labor and Social Security.

4. Conclusions

As stated above, this research contributes to our understanding of the urbanization process, understood not just as mere artificialization of land but also as integration and commercialization of space. This process is currently embracing the whole planet, but it obviously presents notable local differences in intensity, in terms of both space and time. The Iberian Mediterranean coastline is a good example of this phenomenon.

From a methodological viewpoint, our research has enabled us to verify that nighttime satellite images are a useful source for studying the extension, intensity and seasonality of the urban uses of territory. The most obvious conclusions can be summarized in the following six points:

(a) The new sources of nighttime satellite images provide a level of detail in the analysis that is greatly superior to that of even the most recent series previously available. This makes it possible, for example, to fine-tune the correlation between artificialized land and areas with degrees of urban brightness, even though this correlation may partly be due to data from different areas compensating for each other.

(b) As regards the spatial intensity of urbanization, the study of brightness shows that those districts with the greatest extensions of urban light do not necessarily correspond with the most densely populated areas.

(c) Similarly, the absence of urban brightness does not automatically indicate an absence of urban uses. In contrast, areas deprived of this light intensity are in fact characterized by the presence of uses such as energy production activities related to tourism—activities which result from their integration in and interdependence with the urbanization process.

(d) Light intensity can serve as an indicator of efficiency, as regards use of territory and resources, distribution of population and production of goods and services. The diversity of the situations detected on the Mediterranean coastline attests to this.

(e) As regards the intensity of urban uses over time, brightness can again serve as a good indicator. The variations in the intensity of light in territories primarily devoted to tourism makes this clear. Deepening the study of the relationship between spatial intensity and time intensity of urban luminosity is without a doubt, one of the most interesting challenges that this line of research will face in the future.

(f) However, brightness, despite its evident relationship with the evolution of socioeconomic variables (for example, seasonal variations in employment) presents a limited sensitivity to these variations, which suggests that there is still much work to be done on measures aimed at adjusting the intensity of brightness to that of activity.

Nighttime satellite images therefore represent, despite their limitations, an instrument with great potential for both the study of the urbanization process and the provision of information that could underpin territorial, environmental and energy policies.

Author Contributions: Both authors intervened in the conceptualization and general outline of the paper. J.C. was in charge of data correction and preparing the original draft that was their reviewed and edited by both authors.

Funding: This research was funded by Institut d'Estudis Catalans (IEC) as part of the project In Lumine Sapientia. The urbanization process in Catalonia, Valencian Community and the Balearic Islands in the light of nighttime satellite images of the Earth.

Conflicts of Interest: The authors declare no conflict of interest.

References

1. Benevolo, L.; Erbani, F. *La Fine della Città*; Laterza: Bari, Italy, 2011.
2. Hohenberg, P.; Lees, L.H. *The Making of Urban Europe, 1000–1950*; Harvard University Press: Cambridge, MA, USA, 1985.
3. Capel, H. La Definicion de lo Urbano. *Estudios Geográficos* **1975**, *138–139*, 265–301.
4. Nel·lo, O. Los Confines de la Ciudad sin Confines. Estructura Urbana y Límites Administrativos en la Ciudad Difusa. In *La Ciudad Dispersa. Suburbanización y Nuevas Periferias*; Monclús, F.J., Ed.; Centre de Cultura Contemporània de Barcelona: Barcelona, Spain, 1998; p. 223.
5. Harvey, D. Cities or Urbanization? *City* **1996**, *1*, 38–61. [CrossRef]
6. Gambi, L. Ragionando di Confini della Città. In *La Città e il Limite*; Paba, G., Ed.; La Casa Usher: Firenze, Italy, 1990.
7. Indovina, F. *La Città Diffusa*; Istituto Universitario di Architettura di Venezia. Dipartimento di Analisi Economica e Sociale del Territorio: Venice, Italy, 1990.
8. Nel·lo, O. *Ciutat de Ciutats: Reflexions Sobre el Procés d'urbanització a Catalunya*; Editorial Empúries: Barcelona, Spain, 2001.
9. Nel·lo, O.; López, J. El Procés d'urbanització. In *Raó de Catalunya.La Societat Catalana al Segle XXI*; Giner, S., Homs, O., Eds.; Institut d'Estudis Catalans/Enciclopèdia Catalana: Barcelona, Spain, 2016.
10. Soja, E.W. Regional Urbanization and the End of the Metropolis Era. In *Cities in the 21st Century*; Nel·lo, O., Mele, R., Eds.; Routledge: New York, NY, USA, 2016; pp. 41–56.
11. Brenner, N. *Implosions/Explosions: Towards a Study of Planetary Urbanization*; Jovis: Berlin, Germany, 2014.
12. Soja, E. *Postmetropolis: Critical Studies of Cities and Regions*; Blackwell: Oxford, UK, 2003.
13. Indovina, F. *La Metropoli Europea: Una Prospettiva*; Franco Angeli: Milano, Italy, 2014.
14. Aubrecht, C.; León, J. Evaluating Multi-Sensor Nighttime Earth Observation Data for Identification of Mixed vs. Residential Use in Urban Areas. *Remote Sens.* **2016**, *8*, 114. [CrossRef]
15. Bennett, M.M.; Smith, L.C. Advances in Using Multitemporal Night-Time Lights Satellite Imagery to Detect, Estimate, and Monitor Socioeconomic Dynamics. *Remote Sens. Environ.* **2017**, *192*, 176–197. [CrossRef]
16. Jing, X.; Shao, X.; Cao, C.; Fu, X.; Yan, L. Comparison between the Suomi-NPP Day-Night Band and DMSP-OLS for Correlating Socio-Economic Variables at the Provincial Level in China. *Remote Sens.* **2016**, *8*, 17. [CrossRef]
17. Miller, S.; Straka, W.; Mills, S.; Elvidge, C.; Lee, T.; Solbrig, J.; Walther, A.; Heidinger, A.; Weiss, S. Illuminating the Capabilities of the Suomi National Polar-Orbiting Partnership (NPP) Visible Infrared Imaging Radiometer Suite (VIIRS) Day/Night Band. *Remote Sens.* **2013**, *5*, 6717–6766. [CrossRef]
18. Nel·lo, O.; López, J.; Martín, J.; Checa, J. Energy and Urban Form. The Growth of European Cities on the Basis of Night-Time Brightness. *Land Use Policy* **2017**, *61*, 103–112. [CrossRef]
19. Shi, K.; Yu, B.; Huang, Y.; Hu, Y.; Yin, B.; Chen, Z.; Chen, L.; Wu, J. Evaluating the Ability of NPP-VIIRS Nighttime Light Data to Estimate the Gross Domestic Product and the Electric Power Consumption of China at Multiple Scales: A Comparison with DMSP-OLS Data. *Remote Sens.* **2014**, *6*, 1705–1724. [CrossRef]
20. Boira, V.J. L'Eix Mediterrani: Entre les Dinàmiques Locals i la Perspectiva Megaregional. *Documents d'Anàlisi Geogràfica* **2010**, *56*, 91–109.
21. Nel·lo, O. El Arco Mediterráneo: Un Corredor de Luz. In *Grandes Temas de la Vanguardia. El Corredor del Mediterráneo*; Una Apuesta de Futuro: Barcelona, Spain, 2017; pp. 56–64.

22. NOAA. Earth Observation Group. Version 1 VIIRS Day/Night Band Nighttime Lights. Available online: https://ngdc.noaa.gov/eog/viirs/download_dnb_composites.html (accessed on 20 November 2017).

23. Elvidge, C.D.; Baugh, K.E.; Zhizhin, M.; Hsu, F.-C. Why VIIRS Data Are Superior to DMSP for Mapping Nighttime Lights. *Proc. Asia-Pac. Adv. Netw.* **2013**, *35*. [CrossRef]

24. Small, C.; Elvidge, C.D.; Baugh, K. Mapping Urban Structure and Spatial Connectivity with VIIRS and OLS Night Light Imagery. In Proceedings of the 2013 Joint Urban Remote Sensing Event (JURSE), Sao Paulo, Brazil, 21–23 April 2013; pp. 230–233.

25. Levin, N.; Zhang, Q. A Global Analysis of Factors Controlling VIIRS Nighttime Light Levels from Densely Populated Areas. *Remote Sens. Environ.* **2017**, *190*, 366–382. [CrossRef]

26. Liao, L.B.; Weiss, S.; Mills, S.; Hauss, B. Suomi NPP VIIRS Day-Night Band on-Orbit Performance. *J. Geophys. Res. Atmos.* **2013**, *118*, 12705–12718. [CrossRef]

27. Kyba, C.C.M.; Kuester, T.; Sánchez de Miguel, A.; Baugh, K.; Jechow, A.; Hölker, F.; Bennie, J.; Elvidge, C.D.; Gaston, K.J.; Guanter, L. Artificially Lit Surface of Earth at Night Increasing in Radiance and Extent. *Sci. Adv.* **2017**, *3*, e1701528. [CrossRef] [PubMed]

28. Alcott, B. Jevons' Paradox. *Ecol. Econ.* **2005**, *54*, 9–21. [CrossRef]

29. Elvidge, C.D.; Falchi, F.; Hsu, F.-C.; Baugh, K.E.; Ghosh, T. National Trends in Satellite-Observed Lighting 1992–2012. In *Global Urban Monitoring and Assessment through*; Weng, Q., Ed.; Earth Observation. CRC Press: Boca Raton, FL, USA, 2014.

30. Nel·lo, O.; López, J.; Martín, J.; Checa, J. *La Luz de la Ciudad. El Proceso de Urbanización En España a Partir de Las Imágenes Nocturnas de La Tierra*; Grup d'Estudis sobre Energia i Territori. Universitat Autònoma de Barcelona: Bellaterra, Spain, 2016.

31. Instituto Nacional de Estadística. Available online: http://www.ine.es/ (accessed on 12 March 2018).

32. Levin, N. The Impact of Seasonal Changes on Observed Nighttime Brightness from 2014 to 2015 Monthly VIIRS DNB Composites. *Remote Sens. Environ.* **2017**, *193*, 150–164. [CrossRef]

33. Stathakis, D.; Baltas, P. Seasonal Population Estimates Based on Night-Time Lights. *Comput. Environ. Urban Syst.* **2018**, *68*, 133–141. [CrossRef]

34. Mestre, M. *Ciutat i Territori a Mallorca. Una Aproximació a la RelacióeEntre Palma i el Sistema Urbà Mallorquí*; Universitat Autònoma de Barcelona: Barcelona, Spain, 2016.

35. Pons, A. *Turisme, Illeïtat i Urbanització a les Illes Balears (1956–2006)*; Universitat de les Illes Balears: Palma, Spain, 2016.

36. Rullan, O. *L'ordenació Territorial a les Balears: Segles XIX-XX*; Edicions Documenta Balear: Palma de Mallorca, Spain, 2007.

37. Rullán, O. *La Construcció Territorial de Mallorca*; Moll: Palma de Mallorca, Spain, 2002.

38. Aguiló, E.; Sastre, A. La Medición de la Estacionalidad del Turismo el Caso de Baleares. *Estudios Turísticos* **1984**, *81*, 79–88.

39. Ginard, X.; Murray, I. El Metabolismo Socioeconómico de las Islas Baleares, 1996–2010. In *El Metabolismo Económico Regional Español*; Carpintero, Ó., Ed.; FUHEM Ecosocial: Madrid, Spain, 2015; pp. 307–383.

40. López, J.M.; López, L.M. La Concentración Estacional en las Regiones Españolas desde una Perspectiva de la Oferta Turística. *Rev. Estud. Reg.* **2006**, *7585*, 75–106.

urban science

MDPI

Article

Water Management in Urban Sprawl Typologies in the City of Alicante (Southern Spain): New Trends and Perception after the Economic Crisis?

Álvaro-Francisco Morote [1,*], Jorge Olcina [2], Antonio-Manuel Rico [2] and María Hernández [2]

[1]   Department of Didactics of Experimental and Social Sciences, University of Valencia, 46010 València, Spain
[2]   Regional Geographic Analysis and Physical Geography Department, University of Alicante, 03690 Alicante, Spain; jorge.olcina@ua.es (J.O.); am.rico@ua.es (A.-M.R.); maria.hernandez@ua.es (M.H.)
*   Correspondence: alvaro.morote@uv.es

Received: 24 September 2018; Accepted: 2 January 2019; Published: 7 January 2019

Abstract: In recent decades, territorial transformations have occurred on the Spanish Mediterranean coast due to the real estate bubble (1997–2008). The objectives of this research are: (1) to analyse the domestic water consumption trend in the study area ("Beach Sector" of the city of Alicante, Southern Spain) (2000–2017); and (2) explore water use and the characteristics of detached houses and how its residents have introduced water-saving measures to reduce consumption after the economic crisis in the study area. A review and analysis of data on housing and population has been carried out where this urban development type has been implemented. Moreover, surveys of the residents have been conducted in order to determine and analyse water consumption, and the perception and knowledge used to reduce water consumption in detached houses. The results show that consumption decreased between 2000 and 2017 due to different factors and there was no change in the water consumption trend at the end of the economic crisis. In view of the conclusions, it should be mentioned that this reduction has been associated with a greater environmental awareness of the need to save water, the installation of systems that use water more efficiently and water-saving devices. All of this is aimed at reducing the water bill that has been exacerbated by an increase in water prices seeing as this is the type of property that consumes the most water.

Keywords: economic crisis; urban sprawl; consumption; water; Alicante

1. Introduction

The intensive socioeconomic development recorded in European countries since the second half of the twentieth century has, among other aspects, led to a change in lifestyle and an increase in urban-residential areas [1]. In the 2000s, different reports that were prepared by the European Environment Agency such as the State of the Environment [2] and Urban Sprawl [3] highlighted that in the previous twenty years, built-up areas in Europe had grown by 20% and they highlighted the possible repercussions of this dynamic on resources such as land and water, energy demands or the generation of waste [4].

Since the beginning of the twenty-first century, significant morphological and social changes have been taking place in many Spanish cities [5]. During the aforementioned real estate boom, the total number of properties in Spain increased by almost five million (25%) between 2001 and 2011 [6]. Until 2008, in Spain, urbanized and built surfaces increased, together with processes of expansion and the modernization of cities. This has produced contradictions and internal conflicts linked to the overconsumption of resources (land, energy, water) and pollution (air, water, heat islands, urban solid waste) [7–9].

One of the features that characterize the Spanish Mediterranean coast as a result of the recent real estate boom (although its origin has been related to the spread of urban-residential uses since the end of the 1960s) has been the spread and generalization of low-density urban types ("urban sprawl") [10]. In some areas of the Alicante coast, this urban sprawl represents 60% of the total built area [10]. Its expansion is related to the search for less dense, congested urban spaces rather than the town centres and the expansion of residential-tourism development in coastal areas [11]. This type of development is characterized by the presence of outdoor elements, such as gardens and private swimming pools, that consume high amounts of water compared to the traditional compact urban model [12–15]. In this respect, in Australia, Hurd [16] states that approximately half of the water used by these households goes to watering the garden and/or filling up the swimming pool. This development type has also spread in other European Mediterranean countries, such as France [17], Italy and Greece [1], along with in tourist and residential areas of the United States [18], Australia [19], Japan [20] and South America [21].

Despite the significant development of garden areas associated with urban sprawl and their impact on water consumption, the demand generated by these spaces is a topic that has only recently been dealt with in Spanish scientific literature [4]. Relatively little is known about the characteristics of these spaces or the behaviour of their owners. Furthermore, there is a tendency to think that single-family gardens use water in excess as a result of the lack of knowledge about gardening or the low cost of the resource. In Spain, recently, a few studies that consider these lines of research have been carried out in the Metropolitan Area of Barcelona, Girona, Granada, Balearic Islands, Seville, Zaragoza and, in recent years, on the coast of Alicante [4].

The increase in urbanization associated with the real estate boom and the proliferation of urban sprawl development types have demonstrated the unsustainability of the model established due to the high levels of water consumption required [10]. This situation gets worse in periods of drought. However, in the majority of European and Spanish urban agglomerations a drop in water consumption has been observed since the middle of the 2000s [11,22,23].

It is therefore necessary to gain more insight into the factors affecting domestic water consumption and their interrelationships. Studies on water conservation, and especially those on urban water conservation in the developed world [24], have mainly focused on certain areas of North America [25] and Australia [26]. By examining other environmental settings, a wider variety of factors influencing water conservation practices can be assessed more comprehensively. Most notably, the considerable influence of different community water consumption models and the potential of urban and regional planning for water conservation have to be put at the forefront of research and practices on this topic [27]. This is of vital importance in terms of planning future water demand scenarios, taking into account continued urban population growth, episodes of water stress, drought events and the impact of the climate change on the availability of water resources, among other issues [28,29]. Various aspects of the factors affecting the levels of demand for water resources have become priority research topics in recent decades, especially in water-stressed areas that have experienced particularly intensive urban development processes [30]. The relationships between these factors must be analysed along with the changes in water-saving behaviour [31–37]. In the last few years, studies have also been carried out in Europe that analyse the reasons why water consumption has decreased [11]. Numerous studies associated with these results have come up with possible reasons for this decrease that include:

(a) Technological innovation associated with installing new water-efficient appliances as well as water saving devices at home (taps, bathroom fittings, etc.), which have become popular since the late 1990s [22].

(b) Greater environmental awareness among the populace about saving water, thanks to more organized campaigns, especially in times of drought [23,38]. Interesting results have been obtained in the studies about the reduction of water consumption outdoors. In recent years, homeowners have greater environmental awareness. This becomes obvious, for example, in the typology of their gardens, where native species that adapt better to the local environment and require less water are becoming more popular. This was confirmed in a study by Morote and Hernández [39], who reported a change among homeowners from having central and northern European to Mediterranean-type gardens, which adapt better to the climate of the southeast Spanish coast.

(c) The economic crisis has led to a drastic fall in incomes and increased unemployment. One of the strategies used in response to this significant downturn has been to cut back on all domestic consumption, including water, especially among the middle classes [22].

(d) Water rates and prices have increased at a time when family incomes have dwindled.

(e) The efficiency of the Water Company supply networks has improved.

(f) Drinking water has been replaced by non-conventional water sources (reclaimed water and rainwater) for public water, private gardens (in some residential areas) and street cleaning [40].

(g) An aging population. Morote et al. [11] observed that one of the reasons behind the drop in domestic water consumption along the Mediterranean coastline was the increase in the senior population and the loss of a younger population due to migration that was prompted by the economic crisis, which erupted in 2007. These authors reported that a person aged 65 or more consumes 25% less water than the previous population segment (18 to 64 years).

The interest for the topic of study is accentuated in the case of the city of Alicante since water has always been a resource of vital importance in view of its scarcity and the increase in demands as from the second half of the twentieth century [41]. In terms of supply sources, in south-eastern Spain, in order to guarantee the growing demands for water, both for the agricultural sector and for urban-tourism uses, traditional water solutions have opted for the exploitation of aquifers and water transfers [42,43]. Furthermore, more recently, non-conventional sources (desalination and reclaimed treated water) have been used [44]. These measures have been complemented with increased efficiency in the use of water for irrigation and supply [44]. In addition to these factors, there is also a predominance of detached houses. This urban typology represents 60% of the total of the urban areas on the coast of Alicante [10] and it is characterised by high water consumption compared to other urban typologies. Some studies [11,22] point to the fact that more than 1000 L/day are being consumed compared to the 244 L/day in houses of the urban core. This high consumption becomes even more important if we take into account that: (1) the study area is a semi-arid region with a rainfall average of 350 mm/year; (2) the dependence on water resources from other regions (supply by the Tagus-Segura Aqueduct) and the implementation of desalination as "a new water resource" [45]; and (3) the impact of climate change in the study area, which will become apparent through the drop in rainfall and exacerbated extreme events (droughts and heavy rain). Both processes—a drop in rainfall and exacerbated extreme events—will negatively affect the availability of water resources. The growing interest in this factor is highlighted by the necessity to improve water management, the homeowners' perception of this factor (specifically, the level of relevance) and the measures they have adopted or will adopt to reduce water consumption.

As a hypothesis, it has been established that, owing to the increase in urbanization, and especially, the low-density urban development type, in recent years, cities have become less sustainable with regard to the use of natural resources (in this case water). This would have led to an increase in water consumption in the city. However, since the mid-2000s with the economic crisis, the significant increase in the price of water and the recurring drought episodes may have resulted in a change of the property owners' perception of water saving and the water use trend in urban sprawl development types. These changes may have been due to the attempt to reduce the water bill and to consume water more responsibly. Therefore, one of the research questions would be to check to see if water consumption dropped in the detached houses at the end of the economic crisis (2014) or if it continues to drop; that is, highlight the water consumption trend. Moreover, it should be pointed out that the objectives of this research are, first to determine the perception of water use and the consumption of the population, and second, to compare that perception with the real water consumption, namely, the water bills of the owners' homes that were included in the survey carried out by the water supply company. This becomes more interesting thanks to a few papers that have related these two issues and even more so considering the climatic characteristics of Alicante (scarce and irregular precipitations) and a water demand that is higher than the existing supply, which makes this region dependent on external water resources. However, as desalination has been promoted in recent years, perhaps this is the end of the "physical scarcity" of water resources as some authors have stated [46].

The objectives of this research are: (1) to analyse the domestic water consumption trend in the study area (2000–2017), and (2) explore the water use and the characteristics of the detached houses and how property owners and residents in the area have introduced water-saving measures to reduce consumption after the economic crisis. After the introduction, which highlights the characteristics of the study area and the research problem, the materials, methods and results are described. Finally, the discussions and conclusions are presented.

2. Study Area, Materials and Methods

2.1. Period and Study Area

The period analysed in this study covers the series 2000–2017. This period was selected because: (a) it coincides with a period of noticeable decline in urban water demand since 2004–2005 [22], (b) 2008 was the year when the economic crisis erupted in Spain, (c) 2014 is the year that was characterized by the economic recovery [47], and (d) 2017 is the last year for which a full set of consumption data is available. It is worth pointing out that, for certain series of data, the period has been conditioned by the fact that it was made available by the water supply company.

An analysis has been carried out on the sociodemographic characteristics (total population and residential properties) of the study area. This includes the sector of the city of Alicante known as the "Beach Sector". This area includes residential neighbourhoods that are characterized by their obvious residential-tourism component (La Albufereta, Vistahermosa, Cabo de la Huerta and Playa de San Juan) (Figure 1) and the predominance of the detached housing urban development type [11]. With regard to demographic data, the data available at the Department of Statistics of Alicante City Council have been used (total population and evolution of the population between 2000 and 2016). As for data concerning the property type (number and type of properties), the data provided by the Spanish National Statistics Institute (INE) (latest census published of 2011) were used.

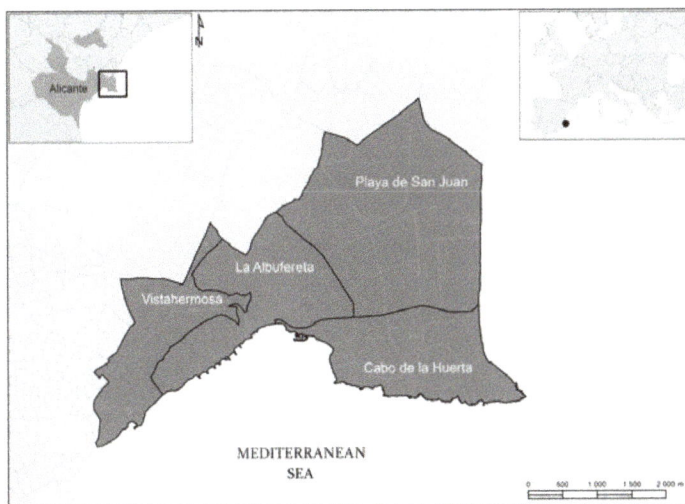

Figure 1. Study area (Beach Sector) (City of Alicante). Source: Compiled by the authors.

2.2. Water Data

The water consumption trend has been analysed, both for the city of Alicante and for the study area. This data was provided by the water supply company, "Aguas de Alicante, Empresa Mixta" (AMAEM) (2004–2017). The first year (2004) is chosen because this is the year that AMAEM began to break down the water consumption data according to the neighbourhoods and by differentiating consumption according to the users (domestic and non-domestic). It should be pointed out that AMAEM and its ownership is divided into equal shares between the City Council of Alicante and the private company *Hidraqua, Gestión Integral de Aguas de Levante S.A.*, a subsidiary of Aquadom (Suez Environment). Although under the supervision of the public partner, Hidraqua enjoys ample autonomy in technical decision-making [22]. Furthermore, according to the World Bank, in 1953, Alicante became the first international example of a successful water company of mixed (public and private) capital under the name of "Aguas de Alicante" [48]. Moreover, the water company has also provided information on the price of water (€/m^3) according to the different consumption tariff blocks for the 2007–2017 period. This period was chosen due to the importance of comparing consumption before and after the economic crisis.

2.3. Questionnaire Development and Distribution

Surveys were conducted (between July and December 2017) among the residents of detached houses in this urban sector in order to ascertain their socioeconomic characteristics, behaviour variables and their perception of water saving and use. The process of conducting the surveys involved visiting the detached houses in the study area. The objectives of the survey were explained to the homeowners and they were informed that their data would be processed anonymously and exclusively for scientific purposes. The survey was conducted in-person with those who were in the house at that moment. Age (over 18 years) was an essential criterion to be able to answer questions in the survey along with parity in the number of respondents.

For the survey on domestic users, the population of Alicante over the age of 18 (273,044 inhabitants in 2016) was taken into account. To calculate the representativeness of the population, the population census of the city of Alicante (Department of Statistics, 2016) was used and the population was divided up according to the neighbourhoods of the different sectors of the city. When selecting the survey sample, a margin of error of 5% and a confidence level of 90% were established. By applying these values and taking into account the global population over 18 years of age of the city of Alicante, for the population selected, a sample of 309 surveys had to be obtained (268 were necessary). For the detached houses (the target of this study), 48 surveys were conducted. Since the population census does not disaggregate between the urban development types analysed (it only differentiates the total population according to the neighbourhoods), the population aged over 18 years was calculated on the basis of the districts predominated by the detached house type (object of study) (Table 1).

Table 1. Number of surveys conducted.

	Population over 18 Years of Age	% of Representativeness	Surveys Necessary (no.)	Surveys Conducted (no.)
Urban core	227,882	81.71	219	142
Block of Flats	27,031	9.69	27	79
Terraced houses	14,292	4.30	11	40
Detached houses	14,292	4.30	11	48
Total	**273,044**	**100**	**268**	**309**

The survey questionnaire was structured into eight sections: (A) socioeconomic aspects; (B) characteristics of the property; (C) characteristics of the outside of the property; (D) characteristics of the garden and irrigation system; (E) indoor uses; (F) water consumption habits in the household; (G) behaviour variables and the perception of water saving and use; and (H) perception of drought, climate change and water scarcity. For this study, the results obtained in sections A, C and G have been used. The results of the surveys form part of the research project "Study of water consumption and smart meters in the city of Alicante. The basis for smart water supply in a smart city" financed by AMAEM. One of the specific aims of that project was to analyse the socioeconomic characteristics and the perception of water use and savings of the population of the city of Alicante by means of conducting surveys.

2.4. Potential and Limitations

To compare the data obtained from the surveys (perception) with the water expenses of the properties, AMAEM provided the water consumption of the houses (m^3/year, 2000–2017) where the surveys were conducted. It is worthwhile highlighting the advantage of being able to use billing data provided by the water supply company. The company does not disaggregate water consumption according to urban development types. What it has done, since 2004, is to differentiate between domestic (homes) and non-domestic (shops, services, restaurants, industries, etc.), according to neighbourhoods.

The limitations involved in research on this scale should be explained and highlighted. It must not be forgotten that the surveys were conducted in the properties themselves and the post code was necessary to subsequently obtain the billing data provided by AMAEM. The signing of a confidentiality agreement with the water company allowed us, according to the postal code, to access (always anonymous data) the water consumption for the period 2000–2017 of the detached houses where the survey had been carried out.

There were a number of advantages of working with real consumption data over other methods such as analyses based on data extrapolation or using information provided by statistical agencies such as the Spanish National Statistics Institute (INE). For example, such data gave us access to information that was not available in conventional statistical sources, which do not disaggregate consumption data beyond large categories (urban, industrial and agricultural). The data analysed was also more accurate and reliable than that obtained by statistical analyses of a small number of real values. Usually, papers on this topic have focused on the population's perception of water consumption (through telephone or street surveys) or on data on average consumption obtained through extrapolations per household. Working with real consumption data is not common in Spain because it is difficult to access this information without knowing the socio-economic characteristics of the residents and their consumption perception. This is one of the main new elements of this research.

3. Results

3.1. Urban Sprawl and Water Consumption in the Beach Sector of the City of Alicante: A Development Type Characterized by High Levels of Water Consumption

The city of Alicante has undergone considerable spatial and socioeconomic transformation since the second half of the twentieth century. The area analysed in this study covers the urban districts of La Albufereta, Vistahermosa, Cabo de la Huerta and Playa de San Juan. They make up what is known as the "Beach Sector", which is distinguished by the predominance of the detached house urban development type [11]. This represents 34.43% of the total urban land of the city, the majority being concentrated in the study area [49]. In 2017, the total population of Alicante came to 329,988 inhabitants. Out of this, around 15% is concentrated in the Beach Sector for which, since the end of the twentieth century, a positive demographic dynamic has been recorded. The registered population doubled between 2000 and 2016, from 28,404 to 53,205 inhabitants, respectively (an increase of 87%). This rise is due to the spectacular increase in the urbanization in this sector, coinciding with the latest real estate boom, which has totally changed the social and landscape physiognomy of this area. With regard to the number of properties, according to the latest census of 2011, the total number of dwellings amounts to 32,745 (17.55% of the total of the city). Out of the 28,707 homes in the city, 10,480 are located in the study area, that is, 36% of the total. This piece of data on second homes becomes more relevant if it is compared with the overall figure for Alicante, where only 15% of total properties are second homes.

In relation to water consumption it should be pointed out that, in general, in the cities of Europe and the developed world, water use has decreased considerably since the end of the 1990s [11]. In Alicante, this has been apparent since 2004 when a quantity of 30.4 hm^3 was supplied. From this date onwards, the decrease in consumption (for both domestic and non-domestic uses) has been continuous, reaching minimum figures of 22.3 hm^3 in 2013 (an approximate reduction of 25%). The slight upturn in economic activity in Spain since 2014 has not resulted in a substantial change in this trend, although it has been observed in tourist municipalities or urban residential-tourism areas owing to higher occupancy and longer stays in the second residences. Likewise, it should be mentioned that during the years 2015 and 2016, the water supplied in the city increased compared to 2014 owing to the climate conditions, such as drought and heat waves, uses related to the watering of both private and public gardens and to the increase in the number of users connected to the network.

In 2017, the total amount for domestic water billed in the study area represents 26.87% compared to the total for the city of Alicante. In the Beach Sector, the water supplied for domestic uses (consumption in households) decreased by 6.18% from 4.02 hm^3 to 3.77 hm^3 (2004–2017). The trend for the city of Alicante is, therefore, reproduced (a decrease of 13.47%), although somewhat more attenuated. When a more detailed analysis is carried out, two very different realities are observed: (1) urban districts where domestic water consumption has been reduced (La Albufereta with −15.50% and Playa de San Juan with −11.81%); and (2) urban districts where its use has remained the same or even increased (Vistahermosa with 0.09% and Cabo de la Huerta with 9.09%) (Figure 2).

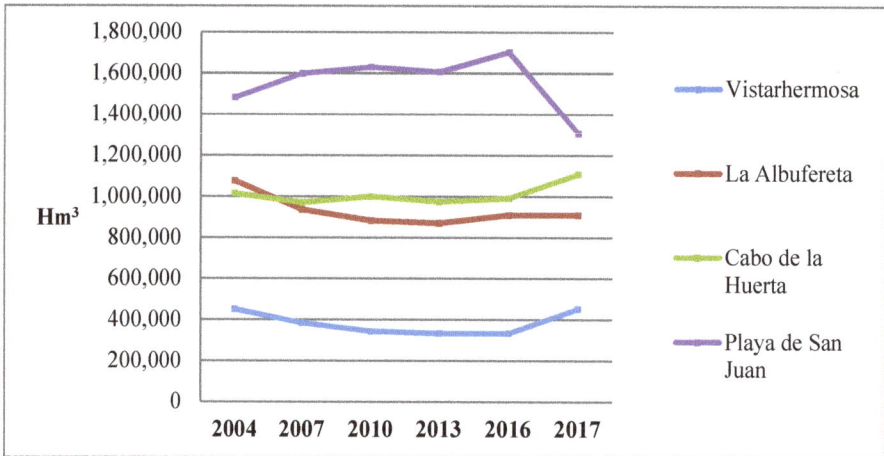

Figure 2. Evolution of domestic water consumption of the Beach Sector (hm^3) (2004–2017). Source: AMAEM. Compiled by the authors.

3.2. Change of Perception, Management and Water Consumption in Detached Houses

After analysing the development characteristics and the water consumption trend in the study area, the socioeconomic characteristics of the residents were examined according to the survey results, a step prior to considering their perception of water use.

The casuistry of conducting the surveys determined the following traits with regard to Section A (Table 2): (a) 100% were Spanish, of whom 56.25% were women; (b) it was an adult population, with cohorts between 35–54 years and over 75 years predominating (35.42 and 33.33%, respectively); (c) from the point of view of the social-employment situation, 52.08% were workers and 23.53% were retired; (d) the level of education demonstrated that this was a high educational level population (33.33% of those surveyed had a university degree). These data are lower than those provided by the CIDES [50] which, for the study area, comes to 50.2%; (e) in relation to the ratio of inhabitants per household, the average was 2.83 and with few changes, since 75% of those surveyed stated that there had been no reduction or increase in the family unit; and (f) the economic income of the households stands at between €3001 and 4500 per month for net income (41.67% of those surveyed) and, in second place, between €1801 and 3000 per month (33.33%). The average income according to the CIDES [50] amounts to €2439. If these data are compared with the average income for the city of Alicante (€1783/month/household), it is obvious that this is one of the sectors where the wealthier classes of the city live [50].

Table 2. Socio-demographic characteristics of the respondents (Section A of the survey).

Variable		%
Age (years)	18–25	8.33
	26–34	6.25
	35–54	35.42
	55–75	16.67
	>75	33.33
Employment	Student	14.58
	Employee	52.08
	Unemployed	0
	Retired	33.33
Level of Education	No studies	0
	Primary education	33.33
	Secondary education	27.08
	Higher education	39.58
Average income per household (€/month)	<600	0
	601–1200	0
	1201–1800	0
	1801–3000	33.33
	3001–4500	41.67
	>4500	25.00

Source: Compiled by the authors.

With regard to the characteristics of the outside of the property (Section C), the average total plot size of those surveyed comes to 1225 m². In order of importance, the plots consist in the garden 35.13% (430 m²) and, second, paved areas taking up 31.35% of the total plot (384 m²). A total of 33.33% of respondents acknowledged having made changes to the outside of their property, and of these, 50% stated that they had made changes outdoors. These include planting succulent plants (vegetation adapted to water scarcity and the Mediterranean climate), replacing the lawn (Atlantic vegetation) with them, paving part of the garden and repairing leaks in the swimming pool. All of these are measures that try to reduce water use. None of the participants surveyed stated that they had increased the garden area. With regard to the supply sources, all the water consumed in the property for the different uses (home, garden, vegetable plot and swimming pool) comes from the drinking water supply network. The objective of the last question in this section ("repercussion of reclaimed water") was to ascertain the perception of the respondents with regard to the use of this non-conventional source. However, since none of them use it (because their properties are not connected to the reclaimed water network owing to the inexistence of the network close by) the results obtained show that 100% are "indifferent" to its impact (Table 3).

Table 3. Characteristics of the outside of the property (Section C of the survey).

Variable		%
	Building	13.7
	Garden	35.13
Plot size	Vegetable plot	5.44
	Swimming pool	2.24
	Paved area	31.35
	Other	12.55
Changes to the property	Yes	33.33
	No	66.67
	Public network	100
Supply sources	Well (groundwater)	0
	Rainwater tank	0
	Reclaimed water	0
	Very positive	0
	Positive	0
Perception of the use of reclaimed water	Indifferent	100
	Negative	0
	Very negative	0

Source: Compiled by the authors.

The purpose of the survey questions related to the variables of water saving and use behaviour (Section G) was to ascertain the respondents' perception of water use and saving and the measures that they have taken in recent years to reduce consumption. The majority (66.67%) compare the water bill with previous ones and they are willing to have a remote meter installed free of charge. This shows that there is an interest in favour of saving water, whether for economic or for environmental reasons. Thanks to the existence of these devices (smart meters), the user can find out about the consumption of the household instantly, and they can also be warned about any anomalous consumption (leak or failure). Therefore, there is greater control of domestic water use. The question relating to the homeowners' awareness of water saving demonstrates that the majority are in favour: 83.33% are moderately aware and 16.67% are very aware (Table 4).

Table 4. Behaviour with regard to water saving and use (Section G of the survey).

Variable		No. of Responses	%
Comparison with previous bills	Yes	32	66.67
	No	16	33.33
Installation of Smart meter	Yes	32	66.67
	No	16	33.33
	Very aware	8	16.67
Awareness regarding water saving	Moderately aware	40	83.33
	Slightly aware	0	0
	Not at all aware	0	0
	It has decreased	0	0
Perception of the consumption trend	It has remained the same	24	50
	It has increased	8	16.67
	Don't know	16	33.33
	Very positive	0	0
	Positive	24	50
Impact of water-saving measures	Indifferent	0	0
	Negative	0	0
	Very negative	0	0
	Don't know	24	50

Source: Compiled by the authors.

The results obtained from this last answer can be considered, to a certain extent, as being "politically correct" in view of the results obtained from other replies. This becomes evident when analysing the consumption trend where 50% state that the water use in their household has remained the same, 16.67% say that it has increased and 33.33% replied that they do not know how much they consume. If these values are compared with the billing data for these houses provided by the water supply company, it appears that, in general, there has been a decrease of 43.27% from 1255 to 712 L/property/day (Figure 3). As the ratio of inhabitants/property in the households surveyed was 2.83, water consumption per capita would amount to 247 L/day. This, in 2000, would be situated (maintaining that ratio) at 503 L. This contradiction highlights the users' considerable lack of knowledge about how much water is consumed in their households and their erroneous perception. The factors that may explain this ignorance are a high level of water consumption and the lack of control in its use as a result of not consulting the water bill or that the price of the water is paid without any economic difficulty. The fact that 33.33% of those surveyed state that they do not know how much water is consumed in their household could vouch for this fact.

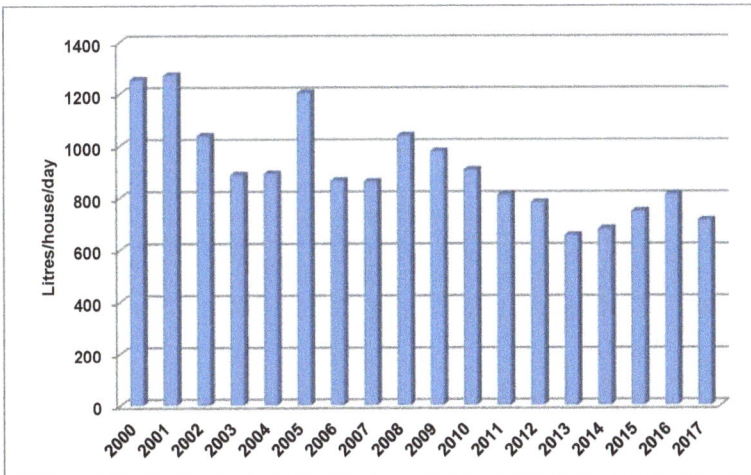

Figure 3. Evolution of water consumption of the detached houses where the survey was conducted (litres/property/day) (2000–2017). Source: AMAEM.

With regard to the impact of the household water-saving measures, 50% replied that they have been positive. However, the rest (the other half), replied that they did not have information or knowledge about this impact. Another one of the questions is related to the different factors that may have affected the reduction in water use at home. According to the answers, the first three factors were: (1) greater environmental awareness, (2) technical innovation (use of domestic appliances or systems that are more efficient in the use of water), and (3) installation of water-saving devices. Factors concerning the increase in the price of water or the economic crisis were in fourth and fifth place, respectively (Figure 4). This order, which is contrary to the results of other neighbourhoods of the city, is explained by the fact that the study area is situated in a high-income sector with a low level of unemployment, thus corroborating the survey data (see section A) and the Survey on Living Conditions and the Employment Situation in the City of Alicante [50]. In terms of future measures to reduce consumption, they reiterate those already adopted. Therefore, when it comes to water-saving devices or more efficient appliances that they consider installing in the future, the majority mention buying eco-friendly washing machines and eco-friendly dishwashers (36.36% in both cases). As for the uses and systems that the participants think consumes the most water at home, these were mentioned in the following order of importance: (1) outdoor elements (watering the garden), (2) washing machine, and (3) shower. Finally, the last questions of this section are related to environmental campaigns. A total of 66.67% remember some campaign, having seen it on the internet (40%) and on television and awareness campaigns by institutions (water company, council, etc.) (30% in both cases).

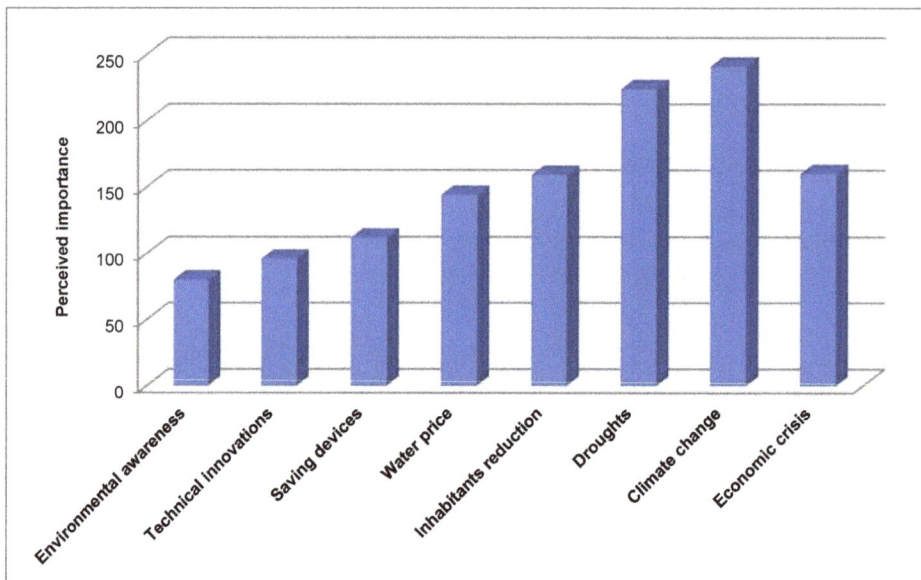

Figure 4. Main perception factors of the water consumption reduction in households according to those surveyed. Source: Results of the surveys. Compiled by the authors. NB: The respondents were required to rate the items on a scale of 1 to 8, the most important being 1 and the least important 8.

The last detail analysed in this study was the annual price paid for the water resource provided by AMAEM. This is of greater interest because water consumption is the highest in these households. In the city of Alicante, billing is quarterly, and it is structured into consumption bands with an increasing price per m^3 as a dissuasive measure against consumption (Table 5). In 2017, the consumption blocks per quarter and price per m^3 (euros) were as follows: (1) from 0 to 12 m^3 (0.01 €/m^3), (2) from 13 to 30 m^3 (0.69 €/m^3), (3) from 31 to 60 m^3 (1.76 €/m^3), and (4) more than 60 m^3 (2.36 €/m^3). It is worth mentioning that this price is final, that is, it takes into account all the service costs (the price of the water, meter maintenance, sewerage, treatment and taxes). It should also be pointed out that, as of 2017, the first two consumption blocks have varied, so has the price per m^3 per block. With regard to the latter (that of the highest consumption), the price per m^3 has increased by 44.78% in the last decade from €1.63 to €2.36. In order to place a property in this band, it would have to consume more than 668 L/property/day.

Table 5. Price of water (€/m^3) per consumption block in the city of Alicante (2000–2017).

Consumption Blocks	2007	2009	2011	2013	2017
From 0 to 9 m^3 per quarter *	0.02	0.02	0.02	0.02	0.01
From 10 to 30 m^3 per quarter *	0.43	0.49	0.49	0.53	0.69
From 31 to 60 m^3 per quarter	1.3	1.52	1.63	1.76	1.76
61 m^3 per quarter and over	1.63	1.92	2.18	2.36	2.36

Source: AMAEM. Compiled by the authors. * NB: As of 2017, the first band of 0 to 9 m^3/quarter has changed to 0 to 12 m^3/quarter, and the second, that of 10 to 30, to 13 to 30 m^3/quarter.

In view of the water consumption data of the households surveyed (712 L/property/day), they are situated in the last block. According to their consumption, the average final amount of the water bill that the residents of the households surveyed pay per year can be calculated. In 2017, this amounted to €613. However, in 2007, with the data provided (price per m^3 in the highest consumption band and consumption that was situated at 861 L/day), this would be €512. If consumption in 2017 had remained the same as that of a decade before, the bill that they would have to pay now (taking into account the new tariff of 2.36 €/m^3), would amount to €741. This means that although water consumption has decreased, water bills have not; on the contrary, they have continued to increase.

4. Discussion

As stated in the initial hypothesis for this research, urban expansion characterized by low-density urban development in the city of Alicante involved implementing an urban model that is not very sustainable; a trait that is exacerbated by the expansion of this development type coinciding with the most recent real estate boom. This study has corroborated the fact that water consumption in these households is high compared to other types. In 2017, water use per detached house amounted to 712 L per day in the study area. Some publications that have analysed water consumption according to residential property types have estimated modules of over 600 L/property/day for houses with private swimming pools and garden modules [11,51,52]. However, other property types characterized by the inexistence of outdoor spaces or where these are very small and arranged in rows as in the case of terraced houses, water consumption is considerably lower. For this type, for example, Rico [53] estimated on the coast of Alicante modules of 456 L/property/day. Regarding the city of Alicante, Gil et al. [22] calculated that consumption was around 387 L in semi-detached or terraced houses, 322 L in properties located in blocks of flats and 244 L in households of the urban core (compact city).

However, despite the significant increase in the urbanized area, a regressive trend has been recorded for urban consumption in the majority of cities in developed countries since the end of the twentieth century [23,54]. On the Spanish Mediterranean coast, Gil et al. [22] explain that this trend is due to an amalgam of factors, among which it is worthwhile mentioning greater environmental awareness in favour of water saving, drought episodes, social and demographic changes (reduction of the population), the increase in the price of the water, more efficient technologies and the effect of the economic crisis since 2008. For the different urban typologies of the city of Alicante, Morote et al. [11] calculated decreases that varied according to economic income and urban development type. In households of the urban core, from 5.86 to 18.84%, in blocks of flats, from 9.18 to 11.89%, in terraced houses from 2.64 to 5.12%. This percentage increases significantly for detached houses (2300 to 1052 L/day) (−54%) to a large extent, as a result of the high starting values and the role played by certain factors (price of water, economic crisis, environmental awareness, incorporation of more efficient technologies, etc.) [11]. This trend, which corroborates the initial hypothesis, makes it necessary to analyse the importance of the role played by those factors in the reduction of consumption by this urban development type in the study area (a decrease of 43.27%).

To examine this matter in more detail, those surveyed were asked about their perception of the different variables that might have influenced this decrease. The three main factors were: greater environmental awareness, technical innovations (domestic appliances and systems that use water more efficiently) and the installation of water-saving devices. According to the answers of those surveyed in this research, environmental awareness is the topic with the greatest repercussion to explain this decrease. It is a factor that is also interrelated with the acquisition of domestic appliances and systems that use water more efficiently, together with the installation of water-saving devices. However, out of the eight factors proposed (from which the respondents had to choose), the price of water was ranked in fourth place and the economic crisis in fifth. These data are opposite to the results obtained by Morote and Hernández [39] in the residential complexes on the coast of Alicante, which are characterized by the presence of a foreign population, where the reasons why changes are made in favour of water saving were the drought and the bad adaptation of Atlantic vegetation that they had planted in their gardens and the high price of water.

The social and economic profile of those surveyed shows that, to a great extent, they have not suffered from the recession, unlike those in other neighbourhoods of the city of Alicante. Other factors, in addition to per capita income, explain the adoption of initiatives aimed at reducing expenses. The increase in the price of water, the adoption of more sustainable consumption habits (for example, using the shower instead of the bath), using more efficient technology in domestic appliances, the environmental awareness associated with water-saving campaigns, or changes in the garden (replacement of Atlantic for Mediterranean plants) play a fundamental role. They have the spending power to acquire efficient, but also more expensive, domestic appliances, or, as a result of their level of education, they are more environmentally aware [22]. The economic crisis may have encouraged these water-saving measures that were taken. The adoption of practices aimed at a more sustainable use of resources is a practice assumed by many echelons of society, becoming a structural fact that is still a personal saving habit.

With regard to the water bill (price of water and other concepts) the data show that, currently, more is paid for this resource than a decade ago, even with less water being consumed. The rise in prices (in addition to the increase in tariffs due to the incorporation of desalinated water and recovery cost related to implementation of the Water Framework Directive) could be a result of the current reduction in water consumption. The operating costs, depreciation, investment, etc., have not decreased. For this reason, to offset the lower consumption of drinking water, the supply company has been obliged to increase the price of water to maintain the service at optimum levels. Morote and Hernández [47] prove that, for a water bill of 30 m^3/quarter, the price paid for this bill has increased by 92% since the year 2000 in the city of Alicante. Furthermore, this has occurred (and therefore the consumers have had to deal with it) in a context of economic recession. In the detached houses of this study the price of water has increased by 44% (2007–2017) (61 m^3 per quarter and over). However, if the evolution of the consumer price index (CPI) and the family's income is compared, the conclusion can be drawn that families have lost their purchasing power in relation to the increase in water prices. For example, according to the data provided by the INE [55], the CPI of the province of Alicante between 2007 and 2017 increased 15.3%, but the income of families dropped 6.85% (25,802 €/year in 2007 and 24,034 €/year in 2017) [56].

The relationship between the increasing water rates and their influence on the consumption drop cannot be considered to be a direct cause. The elasticity of water demand in relation to its price is low in moderate consumption, because a basic minimum consumption of drinking water must be covered (basic needs). Hence, the incorporation of water saving measures does not affect a reduction in the water bill, or the decrease in consumption [57]. In addition to this, the water bill incorporates a series of variables that increases the final price, which are not associated with consumption. The use of consumption blocks as a saving element must provide for the non-elasticity in the price of water in the first blocks of consumption; the last blocks of consumption have a greater impact. This is related to consumption associated with external uses that are not included in the basic supply.

In terms of garden areas, one point that corroborates their effect on the high levels of water consumption is that the participants in the survey state that the main water use in their household is watering the garden. Furthermore, this is mainly due to their size and the presence of Atlantic vegetation. In this respect, it is appropriate to point out that the water requirements of a lawn on the coast of Alicante vary between 1000 and 1200 mm/year (depending on evapotranspiration), and this is exacerbated given that average rainfall in the city amounts to 311 mm/year [58]. Morote and Hernández [59] estimated that a garden on the north coast of the province of Alicante consumed 556.08 L per day (47% of the consumption of a detached house). In the Metropolitan Area of Barcelona (Spain), Domene and Saurí [51] calculated that, in the summer months, 48.8% of total water consumed daily at home was used for irrigation. Higher percentages were recorded in the arid and semi-arid regions of the west part of the USA, where this reached 50% of total household consumption [60]. Authors, such as Loh and Coghlan [61], raise this to 56% in the city of Perth (Australia).

As a result of this research, it has also been ascertained that there has been a change of perception and management of the use of water outdoors, with a predominance of initiatives aimed at reducing consumption. Various processes corroborate this point. First, there is the reduction of gardens. Areas used as gardens stand for 35.13% of the plot, but paved areas have become more popular in the last decade. They currently represent 31.35%. The substitution of plant species is in second place. This is highlighted in the participants' answers concerning the changes made outdoors where 33.33% of those surveyed said that they have replaced the lawn area and plants that require large amounts of water with succulent plants and they have paved part of the garden. These initiatives are complemented by the repair of leaks in the swimming pool. Therefore, these are measures to maintain and reduce consumption from the point of view of demand management. In addition to this, there is the possible impact of awareness campaigns and how they have been able to make a change and improve the environmental awareness of the residents; 66.67% replied that they remember these campaigns.

One of the questions included in the survey was the perception regarding reclaimed treated water. In this case, its use was related to the possibility of using lower quality water for activities that do not require drinking water (watering the garden). Furthermore, in this way, it reduces the pressure on the latter and increases the resilience of the urban model. A total of 100% of those surveyed said they were "indifferent", and this resource was even ruled out. This lack of acceptance may be due to either the perception of the quality of the water or the fact that it is not used since there is no reclaimed water network for the watering of private gardens near their homes. As the reclaimed water distribution network in the different urban sectors of the city is a new concept, a precise evaluation of the role played by this new source in saving drinking water in the city cannot be obtained. Therefore, the survey shows a high value for the option "indifferent", when the increasing importance of this type of resource in the urban use of water as a means of saving drinking water is evident. In the city of Alicante, it should be pointed out that in certain urban areas, reclaimed water is supplied to satisfy watering needs in private properties. According to the calculations of Gil et al. [22], its incorporation, together with other factors, has led to a reduction of 54% in the consumption of drinking water between 2007 and 2013, from 2300 to 1052 L/property/day in detached houses in the urban district of Vistahermosa (city of Alicante).

5. Conclusions

Detached houses represent the urban development type that consumes the highest amount of water due to the existence of uses characterized by high demands such as watering the garden and/or filling the swimming pool. In the city of Alicante since the year 2000, there has been a decrease in water consumption of 43.27% in detached houses, from 1255 to 712 L/day. This process, which forms part of a more sustainable use of resources has not, however, been accompanied by a reduction in the cost of the water bill. On the contrary, users now pay 19.7% more than a decade ago. This demonstrates that, despite the fact that families have made a considerable effort to reduce domestic consumption, this has not led to a reduction in the water bill owing to the increase in the price per m^3 of water (44.78%) and also in the different levies applied to consumption (treatment costs, for example, or charges associated with the maintenance of the service, which the company passes on in the price of the water). This increase has also had a dissuasive effect, since the band in which the price per m^3 has increased the most has been that of the highest consumption (61 m^3 per quarter and over, which applies to detached houses).

The reduction in water use has been a constant since 2004 in the city, as corroborated by the volumes billed by the supply company. However, the results deriving from the surveys highlight that the residents do not know exactly what their consumption is, or their trend is, either because they are not concerned or because they do not monitor their domestic expenditure in detail. They are more concerned (and have greater perception) about matters concerning the adoption of more sustainable practices in the consumption of water resources as corroborated by their responses, and this is shown by the decrease in consumption. The factors that have led to this reduction include, in order of relevance: greater environmental awareness, the existence of systems that use water more efficiently and the installation of water-saving devices. However, their choice, out of a total of eight factors, leads to the question as to whether these three have been influenced by the increase in the price of water and the economic crisis; meanwhile the average annual salary dropped by 6.85% from 2007 to 2017. That is, whether the reason behind adopting practices of this type is to save money owing to the increase in the price of water and the impact of the economic crisis. This has occurred with other domestic expenses that have been reduced. One of the hypotheses of this paper was to see if water consumption in detached houses had recovered after the end of the economic crisis in 2014. Despite the fact that the wealthier population of the city live in these houses (see Reference [11]), the economic crisis has also affected these families. Furthermore, water consumption is no exception. Morote and Hernández [47] have shown that in these households (detached houses), the ratio of fraud in properties connected to the network is similar to that detected in the poorest neighbourhoods of the city of Alicante. The increase in fraud, as these authors explain, is related to the need to save water owing to high levels of water consumption generated in this urban development type, which is exacerbated in periods of drought.

Finally, it is worthwhile pointing out that a change of paradigm and perception is taking place with regard to an improvement in water management with regard to measures for demand management. Perhaps the price of water is an indicator of the control of consumption, which has already been corroborated by other authors [62] and this helps to make cities more sustainable and respectful when it comes to using natural resources [40]. Furthermore, the uncertainty associated with the availability of future water resources must be mentioned, taking into account the climate change scenarios [63–65], along with the need to set a goal to not compromise future generations in terms of the guaranteed availability of water.

Author Contributions: The four authors wrote the paper. Investigation, Á.-F.M., J.O., A.-M.R. and M.H.

Funding: A preliminary version of this article was presented at the XIV Urban Geography Colloquium held at the University of Castilla-La Mancha and the University of Valencia (Spain). The results presented in this article are part of the research projects "Study of water consumption and Smart Meters of the city of Alicante. The basis of the intelligent water supply in a Smart City" (I-PI 27-17) financed by Aguas Municipalizadas de Alicante, Empresa Mixta S.A and "Uses and management of non-conventional water resources on the coast of Valencia and Murcia as an adaptation strategy to drought" funded by the Spanish MINECO under grant number CSO2015-65182-C2-2-P.

Acknowledgments: The authors would like to express their cordial thanks to Aguas Municipalizadas de Alicante, Empresa Mixta S.A. for providing the data on water consumption and especially Asunción Martínez, Francisco Bartual, Francisco Agulló, César Vázquez, Vicent Martínez and Antonio Sánchez.

Conflicts of Interest: The authors declare no conflict of interest.

References

1. Salvati, L.; Venanzoni, G.; Serra, P.; Carlucci, M. Scattered or polycentric? Untangling urban growth in three southern European metropolitan regions through exploratory spatial data analysis. *Int. J. Urban Reg. Environ. Res. Policy* **2016**. [CrossRef]

2. European Environment Agency. *Señales Medioambientales 2002. Referencias Para el Milenio*; Agencia Europea del Medio Ambiente: Copenhagen, Denmark, 2002; Available online: http://www.eea.europa.eu/www/es/publications/environmental_assessment_report_2002_9-sum (accessed on 5 June 2018).

3. European Environment Agency. *Urban Sprawl in Europe. The Ignored Challenge. Informe n° 10/2006*; Agencia Europea del Medio Ambiente: Copenhagen, Denmark, 2006; Available online: www.eea.europa.eu/publications/eea_report.../eea_report_10_2006.pdf (accessed on 9 June 2018).

4. Morote Seguido, A.F. Espacios ajardinados privados en España y su incidencia en el consumo de agua: Estado de la cuestión. *Anales de Geografía de la Universidad Complutense* **2017**, *37*, 415–443. [CrossRef]

5. Burriel, E. La "década prodigiosa" del urbanismo español (1997-2006). *Scripta Nova* **2008**, *XII*, 270.

6.   Ministerio de Fomento. Estimación del parque de viviendas, 2001-2011. 2012. Available online: http://www.fomento.gob.es/BE2/?nivel=2&orden=33000000 (accessed on 5 March 2018).

7.   Lois González, R.C.; Piñeira Mantiñan, M.J.; Vives Miró, S. El proceso urbanizador en España (1990–2014): Una interpretación desde la geografía y la teoría de los circuitos de capital. *Scripta Nova* **2016**, *XX*, 539.

8.   Piñeira-Mantiñan, M.J.; Durán-Villa, F.R.; Taboada-Failde, J. Urban vulnerability in spanish médium-sized cities during the post-crisis period (2009–2016). The cases of A Coruña and Vigo (Spain). *Urban Sci.* **2018**, *2*, 37. [CrossRef]

9.   Romero, J.; Brandis, D.; Delgado Viñas, C.; García Rodríguez, J.L.; Gómez Romero, M.L.; Olcina, J.; Rullán, O.; Vera-Rebollo, J.F.; Vicente Rufí, J. Aproximáción a la Geografía del despilfarro en España: Balance de las últimas dos décadas. *Boletín de la Asociación de Geógrafos Españoles* **2018**, *77*, 1–51. [CrossRef]

10.   Morote, A.F.; Hernández, M. Urban sprawl and its effects on water demand: A case study of Alicante, Spain. *Land Use Policy* **2016**, *50*, 352–362. [CrossRef]

11.   Morote, A.F.; Hernández, M.; Rico, A.M. Causes of Domestic Water Consumption Trends in the City of Alicante: Exploring the Links between the Housing Bubble, the Types of Housing and the Socio-Economic Factors. *Water* **2016**, *8*, 374. [CrossRef]

12.   Leichenko, R.; Solecki, W. Exporting the American Dream: The globalization of suburban consumption landscapes. *Reg. Stud.* **2005**, *39*, 241–253. [CrossRef]

13.   Morote Seguido, A.F.; Hernández Hernández, M. Jardines y patrones de ajardinamiento en las urbanizaciones del litoral de Alicante. *Boletín de la Asociación de Geógrafos Españoles* **2016**, *70*, 31–56. [CrossRef]

14.   Morote, A.F.; Saurí, D.; Hernández, M. Residential Tourism, Swimming Pools and Water Demand in the Western Mediterranean. *Prof. Geogr.* **2017**. [CrossRef]

15.   Llausàs, A.; Hof, A.; Wolf, N.; Saurí, D.; Siegemund, A. Applicability of cadastral data to support the estimation of water use in private swimming pools. *Environ. Plan. B* **2018**, 1–17. [CrossRef]

16.   Hurd, B.H. Water conservation and residential landscape: Household preferences, household choices. *J. Agric. Resour. Econ.* **2006**, *31*, 21–32.

17.   Fernández, S.; Barrado, D.A. El desarrollo turístico-inmobiliario de la España mediterránea e insular frente a sus referentes internacionales (Florida y la Costa Azul): Un análisis comparado. *Cuadernos de Turismo* **2011**, *27*, 373–402.

18.   Robbins, P. *Lawn People: How Grasses, Weeds, and Chemicals Make Us Who We Are*; Temple University Press: Philadelphia, PA, USA, 2012.

19.   Troy, P.; Holoway, D. The use of residential water consumption as an urban planning tool: A pilot study in Adelaide. *J. Environ. Plan. Manag.* **2004**, *47*, 97–114. [CrossRef]

20.   Torrero, A. El final de la burbuja especulativa y la crisis económica de Japón. *Ekonomiaz* **2011**, *48*, 92–127.

21.   Hidalgo, R.; Arenas, F.; Santana, D. Utópolis o distópolis?: Producción inmobiliaria y metropolización en el litoral central de Chile (1992-2012). *Revista de Estudios Urbanos y Regionales* **2016**, *42*, 27–54. [CrossRef]

22.   Gil Olcina, A.; Hernández Hernández, M.; Morote Seguido, A.F.; Rico Amorós, A.M.; Saurí Pujol, D.; March Corbella, H. *Tendencias del consumo de agua potable en la Ciudad de Alicante y Área Metropolitana de Barcelona, 2007–2013*; Hidraqua Gestión Integral: Alicante, Spain, 2015.

23.   March, H.; Saurí, D. When sustainable may not mean just: A critical interpretation of urban water consumption decline in Barcelona. *Local Environ.* **2016**. [CrossRef]

24.   Inman, D.; Jeffrey, P. A review of residential water conservation tool performance and influences on implementation effectiveness. *Urban Water J.* **2006**, *3*, 127–143. [CrossRef]

25.   House-Peters, L.; Chang, H. Urban water demand modelling: Review of concepts, methods, and organizing principles. *Water Resour. Res.* **2011**, *47*. [CrossRef]

26.   Llausàs, A.; Saurí, D. A research synthesis and theoretical model of relationships between factors influencing outdoor domestic water consumption. *Soc. Nat. Resour.* **2016**. [CrossRef]

27.   Saurí, D. Water Conservation: Theory and Evidence in Urban Areas of the Developed World. *Ann. Rev. Environ. Resour.* **2013**, *38*, 227–248. [CrossRef]

28.   Intergovernmental Panel on Climate Change (IPCC). Special Report Global warming of 1.5 °C. 2018. Available online: https://www.ipcc.ch/report/sr15/ (accessed on 9 November 2018).

29.   Chang, H.; Praskievicz, S.; Parandvash, H. Sensitivity of urban water consumption to weather and climate variability at multiple temporal scales: The case of Portland. *Int. J. Geospat. Environ. Res.* **2014**, *1*, 7.

30. Hernández, M.; Morales, A.; Saurí, D. Ornamental plants and the production of nature(s) in the Spanish real estate boom and bust: The case of Alicante. *Urban Geogr.* **2014**, *35*, 71–89. [CrossRef]

31. Chu, J.; Wang, C.; Chen, J.; Wang, H. Agent-Based Residential Water Use Behavior Simulation and Policy Implications: A Case-Study in Beijing City. *Water Resour. Manag.* **2009**, *23*, 32–67. [CrossRef]

32. Hurlimann, A.; Dolnicar, S.; Meyer, P. Understanding behavior to inform water supply management in developed nations—A review of literature, conceptual model and research agenda. *J. Environ. Manag.* **2009**, *91*, 47–56. [CrossRef] [PubMed]

33. Jorgensen, B.; Graymore, M.; O'Toole, K. Household water use behavior: An integrated model. *J. Environ. Manag.* **2009**, *91*, 227–236. [CrossRef]

34. Howarth, D.; Butler, S. Communicating water conservation. How can the public be engaged? *Water Supply* **2004**, *4*, 33–34. [CrossRef]

35. Fielding, K.S.; Russell, S.; Spinks, A.; Mankad, A. Determinants of household water conservation: The role of demographic, infrastructure, behavior and psychosocial variables. *Water Resour. Res.* **2012**, *48*. [CrossRef]

36. Linkola, L.; Clinton, J.A.; Schuetze, T. An Agent Based Model of Household Water Use. *Water* **2013**, *5*, 1082–1100. [CrossRef]

37. Cosgrove, W.J.; Rijsberman, F.R. *World Water Vision: Making Water Everybody's Business*; Routledge: Abingdon-on-Thames, UK, 2014; Available online: http://www.worldwatercouncil.org/index.php?id=961 (accessed on 6 January 2019).

38. March, H.; Hernández, M.; Saurí, D. Percepción de recursos convencionales y no convencionales en áreas sujetas a estrés hídrico: El caso de Alicante. *Revista de Geografía Norte Grande* **2015**, *60*, 153–172. [CrossRef]

39. Morote, A.F.; Hernández, M. Jardines y urbanizaciones, nuevas naturalezas urbanas en el litoral de la provincia de Alicante. *Documents d'Anàlisi Geogràfica* **2014**, *60*, 483–504.

40. Morote Seguido, A.F.; Hernández Hernández, M. El uso de aguas pluviales en la ciudad de Alicante. De Viejas ideas a nuevos enfoques. *Papeles de Geografía* **2017**, *63*, 7–25. [CrossRef]

41. Morales Gil, A.; Gil Olcina, A.; Rico Amorós, A.M. Diferentes percepciones de la sequía en España: Adaptación, catastrofismo e intentos de corrección. *Investigaciones Geográficas* **2000**, *23*, 5–46. [CrossRef]

42. Hernández Hernández, M.; Morales Gil, A. Trascendencia socio-económica del trasvase Tajo-Segura tras 30 años de su funcionamiento en la provincia de Alicante. *Investigaciones Geográficas* **2018**, *46*, 31–48. [CrossRef]

43. Rico Amorós, A.M. La Mancomunidad de los Canales del Taibilla: Un modelo de aprovechamiento conjunto de fuentes convencionales y desalinización de agua marina. In *Libro jubilar en homenaje al profesor Antonio Gil Olcina*; Olcina Cantos, J., Rico Amorós, A.M., Eds.; Publicaciones de la Universidad de Alicante: Alicante, Spain, 2016; pp. 367–394.

44. Gómez Espín, J.M. *El Trasvase Tajo-Segura. Propuestas para su Continuidad y Futuro*; Editorial Académica Española: Saarbrücken, Germany, 2017.

45. March, H.; Saurí, D.; Rico, A.M. The end of scarcity? Water desalination as the new cornucopia for Mediterranean Spain. *J. Hydrol.* **2014**, *519*, 2642–2651. [CrossRef]

46. Morote, A.F.; Rico, A.M.; Moltó, E. Critical review of desalination in Spain: A resource for the future? *Geogr. Res.* **2017**, 1–12. [CrossRef]

47. Morote Seguido, A.F.; Hernández Hernández, M. Unauthorized domestic water consumption in the city of Alicante (Spain): A consideration of its causes and urban distribution (2005-17). *Water* **2018**, *10*, 851. [CrossRef]

48. Cabrera Román, C. *Aguas de Alicante*; Ed Aguas de Alicante: Alicante, Spain, 1999.

49. Morote Seguido, A.F. Transformaciones territoriales e intensificación de la demanda de agua urbano-turística en la provincia de Alicante. Ph.D. Thesis, Universidad de Alicante, Alicante, Spain, 2015.

50. Centro de Investigación y Desarrollo Estratégico (CIDES). Encuesta de Condiciones de Vida y Situación Laboral en la Ciudad de Alicante. 2016. Available online: http://www.alicante.es/es/documentos/encuesta-condiciones-vida-y-situacion-laboral-ciudad-alicante-diciembre-2016 (accessed on 10 April 2018).

51. Domene, E.; Saurí, D. Modelos urbanos y consumo de agua. El riego de jardines privados en la región metropolitana de Barcelona. *Investigaciones Geográficas* **2003**, *32*, 5–17. [CrossRef]

52. Morote Seguido, A.F.; Hernández Hernández, M.; Rico Amorós, A.M. Patrones de consumo de agua en usos turístico-residenciales en la costa de Alicante (España) (2005-2015). Una tendencia desigual influida por la tipología urbana y grado de ocupación. *Anales de la Geografía de la Universidad Complutense* **2018**, *38*, 357–383. [CrossRef]

53. Rico Amorós, A.M. Tipologías de consumo de agua en abastecimientos urbano-turísticos de la Comunidad Valenciana. *Investigaciones Geográficas* **2007**, *42*, 5–34. [CrossRef]

54. Deoreo, W.; Mayer, P. Insights into declining single-family residential water demands. *Journal-American Water World Assoc.* **2012**, *104*, 383–394. [CrossRef]

55. Instituto Nacional de Estadística. Cálculo de Variaciones del Índice de Precios de Consumo. 2018. Available online: http://www.ine.es/varipc/verVariaciones.do?idmesini=1&anyoini=2007&idmesfin=1&anyofin=2017&ntipo=3&enviar=Calcular (accessed on 6 December 2018).

56. Instituto Nacional de Estadística. Renta por Hogar por Comunidades Autónomas. 2016. Available online: http://www.ine.es/jaxiT3/Datos.htm?t=9949 (accessed on 6 December 2018).

57. Del Villar, A. Los precios de los servicios del agua. Un análisis prospectivo de demanda sobre los usos domésticos. *Estudios de Economía Aplciada* **2010**, *28*, 333–356.

58. Agencia Estatal de Meteorología (AEMET). Servicios Climáticos. Datos climáticos. 2018. Available online: http://www.aemet.es/es/portada (accessed on 5 June 2018).

59. Morote Seguido, A.F.; Hernández Hernández, M. El uso y consumo de agua en los jardines de las viviendas unifamiliares del litoral de Alicante. *Cuadernos de Geografía de la Universidad de Valencia* **2016**, *98*, 29–44.

60. St. Hilaire, R.; Spinti, J.E.; Van Leeuwen, D.; Smith, C. *Lansdcape Preferences and Attitudes toward Water Conservation: A Public Opinion Survey of Homeowners in Las Cruces*; New Mexico State University: Las Cruces, NM, USA, 2003.

61. Loh, M.; Coghlan, P. *Domestic Water Use Study: Perth, Western Australia 1998-2001*; Water Corporation: Perth, Australia, 2003.

62. Sánchez García, V.E.; Blanco Jiménez, F.J. El uso sostenible del agua en núcleos urbanos: Las tarifas como herramienta de control del consume. *Observatorio Ambiental* **2012**, *15*, 35–59. [CrossRef]

63. Intergovernmental Panel on Climate Change (IPCC). Climate Change 2013 and Climate Change 2014 (3 vols.). 2014. Available online: http://www.ipcc.ch/ (accessed on 25 March 2018).

64. Agencia Estatal de Meteorología (AEMET). Proyecciones Climáticas Para el Siglo XXI en España. 2015. Available online: http://www.aemet.es/es/serviciosclimaticos/cambio_climat (accessed on 15 August 2018).

65. CEDEX. *Evaluación del Impacto del Cambio Climático en los Recursos Hídricos y Sequías en España*; Ministerio de Agricultura, Pesca, Alimentación y Medio Ambiente y Ministerio de Fomento: Madrid, Spain, 2017; 320p. Available online: http://www.cedex.es/NR/rdonlyres/3B08CCC1-C252-4AC0-BAF7-1BC27266534B/145732/2017_07_424150001_Evaluación_cambio_climático_recu.pdf (accessed on 25 March 2018).

urban science

MDPI

Article

The Failure of Eco-Neighborhood Projects in the City of Madrid (Spain)

Elia Canosa Zamora and Ángela García Carballo *

Department of Geography, Universidad Autónoma de Madrid, 28049 Madrid, Spain; elia.canosa@uam.es
* Correspondence: angela.garcia@uam.es; Tel.: +34-91-497-4290

Received: 22 September 2018; Accepted: 22 November 2018; Published: 27 November 2018

Abstract: The objective of this article is to analyze the implementation of eco-neighborhoods in the city of Madrid. This is a new formulation that joins, within neighborhood scale, purposes of environmental sustainability with social and economic aims. First, we make a general approach reviewing the initiatives proposed in the capital city and then we will make an analysis of the eco-neighborhood of Vallecas, the only one still working. We have looked through the official approach, the present bibliography, the official statements, the interpretations of the technicians, the resident's opinions exposed in websites, social networks and press. The field research and the collection of information through conversations with the agents involved were the keys to verify the real results of the projects. We consider that the development and the conclusion of these initiatives have been a failure. The reasons are in its origin and the process of realization, but mainly in the confused premises that were the foundation of its design and localization. The absence of dialogue with neighbors and associations turned the official speeches and plans in something strange to the citizen's necessities of the southern area, with the lowest rents of Madrid.

Keywords: eco-neighborhood; sustainable urban neighborhoods; Madrid; periphery; urban regeneration; social housing; urban sustainability; social-vulnerability

---

1. Introduction

Environmental sustainability has become extremely relevant for cities today. Scholarly work, political discourse and even marketing campaigns by private promoters have increasingly underscored that ecological concerns are a priority. Within this context, initiatives to promote ecologically sustainable neighborhoods have multiplied in the last few decades and the number of publications related to environmental sustainability too. The focus turning specifically to eco-neighborhoods and their potential to improve the quality of life in our cities.

There are not many initiatives that are actually being carried out and even less those that preserve the essential principles of eco-neighborhoods in Spain. This research focuses on the analysis of the implementation of these initiatives in the Spanish capital. Despite the large initial number of projects (six counted since 2007), and the national and international publicity that has accompanied these initiatives, none has culminated. Its trajectory has been singularly difficult and stormy. The future of these initiatives is extremely uncertain. Several problems have converged to ensure their failure, from their very genesis to the processes adopted to implement them and, especially the confusing premises on which their design and location were based. In 2008, Madrid City Council proposed creating six eco-neighborhoods in areas which had been the object of prior urban regeneration initiatives with enormous difficulties, all without creating a global, dedicated plan. The only project actually launched, though currently paralyses due to fundamental problems, is the eco-neighborhood located in the Puente de Vallecas district. Madrid City Council aimed to build this on land belonging to an existing social housing community (*colonia municipal*) built in the mid-20th century and for which the city had already designed an initial remodeling plan in the 1980s. The eco-neighborhood's development would later be interrupted by changes in the city government, with the corresponding differences in official interests and the adoption of a fully neo-liberal perspective, as well as the economic, social and legal problems associated to the project. The eco-neighborhood project started in an especially complex context which led to the demolition of buildings and the partial relocation of residents without sufficient justification.

This project is the one which has raised the most interest amongst scholars, though their work has systematically eluded any reference to the neighborhood's catastrophic development and the project's adverse results.

The implementation of eco-neighborhoods in Madrid will be analyzed after clarifying the object of study: The basic components, its requirements and characterizing their expansion in Europe. From the comparison of traits, aspirations, and processes, arise the bitter conclusion. The lack of dialogue with residents and negotiations with associations have made the official, well-developed discourse and the initiative itself seem completely alien to the needs and aspirations of the citizens in Madrid's poorer southern districts. The economic crisis, the lack of political will and the added difficulties found in the processes of urban remodeling of very much degraded areas work as final complements for the bankruptcy of the actions.

Many studies approach the theoretical framework of this type of action without having yet achieved a definitive consensus on its definition and which are the essential basic components of eco-neighborhoods. The key to the confusion is based on the evolution of the model from formulas focused exclusively on ecological or environmental components to the most recent, in which a wider context of urban sustainability has been imposed. The success of the denomination of eco-neighborhood, based on its evocative and attractive capacity [1], has prevented from the clearest expression of a sustainable urban neighborhood. Precisely, its poor accuracy and its more flexible and ambiguous use, are the keys of its widespread use. In any case, for our purposes, as the most researchers, technicians and town planners do, we can identify both terms and use them interchangeably. In Spain, as in France, eco-neighborhood has unquestionably triumphed.

In broad strokes, the eco-neighborhood can be established as an urban project, raised at its scale, and based on the three basic dimensions of sustainability: Environmental, social and economic. A greater precision in its description requires clarifying three essential questions: First, the intervention's scale, then second, its components and third the reference model.

The neighborhood as a privileged area for urban planning has also been revealed as being especially sensitive to the objectives of quality of life and sustainability [2–8]. Its scale is considered optimal not only to achieve coherence and socioeconomic and environmental effectiveness (mobility, work, housing, energy, etc.) but also to achieve the necessary coordination of sectorial institutions and policies, in addition to the participation and social cohesion that are essential in these proposals [9]. The concretion in the neighborhood from the city, in the planning of the sustainability [10,11], has allowed substantial advances in different essential subjects, especially related to energy, water and waste. However, some authors criticize its false effect of "island of sustainability", which moves problems (traffic, pollution, housing) to peripheral areas. Of the same way, it has not yet been demonstrated that there may be a transfer of results to the whole city, so its pedagogical capacity in the face of serious environmental problems is in question [12].

The content graphic of the eco-neighborhoods, or sustainable urban neighborhoods, (Figure 1) shows the basic structure of this urban model. There is general agreement to incorporate the three classic dimensions of sustainability: Social, economic and environmental [2,3,7,11,13–18]. The aspects covered by each of them are shown in detail in Appendix A (Table A1). The issues related to the achievement of a sustainable urban metabolism (treatment of energy, water, waste, etc.) are the most elaborate and complete. The economic sustainability is more complex. The best practices should be incorporated together with the uses and mixed activities and a density capable of creating economies of scale, innovative formulas of a collaborative local economy (consumer cooperatives, co-working or local currencies). For its part, social sustainability must guarantee a habitable, diverse and cohesive neighborhood.

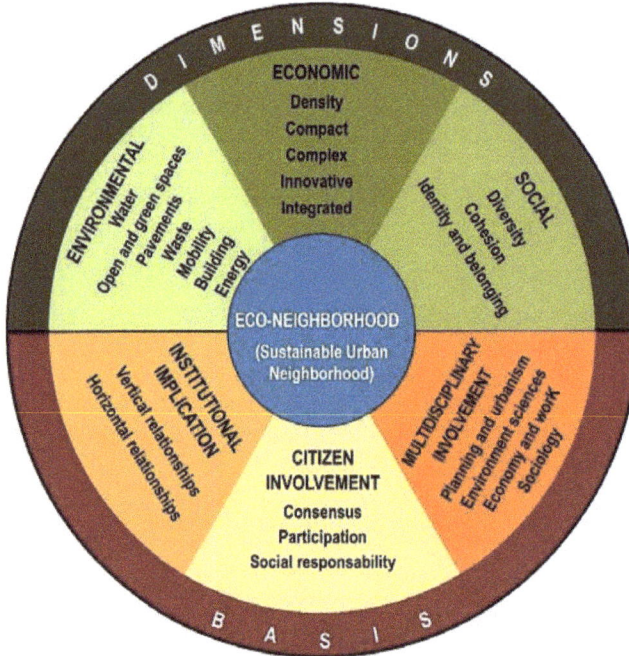

Figure 1. The structure of the eco-neighborhoods. Source: See Appendix A.

The main criticisms are focused on the excessive attention is given to the ecological elements and the high use of technology that these eco-neighborhoods show, converted into showcases for experiments and technological innovations [1,8]. The result of criticism of its limitations is the more recent incorporation of three foundations or pillars as essential conditions for its proper implementation: Institutional, citizenship, academic and technical involvement.

The institutional sustainability refers to the need for special governance applied to very complex interventions [19–21]. It is related to policies, government structures and regulations that, in the Spanish case, are especially relevant. In parallel, the incorporation of social agents in the processes of design and implementation of eco-neighborhoods through participation and consensus has been demonstrated as one of the keys to the success of the most internationally recognized neighborhoods [2,22–24].

The intervention of specialists of complementary fields is another requirement of the eco-neighborhoods, especially in cases of combination with integral urban regeneration [25,26]. The interdisciplinarity, involving urban planners, architects, ecologists, sociologists, economists and other specialists, should be a support in the initial design phase, in the subsequent start-up and during its implementation [27].

A final aspect to which the coherence of sustainability is extended is urban regeneration [2,10,21]. Better than new interventions on vacant land, even with natural values, some want to add a new value such as developing eco-neighborhoods in degraded areas of the consolidated city, residential or industrial. This aptitude for urban regeneration, if it is not well planned, can be converted, given the complexity of the problems linked to these operations, into an impossible burden to overcome. Then, two elements prevent the existence of a single accepted model of eco-neighborhood.

Firstly, the diversity of interpretations existing between planners and specialists and secondly, its excessively recent character, with the first rigorous formulations made in the nineties of the past century. Although there are already many projects around the world, few are really concluded and even less internationally recognized as successful. In Europe, the most complete experiences are located in the countries of the center and north and have been analyzed in depth by different specialists and institutions [6,15,17,22,28]. These are the eco-neighborhoods of Vauban (Freiburg, Germany), Loretto, Mühlen and Französische Viertel (Tübingen, Germany), BedZED (London, Royaume-Uni), Solar City (Linz, Austria), Vesterbro (Copenhagen, Danemark), Hammarby Sjöstad (Stockholm, Sweden), Eco-Viikki (Helsinki, Finland), BO01 and Masthusen (Malmö, Suede). Its emblematic nature is such that some specialists differentiate their conception and development of the Mediterranean model, where the resolution of social, economic and governance problems is more important than purely environmental and technological ones [11,20,29]. In this last area we could mention Aghia Varvara (Athens, Greece), Mata de Sesimbra (Lisbon, Portugal), Sampolino (Brescia Italy) and Claude Bernard and Fresquel Fontarrabie (Paris, France) [30].

In Spain, despite some optimistic accounts [31,32], there are not many eco-neighborhoods, strictly speaking, in progress, although there are more failures and paralyzed initiatives. We must mention the projects, still in the initial phase of Logroño Oeste (La Rioja) [33], La Pinada in Paterna (Valencia) [34], newly created on vacant land and A Ponte in Ourense (Ourense) [35], on a district of the majority of public housing. Barcelona stands out for the pioneering character, in its integration with proposals for urban regeneration, the importance of social participation and its progress, Trinitat Nova [17,18]. Later and somewhat different in its conception is the superblock of San Martí (Barcelona) [24,36], a pilot project on a sector of the neighborhood that, in the future, aims to extend to the entire city. Another case is Sarriguren, in Navarra, whose dimensions and position make it closer to the eco-city concept than to eco-neighborhood [37].

Confronting the reality with the project and determining the keys of an unfavorable implementation will then become the main contributions of this research, away from the more theoretical contents of most existing case studies.

2. Materials and Methods

The assessment of the implementation of the eco-neighborhoods in Madrid has required the use of a special research methodology, in which qualitative techniques have prevailed over other known ways. We have focused attention on fieldwork and the verification of stories, because of the strong divergence between projects and official statements, in relation to the achievements and complaints of residents in areas affected by regeneration processes through eco-neighborhoods. On these bases the analysis has essentially been built, however, we have also incorporated the most usual methods in geographic research (Figure 2).

It has been based on the most relevant bibliography on the subject, which has allowed building the frame of reference on the definition and content of eco-neighborhoods, their insertion in the currents of thinking about city and sustainability, and their development, especially in countries with a strong tradition in environmental concern.

The official planning and intervention documents have also been revised. They are firstly the master plans drafted as modifications to the Plan General de Madrid, approved in 1997 but lacking this environmental aspect. Secondarily, the documentation generated by the Empresa Municipal de la Vivienda y Suelo of Madrid, the owner of the land in most of the projected neighborhoods. This organism is in charge of the maintenance or rehabilitation of former affected municipal suburbs and is responsible for the promotion of new neighborhoods of a municipal initiative. The consultation of the material deposited in its archives, and the conversations held with the officials in charge of the processes of urban regeneration, have been essential.

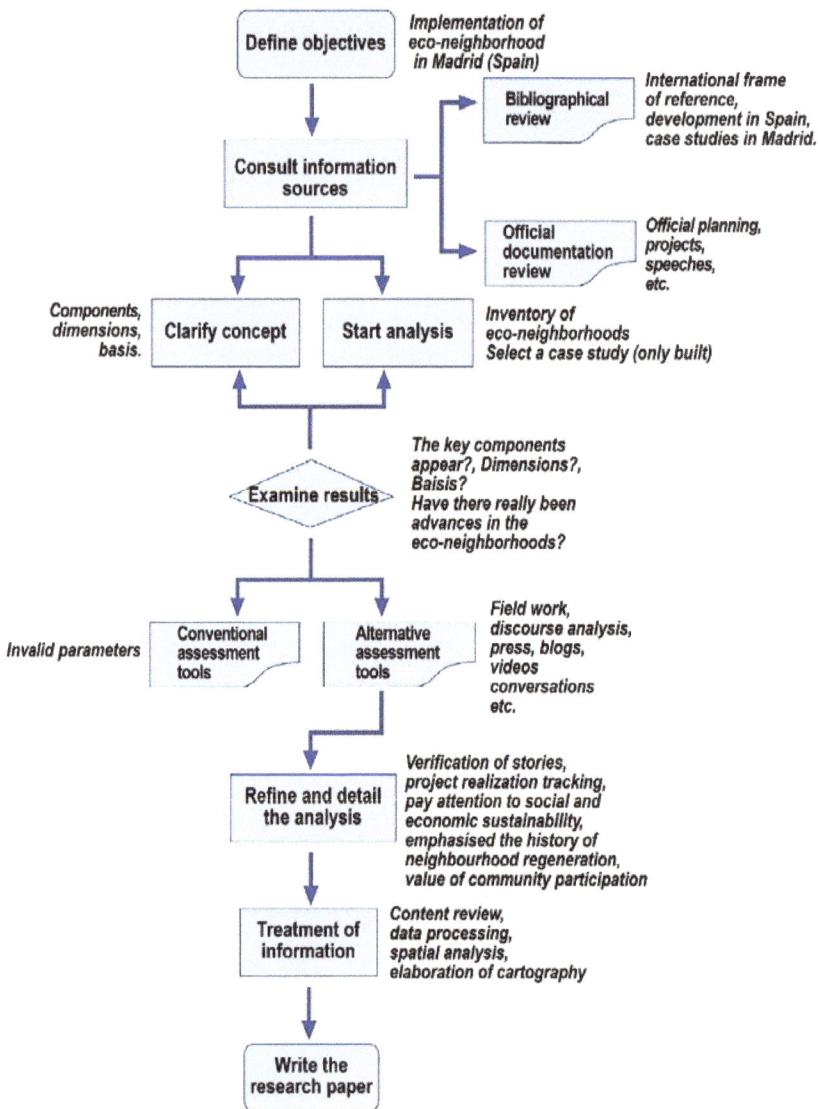

Figure 2. Flowchart of the research methodology. Source: The authors.

The fieldwork, carried out for more than a decade continuously, has been key in this investigation. It has been fundamental to verify plans, official declarations or even the content of some publications to establish a reliable evaluation of this initiative in the spot. This has made possible to carry out an adequate follow-up of the execution of each of the six eco-neighborhoods, of their minimum progress, their misunderstandings and, above all, of the paralysis of most of them and the deterioration of the little that has been done. The direct observation has also facilitated conversations with residents and close neighbors, who have been able to transmit their aspirations, their frustrations and their bewilderment to the impasse that these projects have reached.

Along with this traditional tool of geographic research, we must underline for the relevance of the research, the incorporation of the study of narratives exposed in different documentary sources, such as websites (blogs, corporate sites, portals of official institutions and association's platforms), articles in local and nations media (press, magazines, etc.) and private videos or broadcasts in national tv-shows. The validity of this type of approach has been confirmed by multiple specialists [38–42].

We would like to note that a conventional evaluation of these eco-neighborhoods has not been incorporated. Currently, different neighborhood sustainability assessment tools are being designed and applied. They are established to make certifications and, to a lesser extent, to monitor the project and to formulate improvement actions. The literature is very numerous [15,30,43,44], although, as some specialists have already denounced, little criticism [21,23–45].

In most cases, the tools measure the aspects most linked to strictly environmental sustainability and little to the essential economic and social side of the question. They also highlight its greater adaptation to the new plant projects and not those based on the regeneration of degraded neighborhoods. An additional criticism adds the use of information exclusively derived from master plans. The evaluation methods are based on the analysis of the plans, even though the promotions are in the initial phase or have not even begun. Boyle, Michell and Viruly [21] emphasize the great contrasts existing in the results achieved by the application of different tools to the same eco-neighborhoods. The weighting of each component in each of the assessment tools is very different, which, in some way, calls into question its effectiveness. Generally, the papers dedicated to eco-neighborhood experiences in Europe and in the United States describe success stories and good practices, though, at times, they also focus on projects which have yet to be implemented or those whose results cannot be critically assessed given their recent creation. Consequently, failed projects, the fundamental contradictions and other negative issues regarding their implementation have gone unexplored. The latter is precisely the focus of this paper based on the city of Madrid.

In this way, the eco-neighborhoods of La Rosilla obtained in 2012 BREEAM certificate (Building Research Establishment Environmental Assessment Methodology), of the British company born to certify buildings. Everything was done evaluating the projected sustainability, environmental, social and economic, with the information provided by the detailed study included in the specific plan of the area [46]. It wasn't taken into account neither the rehousing of the former residents of the slum in other more or less distant areas, nor their wishes [47].

The trajectory of Madrid's eco-neighborhoods is so unique that it makes useless the evaluation of projects using the usual tools. Only two of the six municipal initiatives have progressed, and only one has actually been covered a substantial part of the construction and infrastructure program. These facts make impossible to develop a reasonable assessment. In the latter case, in the eco-neighborhood of Vallecas it would not be relevant to use any of the most recognized methods. It has the particularity that its systems of centralized energy supply or waste collection, executed as the vanguard of urbanization, have never been put into operation.

In addition, they have left without maintenance, not only the equipment, but the green zones and the pedestrian itineraries, that show at present a severe deterioration. The primitive proposal, that took as a base the former municipal suburbs and their residents, was not finished. The reason was the constant problems during the relocation and the disagreement between the administration and former neighbors (owners and squatters). Less than half of the original neighbors have been able to occupy new houses that, in addition, some lack basic components of the bioclimatic construction since they had to be supplied by the centralized methods that never worked. Together with them, new middle class cooperative's member and the Roma population from other areas, coexist in differentiated buildings of very unequal quality. Co-responsibility for urban sustainability remains a pure fantasy. The reality contradicts widely the projects, the planning and the official speeches.

3. Eco-Neighborhoods in the City of Madrid

Since the end of the 1990s, municipal policies in Spain have more or less coherently advocated sustainability, livability and quality of life objectives, the standard neo-liberal urban planning goals. These new proposals combine the political will to participate in the new sustainability paradigm inundating a significant part of public and private activity with specific demands from citizens to improve the city's environmental conditions [13]. At the start of the new millennium, the city began considering territorial interventions along with industry-specific actions. This led to different sustainability criteria converging (population density, complexity, urban metabolism efficiency and social cohesion), criteria which city hall had only applied sporadically until then. After choosing the most appropriate neighborhood, the first academic and pragmatic approaches to the so-called eco-neighborhoods emerged. Madrid City Council became interested in these types of projects and issued a publication in 2005 summarizing these types of plans throughout Europe [22].

As of that year, Madrid announced several proposals to build eco-neighborhoods. The first ones were initially independent of each other. As of 2008, the city projected them jointly, though without a single unifying plan. It announced the creation of six pilot projects to create ecological neighborhoods in the periphery of the Spanish capital [48]. However, the sustainability content associated with this proposal was hastily published without any coordination. There were no concrete plans defining the projects, the neighborhoods were excessively large, and the budgets would stretch municipal coffers [49]. Some of the components the city mentioned it would incorporate into these new urban districts included hydrogen-based heating and hot water facilities which were later replaced by biogas or directly by conventional gas. It also mentioned wind power and solar energy. Similarly, it included bioclimatic concerns within building layout and home design elements. In addition, all the proposals alluded to significant improvements in terms of mobility, designing routes for both pedestrians and cyclists even if only minimally. They also mentioned separating grey water and rainfall to be used in green areas. Without doubt, all these announcements represented a "greenwashing" discourse as termed by the Futerra agency [50]. In other words, as evidenced by results, it was a policy that feigned to be a virtuous attempt to encourage environmental sustainability.

Examining the City Council's six proposals as a whole, there are two highly interrelated matters worth noting which will help to better contextualize the case study further below. First is the underlying fallacy of the urban sustainability policy as mentioned above. City Council's political discourse has been full of grand gestures and exemplary declarations of will though providing very little real content. Similarly, the absence of citizen participation has only served to trivialize the social housing projects which have had scant projection. In addition, the municipal wager on environmental sustainability has not exceeded that offered by private housing promotions. Second, the proposed projects represent the failed union of pioneering energy-efficient initiatives and problematic remodeling projects which had already begun previously. This has served to slow down the processes which were already complex in and of themselves and has contributed to increasing the number of irregularities and difficulties associated with the projects.

The choice of areas in which to create these eco-neighborhoods was also simply a question of opportunity (see Figure 3 and Table 1). The selected neighborhoods only shared the fact that they were areas with previous municipal remodeling plans. The latter neighborhoods were extremely necessary due to the poor conditions of the available housing and public spaces. As we have already insisted, operations in these areas were more complex when linking sustainability with urban regeneration. The absence of dialogue and participation are the keys to this problem. In addition, its location in very low-income districts faced, from the beginning of the program, to the neighborhood associations with the municipal administration. The growing social polarization in Madrid [51,52] demanded then, as now, clear and continuous interventions to break the diagonal of poverty that has consolidated in the South-Southeast of Madrid. The realization of this type of experimental projects, was not received properly and it did not have the necessary support for its development. The problems of housing and work are particularly pressing in the South, in the most degraded districts, where new initiatives focusing on the public and private investments are not tested [53].

The difficulties also multiplied in other areas. Only in three cases—San Francisco Javier and Nuestra Señora de los Ángeles, La Rosilla, and Los Olivos—belonged to the city itself, something which should have implied faster and improved management. In addition, ownership of the homes in the first two communities, which were originally municipal, should have been turned over to their residents given that the established date to transfer ownership as part of the original social housing contract had already transpired. This transfer did not occur completely. This was most likely due to an attempt to avoid complications for the urban renewal processes which had already proven to be insurmountable in other neighborhoods and in which adjudicating ownership to resident families had already begun [54].

Also, in the Colonia Lucero community, basic agreements with the new private owners became impossible. In 2008, the homes in this community became private, and achieving the required unanimity of homeowners to implement the remodeling plan was impossible. The said plan included demolishing single-family homes and substituting them with multi-family buildings whose flats could either be bought or rented [55,56].

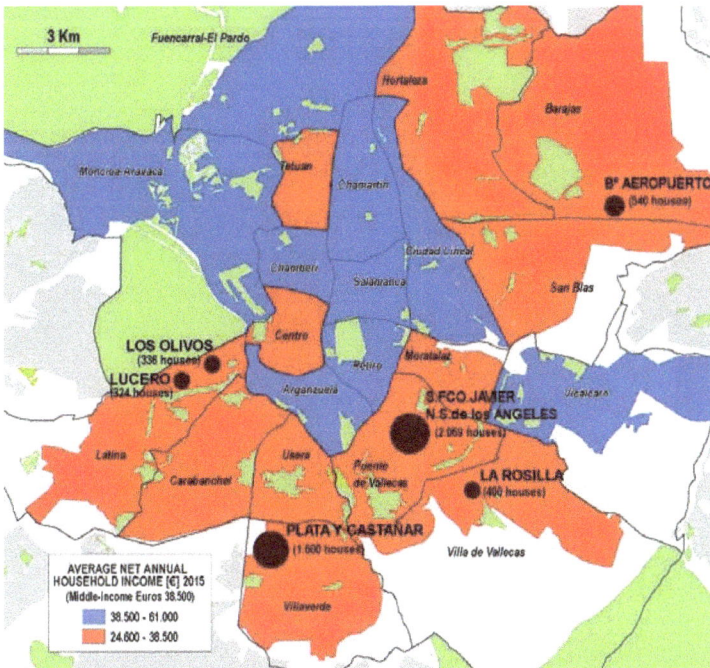

Figure 3. Location of the projected eco-neighborhoods in Madrid. The circles are proportional to the number of planned dwellings. Source: The authors based on Table 1 below and statistical data from Urban Indicators (European Urban Audit Project). Ayuntamiento de Madrid. Área de Información Estadística (Average net annual household income in Madrid. Sub-City District. 2015).

Table 1. Eco-neighborhood projects in Madrid. (B.T.E.: Neighborhoods of Special Typology; neighborhoods of prefabricated houses built outside of urban environments for the Roma population). Source: The authors based on information published in the media and Madrid City Council data (Urban Planning Geographic Data, Madrid City Council).

Neighborhood		San Francisco Javier and Nuestra Señora de los Ángeles	Plata and Castañar	La Rosilla	Los Olivos	Lucero	Aeropuerto
Projected eco-neighborhoods	Num. of dwellings	2069	1600	400	336	324	540
	Surface area (Ha.)	8.3	24.3	3.8	2.24	2.31	8.3
Prior neighborhoods	Type of original promotion	Municipal community	B.T.E.	B.T.E.	Municipal community	Municipal community	Private promotion—protected housing
	Promotion date	1957	1989	1989	1945	1955	1960
	Promoter	Municipal Housing Board	IRIS	IRIS	Municipal Housing Board	Directorate General for Devastated Regions	Roiz S.A.
	Num. of dwellings	1081	100	88	274	228	616
	Start date (first demolitions)	2007	2005	2005	2008	Not started	Not started

A similar problem occurred in the Plata and Castañar areas where remodeling had already begun. In these cases, the City Council, after the demolition of the existing Special Type District (BTE) and relocation of families in other neighborhoods, only owned 49% of the land, the rest being private. Fundamental problems also arose with the Autonomous Community of Madrid's regional government in terms of the land set aside for roads, municipal facilities and green spaces; the regional government would eventually block the eco-neighborhood initiative in this area. The Regional Government imposed, for approval of the plan, a reserve of 90% for local networks (streets, green areas and equipment), which, according to the City Council, would make it impossible "the profitability" of the proposal [57].

Even the Aeropuerto district near Barajas Airport, the only private promotion amongst those selected to transform into eco-neighborhood has not been able to move forward with the plan's implementation. The 2007 collaboration agreement between private individuals and city hall, despite the support of neighborhood associations, has not progressed in any direction [58]. Currently, the neighborhood is included in municipal urban renewal programs, though without receiving any special treatment and no longer referred to as an eco-neighborhood [59].

The two other projects on city-owned land have not had any better luck than the preceding projects. For example, in La Rosilla, after the dwellings were demolished, urbanization projects were initiated though they ended in 2013. Since then, no other initiatives have been launched, and work has been paralyzed [60]. For its part, in Los Olivos, the demolition of two buildings was blocked, and the latter remained in place until 2017, despite being severely affected by cracks and unhealthy conditions in addition to other problems associated to squatters and crime [61].

4. Results of the Eco-Neighborhood Project in the Puente de Vallecas District in Madrid

4.1. Origins of the Nuestra Señora de Los Ángeles and San Francisco Javier Municipal Communities in the Puente de Vallecas District

As mentioned above, the Vallecas eco-neighborhood was designed for the San Francisco Javier and Nuestra Señora de los Ángeles communities originally promoted by the Madrid Municipal Housing Board from 1956 to 1958. These "colonias" are found between Javier de Miguel, Avenida de San Diego, Montes Pirineos and Puerto de la Bonaigua streets and separated by Martínez de la Riva Street. They are located in the Puente de Vallecas district, a part of the former independent town of Vallecas which the city annexed only a few years earlier. At that time, the population in this urban periphery was characterized by working families who had come to the city from other rural areas in Spain, looking for work and a better life.

The first new community comprised 444 dwellings, while the second had 639, representing a total of 1083, of which 187 were single-family homes. They spanned approximately 80,000 square meters. At the outset, they represented a single urban landscape, with similar designs and building styles, comprising a mix of open, five-story multi-family blocks without elevators and single-family row houses [62]. They were organized in blocks, with open spaces in between, many of which were pedestrian areas with planted trees. Short steps served to connect different levels throughout, with elevated platforms to reach some buildings.

When the "colonias" were constructed, they were integrated into the continuum of homes that other residents had previously built for themselves in the area known as Palomeras Bajas. The new communities represented a type of planned areas within the pre-existing urban fabric in which elongated blocks predominated in an irregularly-shaped property originally designated as rural. From the outset, the new neighborhoods included educational centres such as kindergartens and elementary schools, as well as a church. The homes were small, spanning a total of 34 to 42 square meters of useful space, and both the quality of the construction materials and finishes were austere, in keeping with the trends in municipal housing at the time. Some multi-family blocks included access to the homes through external galleries, typical of lower-economic-class dwellings in Madrid, while the single-family homes featured small patios. It goes without sayinf that the families to whom these homes were adjudicated belonged to the lower-income brackets. They signed deferred-ownership contracts which included small monthly payments for forty years. In some cases, the contracts dated back to 1957, implying that those living there would have paid off their debts as of 1997 and could officially request ownership of their homes [63].

Their construction did not adhere to high quality standards; nor did they include the necessary investment to ensure that they were correctly maintained. By the 1980s, the entire area's decline was palpable: A good part of its open spaces was being used as a car park; the green spaces were deficiently maintained and cleaned; and the buildings had deteriorated significantly. When the city transferred the communities' ownership to the new Madrid Municipal Agency for Housing and Land (*Empresa Municipal de la Vivienda y Suelo de Madrid*, EMVS) in 1982, a body created by the new democratic government elected during the first free elections in 1979, the city council clearly advocated the need to remodel the area [62]. In 1985 it began carrying out a census on the resident families to relocate them nearby and begin remodeling the old "colonias". However, the census would first have to identify the families with the right to a new home. There were several problems with this process: In some cases, contracts had been transferred from parents to children or other family members after the original titleholders had died, and there were also problems with sublet flats and squatters [64]. This led the EMVS to define 1991 as the final date for residents to demonstrate their legal rights over the homes in question after signing contracts with the city [65].

After deciding to remodel these communities, it is worth noting that city hall did not include them in its 1979 Neighborhood Remodeling Program which affected more than 39,000 homes, 150,000 people and approximately 830 hectares of which 460 were in the Palomeras area adjacent to these "colonias" [66]. Incorporating them into this large-scale programme to effectively improve sub-standard housing in Madrid would have avoided delays in remodeling these "colonias" and the area's spiraling abandonment and deterioration. That notwithstanding, the 1979 program helped transform the "colonias" through two promotions that the EMVS carried out in the Madrid Sur promotion nearby, just 50 m away, where some families from the San Francisco Javier community were relocated from 1994 to 1998 when their homes were demolished. At the same time, the new initiative also implied the construction of homes for families with higher income levels next to Madrid Sur and where the Autonomous Community regional government, would eventually build its new parliament (see Figures 4 and 5).

Some of the obstacles the community renewal project faced included urban planning norms and other legal requirements, given that the project did not comply with the Madrid General Urban Planning Plan. This was resolved in 1997 with the approval of a new Special Interior Reform Plan which permitted the first buildings to be demolished, restructure streets to adapt them to the plan, develop new areas and build the first residential blocks in the San Francisco Javier community.

In 2006, when demolition was well underway and three new buildings had been built in San Francisco Javier, city hall modified the Special Interior Reform Plan, indicating that single-family homes would no longer be preserved (permitted in the first plan in the 1980s). In addition, the modified plan included creating new streets to improve communication with adjacent areas, the argument being that the "colonias" suffered from a "plug effect" which made mobility throughout the general surrounding area difficult. In addition to these important changes, another factor was the plan to create new infrastructures to provide centralized heating and hot water for all the buildings, as well as the installation of an underground solid waste collection system [67].

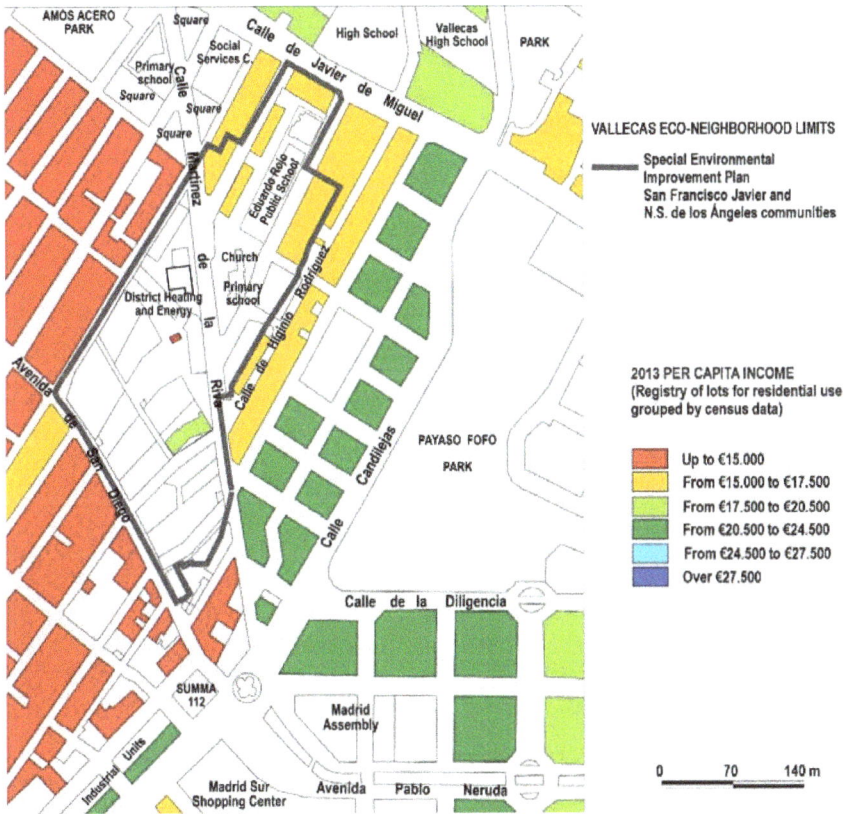

Figure 4. Vallecas eco-neighborhood limits and income levels in surrounding areas. Source: The authors based on Madrid City Council data, 2017 [51].

In addition to the centralized services based on new technologies, the seed of what would soon be referred to as an eco-neighborhood project, the new proposal included building homes in the area created after demolishing the 2069 existing buildings. This implied doubling the number of dwellings though without doubling the number of facilities and public spaces.

4.2. The Sustainability as a Response to Housing Problems and Social Conflict

In 2007 city hall began to use the *eco-neighborhood* label to refer specifically to the remodeling of the San Francisco Javier and Nuestra Señora de los Ángeles communities based on the modifications included in the 2006 Special Interior Reform Plan. The press also began to talk about the new features which made this project an eco-neighborhood. In essence, the central element which justified the label was the "district heating" plant, featuring condensation technology, thermal solar energy and fuel cells. It would work thanks to the use of biogas created by treating waste. To this was added the installation of an automated solid waste collection system. Environmental sustainability was justified due to the reduction of CO_2 emissions achieved as follows: New centralized facilities, planting autochthonous trees and shrubs to enable the "creation of micro-climates", establishing guidelines for the construction of future buildings and other bio-construction conditions, the creation of "large green spaces", limited road traffic and investment in pedestrian streets and bike lanes [68].

Figure 5. The Nuestra Señora de los Ángeles community in 2008. Some homes are still occupied, while others have been sealed after relocating residents and others have been demolished. (CARTEL: This block is included in the plan to remodel the Nuestra Señora de los Ángeles community. As of May 1991, any occupation of a home without the proper legal title does not imply the right to have a new home adjudicated if applicable). Source: The authors.

At the time, pretentious discourse included statements by those in charge of Madrid's EMVS regarding the avant-garde thermoelectric plant, declaring that the only other examples were in Tokyo and in the United States, and their announcement that electricity, heating and hot water bills would drop for homes, highlighting the creation of surplus energy which could then be sold [69]. At this point in time (2007), the demolitions were well underway, and approximately 800 families had already been relocated. In addition, five new housing blocks had been built in the San Francisco Javier community; by contrast, demolitions in the Nuestra Señora de los Ángeles "colony" had barely begun [70].

One year later, when Spain would feel the brunt of the economic crisis and 25 years after the original renewal projects had been presented, the eco-neighborhood initiative came to an abrupt halt [71]. The area's and buildings' deterioration worsened, while the illegal occupation of homes intensified and drugs were increasingly being sold in the neighborhood. The stigmatization of this working-class and impoverished area reached its peak with numerous references in the media highlighting the problem with drugs and delinquency [72].

In 2009 demolition began again in the Nuestra Señora de los Ángeles community which had followed behind San Francisco Javier throughout the process. However, there were numerous obstacles and problems with the prior process of evicting residents. Delays in remodeling coincided with the final contract dates, and some families demanded ownership of their then-current homes to thus receive a newly built home that they would also own. In addition to the long wait to see improvements in the neighborhood, the unimplemented plans and the inevitable suffering caused by extremely poor living conditions and a public space in ruins, many residents now had to face the added disappointment of having to take on new payments to access newly-built homes after having made constant monthly payments for nearly forty years.

City Council reached individual agreements to evict families, without a collective bargaining framework. This also led to conflicts between neighbors within the communities. The new buildings included rental and for-sale properties, with variable payment schemes according to the residents' purchasing power. For example, the need to leave partially blocked-off buildings full of damp stains and surrounded by debris led many pensioners to accept contracts for new homes, though this implied paying 200 euros a month for 25 years in order to have access to decent housing [71]. Meanwhile, numerous other neighbors refused to leave their homes and took legal action, successfully blocking the demolition of their homes with court orders. For its part, city hall attempted to speed up evictions by declaring the "ruinous" state of the buildings to thus proceed with their immediate demolition [73]. Legal battles were particularly intense for some single-family homes and several multi-family buildings, with many of the homes abandoned and blocked up. The social conflict and urban drama characterizing the neighborhood intensified as a result.

Within the context of these confrontations with city hall, one of the community's neighborhood associations, *Asociación Vecinal VK Sierras*, launched a campaign against the thermoelectric plant whose construction was already underway with financing from Spain's National Economic and Employment Stimulation Plan (known as *Plan E*) and other national funds. This association alluded to the possible negative health effects from the gases produced and emitted by the thermoelectric plant; its aim was to try to achieve popular support to paralyze the plant [74]. Upon reading the association's press releases, it also aimed to combine concern for this plant with the declaration of the non-habitability of homes, demolitions, forceful evictions and the EMVS' refusal to grant ownership of new homes and failure to carry out maintenance work in the community [75]. However, all this "noise" was unable to stop the demolitions or the construction of the thermoelectric plant. These initiatives slowly progressed, and the media no longer mentioned the conflict.

In 2010 City Council's support for the eco-neighborhood and the issue of sustainability would appear in the media again after the municipal government approved two new plans: The Plan Especial de Mejora del Medio Urbano and the Plan Especial de Mejora Ambiental [63]. Both included novel features compared to previous projects, the most noteworthy being that they made urban planning conditions more flexible to optimize the focus and energy efficiency of future buildings, joining several residential lots and restructuring certain pedestrian areas. The plans included very detailed building requirements and new zoning plans and land-use restrictions, reserving space for the centralized electrical and heating facilities (see Figure 6). As for the rest, the surface area dedicated to residential use remained unchanged though dedicated solely to new social housing without, including any new facilities or public services in the neighborhood [67].

After approving the 2010 plans and once 75% of the affected families had been relocated, city hall began talking about the project's supposed virtues again, organizing a dedicated exhibit on the eco-neighborhood to attempt to mitigate the lack of information and dialogue which had characterized the prior stage. However, the exhibit was held in the Matadero de Madrid Design Centre, far-removed from Puente de Vallecas though considered a prestigious cultural center of reference in the city [76].

Special Plan for the Environment of the San Francisco Javier and Nuestra Sra. de los Ángeles communities

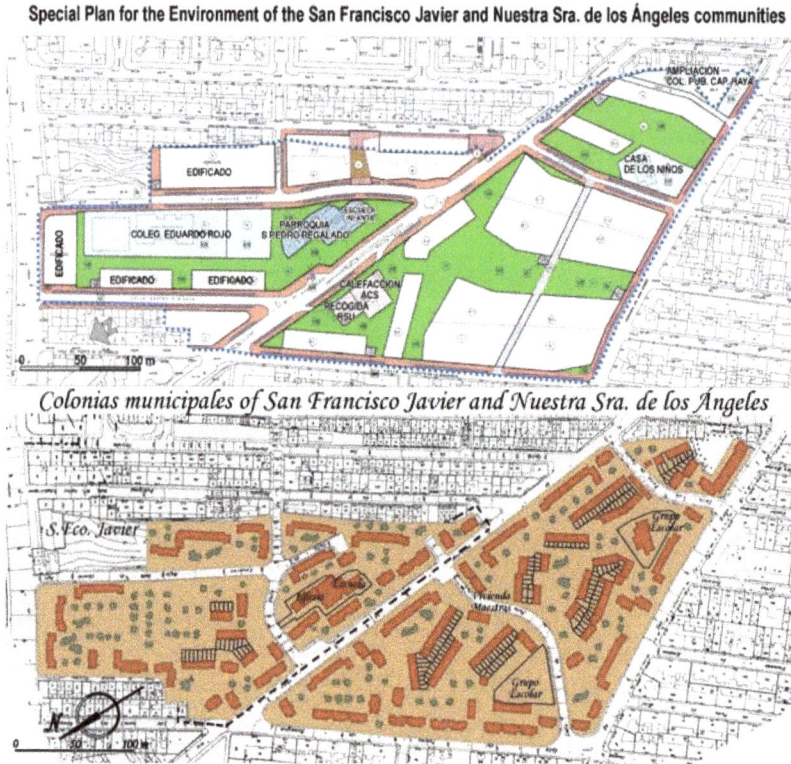

Figure 6. Top: Map of the eco-neighborhood included in the 2010 environmental improvement plan; **bottom**: Map of the old "colonias municipales". Source: See Table 2.

Table 2. Comparison of land use in the San Francisco Javier and Nuestra Señora de los Ángeles communities through the eco-neighborhood project. * Eco-neighborhood facilities: Heating-hot water and solid waste collection, 1067 m²; energy transformation center, 353 m²; fuel supply, 33 m². Source: Municipal data on said communities in cadastral map 1982 and 2006. EMVS [62,69].

| Land Use | Historical Municipal "Colonias" | | | | | | Eco-Neighborhood 2006 | |
| | Colonia S.Fco.Javier | | Colonia N.S. Ángeles | | Total | | | |
	Total	Surface Area (m²)	Total	Surface Area (m²)	Total	Surface Area (m²)	Total	Surface Area (m²)
Residential (number of buildings)	444	6122	639	13,160	1083	19,282	2069	31,147
Multi-family	420/28 blocks	4879	476/27 blocks	6145	896/55 blocks	11,024	2069/20 blocks	31,147
Single-family	24	1243	163	7015	187	8258	0	0
Facilities		1374		2754		4128		9831
Infrastructure								1454 *
Green/open spaces		23,090		28,519		51,609		19,790
Road		2914		5641		8555		19,188
Main public road				2712		2712		1651
Secondary public road		2914		2929		5843		17,537
Parking area-pedestrian preferred street								1040
Parking area-garden area								462
Total		33,500		50,074		83,574		82,912

This is also when the project was Internationalized and presented at the 2011 Ibero-American Conference on Sustainable Development (*Encuentro Iberoamericano sobre Desarrollo Sostenible de Sao Paulo*) held in Sao Paolo in which EMVS directors announced Madrid's wager on environmental sustainability through actions, such as the Vallecas Eco-Neighborhood [77]. At the same time, the project began to receive numerous awards, such as from the Spanish Association of Public Promoters of Housing and Land in 2010 due to the project's good practices regarding protected housing. City hall also multiplied the number of documents explaining the thermoelectric plant's possibilities and future residential buildings incorporating sustainable design criteria. The greatest recognition for the project came in 2014 when the eco-neighborhood was chosen by the Spanish Habitat Committee as part of the International Best Practices Competition held in Dubai in 2014 within the framework of the second United Nations Human Settlements Program (HABITAT II). City Council's discourse [78] at these events insisted that the eco-neighborhood initiative fomented the "families' social development", as well as "cushioned deteriorated neighborhoods and introduced green spaces in highly dense, poorly planned areas" when, paradoxically, the eco-neighborhood plan did not in fact increase the area dedicated to open spaces and building density worsened (see Table 2).

This discourse and external recognition contrasted with the reality in the neighborhood at the time. In 2010, the waste collection station and thermoelectric plant with its six 40-meter-tall chimneys were completed, representing the aesthetic landmark for the operation. Meanwhile, the last buildings were demolished, leaving the Nuestra Señora de los Ángeles area akin to a mudflat in which the newly created gardens and pedestrian areas were beginning to deteriorate due to a lack of maintenance.

Two more building blocks were constructed in the San Francisco Javier "colony" in 2011 and 2014 which, in addition to the previous four, encompassed a total of 446 homes. This is when the then city council run by the conservative party began considering a change in the promotion of social housing, announcing that it would no longer assume responsibility for the construction of the remaining buildings. In other words, this affected all the vacant lots in the Nuestra Señora de los Ángeles community, opening the door for private promoters to continue the work [62]. However, only the housing co-op, VITRA, belonging to the Comisiones Obreras labour union purchased a lot on which it immediately built a 9-storey building with 81 homes, finalizing in 2016 and successfully selling the flats at prices ranging from €125,000 to €175,000 [54,60]. These positive results led VITRA to begin negotiations to buy a contiguous lot to raise a second building. However, after the 2015 elections, the new city council led by the left-leaning Ahora Madrid party halted the sale and blocked the arrival of families with higher income and their contribution to furthering the area's social diversity [79].

In fact, in 2016 the new city council decided to re-launch the eco-neighborhood projects which the previous government had abandoned, announcing the construction of 1500 council flats for rent in the San Francisco Javier community. The entire area continued abandoned and was clearly deteriorating due to the lack of cleaning and maintenance. City hall energetically took up the eco-neighborhood project, and its public announcements began mentioning the thermoelectric heating and hot water plant and waste collection system as the cornerstones of the project and environmental sustainability. The city had already invested approximately 9.5 million euros in those infrastructures, though they still did not provide services to the neighborhood given that the minimum threshold of 7000 connected homes had still not been achieved, the minimum required to ensure the infrastructures' effective performance [80].

City hall began to define its new initiative with the presentation of a project to build on three lots and the announcement that it would introduce the concept of "intergenerational housing", providing housing for youth and seniors alike. The aim was to facilitate the former's access to housing and improve the quality of life of the latter [81]. What was presented as an extremely novel approach to social intervention appeared to be no more than dedicating a few buildings to youth and others to seniors though with shared common spaces [82]. The work has currently begun on this last project, though the public spaces still lack the required care. Meanwhile, the last single-family home in the original municipal "colony" still remains standing (see Figure 7).

Figure 7. The situation of the eco-neighborhood in April 2008. Publicity for the construction of 1150 homes; the award-winning building found in Peña Gudina Plaza; the thermoelectric plant chimneys; abandoned public areas; and the last single-family home to have resisted demolition. Source: The authors.

Madrid City Council has thus resuscitated the triumphant discourse regarding the eco-neighborhood though hiding the reality of failures affecting the now forty-year-old remodeling project, an initiative which remains bogged down with no foreseen end date in sight. There is no critical reflection, and the plan still increases the density of an already impoverished and congested neighborhood. Nor does it resolve the lack of schools, healthcare and cultural facilities and access to public transport. Mobility and available parking in the area will continue to be a problem once the 2069 planned homes have been finished and occupied given that no significant changes have been made to the network of narrow roads.

By re-launching the eco-neighborhood project without reconsidering and adjusting the premises on which it was founded, city hall has missed yet another opportunity to introduce real and significant improvements and diversify the social make-up of one of the city's most impoverished areas. Once more, the area will include social housing but without any specific plan to support the families at risk of social exclusion who move there.

5. Conclusions

The follow up of the implementation of the eco-neighborhoods in the city of Madrid has shown the enormous gap between the projects and their realizations, between official statements and urban practices and finally, between the wishes of politicians and technicians and the aspirations of citizens. Specifically, the results of the research can be gathered into three essential axes.

The first one, generally, refers to the global challenges for the failure of the sustainability policy applied to areas in the Madrid consistory. The fallacies of a municipal initiative not attentive to the complex situations of some highly degraded areas are here mixed with the absence of involvement of the population in this type of proposals of sustainable urbanism. Generally, none of the bases, indicated in Annex 1, present as keys of the successful implementation of this type of neighborhood, or have had a solid or continuous presence. The projects were so little elaborated on that they did not adapt to the current planning, or to the demands of the process of urban regeneration in which they are used (such as deadlines, rehousing purposes, rehabilitations purposes). The sufficient institutional support neither existed, nor was the process opened up to the collaboration of more technicians or specialists. Similarly, neighbors and agents involved remained absent of the procedure. The economic crisis that began in 2008 must be considered together with the lack of foresight, the cause of the paralysis or revocation of almost all the initiatives. Previously, for years, the interventions in the working-class vicinity, now selected to be eco-neighborhood had not been addressed with rigor and continuity. The serious physical and social problems they faced were excessive for unsound projects. One reason is the lack of true commitment of public authorities, the other one was that the funding was more reduced and therefore restricted to isolated actions. Almost all the plans were abandoned in just over six years.

One more supplementary question, on this particular matter, is whether the pretentious rhetoric we attribute to city officials might be assigned to more general emptiness and purposefulness in the current jargon of 'sustainability' itself. In political discourse, as in the marketplace, 'sustainable' and 'eco-' may serve as empty labels intended to make people feel really good about something, regardless of whether the product or project really is sustainable. It is necessary to deepen in the arguments of greenwash that different public and private agents are using.

The second axis of the research describes all the shortcomings of the design and the construction process of the Vallecas case, the only eco-district still underway. The review of the fundamental components of these areas, listed in Annex 1, reveals that many of the requirements to make this an eco-neighborhood in the full sense of the word have not been met. There is lack of social diversity, no substantial mobility improvements have been made, the design of the public spaces does not include any new innovations, there hasn't been citizen participation and the promised reduction in pollution remains to be seen. Furthermore, the thermoelectric plant and the pneumatic collection of garbage haven't been ever in operation. The equipment and the infrastructures developed: Green areas, interior pedestrian paths and urban furniture have been abandoned and damaged. As a balance, this project represents a clear example of the absence of coherence between public administration discourse of sustainability of the urban planning and the physical reality of the projected neighborhood.

The third axis, in the mentioned eco-district of Vallecas, focuses on the lack of residents' participation that has burdened the entire process, even the start-up of the built elements. The community participation during the development has shown their very positive impacts when it is encouraged from the initial phase, prior to the final project. Their contribution would have been a basic support for the proposal and the implementation of the project. Involving residents, traders and entrepreneurs would have strengthened the initiative and this would have made it more resistant to short-term problems, such as the economic crisis, or structural ones as the problematic social insertion in a process of urban renewal. It should be emphasized that there hasn't been parallel social work to improve the quality of life of the inhabitants, meanwhile it would have been incorporated sustainability criteria. There haven't been planned sustainable development workshops that have been successful in other neighborhoods and that would have guaranteed to the low-income population a satisfactory and affordable access to benefits of sustainability.

Author Contributions: Both authors were equally involved in the conception of the work, in all phases of the research, in drafting and writing the article, and its edition.

Funding: This research received no external funding.

Conflicts of Interest: The authors declare no conflict of interest.

Appendix A

Table A1. Synthesis of the components of the eco-neighborhoods. Source: Realized through the criterions of the specialists referred to the bibliography. The most renowned authors that make a systematization of the basic characteristics of the eco-neighborhoods have been included [2,7,17,18,22, 83]. We also include the criterions of evaluation used by the Madrid City Council in his document of Bioclimatics good practices [28].

Three Dimensions of the Sustainability. Requirements		
Environmental Components	**Economic Basis**	**Social Matters**
Closure of the water cycle: Efficiency in the consumption, optimization of the water distribution and purifying system, use of the flooding rain, etc. Comprehensive planning of free spaces in the city, green areas and ecosystem services. Irrigation control and gardening with plants that need little water (xerojardinería). Provide comfort and attraction to create public spaces. Pavement: Use of ecological photocatalytic pavements, permeable covers, etc. Waste management: Pneumatic waste collection, underground containers, etc. Mobility: Reduction in motorized journeys through an integrated network of footpaths and cycleways Building: Maximum exploitation of sunlight, good insulation, cross ventilation of rooms, thermal inertia, etc. Energy efficiency installations: A centralized system of power generation (natural gas, biogas, biomass) or energy self-efficiency buildings. District heating, cooling and hot water systems.	Appropriate density of population: to stimulate local trade, to access to centralized energy generation systems, etc. Compact urbanization morphology. Avoid dysfunctions of dispersed urbanization and favor the reduction of displacements through proximity of uses and accessibility. Economic activities diversity but with a balanced distribution of equipment and services and an integration of residential areas. Innovative economic base: Promotion of the circular economy that integrates retail and craft pre-existing trades with new incorporations. Creation of collaborative spaces, such as coworking spaces or makerspaces. Good access to the city center with public transport and reasonable connection with bordering areas and other neighborhoods.	Creation of conditions to establish social stability, and equal opportunities. Social diversity: Intergenerational, interethnic, interclass. With these purposes, to guarantee the mixture of housing tenure (property and rent), types (multi-family and single-family building), sizes and adapted for disabled or elderly people. To encourage public and private promotions. Identity and legibility: To build a friendly neighborhood, and improve the feeling of belonging.

Three Basis for an Optimal Development		
Public Participation	**Citizen Involvement**	**Multidisciplinary Involvement**
Vertical involvement between authorities: Central government, autonomous regions and city councils. Different sources of funding and complementary subsidies. Horizontal involvement between entities that have the duty to cooperate: Housing, power, social inclusion and employment.	Consensus between public and private entities, residents, citizens etc. Participation of the residents in the design and management of the neighborhood. To urge social responsibility in a new culture of environmental sustainability.	To incorporate professionals of the design and construction sector (architects, urban planners, environment and ecology specialists, geographers) together with sociologists and social workers.

References and Notes

1. Boutaud, B. Quartier durable ou éco-quartier? *Cybergeo Eur. J. Geogr.* **2009**. Available online: http://journals.openedition.org/cybergeo/22583 (accessed on 7 September 2018).
2. Hernández Aja, A.; Velázquez, I.; Verdaguer, C. Ecobarrios para ciudades mejores. *Ciudad y Territorio Estudios Territoriales* **2009**, *41*, 543–558. Available online: http://oa.upm.es/5841/1/CyTET_161_162_543.pdf (accessed on 7 September 2018).
3. Choguill, C. Developing sustainable neighbourhoods. *Habitat Int.* **2008**, *32*, 41–48. [CrossRef]
4. Rohe, W.M. From Local to Global: One Hundred Years of Neighborhood Planning. *J. Am. Plan. Assoc.* **2009**, *75*, 209–230. [CrossRef]
5. Mongil, D. Intervención integral en barrios: Conceptos, instrumentos y elementos de mejora. *Ciudades* **2010**, *13*, 139–161. [CrossRef]
6. Rey, E. *Quartiers durables. Défis et opportunités pour le développement urbain*; Office Fédéral du Développement Territorial ARE/Office Fédéral de l'Énergie OFEN: Berne, Suisse, 2011; Available online: https://www.are.admin.ch/are/fr/home/media-et-publications/publications/developpement-durable/nachhaltige-quartiere---herausforderungen-und-chancen-fuer-die-u.html (accessed on 7 September 2018).
7. Charlot-Valdieu, C.; Outrequin, P. *Ecoquartier-Mode d'emploi*; Editions Eyrolles: Paris, France, 2011; ISBN 212126018.
8. Sturgeon, D.; Holden, M.; Molina, A. What does neighborhood theory mean for ecourbanism? Introduction to the themed issue on 'Ecourbanism Worldwide'. *J. Urban Res.* **2016**, *14*. Available online: http://journals.openedition.org/articulo/3128 (accessed on 7 September 2018).
9. Albors, J. La mejora urbana desde los barrios: Marco instrumental, intervención integral y oportunidades. In *Ciudades en (re)construcción: Necesidades Sociales, Transformación y mejora de Barrios*; Colección_Estudios—Diputació Barcelona: Barcelona, Spain, 2008; pp. 267–278, ISBN 978-884-9803-580-3. Available online: https://www1.diba.cat/uliep/pdf/42942.pdf (accessed on 7 September 2018).
10. Sharifi, A. From garden city to eco-urbanism: The quest for sustainable neighborhood development. *Sustain. Cities Soc.* **2016**, *20*, 1–16. [CrossRef]
11. Medved, P. A contribution to the structural model of autonomous sustainable neighbourhoods: New socio-economical basis for sustainable urban planning. *J. Clean. Prod.* **2016**, *120*, 21–30. [CrossRef]
12. Bonard, Y.; Matthey, L. Les éco-quartiers: Laboratoires de la ville durable. Changement de paradigme ou éternel retour du même? *Cybergeo: Eur. J. Geogr.* **2010**. Available online: https://journals.openedition.org/cybergeo/23202 (accessed on 7 September 2018).
13. Verdaguer, C. De la sostenibilidad a los ecobarrios. Documentación Social. *Revista de Estudios Sociales y Sociología Aplicada* **2000**, *119*, 59–78. Available online: http://oa.upm.es/5827/ (accessed on 7 September 2018).
14. Rudlin, D.; Falk, N. The sustainable urban neighbourhood. In *Building the 21st Century*; Architectural Press: Oxford, UK, 2009; pp. 147–168, ISBN 0 7506 2528 7.
15. ARENE (Agence Régionale de l'Environnement et de l'Énergie d 'Ile de France). *Quartiers Durables–Guide d'expériences Européennes*; IMBE: Paris, France, 2005; Available online: https://rue-avenir.ch/fileadmin/user_upload/resources/Guide-quartiers-durables--ARENE-.pdf (accessed on 7 September 2018).
16. Luederitz, C.; Lang, D.; Von Wehrden, H. A systematic review of guiding principles for sustainable urban neighborhood development. *Landsc. Urban Plan.* **2013**, *118*, 40–52. [CrossRef]
17. Flurin, C. Eco-districts: Development and Evaluation. A European Case Study. *Procedia Environ. Sci.* **2017**, *37*, 34–45. [CrossRef]
18. Gea21. *Ecobarrio de Trinitat Nova. Propuestas de sostenibilidad urbana. Documento de síntesis de los estudios sectoriales de sostenibilidad*; Pro Nou Barris: Barcelona, Spain, 2004; Available online: http://www.gea21.com/_media/proyectos/trinitat/ecobarrio_trinitat_nova_documento_sintesis_2004.pdf (accessed on 7 September 2018).
19. Komeily, A.; Srinivasan, R.S. A need for balanced approach to neighborhood sustainability assessments: A critical review and analysis. *Sustain. Cities Soc.* **2015**, *18*, 32–43. [CrossRef]
20. Medved, P.A. Leading sustainable neighbourhoods in europe: Exploring the key principles and processes. *Urbani Izziv* **2017**, *28*, 107–121. [CrossRef]

21. Boyle, L.; Michell, K.; Viruly, F. A Critique of the Application of Neighborhood Sustainability Assessment Tools in Urban Regeneration. *Sustainability* **2018**, *10*, 1005. [CrossRef]
22. Rueda, S. *Eco-barrios en Europa. Nuevos entornos residenciales*; Ayuntamiento de Madrid, EMVS: Madrid, Spain, 2005; ISBN 84-934362-7-5.
23. Westerhoff, L.M. Emerging Narratives of a Sustainable Urban Neighbourhood: The Case of Vancouver's Olympic Village. *J. Urban Res.* **2016**, *14*. [CrossRef]
24. Oliver, A.; Pearl, D.S. Rethinking sustainability frameworks in neighbourhood projects: A process-based approach. *Build. Res. Inf.* **2018**, *46*, 513–527. [CrossRef]
25. Belchior Rocha, H. Social work practices and the ecological sustainability of socially vulnerable communities. *Sustainability* **2018**, *5*. [CrossRef]
26. Talen, E. Social science and the planned neighbourhood. *Town Plan. Rev.* **2017**, *88*, 349–372. [CrossRef]
27. Lehmann, S. Green urbanism: Formulating a series of holistic principles. *S.A.P.I.EN.S. Sur. Perspect. Integr. Environ. Soc.* **2010**, *3*, 2. Available online: https://journals.openedition.org/sapiens/1057 (accessed on 7 September 2018).
28. Higueras, E. *Buenas prácticas en arquitectura y urbanismo para Madrid. Criterios bioclimáticos y de eficiencia energética*; Ayuntamiento de Madrid, Área de Gobierno de Urbanismo y Vivienda: Madrid, Spain, 2009; ISBN 978-84-7812-718-4. Available online: https://www.madrid.es/UnidadesDescentralizadas/UrbanismoyVivienda/Vivienda/Buenas%20pr%C3%A1cticas%20en%20Arquitectura%20y%20Urbanismo.pdf (accessed on 7 September 2018).
29. Kyvelou, S.; Sinou, M.; Papadopoulos, T. Developing a south-European eco-quarter design and assessment tool based on the concept of territorial capital. In *Sustainable Development. Authoritative and Leading Edge Content for Environmental Management*; Curkovic, S., Ed.; InTech Open: Rijeka, Croatia, 2012; pp. 561–588. [CrossRef]
30. Chastenet, C.A.; Belziti, D.; Bessis, B.; Faucheux, F.; Le Sceller, T.; Monaco, F.X.; Pech, P. The French eco-neighbourhood evaluation model: Contributions to sustainable city making and to the evolution of urban practices. *J. Environ. Manag.* **2016**, *176*, 69–78. [CrossRef] [PubMed]
31. Castillo, H.A. Evaluación de ecobarrios en Europa y su posible traslación al contexto Latinoamericano. Caso de la Ciudad de Santo Domingo. Ph.D. Thesis, Universidad Politécnica de Madrid-ETS Arquitectura, Madrid, España, 2013. Available online: http://www2.aq.upm.es/Departamentos/Urbanismo/institucional/en/tesis-leida/evaluacion-de-ecobarrios-en-europa-y-su-posible-traslacion-al-contexto-latinoamericano-caso-de-la-ciudad-de-santo-domingo/ (accessed on 7 September 2018).
32. Valenzuela, M. Ciudad y sostenibilidad el mayor reto urbano del siglo XXI. Lurralde. *Investigación y espacio* **2009**, *32*, 405–436. Available online: http://www.uam.es/gruposinv/urbytur/documentos/32valenzuela.pdf (accessed on 7 September 2018).
33. Marzo, R.; López, B. *Propuesta para un ecobarrio en Logroño*; Logroño Oeste. Coderisa: Logroño, Spain, 2008; Available online: http://www.lopezmarzo.com/proyectos/ecobarrio_oeste_web.pdf (accessed on 7 September 2018).
34. La Pinada, Europa se fija en el eco-barrio La Pinada como modelo sostenible contra el cambio climático. Nota de prensa. 2017. Available online: https://www.barriolapinada.es/wp-content/uploads/2017/06/la-pinada.pdf (accessed on 7 September 2018).
35. OURENSE.EP. El ecobarrio de Ourense será "modelo de las ciudades europeas del futuro". 13 March 2018, El Correo Gallego.es. Available online: https://www.elcorreogallego.es/galicia/ecg/ecobarrio-ourense-sera-modelo-ciudades-europeas-futuro/idEdicion-2018-03-19/idNoticia-1105807/ (accessed on 7 September 2018).
36. Rueda, S. *Àmbit Pilot de Superilles Districte de Sant Martí. Barri del Poblenou*; Informe Diagnòstic. Agència d'Ecologia Urbana de Barcelona: Barcelona, Spain, 2015; Available online: http://ajuntament.barcelona.cat/superilles/sites/default/files/20150217%20%20Diagnostic%20Superilla%20Poblenou%201.pdf (accessed on 7 September 2018).
37. Metrópoli, F. Sarriguren Ecociudad Ecocity. In *Departamento de Vivienda y Ordenación del Territorio*; Navarra de Suelo Residencial S.A.: Pamplona, Navarra, 2009; ISBN 978-84-613-2568-9.
38. Lees, L. Urban geography: Discourse analysis and urban research. *Prog. Hum. Geogr.* **2004**, *28*, 101–107. [CrossRef]

39. Mcdonogh, G. Learning from Barcelona: Discourse, power and praxis in the sustainable city. *City Soc.* **2011**, 23, 135–153. [CrossRef]

40. Ivalua (Institut Català d'Avaluaciò de Polìtiques Pùbliques). *Guía Práctica 8. La Metodología cualitativa en la evaluación de políticas públicas*; Obra Social la Caixa Iválua: Barcelona, Spain, 2013; Available online: http://www.dgfc.sepg.minhafp.gob.es/ (accessed on 7 September 2018).

41. Morange, M.; Schmoll, C. *Les outils qualitatifs en géographie: Méthodes et applications*; Armand Colin: Paris, France, 2016; ISBN 978-2-200-61721-9.

42. Mannay, D. Métodos visuales, narrativos y creativos en investigación cualitativa. In *Narcea Ediciones-Ministerio de Educación*; Cultura y Deportes: Madrid, Spain, 2017; ISBN 978-84-277-2338-2. Available online: https://sede.educacion.gob.es/publiventa/PdfServlet?pdf=VP18427.pdf&area=E (accessed on 7 September 2018).

43. Sullivan, L.; Rydin, Y.; Buchanan, C. *Neighbourhood Sustainability Frameworks—A Literature Review*; Working Paper Series, Number: 001; UCL Centre for Urban Sustainability and Resilience: London, UK, 2014; Available online: http://discovery.ucl.ac.uk/1428696/1/001_USAR_WPS_SULLIVAN_DRAFT_LS_2014-05-07_FINAL2.pdf (accessed on 7 September 2018).

44. Momoh, J.; Medjdoub, B. A Global Review of the Emerging concepts of Sustainability Assessment and Sustainability Indicators". In *Urban Neighbourhood. Inclusive City Growth and the Poor, Policies, Challenges and Prospects*; Zubairu, S.N., Adedayo, O.F., Eds.; Community Participation Research Group (COPAREG): Minna, Nigeria, 2018; Volume 1, pp. 125–147, ISBN 978-978-54580-9-1. Available online: https://www.researchgate.net/project/Call-for-Book-Chapter-on-INCLUSIVE-CITY-GROWTH-AND-THE-POOR-Policies-Challenges-and-Prospects (accessed on 7 September 2018).

45. Simón-Rojo, M.; Hernández-Aja, A. Herramientas para evaluar la sostenibilidad de las intervenciones urbanas en barrios. *Informes de la construcción* **2011**, 63, 41–49. Available online: http://informesdelaconstruccion.revistas.csic.es/index.php/informesdelaconstruccion/article/view/1273/1357 (accessed on 7 September 2018). [CrossRef]

46. Pereiro, P.; Sanguiao, M.P. *Requisitos para un Urbanismo Sostenible: Aspectos económicos, sociales y Medioambientales*; Congreso Nacional del Medioambiente (CONAMA): Madrid, Spain, 2012; Available online: http://www.conama11.vsf.es/conama10/download/files/conama11/CT%202010/1896705643.pdf (accessed on 7 September 2018).

47. EMVS (Empresa Municipal de la Vivienda y Suelo). Ecociudad en La Rosilla. Diagnóstico, 2009, Historical Archive (Box, A3/05).

48. Muñoz, B. El Ayuntamiento de Madrid proyecta 5.269 casas en seis barrios que serán ecológicos. *El Mundo. Su Vivienda*. 30 May 2008. Available online: http://www.elmundo.es/suplementos/suvivienda/2008/541/1212075054.html (accessed on 15 July 2018).

49. EMVS (Empresa Municipal de la Vivienda y Suelo). Propuesta medioambiental para cuatro ecobarrios: La Rosilla, San Francisco Javier y Nuestra Señora de los Ángeles, Barrio del Aeropuerto y Plata y Castañar. 2008, EMVS, Dirección General de Producción. Dirección de proyectos de innovación residencial. Historical Archive (Box, A2/01).

50. Horiuchi, R.; Schuchard, R.; Shea, L.; Townsend, S. *Understanding and Preventing Greenwash: A Business Guide*; Futerra Sustainability Communications: London, UK, 2009; Available online: https://www.bsr.org/reports/Understanding%20_Preventing_Greenwash.pdf (accessed on 7 September 2018).

51. Ayuntamiento de Madrid. *Renta per cápita 2013. Parcelas catastrales de uso residencial agrupadas por secciones censales*; Dirección General de Estrategia de Regeneración Urbana; Departamento de Análisis Urbano: Madrid, Spain, 2017; Available online: https://www.madrid.es/UnidadesDescentralizadas/UDCUrbanismo/ComunicacionYDifusion/Publicaciones%20del%20%C3%81rea/Renta%20Per%20C%C3%A1pita%202013.pdf (accessed on 15 June 2018).

52. Denche, C. La ciudad segmentada y el cambio social. Un proceso en proceso. Blog RE-HAB. Crisis urbana, rehabilitación y regeneración. Departamento de Urbanística y Ordenación del Territorio. Escuela Técnica Superior de Arquitectura—Universidad Politécnica de Madrid. 2017. Available online: http://www2.aq.upm.es/Departamentos/Urbanismo/blogs/re-hab/files/2017/12/Concha-Denche-Fragmento-y-segregaci%C3%B3n.pdf (accessed on 7 September 2018).

53. Leung, C.K.Y.; Sarpca, S.; Yilmaz, K. Public housing units vs. housing vouchers: Accessibility, local public goods, and welfare. *J. Hous. Econ.* **2012**, 21, 310–321. [CrossRef]

54. VallecasVa. VITRA pone en marcha el ecobarrio. *VallecasVa*. 2–23 April 2014. Available online: https: //vallecas.com/el-ecobarrio-y-vitra/ (accessed on 7 September 2018).

55. Roces, M. Áreas y zonas de rehabilitación, experiencias de las asociaciones de vecinos de Madrid en 2004. Ponencia de presentada por la Federación Regional de Asociaciones de Vecinos de Madrid (FRAVM) para las Jornadas Estatales sobre Vivienda Social. Valencia, 19–21 November 2004. Available online: http://docplayer.es/7316409-Areas-y-zonas-de-rehabilitacion-experiencias-de-las-asociaciones-de-vecinos-de-madrid-en-2004.html (accessed on 7 September 2018).

56. Ayuntamiento de Madrid. *Memoria de Gestión 2006*; Área de Gobierno de Urbanismo y Vivienda: Madrid, Spain, 2006; Available online: https://www.madrid.es/UnidadesDescentralizadas/UrbanismoyVivienda/ Urbanismo/MemoriaDeGestion2006/Vivienda/Ficheros/E02.pdf (accessed on 15 July 2018).

57. Adiós al ecobarrio de Plata y Castañar. *ABC*. 20 February 2013. Available online: https://www.abc.es/local-madrid/20130220/abci-ecobarrio-plata-castanar-201302201300.html (accessed on 15 July 2018).

58. EMVS (Empresa Municipal de la Vivienda y Suelo). (2008). Barrio del Aeropuerto (APR 21.02). Estudio Socioeconómico. 2008. Historical Archive.

59. Ayuntamiento de Madrid. *APIRU (Área Preferente de Impulso a la Regeneración Urbana)*; Ayuntamiento de Madrid: Barrio del Aeropuerto, Spain, 2017; Available online: https://aeropuertoparticipa.es/data/ documents/APIRU-de-Gestion-21.01-Barrio-del-Aeropuerto.pdf (accessed on 7 September 2018).

60. Belver, M. El 'triángulo de las Bermudas' de Vallecas. *El Mundo*. 26 March 2014. Available online: http: //www.elmundo.es/madrid/2014/03/26/5331d85ae2704ea50e8b4587.html (accessed on 15 July 2018).

61. Serrano, F. El infierno continúa en la colonia de Los Olivos. 30 familias siguen malviviendo en unas condiciones deplorables. *Cadena Ser*. 10 March 2017. Available online: http://cadenaser.com/emisora/2017/ 03/10/radio_madrid/1489171030_150516.html (accessed on 15 July 2018).

62. EMVS (Empresa Municipal de la Vivienda y Suelo de Madrid). Colonias municipales de San Francisco Javier y Nuestra Señora de Los Ángeles. Una actuación de regeneración urbana. Urban-e 2013. Available online: http://habitat.aq.upm.es/dubai/14/bp-50.html (accessed on 15 July 2018).

63. Ayuntamiento de Madrid. Planes Especiales en las Colonias Municipales de San Francisco Javier y Nuestra Señora de los Ángeles. In *Memoria de Gestión*; Área de Gobierno de Urbanismo y Vivienda: Madrid, Spain, 2009; pp. 343–345. Available online: https://www.madrid.es/UnidadesDescentralizadas/ UrbanismoyVivienda/Urbanismo/MemoGest2009/6OtrasActuaciones/ficheros/10coloniasmunicipales. pdf (accessed on 15 July 2018).

64. Canosa, E.; García, A. Conservar la memoria de la periferia para entender su paisaje. Fotografía urbana de fragmentos de ciudad. In *Paisajes pintados, paisajes fotografiados*; Ortega, N., Martíez de Pisón, E., Eds.; Fundación Duques de Soria-Universidad Autónoma de Madrid: Madrid, Spain, 2017; pp. 267–300, ISBN 9788483445907.

65. Ayuntamiento de Madrid. *Buenas prácticas de la ciudad de Madrid. Catálogo para la promoción internacional de la Ciudad. Título de la Práctica: Una Actuación de Regeneración Urbana. Colonias Municipales de San Francisco Javier y Ntra. Sra. de los Ángeles. Puente de Vallecas*; Área de Gobierno de la Vicealcaldía, Coordinación General de Relaciones Institucionales e Internacionalización: Madrid, Spain, 2012; Available online: https://www.madrid.es/UnidadWeb/Contenidos/Publicaciones/RelacionesInternacionales/ CatalogoBuenasPracticas/MedioAmbiente/RegeneracionUrbanaySocialdeColoniasMunicipales.pdf (accessed on 15 July 2018).

66. López de Lucio, R. Los nuevos tejidos residenciales, la supresión del suburbio y el cambio de paradigma de ordenación de la ciudad del bloque abierto a los nuevos ensanches. In *Madrid 1979–1999. La transformación de la ciudad en veinte años de ayuntamientos democráticos*, López de Lucio, R; Ayuntamiento de Madrid: Madrid, Spain, 1999; pp. 134–158, ISBN 8478124861.

67. RUA (Rehabilitación, Urbanismo y Arquitectura). *Memoria del Plan Especial de Mejora Ambiental: Colonias de San Francisco Javier y Nuestra Señora de los Ángeles, Vallecas*; RUA (Rehabilitación, Urbanismo y Arquitectura): Madrid, Spain, 2010; EMVS (Empresa Municipal de la Vivienda y Suelo), Historical Archive.

68. Ayuntamiento de Madrid. *Plan de Uso Sostenible de la Energía y Prevención del Cambio Climático de la Ciudad de Madrid*; Ayuntamiento de Madrid: Madrid, Spain, 2008; Available online: https://www.madrid.es/ UnidadesDescentralizadas/Sostenibilidad/EspeInf/EnergiayCC/02PECCH/Ficheros/PECCH2020.pdf (accessed on 15 July 2018).

69. EMVS (Empresa Municipal de la Vivienda y Suelo). Elaboración integrada de datos sobre las colonias municipales. Nuestra Señora de los Ángeles, San Francisco Javier, Los Olivos y Colonia Lucero. 1990. Historical Archive (several boxes).

70. Medialdea, S. El biogás de la basura dará luz y calor a los pisos del primer ecobarrio. *ABC.* 2 September 2007. Available online: https://www.abc.es/hemeroteca/historico-02-09-2007/abc/Madrid/el-biogas-de-la-basura-dara-luz-y-calor-a-los-pisos-del-primer-ecobarrio_164625589826.html (accessed on 15 July 2018).

71. PSOE. *Gallardón abandona el proyecto de "Ecobarrio" en Puente de Vallecas*; Notice: Madrid, Spain, 6 February 2008; Available online: http://www.psoeaytomadrid.es/notas_de_prensa/view/gallardon_abandona_el_proyecto_de_quot_ecobarrio_quot_en_puente_de_vallecas.html (accessed on 15 July 2018).

72. López, S. La caída de los Ángeles. In Callejeros, episode 187. 2010. Available online: https://www.cuatro.com/callejeros/Callejeros-caida-angeles_4_975510001.html (accessed on 7 September 2018).

73. Gutiérrez, C.M. Esta casa de Vallecas no es una ruina. *Madridiario.* 21 January 2010. Available online: https://www.madridiario.es/noticia/181606/madrid/esta-casa-de-vallecas-no-es-una-ruina.html (accessed on 15 July 2018).

74. Europa Press. Ayuntamiento acusa de "confundir" a los que critican la central de Vallecas, pues sólo busca reducir la contaminación. *EcoDiario.es.* 25 January 2010. Available online: http://ecodiario.eleconomista.es/espana/noticias/1858189/01/10/Ayuntamiento-acusa-de-confundir-a-los-que-critican-la-central-de-Vallecas-pues-solo-busca-reducir-la-contaminacion.html (accessed on 15 July 2018).

75. Blog VK Sierras neighbourhood association. Available online: http://vksierras-centraltermicavallekas.blogspot.com.es/ (accessed on 15 July 2018).

76. EMVS (Empresa Municipal de la Vivienda y Suelo de Madrid). Un ecobarrio en Puente de Vallecas. El coordinador general de Gestión Urbanística inaugura una exposición sobre las colonias de San Francisco Javier y Nuestra Señora de los Ángeles. *Portal de Comunicación.* 27 September 2011. Available online: https://www.emvs.es/Comunicacion/Noticias/Paginas/ExpoColoniasMunicipales_270911.aspx (accessed on 15 July 2018).

77. Ayuntamiento de Madrid. Durante el Encuentro Iberoamericano sobre Desarrollo Sostenible que se celebra en Sao Paulo. El Ecobarrio de Vallecas, modelo de sostenibilidad. *Portal de Comunicación.* 23 October 2011. Available online: https://www.madrid.es/portales/munimadrid/es/Inicio/Actualidad/Noticias/El-Ecobarrio-de-Vallecas-modelo-de-sostenibilidad/?vgnextfmt=default&vgnextoid=a40a2d3544623310VgnVCM1000000b205a0aRCRD&vgnextchannel=a12149fa40ec9410VgnVCM100000171f5a0aRCRD (accessed on 15 July 2018).

78. EMVS (Empresa Municipal de la Vivienda y Suelo de Madrid). *Memoria de Gestión de la EMVS*; Ayuntamiento de Madrid: Madrid, Spain, 2016; Available online: https://www.emvs.es/Transparencia/PyE/Documents/Memoria%20de%20Gesti%C3%B3n%202016.pdf (accessed on 15 July 2018).

79. Gutiérrez, C.M. Cooperativistas de Vitra reclaman al Ayuntamiento que desbloquee la venta de dos parcelas. *Madridiario.* 19 December 2016. Available online: https://www.madridiario.es/439830/cooperativistas-vitra-reclaman-parcelas-madrid (accessed on 15 July 2018).

80. Belver, M. De ecobarrio a 20 millones de 'ecofiasco. *El Mundo.* 8 March 2014. Available online: http://www.elmundo.es/madrid/2014/03/08/531a5a19268e3e39658b4583.html (accessed on 15 July 2018).

81. Uche, L. Las viviendas intergeneracionales llegan a Madrid: Reducciones en el alquiler a jóvenes que se ocupen de los mayores. *Eldiario.es.* 12 August 2017. Available online: https://www.eldiario.es/madrid/viviendas-intergeneracionales-alquileres-reducidos-cuidados_0_674732659.html (accessed on 15 July 2018).

82. EMVS (Empresa Municipal de la Vivienda y Suelo de Madrid). Las intergeneracionales del Ayuntamiento de Madrid, mucho más que unas viviendas. *EMVS.* 26 January 2018. Available online: https://www.emvs.es/Comunicacion/Notas/2018/Paginas/intergeneracionales0126.aspx (accessed on 15 July 2018).

83. Mateo, C.; Cuñat, A. Guide of strategies for urban regeneration: A design-support tool for the Spanish context. *Ecol. Indic.* **2016**, *64*, 194–202. [CrossRef]

urban science

MDPI

Article

Urban Projects and Residential Segregation: A Case Study of the Cabanyal Neighborhood in Valencia (Spain)

Roxana-Diana Ilisei and Julia Salom-Carrasco *[iD]

Inter-University Institute for Local Development, University of Valencia, 46010 Valencia, Spain;
rodiai@alumni.uv.es
* Correspondence: julia.salom@uv.es; Tel.: +34-963-983-909

Received: 27 September 2018; Accepted: 11 December 2018; Published: 13 December 2018

Abstract: In this paper, we study the consequences of neoliberal urban policy, in terms of the segregation and social changes experienced in the Cabanyal neighborhood located in Valencia, Spain. In doing so, we analyze the process of residential mobility that has affected the neighborhood during the last decade, resulting in a segregation of space. This neighborhood had been affected, since 1988, by an urban project that was to bring about its partial destruction. Despite having been stopped, the project has caused a dynamic of physical and social degradation of the neighborhood against which the local government has only very recently started to intervene. Using microdata from the Residential Variation Statistics provided by the Statistical Office of the City of Valencia, we analyze the demographic profile of the mobility inside the Cabanyal neighborhood and also the origin of the arrivals and the destination of the departures from 2004–2016. The aim is to identify the territorial pattern of the socio-demographic changes that have affected the neighborhood. The results indicate that during the period under analysis, in which the area was affected by the urban project, a progressive loss in the Spanish population was occurring, as well as a substitution of non-EU immigrants, who were predominant at the beginning of the period, with EU immigrants. This process has produced a high level of residential segregation, since immigrants from the European Union are viewed more negatively than immigrants from outside of the European Union, which, along with their lower level of education and employment in low-skilled and poorly paid jobs, makes their social integration and interaction more difficult.

Keywords: neoliberal urban policy; residential mobility; foreign immigration; Cabanyal; Valencia

---

1. Introduction

Mobility is a concept that has been used in geography for a long time but, in the last decades, it has been associated with new connotations and has become more complex with the globalization and expansion of technology and transport. It became a "core geographic concept" [1], which is widely researched in various fields of work. It is determined by a large number of diverse factors related to dwellings [2], neighborhood [3], individual features [3,4], political factors, etc., and its consequences can be observed at many levels, as it can influence the life of the individual, family life, social groups, land use patterns, urban landscapes, transportation, etc. [5]. However, all the factors of mobility can be linked to a single element: the existence of inequalities, which can be social, economic, or demographic [6], and force people to move from one place to another in order to achieve relative balance in their lives. Public or private intervention, through urban renewal projects, can also influence residential mobility by encouraging the arrival or the departure of determined social groups in the intervention area [7], the consequent actions of which have an impact on the balance in people's lives. Thus, many cities have been affected by political actions and decisions and private interventions that have led to a loss in population or, on the flip-side, a high level of immigration. Even though inequalities are a key factor of mobility, they are also a consequence of this process, as migrants with different characteristics end up living in the same territory. In this situation, the contrasts between the departure and the arrival places are more obvious, while the contrasts between the local population and the new population entering the host area can contribute to an increase in the level of segregation.

In this article, we use the concept of segregation as the unequal distribution and the territorial separation [8] of different social groups in an urban area based on criteria such as ethnicity and level of education as indirect indicators of income level. Even though there might not exist a physical limit that marks the territorial separation, we consider a group to be segregated if its members live in a certain part of the area which is considered their own territory and where they represent the majority, as they usually do not have any sort of interaction with the others.

Since the 1970s, and especially since the 1980s, European cities have been increasingly engaged in exploring new ways of driving local development and employment growth in order to counteract the erosion of their economic and tax bases, a result of global socio-economic changes. In most cases, this has involved the implementation of an urban development policy that has been called "entrepreneurial" to distinguish it from previous "managerial" policies typical of the 1960s, which focused on the local provision of services, facilities, and benefits for the population [9].

These new policies are the urban expression of the 'New Economic Policy', the political platform of conservative liberalism which seeks to reorient state intervention away from monopoly market regulation and towards marshalling public resources for the social, physical, and geographical infrastructures that support, finance, subsidize, or promote new forms of capital accumulation.

This entails a shift from distributive policies, which give priority to welfare considerations and direct service provision, towards market-oriented and market-dependent approaches aimed at economic promotion and competitive restructuring. As a result, urban renewal becomes an intermediate objective, being a necessary precondition for economic regeneration [10]. This approach leads to highlighting the importance of re-imagining and recreating an urban space, not only from the perspective of planners and residents, but mainly with regards to foreigners, investors, business people, and wealthy tourists. Consequently, strategies are not merely economic, as they are also concerned with handling the symbolic dimension and the construction of identities. Therefore, major emblematic projects promoting events with great media impact and place marketing constitute a fundamental tool to attract investment capital and enhance urban vigor [11].

In terms of the social implications, Swyngedouw et al. (2002) [10], based on their analysis of large-scale urban development projects in twelve European Union countries, concluded that most of the projects heighten social polarization through the operation of real estate markets (rising prices and displacement of low-income and social housing). Additional factors included changes in public spending priorities, moving away from social objectives towards investment in the built environment, and the restructuring of the labor market. Firstly, the inclusion of workers in new economic activities is very hard or even impossible due to training programs tending to be unsuccessful. Secondly, the newly-built environments with their associated rent increases create urban islands, a patchwork of discrete spaces with particularly sharp boundaries. The overall outcome is the amalgamation of a fragmented city.

Trop (2017) [12] identifies the fact that during the first phases of many urban projects, the social impacts are only analyzed after the project has started to be developed. That is a reason why this project's base strategy is also very controversial: it generates effects that were initially not expected. Eventually, problems appear when the contrasts between project aims and the current needs of the community become visible, due to the fact that the latter are not considered at the beginning and do not constitute the basic principle of the project itself.

Another undesired effect of these projects is the marginalization of the population [13], as some buildings are abandoned and then used by the poor or homeless who have no other option but to live in poor, unsanitary, and dangerous conditions. In view of this situation, a rise in social fragmentation can be observed in neighborhoods where these kinds of projects are developed. This explains why these kinds of projects provoke a high degree of social response, materialized in social movements [14]. The occurrence of social conflict is, thus, caused by the division of neighborhoods into groups in favor or against the project, with the result that social cohesion is weakened.

Financial problems should be also mentioned when discussing urban-projects and mega-events, firstly because these often do not manage to achieve the economic benefit expected at the beginning [15] and, secondly, because of the displacement of public funds [16]. In addition, the gap between rich and poor tends to widen, as the projects have generally encouraged the gentrification process, which, consequently, limits access for those less well-off. The rise in property value [16] is a first step to trace the boundaries between social groups based on economic criteria.

Since the 1980s, many Spanish cities have opted for economic promotion and urban image models as a strategy to overcome the recession, loss in economic competitiveness and the restructuring of urban systems arising from the new socioeconomic context and increasing globalization [17]. In most cases, these policies have exacerbated inequalities and have encouraged social fragmentation in the urban area [18].

In the case of Spain, this process was sharpened by the acceleration of international migration during the last years. Migration in Spain was marked by different phases, characterized by internal movements during the 1950s and 1960s and by the predominance of foreign immigrants during the 1990s [19]. This last phase was extended throughout the decade prior to the crisis, when Spain became the second member of the OECD to receive immigrants [20]. In Spanish society, the stark contrast in the perception of immigrants based on whether or not they come from an EU country [19], creates more or less important premises for the occurrence of segregation. However, migration has determined a greater structural and social complexity in the host cities [21], which justifies the need to analyze the residential changes in order to identify the patterns that characterize the movements, the factors that determine these movements, and the profile of migrations.

As it has been the case in other Spanish cities (Barcelona, Bilbao, Madrid, etc.), since the mid-1980s, and particularly following the triumph of the conservative party in local (1991) and regional (1995) elections, the city of Valencia had implemented an urban development policy based on public investment in mega-events, major projects, and very large infrastructures. This policy was designed to overhaul its economy following the decline of agriculture and the loss in dynamism in its industry. In addition, by building an attractive environment that would draw external investment, professionals, and tourists, it aimed to enhance its international visibility and role, which were seen to have been significantly impaired by the economic crisis. Despite the tourist attractivity of the cities registering an increase, the urban policy also had a strong social impact, mainly a negative one, indicated by an increase in poverty, unemployment, precarious work for vulnerable groups, and an increase in cadastral value in the real estate sector [22]. Another effect of this policy, frequently mentioned in the literature, is the increase in spatial segregation and urban inequalities from one generation to another or the promotion of residential mobility in the processes of gentrification and abandonment. Although there are many critical studies that point out these social effects in Spanish cities, there are very few empirical studies that analyze, at a detailed level, how these processes are developed and the role played by them in the residential mobility of the different sociodemographic groups.

In Valencia, the year 1989 marks the beginning of this new process, with the construction of the City of Arts and Sciences, which in 2007 won the competition of the 12 Treasures of Spain [22], while other initiatives were carried out at a local and neighborhood level. Basically, the main areas where this kind of policy was carried out were at the mouth of the River Turia and the port [23]. The interventions exercised in the second area affected an important part of the coastline, which includes the Poblados Marítimos district and the Cabanyal neighborhood.

Cabanyal was previously an old village populated by sailors and fishermen registered in historical documents from the fifteenth century. From 1837–1897 it was an independent town called Poble Nou de la Mar, and in 1897 it became a neighborhood of the City of Valencia [24]. The neighborhood maintained its feature as a settlement for sailors and fishermen until 1970, which marked the industrial crisis. In 1990 the district of Poblados Marítimos, to which Cabanyal belongs, was the district with the most problematic socio-economic situation in the entire city [25].

Due to its location, the Cabanyal neighborhood was strongly affected by the urban projects and mega-events that formed part of the global marketing strategy related to the neoliberal urban policy mentioned before, which pursued the creation of a brand for the City of Valencia and its placement on the global map of elite spaces. These events include the Balcón al Mar project, the America's Cup and the Formula (1) European Grand Prix [24], however, the extension project of Blasco Ibáñez Avenue had the greatest impact.

This project has a long history, which began in 1931, but its most recent history started in 1988, when it was included in the General Urban Zoning Plan of 1988. This project aimed to construct a connection between the City of Valencia and the beach, which would mean the division of the historical location into two different parts and the destruction of 1651 houses and two symbolic buildings in the old town [26]. As a response against the municipal plans and with a view to protecting the neighborhood, considered an historical location by its patrimony in popular architecture, the regional government declared it in 1993 as an Asset of Cultural Interest, thus resulting in the paralysis of the project. Despite this, the City Council developed and approved in 2001 a Special Plan for Protection and Interior Reform (PEPRI) of the Cabanyal-Canyamelar neighborhood, which maintained the extension of the avenue to the beaches, although of a somewhat smaller width (48 m), which would mean the demolition of 575 properties (see Figure 1). This decision was met with strong opposition and the emergence of a citizen movement that, with the slogan "Salvem el Cabanyal", confronted the project head-on and even went so far as to obtain the declaration of "cultural plunder" by the Spanish Ministry of Culture in 2009. This aimed to stop the plans of PEPRI from being executed, as well as to reverse the suspension made by the City Council of Valencia of granting rehabilitation licenses in the affected area until this decision had been resolved. Meanwhile, the Council continued with the process of public acquisition and demolition of homes.

The uncertainty associated to this decision led to a strong retreat of private investment in the construction and rehabilitation of housing. This, together with the limitations in the granting of municipal works licenses, in a process that was considered real estate mobbing by the resident population, is one of the main causes for the physical degradation of the area, potentially affected by the extension. According to the Citizen Platform Salvem el Cabanyal, "the methods of the City Council and associated companies is to reach specific agreements with the neighbors to acquire the properties. Once acquired, these buildings are demolished to leave open lots, or are rented to a marginal population, or left in a state of abandonment. In this way the neighborhood is degraded" [27]. Furthermore, the Strategy of Sustainable Urban Development created for the neighborhood in 2015, states that the aforementioned real estate mobbing would be responsible for the current situation, characterized by the deterioration of buildings and public spaces, the forced sale of property to the administration, the irregular occupation of numerous buildings, the abandonment of the neighborhood by its native population and its replacement by a population at risk of exclusion, the disappearance of productive activity, and a strong deterioration of the coexistence and the image of the neighborhood both internally and in the city [28]. According to the same source, in 2015, 10% of the neighborhood plots were empty lots (128 of them public property), and 11% had abandoned or dilapidated homes (368 of them public property).

This stage of uncertainty ended when, after the political change experienced after the 2015 elections, the new municipal government decided to abandon the idea of extension and instead opted for the rehabilitation and regeneration of the neighborhood, starting in 2017 the project Va Cabañal! which promised regeneration, revitalization and urban restructuring. However, as will be observed later, the results to date are still not evident.

Hence, the uncertainty regarding the future of the Cabanyal neighborhood has contributed to its classification by the Ministry of Development as a vulnerable neighborhood from 1991, a period when only two other neighborhoods in the city were considered vulnerable, until 2011, when the number of vulnerable neighborhoods ascends to 39. It is registered among the neighborhoods with greater socio-economic and residential vulnerability, with an increase in criminal incidences and a small surface area of green spaces [29]. On the other hand, a study conducted by the City Hall of Valencia for the year 2015 places the Cabanyal neighborhood among the potentially vulnerable neighborhoods, with major socio-economic vulnerability and average values in terms of indicators related to demographic and equipment vulnerability. Among its main problems, compared to other neighborhoods of the city, there can be mentioned: restricted accessibility to health services and social services centers, lack of green areas, an ageing population, predominance of a population with a low level of education and lack of tourist services [30]. It should also be noted that the district of Poblados Marítimos, which is included in the study, remained during the period 2001–2011 among the urban areas at a low economic level, characterized by high unemployment rates, a large proportion of non-EU immigrants, a high level of illiteracy among the population and small, poorly-equipped homes [31].

In this article we study the process of residential changes which the Cabanyal neighborhood of Valencia City has experienced during the last decade, a process that has resulted in the constitution of a strongly segregated space owing to the impact of the extension project and its posterior paralysis on the area. We start from the hypothesis that the launch of the project, economically-focused and without consideration for the social and territorial variables, together with the lack of local government action when social resistance and protection regulations paralyzed it, has generated in the area directly affected by the project (what we call zone 0) a series of demographic changes. These include the breaking up of the existing social structure and the consequent formation of a socially conflictive space which has proved difficult to recover by incipient regeneration plans.

The next section will include the objectives and the methodology. Afterwards, we will present the results, describing the demographic dynamics of the neighborhood, the changes in the composition of migration and the profile of the immigrants. Finally, our conclusion will highlight the main elements identified during the research.

2. Materials and Methods

The purpose of this paper is to conduct a research of the demographic dynamics and residential changes that have taken place in the Cabanyal neighborhood, in order to identify to what extent the extension project of Blasco Ibáñez Avenue has contributed to the increase in segregation and physical and social degradation of the neighborhood. In order to do this, we used microdata from the Residential Variations Statistics provided by the Statistical Office of Valencia City over the period 2004–2016, which contain information about sex, age (under 16 years old, between 16 and 25, 25 and 45, 45 and 65, inclusively, and greater than 65 years old), and nationality of the migrant (Spanish, EU resident, non-EU resident). For the 2014–2016 period, details concerning the level of education are also provided: under 18 years old; they do not know how to read or write; lower degree to secondary school level; secondary school level or equivalent; Bachelor, FP second degree or equivalent or higher degrees. The residential variations are registered through seven types of movements: inputs based on immigration, inputs based on childbirths, inputs based on other reasons, outputs based on emigration, outputs based on deaths, outputs based on other reasons and changes of address, but for the present investigation, only the data related to immigration, emigration and the changes of residence were used. These data include the number of movements that correspond to common characteristics at the census tract, and indicate, in addition to the demographic profile of the migrant, the census section of origin (for the inputs) and destination (for the outputs).

In order to highlight the disparities that characterize the Cabanyal neighborhood, we have divided the study area into two sectors: the first one corresponds to "zone 0", the most degraded part, directly affected by the extension project (although zone 0 corresponds to a part of several census sections, due to the restrictions of the date source used, we have incorporated in the study the complete sections, so that the zone 0 includes five census sections: 21, 22, 24, 26, and 27; the other 14 census sections that make up the neighborhood are included in the second analysis sector) and the second one includes the rest of the neighborhood (see Figure 1). Regarding the places of origin and destination of the movements, these have been grouped into seven categories:

- Abroad
- The rest of Spain, which includes municipalities outside the Valencian Community
- The rest of the Valencian Community (CV), which includes the municipalities of the region (NUTS 2), outside the Metropolitan Area of Valencia
- Metropolitan Area of Valencia (AMV), which includes 75 municipalities selected according to criteria of alternating residence-work mobility [32] (for aspects related to the data source, please see [32])
- City of Valencia, which includes the districts of the city, except for the district to which the neighborhood belongs
- Poblados Marítimos District, which includes movements with origin or destination in neighboring neighborhoods
- The Cabanyal neighborhood, which includes internal movements, between census sections of the neighborhood

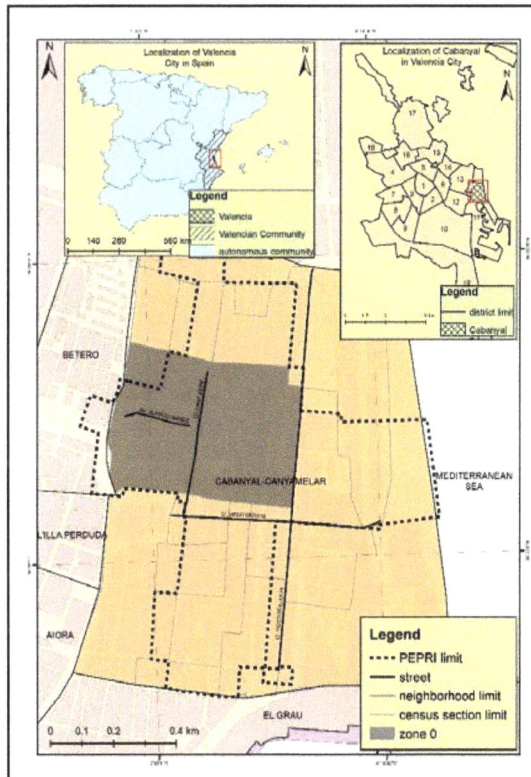

Figure 1. Localization of the Cabanyal neighborhood and zone 0. Data source: [33,34].

For each of the mentioned sections, the following have been calculated: the total of the inputs, the total of the outputs, the total migratory balance and the migratory balance according to the demographic profile of the persons who change their residence. We have also calculated annual rates of immigration, emigration, and balance, taking as reference the population of the census corresponding to the first year of the period under analysis. Since the period under analysis has been marked by several events with strong impact in the study area, we have decided to divide it into four intervals: 2004–2007, prior to the economic and social crisis, characterized by the massive influx of immigrant population; 2008–2009, interval included between the time of the beginning of the crisis and the moment of suspension, by the municipality, of the rehabilitation and construction licenses, which accelerates the process of physical and social degradation of the neighborhood; 2010–2013, a period of economic crisis, of strong changes in migration trends and 2014–2016, a period of slow revitalization after the crisis and changes in the territorial policies of Cabanyal.

3. Results

Valencia City was characterized, over the period from 2001–2016, by a process of population growth, interrupted only in the period 2008–2013 due to the economic crisis. The demographic growth was largely due to the increase in the immigrant population, whose percentage in the total population has registered in this period a rise of 10%, the maximum value corresponding to 2009, the year which marked the beginning of the economic crisis (15.06%). If at the beginning of the period only in one section of the Patraix neighborhood the number of immigrants exceeds 30%, in 2008 the number of sections with this characteristic ascends to 21 and in 2016 declines to 16. We can also observe that at the end of the period the immigrant population begin to be distributed throughout the entire territory, with peripheral districts gaining in importance (Figure 2).

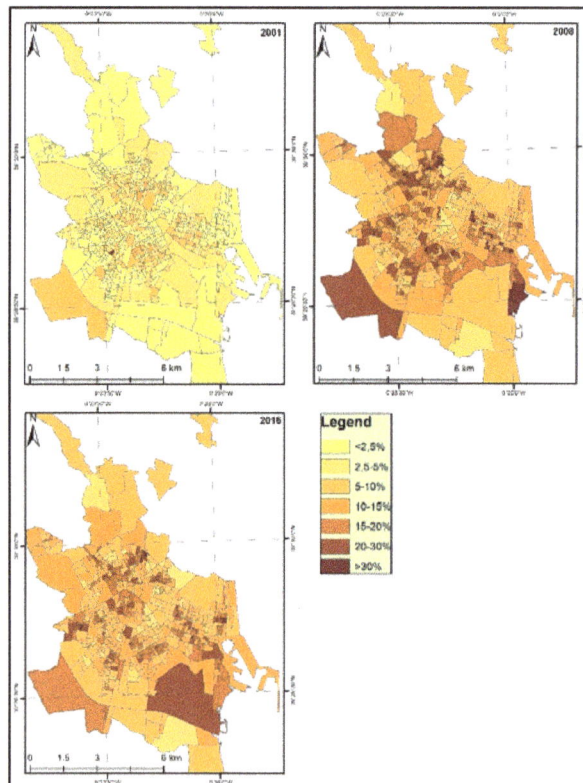

Figure 2. Immigrants' percentage in Valencia City, at census section level, 2001–2016.

In order to provide a better understanding of the situation of the Cabanyal neighborhood and zone 0 at a regional and national level, Table 1 offers a general image of some indicators regarding the population structure. In 2016, it can be noticed that zone 0 registered a higher number of immigrants compared to the ones registered in Spain, Valencia and even the neighborhood of Cabanyal. Furthermore, during the period corresponding to the project development, it registered the highest increase in terms of immigrants' percentage and also the greatest loss in Spanish population. Moreover, even when the proportion of the elderly was diminishing, it still remained higher in the Cabanyal neighborhood (see Table 1).

Table 1. Socioeconomic criteria in different analysis areas.

Criteria	Spain			Valencia			Cabanyal			Zone 0		
	2001	2016	Rate (%)	2001	2016	Rate (%)	2001	2016	Rate (%)	2001	2016	Rate (%)
1	41,116,842	46,557,008	13.23	738,441	790,201	7.01	19,651	20,418	3.90	5030	5051	0.42
2	96.15	90.49	5.52	95.82	87.97	−1.76	97.09	85.09	−8.94	97.10	75.05	−22.38
3	3.85	9.51	236.96	4.18	12.03	207.99	2.91	14.91	432.17	2.90	24.95	763.01
4	17.04	18.72	23.02	17.61	20.14	21.01	24.18	20.89	−10.23	24.95	20.19	−18.73
5	14.16	18.50	4.34	14.19	17.32	3.13	No data	No data	No data	No data	No data	No data

Criteria: 1—Total population; 2—Spanish population (%); 3—Immigrants (%); 4—Population >65 years (%); 5—Unemployment rate (%). Data source: [33].

The Cabanyal neighborhood, similar to all the components of the City of Valencia, is characterized by a general trend of demographic growth, interrupted only in short periods. A fundamental difference when compared to the trends registered in Valencia City and in the rest of the Poblados Marítimos district, is the relative delay in the display of the consequences of the economic crisis, given the fact that the greatest loss in population in the neighborhood corresponds to the period 2013–2016, due to a decrease in the migratory balance that occurs when the city and district already begin to recover. This population growth occurs in parallel with an intense process of population substitution, as we will see in the following paragraphs.

During the whole period under analysis, the migration balance of the Cabanyal neighborhood was always positive, with an alternating evolution from one year to another. To explain this result, of positive migratory balance, there are some facts, especially the movements originated from outside of Valencia City, while the changes of residence, related to internal movements, have generally experienced a negative balance or very low values (Figure 3). Therefore, we are witnessing a substitution of the local population, that leaves the neighborhood due to its problems, with a new population, recently arrived, that is in a phase of searching for cheap housing.

With regards to the spaces of origin and destination, most of the arrivals are made up of a foreign population, while the departures consist of a population which is oriented towards towns in the Metropolitan Area of Valencia. In terms of population movements in the area of the City of Valencia, it is worth mentioning the change in orientation that occurs with the economic crisis, so that, while Cabanyal receives population from the rest of the city before the crisis, after that, it begins to lose its population in favor of the rest of the neighborhoods in the city (Figure 4a).

This geographic pattern is related to the sociodemographic profile of the population that moves. In effect, during the period under analysis, the neighborhood continuously lost Spanish population, while it gained immigrant population, so that the proportion of foreigners reaches almost 15% of the total in 2016 (the maximum value, 15.19%, was registered in 2013). The continuous loss in Spanish population is progressively reduced, with the largest negative balances corresponding to the 2004–2007 interval (−0.86%/year).

In addition, throughout the studied period we also observe a fundamental change in the composition of this immigration. The migration analysis according to nationality shows strong discrepancies between the migratory behavior of Spaniards, of EU migrants and of non-EU migrants.

As can be observed in Figure 5, there is not only a loss in Spanish population, but also a substitution of non-EU immigrants, who form the majority during the 2004–2009 interval, with immigrants from the EU, who predominate during the 2010–2016 period. Consequently, while in 2006 the non-EU immigrants born in Colombia (14.01%) and Ecuador (11.72%) predominate in the composition of the population, in 2016, Romanians represent almost half of the population born outside Spain (42.44%). The process of substituting non-EU immigration with EU immigration is notably more intense than in the rest of the City of Valencia. Thus, while in the City of Valencia the percentage of the Romanian population over the total number of immigrants in 2016 was 12.83%, in the neighborhood it exceeded 40%. Even though in Valencia there were also other neighborhoods with high percentages of immigrants, in Cabanyal, the problem was exacerbated by the degradation of the neighborhood and the attitude of the local authorities towards it. As a result, there exists a stronger negative perception towards the Romanian population in Cabanyal, due to the fact that they are considered a part of the political strategy for demolishing the neighborhood and for putting pressure on the local population to leave the neighborhood. There is also competition between Romanians and the local population for resources, specifically jobs, social assistance and aid which, in this neighborhood, is more emphasized due to the general situation. Furthermore, taking into consideration that they are the last immigrants to arrive in the neighborhood, they have no representatives or leaders in the community, which again contributes to their segregation and abandonment (Source: interviews developed in the neighborhood).

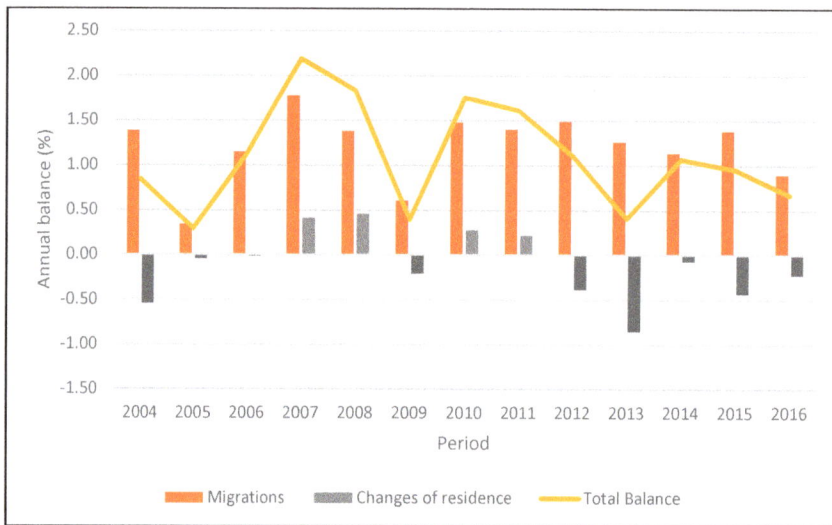

Figure 3. Migration balance in the Cabanyal neighborhood, 2004–2016.

This change in the composition of the immigrant population has important consequences in the field of segregation. A fundamental difference between EU and non-EU immigrants is their contact with the neighborhood and the degree of stability. For EU immigrants, Cabanyal is their first contact with Spain, the neighborhood corresponding to their first settlement in this country. On the other hand, non-EU immigrants settle initially in other neighborhoods of the city and then choose Cabanyal as their second or third destination. In addition, EU immigrants settle in the neighborhood and tend to stay there, with few departures to other neighborhoods or towns. Conversely, non-EU immigrants show a higher mobility, not only because Cabanyal is not the first settlement destination, but also because, after a while, many of them go to other neighborhoods or other towns in the metropolitan area (see Figure 6a,b). One drawback of the analyzed data is the division of nationalities into only these three categories, which do not allow us to distinguish between North Americans, Latin Americans,

Africans (for non-EU immigrants), or those from Western Europe, from Central Europe, or from Eastern Europe (for the EU immigrants). However, the census data allow us to observe that among the non-EU immigrants, Latin Americans predominate and among the EU immigrants those from Eastern Europe form the majority. This could justify the choice of both settlements: the Cabanyal neighborhood for its cheap housing, but also the city with its accessibility to various services.

According to other demographic aspects, the composition of the migration indicates a greater number of arrivals by members of the male population than the female population. According to age, there is a continuous loss in the over-65 population, while, at the same time the 25–44 population, which represents the working age, is seen to be entering the neighborhood. In the period of economic crisis in the neighborhood, families also enter, this fact being confirmed by the increase in the under-16 population.

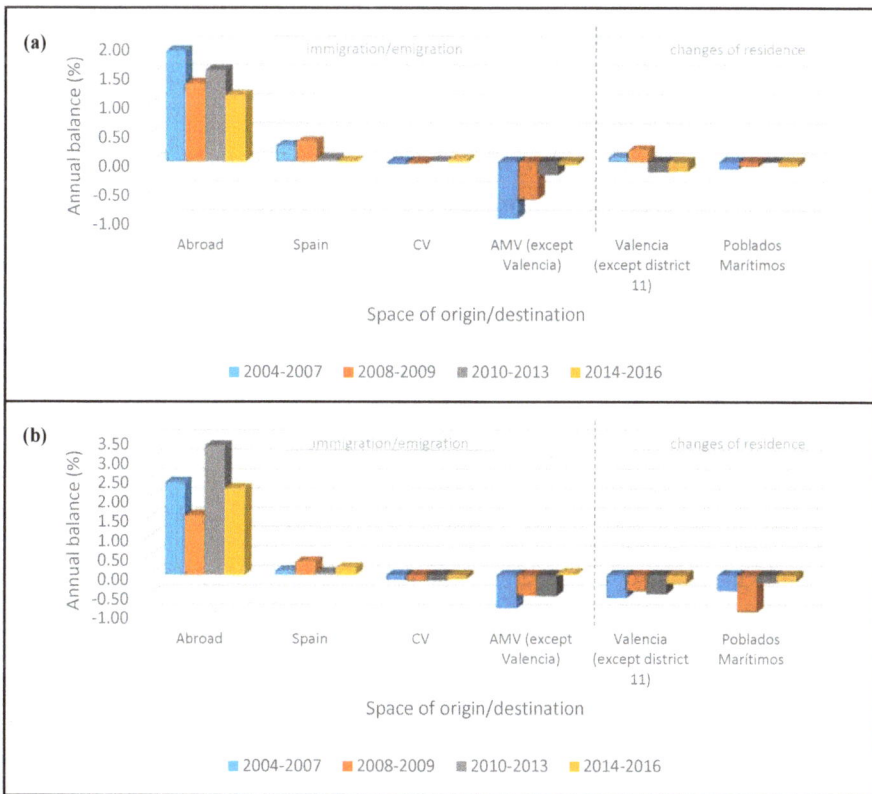

Figure 4. Total balance in Cabanyal (**a**) and in zone 0 (**b**) according to spaces of origin and destination, 2004–2016.

To demonstrate this point further, the available data allow us to analyze the mobility in the Cabanyal neighborhood according to the level of education only from the period 2014–2016, a period of reinvigoration after the economic crisis. An important fact to be highlighted regarding the level of education is the differences that it shows according to nationality. Regarding this, the major difference is that the EU immigrants are associated, based on the statistical data, to the population with a low level of education that comes to the neighborhood, while the non-EU immigrants have at least a secondary education level or equivalent or high level of education. Spanish migrants that come to the neighborhood are similar to non-EU immigrants based on these categories relating to levels of education, but the percentages are higher.

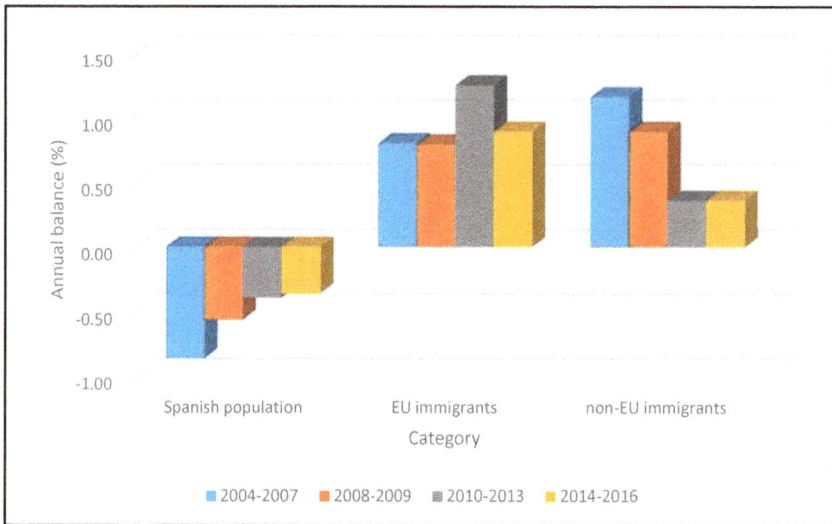

Figure 5. Migration balance according to nationality in Cabanyal, 2004–2016.

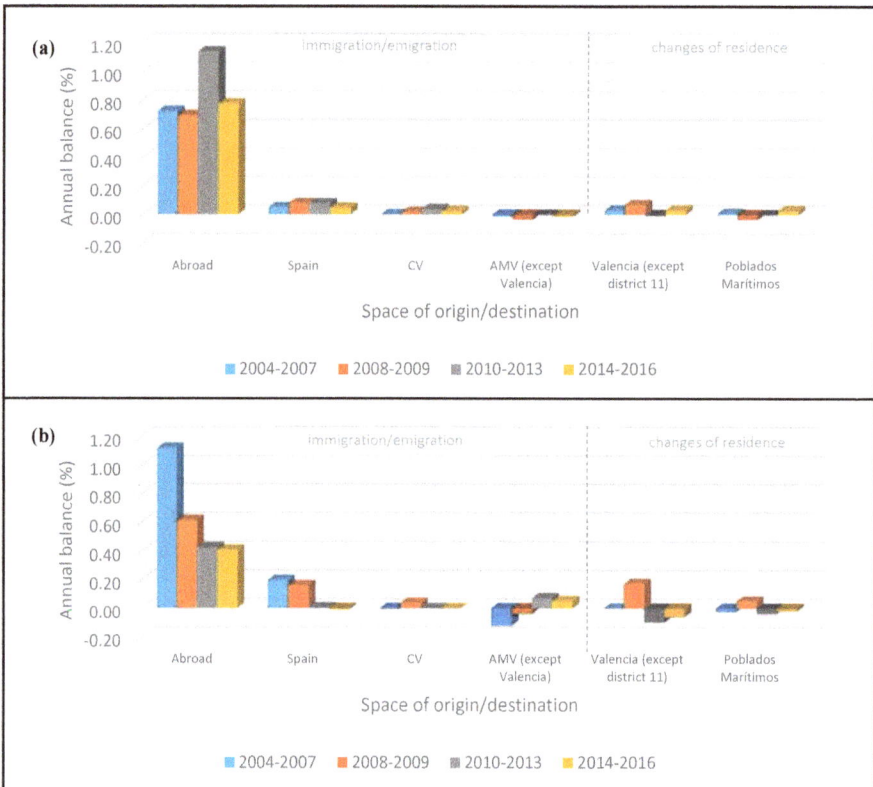

Figure 6. Total balance of EU immigrants (**a**) and non-EU immigrants (**b**) in Cabanyal, according to spaces of origin and destination, 2004–2016.

Although the period is quite reduced, a trend of social renewal of the neighborhood can be observed, which sees an increase in members of the population with a Bachelor's or other high level of education, but also in the under-18 population, which indicates the settlement of families (Figure 7a).

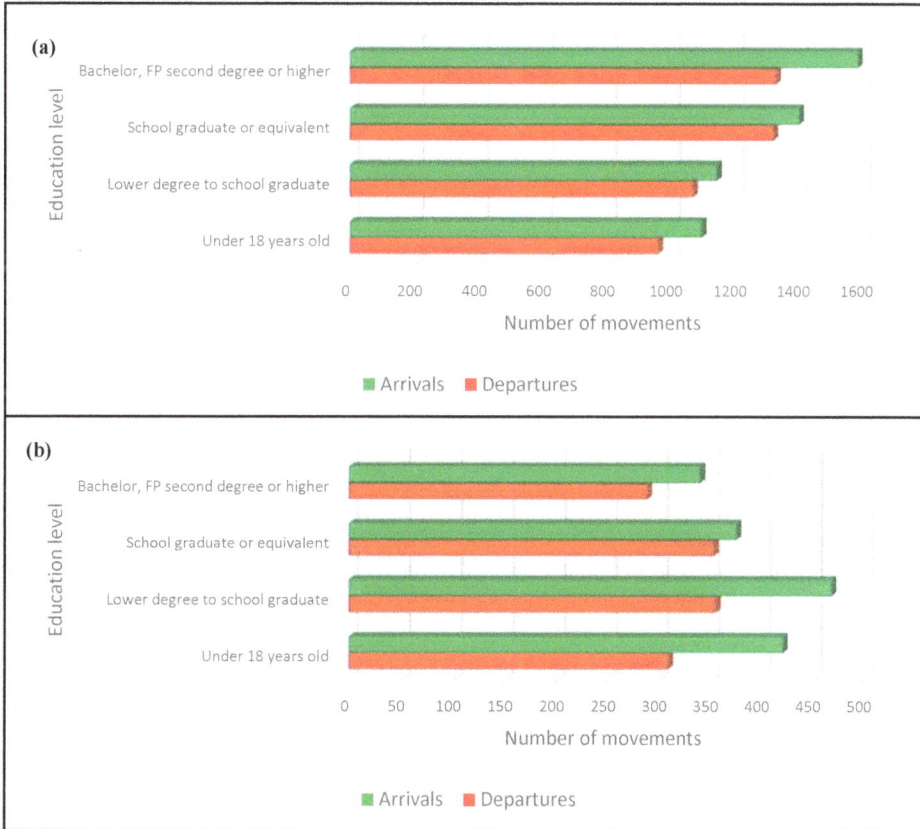

Figure 7. Migration balance in Cabanyal (**a**) and zone 0 (**b**) based on education level, 2014–2016.

In this context, the impact of the project can be observed when we analyze these processes at a more detailed level. Indeed, zone 0 shows a different behavior, since the impact of the extension project of Blasco Ibáñez Avenue generates a regressive dynamic in the affected sections. Firstly, while the demographic balance of the neighborhood as a whole is, as we have already said before, positive, zone 0 registers a continuous loss in population until 2013. The contrasts existing in the neighborhood are evident on the map (see Figure 8), especially in the surroundings of zone 0, where there are neighboring sections with minimum and maximum values of demographic balance.

Secondly, and regarding the spaces of origin, the positive balance of the movements originating from abroad is significantly greater in zone 0 than the one registered in Cabanyal neighborhood as a whole (see Figure 4a,b). In this area, there are also recorded arrivals of migrants from the rest of Spain, although to a lesser extent. On the other hand, the majority of those who leave zone 0 of the neighborhood are directed, in the initial period (2004–2007), towards the towns of the metropolitan area and, subsequently, to the rest of Poblados Marítimos district and other neighborhoods of the city. It is especially significant that during the period between 2008 and 2009, corresponding to the suspension of the rehabilitation and construction licenses in the neighborhood by the municipality, the greatest number of population outflow is directed towards the neighboring residential areas of the

Poblados Marítimos district, which indicates the repercussions that this action had on the population of the neighborhood (see Figure 4b).

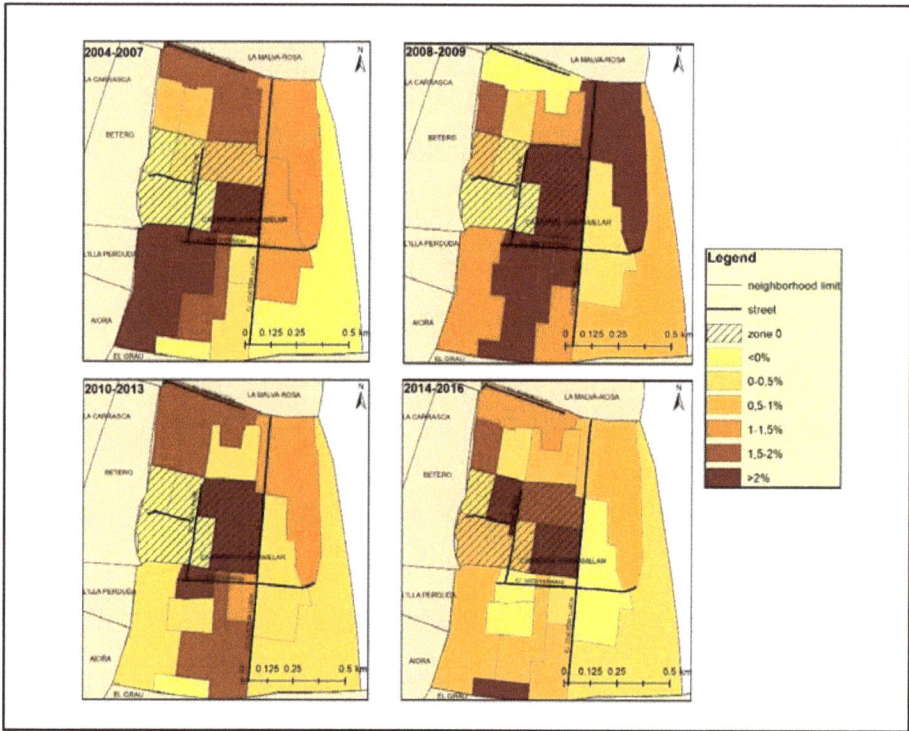

Figure 8. Migration balance in Cabanyal and zone 0, 2004–2016 [35].

The three categories of nationalities show a markedly different attitude towards zone 0: the Spanish population avoids this sector, leading to a greater number of departures; the non-EU population chooses this sector in the period 2004–2007, but then the sector becomes neutral according to their preferences (migratory balances near the value 0); for immigrants from the EU, zone 0 becomes a preferred space from the period 2010–2016. Therefore, EU immigrants have a greater tendency for segregation, since they are concentrated in well-defined spaces (after the crisis they choose even the most degraded ones), establishing few relations with the other residents.

Finally, if we take into consideration the educational level of the population that changes its residence, zone 0, due to its advanced state of degradation, is characterized by a completely different situation compared to the whole neighborhood. In the period between 2014 and 2016, the economic recovery phase, most of the neighborhood lost members of its population who had less than a secondary education and gained a population with a higher education level, evidencing, as previously stated, a social revitalization. Zone 0 demonstrates the inverse behavior through the registering of the highest value of the migration balance for the population with a low education level, while the population with a higher level of education either decreases or does not register any significant changes. Figures 9 and 10 clearly show the contrast between the gentrification processes that affect certain sectors of the neighborhood in this phase of economic recovery, particularly the northwest sector, but also, with lower intensity, the southwest area and the maritime strip, and the concentration of population with fewer resources in the area affected by the extension project.

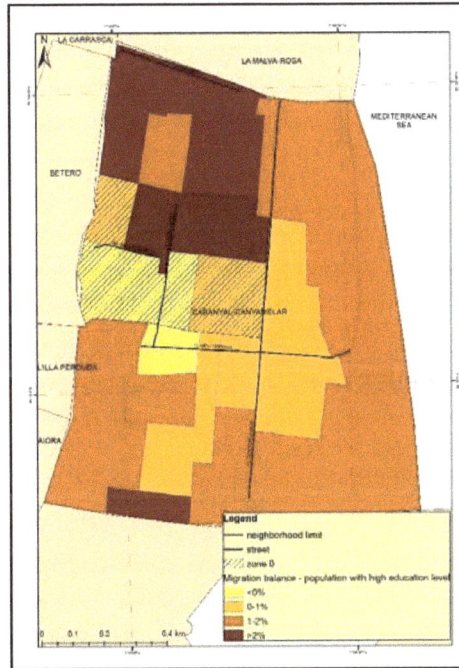

Figure 9. Migration balance of population with high education level in Cabanyal and zone 0, 2014–2016.

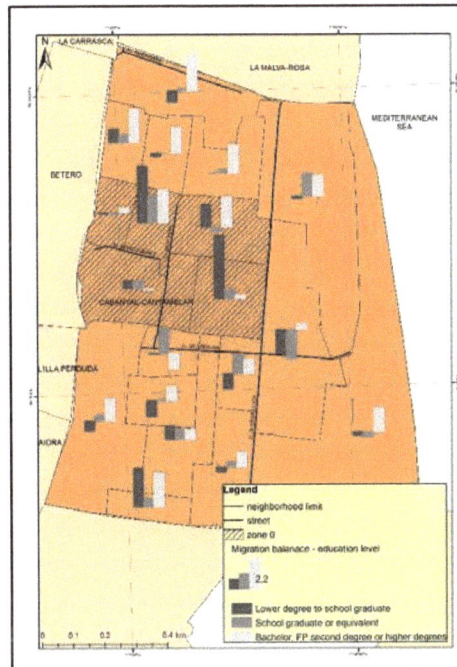

Figure 10. Migration balance in Cabanyal and zone 0 based on education level, 2014–2016

Based on our analysis, we can conclude that the extension project of Blasco Ibáñez Avenue affected the neighborhood to a great extent. Basically, there were three phases of the project: the initial project of extension, the paralysis of the local government's actions and the current re-urbanization project, each phase being identified by different types of consequences. The initial phase was the one that introduced the main changes in the social structure of the neighborhood, causing, thus, a break in the pre-existent social structure, by compelling the Spanish population to leave the neighborhood and favoring the settlement of immigrants in abandoned house. The second phase, characterized by the paralysis of the local government's actions, is characterized by the conversion of zone 0 in the home of the immigrants from the European Union. This means a change of population that adds to the physical degradation of the neighborhood also the increase in segregation level. The last phase, that started in 2015, is a period of new opportunities and expectations, but related mostly to the neighborhood, not to the zone 0. The neighborhood has been affected in this period by a gentrification process, which seems to generate another social conflict, since housing and rent prices are rising, forcing the Spanish population that managed to cope during the difficult periods of the extension project to once again leave the neighborhood in favor of tourism development. Furthermore, for the moment, this process seems to affect only the Spanish population, not the immigrants that settled in the neighborhood in the previous years, due to the fact that zone 0 is not yet included in the process.

4. Discussion and Conclusions

According to our results, in the study area, we can observe the negative effects that have been pointed out by different authors as a consequence of project planning that aims to improve the image and global positioning of the city without previous reflection on the social consequences. That is, the displacement and marginalization of the local population [13] and the confrontation between the interests of the community and the project's objectives [12] that generates an important social response [14] and leads to polarization and social fragmentation [10]. The dynamics of segregation and gentrification thus created lead to a greater fragmentation of the urban space. This paper constitutes an empirical contribution to the knowledge of the way in which these processes are produced in a specific space. In particular, it shows how not only the continuous action of the administration, but also its lack of action can lead to a situation of deterioration difficult to reverse, which once catalyzed the process of marginalization in the urban space. Although the Cabanyal neighborhood has been affected by other general processes, such as the economic crisis and the massive influx of immigrants, the specific impact of the project in the generation of this dynamic is evident through the observations into the different evolutionary processes between the area directly affected by the extension of the avenue and the surrounding areas.

The Spanish state has been affected by a massive influx of immigrants since the end of the 20th century, a tendency that continues into the current period. This phenomenon is relatively new in Spain if we compare it with other European countries, and, in this context, the country has had to adapt very quickly to these new trends, without having enough time to assimilate the new process that was characterizing it. This situation was observed with greater intensity in the large cities, which constituted poles of attraction for the immigrant population. Therefore, Valencia also followed these trends and received a large number of immigrants in a relatively short period of time. The migration dynamics, along with political decisions and the economic crisis, have had a strong impact on the territory and on the population, concerning coexistence and lifestyle. In addition, the economic crisis was one of the most important temporary nodes, which have determined on one hand changes of tendencies and on the other hand an increase in the existing trends.

The Cabanyal neighborhood is an example of the interaction of both factors, but also of the consequences of an urban policy focused on economic interests that paid little attention to social issues. In the period between 2004 and 2016 its number of immigrants has increased due not only to the migratory dynamics that characterized the entire city, but also to the situation in which it is after the paralysis of the extension project of Blasco Ibañez Avenue. However, the migratory dynamics did not have the same tendencies during the whole period, but it was characterized by different trajectories of evolution according to the temporality of the project.

In this context, the Cabanyal neighborhood lost part of its Spanish population especially through residential mobility, while it received a foreign population in return. If the loss in the Spanish population is continuous, the EU and non-EU population entries are identified by different guidelines in each period. In the period 2004–2007, the non-EU population was clearly the majority among the immigrant population, but in the period 2008–2009 the balance of the EU and non-EU population tends to be similar. The period 2010–2013, corresponding to the real estate, economic, and social crises, is the one that introduces the greatest changes, as it determines the reversal between the two categories of immigrants. After this interval, the EU immigrants become predominant, replacing, to a large extent, the non-EU immigrants.

The weight of the project in the generation of this dynamic is evident when we consider the different ways in which the area directly affected by the extension of the avenue evolved along with the surrounding areas. Thus, during our analysis we observed in zone 0 not only the greatest loss in Spanish population from the whole neighborhood or the greatest increase in the percentage of immigrants, but also a change in the social structure of the population in terms of education level, due to the area being populated by immigrants with a low level of education. Furthermore, this area is the most degraded in the neighborhood, owing to the expected extension of Blasco Ibañez Avenue, which made it a strategic place for change. That is why, for the moment, even though the regeneration process has started in the neighborhood, in this area the consequences of the project and the social problems caused can still be observed: degraded buildings or walled houses, abandoned places, poverty, litter, drug trafficking, etc.

In this context, the extension project of Blasco Ibañez Avenue has contributed to the increase in segregation, by encouraging the settlement of social groups with more obvious segregation dynamics. The main problem here is not, however, the settlement of a certain social group, but the fact that they live in very deteriorated housing conditions, without basic installations and utilities. They also have a low level of education and low-skilled and poorly paid jobs and this situation makes their social integration even more difficult. This process was not spontaneous, it was encouraged by local authorities, who, by their own efforts, allowed and contributed to the physical degradation of the neighborhood.

Cabanyal became, therefore, an attractive space for the immigrants coming from the European Union, especially for those from Eastern Europe with few economic resources. The non-EU immigrants, mostly from Latin America, with similar linguistic and cultural characteristics to the Spaniards, were replaced by the EU immigrants, admittedly closer from a geographical point of view, but with a different culture and lifestyle. Based on this settlement of people with different customs and traditions, who maintain few social relations with the local population, there is a tendency of increasing social segregation through the tracing of a perceptible boundary in the territory.

The dynamics of residential changes in the area during the recent years indicate that the processes of residential segregation have created a strong social inertia and resistance towards the urban revitalization policies implemented by the new municipal government. The case studied here illustrates how unwise public action can sharpen the tendency towards the formation of highly focused territorial inequalities in the urban areas, inequalities that are very difficult to reverse later, even in favorable circumstances characterized by economic recovery and the implementation of urban revitalization strategies. The main lesson on urban public policies that this case study provides us with is the importance of incorporating the analysis of social factors and community life in the neighborhoods in intervention projects as one of its most relevant aspects ahead of architectural aspects or the creation of an "urban scene". The challenge that the new managers of the city are facing is how to intervene and promote regeneration without causing additional problems in an area that, as we have seen, currently suffers from strong contrasts in sociodemographic dynamics.

Urban Sci. **2018**, *2*, 119

Thus, the current government's responsibility is quite demanding, as it has to resolve an enduring problem, but without sparking off another social conflict and movement. It has to facilitate the immigrants' social integration, by improving the quality of the buildings, but without transforming the neighborhood into a tourist one. It must, therefore, create a balance which ensures that the neighborhood's attraction and specific lifestyle is not lost. According to the interviews made with members of the neighborhood, this is now one of the greatest fears of the local population: that the neighborhood will lose the distinctive features that they wanted to preserve, due to cohabiting with people who lack a sense of inclusion.

Consequently, public intervention should not be limited to the physical recovery of the neighborhood but should also be proactive in its social and economic rehabilitation. For this purpose, it currently has a public land patrimony acquired during the process, that would allow implementing public housing policies that favor the mix and reconstruction of the social structure, avoiding the risk of tourism gentrification in the neighborhood, that already seems forecast. In order to ensure this result, the process is dependent on the active group of local collectives created by the citizens' initiative during the period of the conflict.

Author Contributions: Conceptualization: R.-D.I. and J.S.-C.; methodology: R.-D.I. and J.S.-C.; software: R.-D.I.; validation: R.-D.I. and J.S.-C.; formal analysis: R.-D.I.; investigation: R.-D.I. and J.S.-C.; resources: R.-D.I. and J.S.-C.; data curation: R.-D.I. and J.S.-C.; writing—original draft preparation: R.-D.I. and J.S.-C.; writing—review and editing: R.-D.I. and J.S.-C.; visualization: R.-D.I. and J.S.-C.; supervision: R.-D.I. and J.S.-C.; project administration: J.S.-C.; funding acquisition: J.S.-C.

Funding: This research was funded by Agencia Estatal de Investigación (AEI) and Fondo Europeo de Desarrollo Regional (FEDER) in the State Program for Research, Development and Innovation Oriented to the Challenges of Society, within the framework of the State Plan for Scientific and Technical Research and Innovation 2013–2016, call for 2016, within the framework of the project "Social Sustainability, Global Connectivity and creative economy as development strategies in the metropolitan area of Valencia" (CSO2016-74888-C4-1-R).

Acknowledgments: We would like to thank the Statistical Office of Valencia City for providing the microdata used in this study.

Conflicts of Interest: The authors declare no conflict of interest. The funders had no role in the design of the study; in the collection, analyses, or interpretation of data; in the writing of the manuscript; or in the decision to publish the results.

References

1. Kwan, M.-P.; Schwanen, T. Geographies of Mobility. *Ann. Am. Assoc. Geogr.* **2016**, *106*, 243–256. [CrossRef]
2. Coulton, C.; Theodos, B.; Turner, M.A. Residential Mobility and Neighborhood Change: Real Neighborhoods Under the Microscope. *Cityscape* **2012**, *14*, 55–89.
3. Hasan, S.; Schneider, C.M.; Ukkusuri, S.V.; González, M.C. Spatiotemporal Patterns of Urban Human Mobility. *J. Stat. Phys.* **2013**, *151*, 304–318. [CrossRef]
4. Kang, C.; Gao, S.; Lin, X.; Xiao, Y.; Yuan, Y.; Liu, Y.; Ma, X. Analyzing and geo-visualizing individual human mobility patterns using mobile call records. In Proceedings of the 2010 18th International Conference on Geoinformatics, Beijing, China, 18–20 June 2010; pp. 1–7.
5. Eluru, N.; Sener, I.; Bhat, C.; Pendyala, R.; Axhausen, K. Understanding Residential Mobility. *Transp. Res. Rec. J. Transp. Res. Board* **2009**, *2133*, 64–74. [CrossRef]
6. United Nations Millennium Development Goals. Available online: http://www.un.org/millenniumgoals/ (accessed on 6 February 2017).
7. Rojo-Mendoza, F. La gentrificación en los estudios urbanos: Una exploración sobre la producción académica de las ciudades. *Cadernos Metrópole* **2016**, *18*, 697–719. [CrossRef]
8. van Ham, M.; Tammaru, T. New perspectives on ethnic segregation over time and space. A domains approach. *Urban Geogr.* **2016**, *37*, 953–962. [CrossRef]
9. Harvey, D. From Managerialism to Entrepreneurialism: The Transformation in Urban Governance in Late Capitalism. *Geogr. Ann. Ser. B Hum. Geogr.* **1989**, *71*, 3–17. [CrossRef]
10. Swyngedouw, E.; Moulaert, F.; Rodriguez, A. Neoliberal Urbanization in Europe: Large–Scale Urban Development Projects and the New Urban Policy. *Antipode* **2002**, *34*, 542–577. [CrossRef]

11. Díaz Orueta, F.; Fainstein, S.S. The New Mega-Projects: Genesis and Impacts. *Int. J. Urban Reg. Res.* **2008**, *32*, 759–767. [CrossRef]

12. Trop, T. Social Impact Assessment of Rebuilding an Urban Neighborhood: A Case Study of a Demolition and Reconstruction Project in Petah Tikva, Israel. *Sustainability* **2017**, *9*, 1076. [CrossRef]

13. Carrero, R.; Malvárez, G.; Navas, F.; Tejada, M. Negative impacts of abandoned urbanisation projects in the Spanish coast and its regulation in the Law. *J. Coast. Res.* **2009**, *5*, 1120–1124.

14. Díaz Orueta, F. Madrid: Urban regeneration projects and social mobilization. *Cities* **2007**, *24*, 183–193. [CrossRef]

15. Hall, C.M. Urban Entrepreneurship, Corporate Interests and Sports Mega-Events: The Thin Policies of Competitiveness within the Hard Outcomes of Neoliberalism. *Sociol. Rev.* **2006**, *54*, 59–70. [CrossRef]

16. Pillay, U.; Bass, O. Mega-events as a Response to Poverty Reduction: The 2010 FIFA World Cup and its Urban Development Implications. *Urban Forum* **2008**, *19*, 329. [CrossRef]

17. Romero, J.; Melo, C.; Brandis, D. The neoliberal approach to Valencia and Madrid. In *Cities in Crisis. Socio-Spatial Impacts of the Economic Crisis in Southern European Cities*; Knieling, J., Othengrafen, F., Eds.; Routledge: London, UK, 2016; pp. 73–93, ISBN 9781138850026.

18. Observatorio Metropolitano. *Paisajes Devastados. Después del ciclo Inmobiliario: Impactos Regionales y Urbanos de la Crisis*; Traficantes de Sueños: Madrid, Spain, 2013; ISBN 9788496453807.

19. Torres-Pérez, F. *Nous Veïns a la Ciutat: Els Immigrants a València i Russafa*; Publicacions de la Universitat de València: València, Spain, 2007; ISBN 978-84-370-6709-4.

20. Pérez, F.T.; Montesinos, M.E.G. *Crisis, Inmigración y Sociedad*; Talasa: Madrid, Spain, 2015; ISBN 978-84-96266-46-9.

21. Cucó-Giner, J. *Metamorfosis Urbanas: Ciudades Españolas en la Dinámica Global*; Icaria, Institut Català d'Antropologia: Barcelona, Spain, 2013; ISBN 978-84-9888-478-4.

22. Salom-Carrasco, J.; Pitarch-Garrido, M.-D. Análisis del impacto en el turismo de la estrategia de desarrollo urbano basada en megaproyectos. El caso de la ciudad de Valencia. *Cuadernos de Turismo* **2017**, 573–598. [CrossRef]

23. Salom Carrasco, J.; Pitarch Garrido, M.D.; Albertos Puebla, J.M. Desired and undesired effects of the tourism development policy based on megaprojects: The case of Valencia (Spain). In Proceedings of the International Conference Building Urban Tourism through Place Making and Urban Regeneration in Central and Eastern European Countries, Timişoara, Romania, 19–20 May 2017.

24. Cucó-Giner, J. *La Ciudad Pervertida: Una Mirada Sobre la Valencia Global*; Anthropos Editorial: Barcelona, Spain, 2013; ISBN 978-84-15260-74-5.

25. Del Romero-Renau, L.; Trudelle, C. Mega Events and Urban Conflicts in Valencia, Spain: Contesting the New Urban Modernity. *Urban Stud. Res.* **2011**, *2011*. [CrossRef]

26. Salvem el Cabanyal-Canyamelar-Cap de França | El Cabanyal es el Barrio Marinero de Valencia, España, Amenazado Desde el 24 de Julio de 1998 por un Proyecto de Prolongación de la Avenida Blasco Ibáñez que Partirá el Barrio en dos y que Supone la Destrucción de 1651 Viviendas. Available online: http://www.cabanyal.com/nou/?lang=en (accessed on 18 September 2017).

27. Plataforma Salvem el Cabanyal, El PEPRI, un Plan de Reforma Interior sin Protección. Available online: http://www.cabanyal.com/nou/el-pepri-un-pla-de-reforma-interior-sense-proteccio/?lang=es (accessed on 1 November 2018).

28. Ajuntament de Valencia. *Estrategia de Desarrollo Urbano Sostenible e Integrado del Barrio Cabanyal-Canyamelar-Cap de França*; Ajuntament de Valencia: Valencia, Spain, 2015; 217p.

29. Portada Fomento | Ministerio de Fomento. Available online: https://www.fomento.es/ (accessed on 19 January 2018).

30. Oficina de Estadística. Ayuntamiento de Valencia. Available online: http://www.valencia.es/ayuntamiento/catalogo.nsf/CatalogoUnTitulo?readForm&lang=1&serie=60&titulo=%C1reas%20vulnerables%20en%20la%20ciudad%20de%20Valencia%202016&bdOrigen=ayuntamiento/estadistica.nsf&idApoyo=58FB3C7A3D56E414C1257DD40057EB6C (accessed on 6 November 2017).

31. Salom, J.; Fajardo, F. Cambios recientes en la estructura territorial sociodemográfica del área metropolitana de Valencia (2001–2011). *Boletín de la Asociación de Geógrafos Españoles* **2017**. [CrossRef]

32. Feria-Toribio, J.M. Un ensayo metodológico de definición de las áreas metropolitanas en España a partir de la variable residencia-trabajo. *Investigaciones Geográficas* **2008**, *46*, 49–68. [CrossRef]

33. Instituto Nacional de Estadistica. (Spanish Statistical Office). Available online: http://www.ine.es/ (accessed on 26 September 2017).
34. Portal Transparencia y Datos Abiertos Valencia. Available online: http://gobiernoabierto.valencia.es/es/ (accessed on 22 September 2017).
35. Ilisei, R.-D. Mobility and segregation in Valencia City. Case study: Cabanyal neighborhood. *Geogr. Timisiensis* **2016**, *25*. Available online: https://geografie.uvt.ro/wp-content/uploads/2018/05/ilisei-format.pdf (accessed on 22 September 2017).

urban science

MDPI

Article

Foreclosures and Evictions in Las Palmas de Gran Canaria during the Economic Crisis and Post-Crisis Period in Spain

Juan M. Parreño-Castellano [1,*], Josefina Domínguez-Mujica [1], Maite Armengol-Martín [1], Tanausú Pérez García [2] and Jordi Boldú Hernández [2]

[1]   Department of Geography, University of Las Palmas de Gran Canaria, 35003 Las Palmas de Gran Canaria, Spain; josefina.dominguezmujica@ulpgc.es (J.D.-M.); matilde.armengol@ulpgc.es (M.A.-M.)
[2]   G.I. Sociedades y Espacios Atlánticos, University of Las Palmas de Gran Canaria, 35003 Las Palmas de Gran Canaria, Spain; tanausupg@gmail.com (T.P.G.); jordi.boldu@geografos.org (J.B.H.)
*   Correspondence: juan.parreno@ulpgc.es; Tel.: +34-928-452-776

Received: 23 October 2018; Accepted: 18 November 2018; Published: 22 November 2018

Abstract: At the beginning of the economic crisis in 2008, the number of foreclosures and evictions increased dramatically in Spain. The severe economic situation and the lack of mitigation measures by public institutions seemed to be the main causes. However, the start of a period of economic recovery since 2014 has meant that the number of the evictions continues to increase. In this article, we analyze in detail this phenomenon in the city of Las Palmas de Gran Canaria. Based on the disaggregated judicial data on the records of ejections and transfer of possession by foreclosures and evictions for the period 2009–2017, we carry out a study according to judicial procedures and proceedings and nature of the parties affected from a time-based and spatial perspective. This information allows us to discern that the causes that have led to the loss of housing are more varied than expected; that these circumstances have affected both societies and individuals, diverging on the period of incidence; and that the loss of housing has a different spatial impact in each stage. We conclude that both dispossession and loss of use are two structural occurrences coherent with the capitalist model of secondary accumulation developed in the world in the last 20 years. In the case of Spain, we have recognized these phases and modes of accumulation beyond the incidence of the crisis, revealing the structural character of the phenomenon analyzed.

Keywords: foreclosure; eviction; economic crisis; post-crisis; housing vulnerability; Spanish city; housing bubble; financialization; holiday home; housing market

1. Introduction

Since the middle of the 1980s, Spain's economic policy backed property construction as the main instrument for generating wealth and economic growth. This enabled its productive system to consolidate and allow property investment to become the main source for the creation of surpluses for economic agents and savings for the population [1]. Since the end of the nineties, bank credits boosted this circuit, facilitating financing for the purchase of homes for a large part of the population. For this purpose, the mechanism used was the securitization of loans on secondary markets, as in most developed countries [2], which led to a spectacular increase in the prices of the homes and to a high level of private indebtedness.

When the global crisis began in 2008, with the consequential collapse of the credit markets and the increase in asset interest rates, property demand fell speedily, triggering difficulties for many property transactions underway for the sale of property and causing residential investments to fall sharply. This new scenario struck a hard blow to the stability of many companies and caused a fast increase in unemployment rates, which, in turn, reduced internal consumption. In this context, difficulties for the payment of mortgages and rentals by companies and individuals became widespread, with legal processes for dispossession and loss of use of properties increasing through both judicial and extrajudicial means.

The severity of the situation is explained by the crisis, but also by the fact that no public policy was put in place to alleviate the social impacts of this situation, with measures aimed at transferring rentals or the flexibilization of payment terms and conditions [3]. On the other hand, public policies since 2011 focused its actions to reactivate the economy on an increase in export competitiveness, through labor devaluation and the re-floating of the banks that accumulated non-performing or toxic assets, in other words mortgage loans that the borrowers had stopped paying. In this regard, the first measures financed through the Orderly Bank Restructuring Fund had already been adopted by 2010 and, two years later, this policy continued with the nationalization of Bankia and Catalunya Bank and with the creation of the Bank Restructuring Assets Management Company (Spanish acronym: SAREB).

The difficulties involved in selling toxic assets in a housing market with devalued prices meant that, since 2013, a policy was implemented to attract foreign purchasers, with the approval of the law entitled "Act for the support of entrepreneurs and their internationalization" (Law 14 dated 27 September 2013). With this Act, international investment companies obtained tax breaks and bureaucratic barriers were simplified so that they could purchase property in Spain. In the case of private individuals not resident in Spain, they were offered the possibility of obtaining a visa and a residence permit for house purchases for amounts in excess of €500,000. As a consequence of all of the above, some private individuals and, above all, investment funds (the so-called vulture funds) began to acquire part of the assets held by the SAREB and the rest of the financial institutions at highly advantageous prices, through such instruments as Property Investment Companies (FII or SII), Servicers and REITs (in Spain, SOCIMIs) [4].

Part of the homes acquired by the international investment funds and non-resident individuals have since been sold off at higher prices as and when the market has begun to be revalued, but the vast majority of these properties have been put to a secondary use or to rental, as there is growing international demand to acquire or lease these properties, at the same time as holiday homes is becoming a consolidating sector. All this has meant that the prices, which started at low levels as a result of the crisis, have begun to increase in coastal areas and in the central areas of large cities, especially since 2015. This price growth has transferred to the rest of the traditional rental market located in these areas, thanks to the approval of Law 4/2013 on measures for the flexibilization and encouragement of the home rental market, which enabled owners to increase the rental received or use their properties as holiday homes in a much simpler way. In consequence, we have seen over the last few years what is beginning to be considered a bubble in the rental prices of certain areas offering demand and centrality conditions in this new market.

In this context concisely summarized above, dispossessions and losses of use are elements of great economic and social relevance. Official statistics enable us to know quite accurately the magnitude of the mortgage foreclosures carried out in Spain thanks to the publication of aggregated data by the General Council of the Judiciary. As can be seen in Figure 1, mortgage foreclosures begun and entered on the Property Registries increased exponentially between 2008 and 2010, growing from total figures of less than 20,000 foreclosures begun in the first year mentioned to values close to 100,000 in the second. The number of new annual entries recorded stabilizes around this value, with a slight upturn in 2012 with the start of the second phase of the crisis in Spain or the debt crisis. Since then, and especially since 2015, registry entries have been gradually declining, but the number of foreclosures noted still in 2017 was higher than that recorded before the start of the economic crisis.

In the case of evictions due to non-payment of rental, data are scanter. The series published by the Spanish Statistical Office (INE) do not go back beyond 2005. In the period from 2009–2016, in urban leases of main homes due to non-payment of rental or deposits, the trend in the judicial rulings with a positive pronouncement (whether total or partial) in favour of the plaintiff reflects a peak in 2010, the highest figure in the series, before then beginning a marked decline until 2014. The information about recent years begins to reflect an upturn in the number of judgements for Spain as a whole (Figure 2).

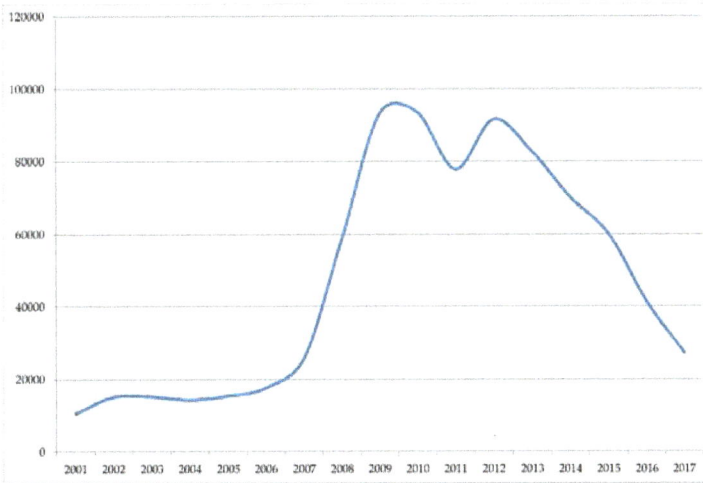

Figure 1. Number of the foreclosures initiated on homes per year in Spain. Data: General Council of the Judiciary. Own production.

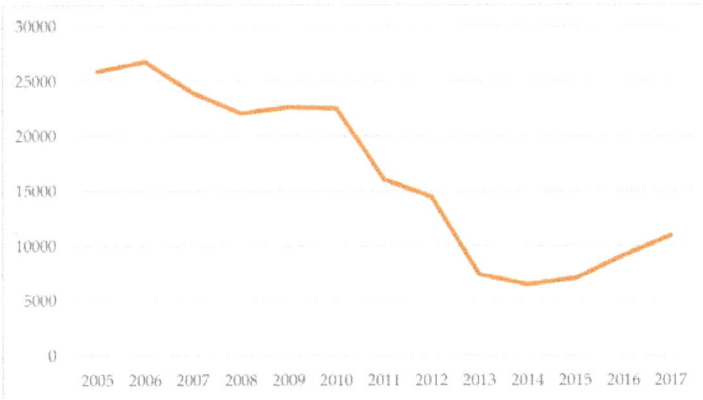

Figure 2. Number of evictions due to non-payment of rental or deposits per year in Spain. Data: General Council of the Judiciary and INE. Own production.

The most important thing here is to reveal to what extent this sequence of events reflects the fact that the loss of a home is a cyclical or circumstantial element or a structural element of Spain's new economic model. In order to approach this response, we believe it is necessary to understand the phenomenon from the perspective of its incidence on an infra-municipal scale, a dimension that may indicate, from a geographical perspective, who are affected by these dispossession and loss of use processes. For this purpose, the goal of this article focuses on exploring the territorial impact and trend of mortgage foreclosures and evictions in the urban space of Las Palmas de Gran Canaria from 2009 to 2017. We are starting from the premise that this phenomenon is tightly linked to the economic crisis and to the political measures adopted, as highlighted in the pre-existing literature, but we believe that the analysis of this case will allow us to demonstrate that the end of the crisis has not meant that the loss of homes has a lower incidence for certain social groups. The way in which the crisis has been handled and the characteristics of the post-crisis period have benefited some population segments more than others, and this can also be seen in the right to accommodation.

The study of Las Palmas de Gran Canaria is of interest because it implies focusing the analysis on an island space that is highly attractive for international property demand. The city, one of the two capitals in the Canary Island region, had a registered population of 377,650 inhabitants in 2017, making it the most populous city in the Islands. Located in a European ultra-peripheral region, its economy is clearly specialized in services, many of them related to tourism, and port activities. It was particularly impacted by the economic crisis, to the extent that the unemployment rate rose from 15.8% in 2007 to 31.2% in 2013 according to the estimates of the Active Population Survey (EPA), therefore the lack of solvency of part of the population led to non-payment of housing-related debt due to the economic recession. The recovery that seems to be taking place since 2015 has not allowed the levels of employment to come close to those that existed prior to the crisis, nor has the capacity for expense on housing increased among the population at the same pace as rentals. The difficulties to satisfy the legitimate right to housing are, nowadays, a reality for a large part of the city's population, which has suffered a process of impoverishment over the last decade.

2. Current Status of the Issue

The social impact since 2008 seen in the accelerated increase in mortgage foreclosures and evictions has led to the emergence of considerable studies from disciplines such as Geography, Economics or Sociology. Some schools of thought interpreting this phenomenon explain it from the perspective of the evolution of the capitalist system. Against this background, Critical Urban Theory considers late capitalism or post-Fordist capitalism to have its bases in the "New Urban Enclosures" and conceives the loss of housing as one of its clearest expressions, as a consequence of the reduction in the guarantees in accessing social reproduction mechanisms [5–8].

In a similar logic, another interpretative approach relates the development of the secondary accumulation system with dispossession [9,10], which is considered in and of itself as a tool inherent to the economic system to facilitate the accumulation of earnings for certain social groups and economic agents [11].

Other complementary works focus, however, on the dynamic of the mechanisms in the late capitalist productive system as a factor explaining dispossession. Economic financialization (or the conversion of land and housing into financial assets) and the securitization of credits are considered to have been the main tools that have facilitated dispossession [12–14], insofar as they imply continuous revaluation and this, in turn, implies the expulsion of residents.

In this line, in American literature on foreclosures, these link with the flexibilization of mortgage markets or high risk (subprime) mortgages [15,16]. This approach has meant that several studies have related the geography of evictions to other socio-spatial variables [17], since some social groups were the ones who benefited from flexibilization in the terms and conditions for granting mortgage loans. In the specific case of island geographic contexts with a strong implantation of tourism, as is the case of the Balearic Islands, the touristification of the urban space has been conceived as a specific factor for the dispossession of homes [18].

The preceding lines of argument are not mutually exclusive, therefore our analysis of the dispossession process in Las Palmas de Gran Canaria is carried out from an integrating perspective.

Geographical research into dispossession in Spain does not come from a long tradition. The first studies made use of foreclosure data, provided by the General Council of the Judiciary, from the 431 judicial districts existing in Spain [19–22]. These data make it possible to observe the process in the whole of Spain but on a judicial district scale, meaning that they do not distinguish houses from other types of real estate assets nor do they allow researchers to analyze evictions or to conduct urban studies. Similar studies were performed in subsequent years for Spain as a whole [23] or in particular for the Canary Islands [24].

Complementary to this, other studies have been carried out based on the disaggregated analysis of judicial records of foreclosures and evictions from specific judicial districts. This is the case of the studies conducted on the judicial districts of Palma in Majorca [18,25], Maó in Menorca [26] and Las Palmas de Gran Canaria [27]. The advantage of such a micro-scale approach is that it makes urban geographical analysis easier, given that the address is provided for each of the properties affected by dispossession or eviction and a larger number of variables can be obtained for analysis.

A different line of research draws on the systematic examination of housing advertisements of real estate agencies that are linked to banks. It is estimated that around 30% of these properties derive from dispossession processes (not necessarily judicial ones). This fact has given rise to a series of geographical studies on the cities of Lleida [28], Tarragona, Terrassa and Salt [29–31], Alicante, Murcia and Zaragoza [32]; Madrid [33] as well as the total of housing properties owned by SAREB in all Spanish municipalities [34]. With a similar approach, some insights offered from other fields are also worth mentioning, as is the case of Raya [35], whose research focuses on the autonomous communities of Madrid and Valencia. The drawback of these papers is that they do not allow the reader to identify the year of each foreclosure; they do, however, provide information on the characteristics of the property and on the bank that owns it.

Finally, the studies of Gutiérrez and Vives-Miró [36,37] make use of the registry of empty houses in the hands of financial entities created by the Catalonian Regional Government in 2016. The aim of this initiative was the creation of a special tax to be applied on these assets. This source makes it possible to find out the total number of houses accumulated by banks through foreclosures in Catalonia, providing information on the census area each property is located in and the entity that owns it.

The work we have carried out, and which we defend in this article, follows the path of those already mentioned who use judicial sources to analyze the geographical dimension of dispossession and loss of use. Nonetheless, it contains certain peculiarities that are commented on in the section on materials and methods and that enable us to reach relevant results.

3. Materials and Methods

The source of the information on which this study is based is the register of actions carried out by the Common Service of Notifications and Liens of the Judicial District for Las Palmas de Gran Canaria, comprising the municipalities of Las Palmas de Gran Canaria, Santa Brígida and Vega de San Mateo.

Spanish judicial districts of a larger size in demographic terms have what are known as Common Services, a court service unit that was set up based on Fundamental Law 19 dated 23 December 2003, and was subsequently developed by Regulation 2/2010. This Regulation specifies that Common Services perform the notification and enforcement acts with which they are charged by the Courts, such as evictions, liens and removal of deposit holders. Since they are also charged with registration and distribution functions, at the same time, they have to use an application that enables them to process documents electronically.

In the case of the Canary Islands, there are only two Common Services of Notifications and Liens, namely those for the judicial districts of Las Palmas de Gran Canaria and Santa Cruz de Tenerife. They both use the same type of register, within the framework of the computerized procedural management system used by the Administration of Justice in the Canary Islands, known as Atlante, similar to that in place in other autonomous regions.

The information from these registers is generally published by the High Courts of Justice in the various regions and by the General Council of the Judiciary. The original extensive information is only available for the members of the courts themselves or the Common Services. In our case, we were granted authorization to consult it.

The fields contained in the register for each of the notes include the note number, the party involved, type of action, courts ordering the action, address, legal proceedings, date of registration, date of action, and current status. This information refers to both homes and other premises.

In the case of the different types of actions taken, the ones we considered were evictions and memoranda for taking possession. Eviction is the legal act whereby the lessee or owner of the property is removed, at the same time as, in the latter case, the owner loses his or her property rights in favour of the new acquirer by order of the judicial authority. Memoranda for taking possession are actions whereby an owner loses the ownership of a property in favour of a new acquirer by judicial order, without the need for eviction. Liens, as they do not entail the loss of ownership in and of themselves nor any eviction, were not taken into account.

The consultation of the register of the Common Service of Notifications and Liens for the judicial district of Las Palmas de Gran Canaria has enabled us to create a database adapted to our purposes, which only considers those records with a positive status, that is to say those in which the processes for eviction or taking of possession were culminated. Prior to processing, we eliminated 94 records since we detected situations of duplication. The information was homogenized and the postal addresses confirmed. The cartographic representation of the losses of ownership and use were elaborated using the postal addresses and generating kernel density maps.

The kernel density analysis calculates the territorial density of a phenomenon (point or linear) in a raster pattern using parameters of distance and neighborhood by a quadratic function. The calculation must take in account the bandwidth or distance, the size of the pixel and the possible existence of attributes for each entity. The result for each pixel is the sum of the values obtained with the different calculations for each raster unit. In our analysis, we used this method as a simplified cartographic modelling tool, generating maps with exit cells of 10 m and calculation radii of 200 m (bandwidth).

4. Results

Between 2009 and 2017, a total of 4138 case files aimed at the forcible deprivation of use and ownership were executed in the judicial district for Las Palmas de Gran Canaria, i.e., an average of 460 case files per year. Taking the mean registered population in the period as a reference, we obtained a proportion of a little over one case file (1.2) per thousand inhabitants. This figure does not apparently seem very high, however we must remember that deprivation of use and dispossession by judicial order must be considered as the tip of the iceberg of this phenomenon, since the parties involved generally agree to early sales, voluntary abandonment of the property or out-of-court settlements in order to resolve the conflict in a less costly way, and, in all cases, to avoid a judicialized solution to the problem.

In our study of the actions taken in Las Palmas de Gran Canaria, we have been interested in exploring the procedures involved, the types of action used, the nature of the parties involved and the intra-urban location of the properties affected. We will discuss the study of these variables from a time-based analysis, as this will enable us to provide useful comments in order to understand better the reality of deprivation of use and dispossession. We shall offer our results on the basis of these criteria, but first we will present the evolution over time of dispossession and loss of use processes as a whole.

4.1. Evolution over Time

As reflected in Figure 3, the crisis in Las Palmas de Gran Canaria gave rise to an increase in judicial actions related to dispossession and evictions, as shown by the fact that the number of positive actions in 2009 (239) rose to 620 in 2011. The growth curve in these three years can be explained by two fundamental reasons: The first is that judicial proceedings, particularly in dispossession actions, take place over a long period of time. Judicial intervention is not immediate, and the procedural protocols established have to be followed, thus delaying the expression of the crisis in the actions analyzed until about two years after the start of legal proceedings. The second reason is that, with the start of the crisis, the Spanish government adopted palliative measures attempted to maintain a higher level of solvency among the population, despite the increase in unemployment. The so-called "Plan E" which tried to inject liquidity through an ambitious and costly infrastructure plan controlled by local governments is a paradigmatic example. The measures remained in force until the end of 2010 in some cases, which delayed non-payments.

From 2011 and until 2013, the figures remain very high but with a slight downward trend. These are years in which the loss of homes takes on great media significance. This stage corresponds with the second phase of the economic crisis in Spain, which has become known as the "debt crisis," in which the high level of public indebtedness generated in the preceding years provoked a change in the State's economic policy, leading to the start of wage devaluations, budgetary austerity, and deficit control in the context of the adjustment measures adopted by the European Commission, the European Central Bank and the International Monetary Fund.

Starting from 2013, the figures for legal proceedings tend to stabilize at above 400, with this figure improving slightly in 2017, which might be seen as a delayed symptom of the mild economic recovery begun in Spain in 2015. Nonetheless, just as a clear relationship can be appreciated between the number of judicial proceedings and the crisis, the figures did not demonstrate with the same forcefulness as might be expected the association between the number of legal actions taken and the economic recovery.

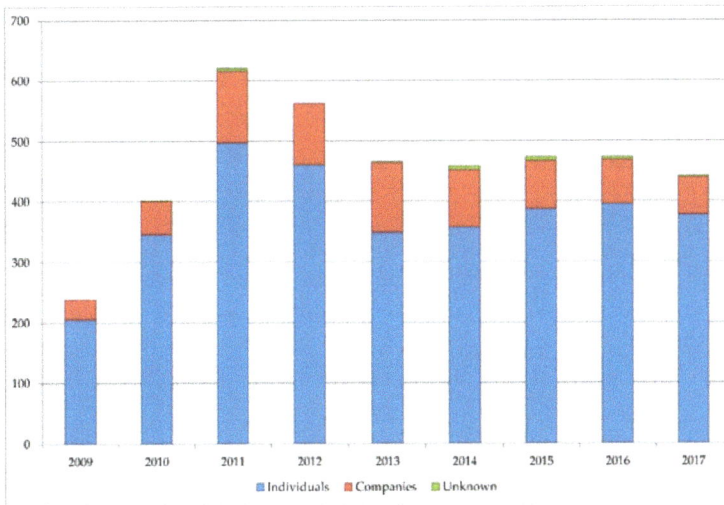

Figure 3. Number of Positive Judicial Actions of the Common Service of Las Palmas de Gran Canaria by category of the party involved and year. Data: Common Service of Notifications and Liens of the Judicial District for Las Palmas de Gran Canaria. Own production.

4.2. Judicial Procedures

From the perspective of the procedures applied, for the purposes of an overview, we have grouped together, on the one hand, those representing dispossession, in the majority foreclosures of title, and, on the other hand, those that only represent deprivation of use. The most abundant actions between 2009 and 2017 were those implying loss of ownership (59.9% of positive enforcement actions). Those intended for deprivation of use represented, therefore, 40.1%. The most frequent among the first group were enforcement of judicial title and mortgage foreclosures, which only represent 25% of all case files. We also found other grounds for dispossession that gave rise to different civil, criminal, insolvency and arbitration proceedings. Therefore, loss of ownership cannot only be interpreted as the result of the impossibility to pay a mortgage loan, but also as the consequence of general economic insolvency. We must also not forget that dispossession is sometimes related to family break-ups, conflicts in the acceptances of inheritances, criminal actions, etc.

Deprivation of use is instrumented in most cases through oral trials and, fundamentally, by appealing to article 250.1.1 of the Civil Procedure Act (Law 1 dated 7 January 2000), as amended by Law 19 dated 23 November 2009, on measures for encouraging and speeding up the process for rental and energy efficiency of buildings. Article 2.8 of this Act specifies that oral hearings must be used for those cases "dealing with claims for amounts relating to non-payment of rental and sums owed and, similarly, those based on the non-payment of rental or sums owed by the lessee, or on the expiry of the term established contractually or by statute, and intended for the recovery of the possession of property by the owner, usufructuary or any other person entitled to own a rural or urban property granted under a lease, whether ordinary or financial, or under a crop sharing agreement."

Nonetheless, in addition to this more generalized widespread situation, namely the use of oral hearings for non-payment of rental, we also find proceedings for unregistered assignments (250.1.2); summary protection for the possession of real estate (250.1.4); claims by holders of in rem rights (250.1.7) and for petty amounts (250.2). These claims for unregistered occupation, summary protection for possession or to re-establish in rem rights are usually aimed at recovering properties that have been occupied without any prior contractual relationship. In fact, most of these occupancies arise after a contract, therefore many of these situations are judged through article 250.1.1 [38].

We are of the opinion that it is of great interest to show the time sequence of the positive proceedings for loss of property and of use in different ways in order to understand better the phenomenon under study. As can be observed in Figure 4, the case files for deprivation of use and ownership grow in parallel and intensely in the early years of the crisis (2009–2011). However, after 2011, there is a distinct behaviour over time between the different types of proceedings. The evictions (deprivation of use) maintain stable data in the next three years before showing, after 2014, with an alleged "post-crisis" situation, a constant increase in their number to the point where there are more positive proceedings for loss of use in the last two years than for loss of ownership. On the other hand, dispossession proceedings show a descending curve from 2011 until 2013, before stabilizing and once more recording a major decline in the last two years, between 2016 and 2017. During this last period, the number of properties affected is lower than that recorded in 2009.

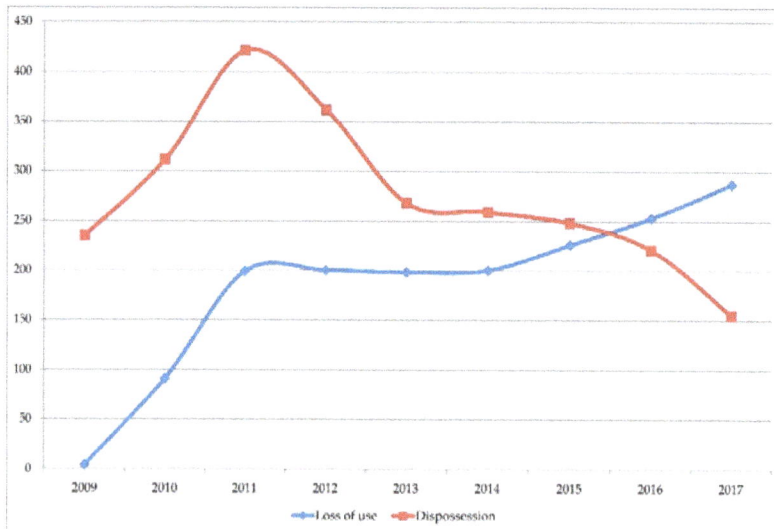

Figure 4. Number of Positive Judicial Actions of the Common Service of Las Palmas de Gran Canaria by type of procedure and year. Data: Common Service of Notifications and Liens of the Judicial District for Las Palmas de Gran Canaria. Own production.

With respect to the loss of ownership, it can be inferred that this differential evolution is related to the early stage of the inability to pay caused for many households and companies by the economic crisis. In the second stage, after 2011, the smaller number of actions correlates with the gradual reduction in private indebtedness, due above all to the greater difficulty in accessing third-party finance for the purchase of property, due to the hardening of the mortgage conditions imposed by credit institutions. Therefore, the evolution in dispossessions reflects the peculiar sequence of the economic crisis and the policies applied as a consequence of the same in Las Palmas de Gran Canaria.

On the other hand, the evolution in the deprivation of use proceedings is an indicator of the vulnerability of the population with regard to accommodation in Las Palmas de Gran Canaria, during both the crisis and post-crisis periods. In this sense, it must be understood that, since 2011, a series of interrelated events have taken place that explain the situation and also explain why the economic improvement in recent years has not been reflected in a reduction in the number of evictions. In this sense, we can cite such factors as: (a) The increase in demand for rental properties, as a result of the toughening of the conditions for accessing bank loans for home purchases and the insecurity of potential buyers following their experience during the years of the crisis; (b) the employment market has become more and more precarious with the successive wage devaluations and the worsening of employment conditions, within the framework of the strategy to increase competitiveness through the devaluation of the labor factor; (c) non-resident individuals and foreign investment funds have begun to control a growing part of the market for rental properties, facilitated by the liberalization measures intended to clean up the banks' toxic assets; (d) holiday homes have grown spectacularly in Las Palmas de Gran Canaria without any effective regulation having been sanctioned in the Canary Islands; and (e) as a result of the approval of Law 4/2013 on Measures for the flexibilization and encouragement of the home rental market, lessors now have conditions enabling them to increase rents or terminate contracts on advantageous conditions. In short, this indicates the persistence of economic weakness in a segment of the population even at times of supposed recovery, and expresses the way in which an attempt has been made to overcome the crisis by means of the exclusion of a large part of the population through the lack of compensating public policies.

4.3. Judicial Proceedings

From the standpoint of the type of legal practice applied, it must be remembered that the enforcement of title is not synonymous with eviction proceedings. This can also be extrapolated to oral hearing proceedings, albeit exceptionally (a little less than 2% in our case). If we analyze the practices applied and group them into the categories of memoranda for taking possession and evictions, it can be seen that the number of evictions predominated over the recovery of possession in a proportion of three out of every four actions and, in the specific case of enforcement proceedings (enforcement of title, mortgage foreclosure, etc.), 62.8% implied evictions. In other words, abandonment, free handover or making the property available to the claimant has occurred in a smaller number of cases. The fact that eviction is the most common judicial action adopted is an indicator of the severity and drama of the situation that people have been living through in the last decade in the city of Las Palmas de Gran Canaria.

The evolution over time of evictions and recovery of possession follows approximately the same sequence as mentioned above with respect to the actions as a whole (Figure 5), with the only difference that evictions have been increasing since 2013 (not the case of memoranda for taking possession), and this is due, to a large extent, to the increase in evictions for non-payment in recent years. It is therefore paradoxical that, in the economic recovery stage, the number of evictions is coming closer and closer to the figures shown in the hardest years of the crisis.

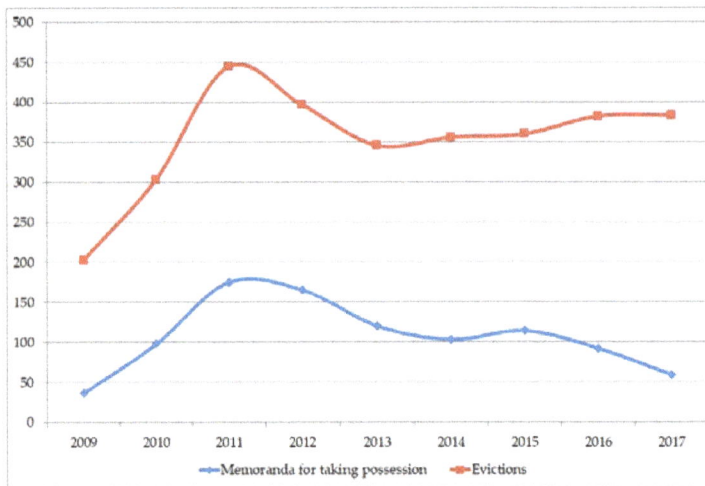

Figure 5. Number of Proceedings of the Common Service of Las Palmas de Gran Canaria per year. Data: Common Service of Notifications and Liens of the Judicial District for Las Palmas de Gran Canaria. Own production.

4.4. Nature of the Parties Affected

The registers for the actions carried out in the judicial district for Las Palmas de Gran Canaria has enabled us to identify whether the party affected by dispossession or eviction proceedings is a company or a private individual. As can be seen in Figure 3, most of the actions affect natural persons. If we take into account the impact over the period analyzed, it is possible to observe in this sequence that the case files for companies peak between 2011 and 2014, in other words during the debt crisis period. The figures subsequently decline gradually, showing a clear trend in the economic recovery and a lower degree of vulnerability in the post-crisis period. However, among natural persons, always more affected, the trend for legal action to diminish with the economic recovery is less clear.

This disparity in the impact and in the time sequence of the data available informs us of a single phenomenon, the loss of ownership and use of property, but two different scenarios, each one with distinct causes. In the first case, the one that occurred during the crisis period, the economic difficulties brought about by the recession drove both legal and natural persons into situations of eviction. In the second scenario, it is the way in which the country has emerged from the crisis that justifies the divergences in the impact on companies and on private individuals.

4.5. Urban Location of the Proceedings

The territorial distribution of the legal actions adopted are generally concentrated in the city's central spaces, those included within the surroundings of the port area and Las Canteras beach (La Isleta, Puerto, Santa Catalina and Guanarteme neighborhoods) to the north of the city and the quarters of Triana, Arenales and Lugo, close to the foundational core of Las Palmas de Gran Canaria. These two areas constitute urban centers as they concentrate the largest part of the city's private service activities, public administrative functions, regulated tourism offerings and holiday homes, as well as being the sectors with the best connectivity to the rest of the urban space. Nonetheless, as can be seen in Figure 6, the incidence of dispossession and rental-related evictions overflowed these spaces and also affected intensely the urban periphery.

However, we can appreciate an inverse territorial tendency in the distribution of dispossessions and evictions. In the first case, the presence in the city's central spaces and the sprawl in the urban periphery is higher until 2013. On the contrary, the evictions have a greater territorial presence in recent years in the periphery and, especially in the urban centre, linked to the acquisition of holiday homes.

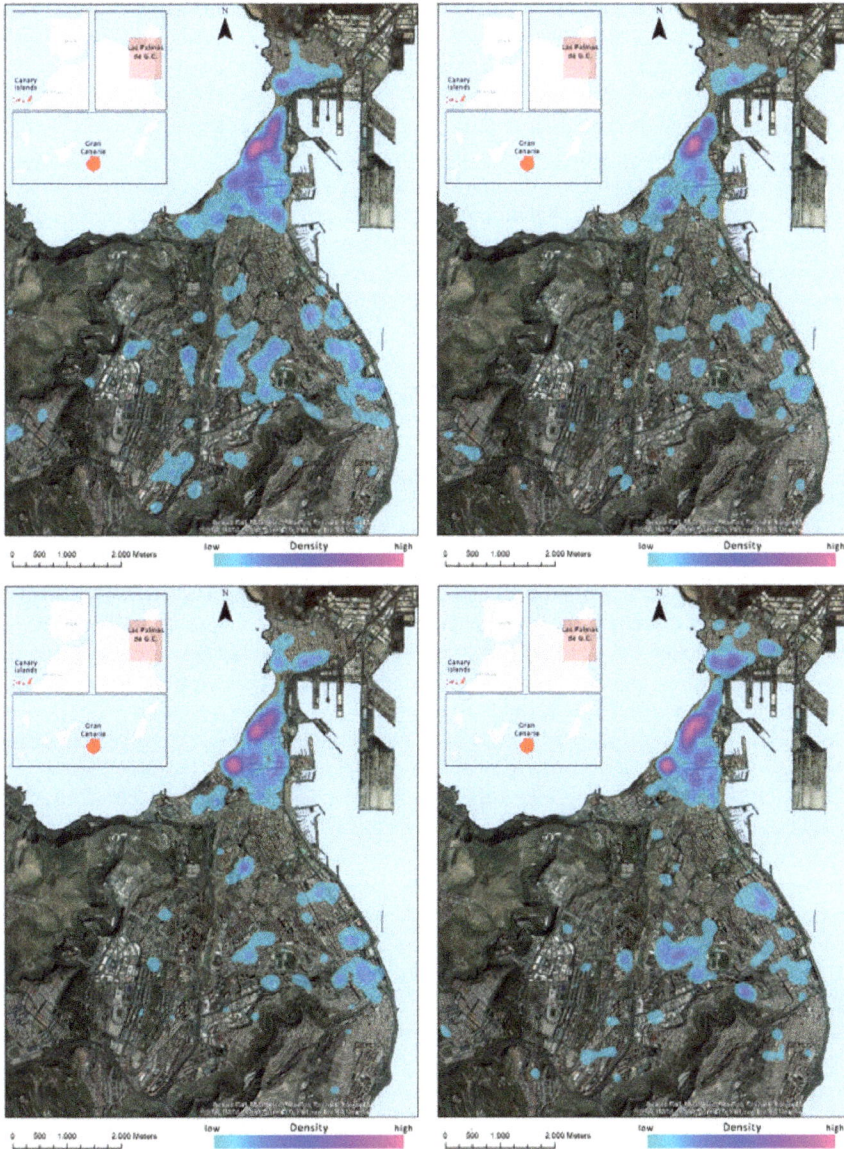

Figure 6. Distribution of the dispossessions between 2009 and 2013 (**top left**) and 2014 and 2017 (**top right**) and the losses of use between 2009 and 2013 (**bottom left**) and 2014 and 2017 (**bottom right**) in Las Palmas de Gran Canaria. Data: Common Service of Notifications and Liens of the Judicial District for Las Palmas de Gran Canaria. Own production.

5. Discussion and Conclusions

In summary, dispossession in Las Palmas de Gran Canaria was concentrated in the early years of the crisis, whereas loss of use has affected the more recent period, the incipient post-crisis. For this reason, while the problem, in the first few years, affected more those who could not pay the loans with which they had bought their homes, it has now spread more generally to those groups unable to pay their rent due to unemployment, the impossibility to obtain a stable or fairly-paid job, or due to the increase in rental prices. Similarly, we have seen that the situations underlying dispossession or eviction processes are more diverse than might have been expected, as they are not always associated with mortgage foreclosures or non-payment of rent. Furthermore, these circumstances affected both companies and individuals during the crisis, as it was a widespread situation of insolvency and there was no policy implemented to compensate either side. The post-crisis, however, is having a particular impact on certain households with a lower level of income, so the situation is now more selective.

The sequence of these processes correlates with their territorial impact. With the crisis, legal actions affect a large part of the city, with numerous interventions in areas of its most recent expansion, where the mortgage foreclosures for non-payment occur, whereas, in the last few years, the judicial proceedings are focused on certain central areas, those recording the largest number of evictions, a phenomenon paralleling the revaluation of property rentals.

As a consequence, the maximum intensity of the dispossession processes recorded during the crisis years, and the dramatic situations that accompanied it, must not make us forget that there is still a persistent social vulnerability, albeit with a new face, namely evictions, as a reflection of the inability of a wide sector of the population to resolve their housing problem. It could be said that, in the face of a "hard" situation, namely the loss of a home and the instalments paid under the mortgage contracts signed with the banks, the vulnerability in the post-crisis period has emerged in "soft" situations, related to the difficulty in accessing a rented home with all of the new formats of job flexibilization and precarious contracts.

The results obtained in the time-trend study of mortgage foreclosures and evictions in Las Palmas de Gran Canaria are consistent with the aggregate figures known for Spain as a whole, although they present some nuances that enable us to understand that the loss of a home is not as homogeneous a phenomenon as the forcefulness of the figures seems to indicate. In other words, the phenomenon is much more heterogeneous and multi-faceted, despite which it could be interpreted as a circumstantial and also structural consequence of the capitalist system.

Specifically, the dispossession enforcements resolved present a similar trend as in the series of enforcement actions begun for the country as a whole, except for the time delay caused by the judicial proceedings. In Spain overall, the case files opened reflect two periods of growth: 2008–2010 and 2012. In the judicial district for Las Palmas de Gran Canaria, there is only one period of decline recorded, namely from 2010 to 2011. In the case under study, therefore, the first stage of the crisis had a greater impact than the subsequent debt crisis. The reason is not so much an improvement in the economic situation in the Canary Islands compared to other regions of Spain during the second stage of the crisis, but rather a lower level of private indebtedness in the Islands.

The analysis over time of evictions due to non-payment of rent has fewer benchmark studies, as the urban analyses usually group together the data for multiple years, either focusing on short periods or else contrasting figures from specific years [18,20,25]. While the figures from the National Statistics Institute at national level, as already mentioned, recorded accelerated growth until 2011, followed by a stop-start decline in recent years, the initial growth in the judicial district for Las Palmas de Gran Canaria lasted somewhat longer, until 2012, when the figures stabilize until 2015 before recording growth since then, attaining absolute values even higher than those in the years of the first crisis. This difference in how the series evolves, leaving aside the distortions that might arise from the fact of not comparing completely identical variables, is due to the contrasting of distinct socio-economic structures, that of Spain and that of the Islands, that were affected to a different extent and pace by the crisis and the adjustment measures. This speaks once more, as in the case of dispossessions, to the heterogeneity of the process.

In the case of Las Palmas de Gran Canaria, the recovery policies based on rental market flexibilization, the deregulation of holiday homes and the internationalization of the housing market have given rise to the expected results, making transactions more dynamic and triggering the revaluation of the properties, associated with the loss of use of habitual homes. The harmful effects of the new focus of the rental market are particularly serious if we take into account the unfavourable situation of the city in such aspects as per capita income, the unemployment rate, precarious labor contracts or the proportion of the population at risk of poverty or social exclusion [39].

As a consequence, this differentiation of the case analyzed with respect to the State as a whole can also be extrapolated to those affected. During the crisis, dispossession processes had a major impact on both legal and natural persons. In the recent years of the recovery, however, it is the private individuals, i.e., householders, who have been most harmed compared to companies, who seem to have adapted more successfully to the new economic scenario. In a daring interpretation, we might say that everyone, businesses and households alike, were doubly impacted by the situation of the property market insofar as their assets were devalued and they suffered losses of both ownership and use, at the same time as they have had to remediate the financial institutions by backing, through the State, the loan granted for the purpose by the European Central Bank.

Lastly, the study of the housing loss in Las Palmas de Gran Canaria has provided elements for reflecting on the circumstantial or structural nature of the process. A strictly circumstantial vision would be based on a scenario characterized by an increase in legal proceeding for dispossession and eviction at times of crisis and a contrary behavior during economic booms. With this logic, if the period of prosperity generated an excessive valuation of properties and greater indebtedness, then the recession should be manifested through a more acute process of housing loss, which is in line with the logic of those explanations based on market operation. As we have seen in our study, however, this is not what has happened, so the purely circumstantial explanation is not completely satisfactory.

From a structural perspective, the excessive financialization of the property market, through the granting of high-risk mortgages, and the securitization of these financial assets are the structural elements explaining the increase in dispossessions since 2008, although it was the start of the crisis that highlighted this situation, as has been indicated in the pertinent literature. In this line, financialization and securitization are once more the structural factors of late capitalism that explain the situation arising in the years of economic recovery, except that, in this case, it is through the internationalization and flexibilization of rental markets.

The persistence of these structural elements defines different stages in secondary accumulation over the last two decades. An initial growth stage through property possession (from the end of the 1990s until 2008); a second growth stage through dispossession (the crisis, from 2009 until at least 2013), already stated by Harvey [6]; and a final growth stage through repossession, in recent years, as was expressed by Janoschka [40]. These global structural trends must be nuanced in the light of the peculiar features of each territory, but they seem to explain, in a more precise way, the importance of dispossessions in the past and, in recent years, of evictions due to non-payment of rent. This latter situation negates the fact that, after the crisis had passed, the difficulties for satisfying the accommodation problems for extensive collectives within the population had also been overcome. In fact, these difficulties remain because they form part of the structure of the current housing market.

Author Contributions: Conceptualization, J.M.P.-C. and J.D.-M.; Data curation, T.P.G. and J.B.H.; Formal analysis, T.P.G. and J.B.H.; Investigation, J.M.P.-C., J.D.-M. and M.A.-M.; Resources, J.M.P.-C., J.D.-M and M.A.-M.; Visualization, J.M.P.-C. and T.P.G.; Writing—original draft, J.M.P.-C. and J.D.-M.

Funding: This research was funded by the State Research Agency (AEI) and the European Regional Development Fund (ERDF) with R&D project "Crisis and vulnerability in Spanish island cities: transformations in social reproduction spaces" (CSO2015-68738-P).

Acknowledgments: We would like to express our gratitude to Common Service of Notifications and Liens of the Judicial District for Las Palmas de Gran Canaria and to its head, for the support given.

Conflicts of Interest: The authors declare no conflict of interest. The funders had no role in the design of the study; in the collection, analyses, or interpretation of data; in the writing of the manuscript, or in the decision to publish the results.

References

1. Boyer, R. Is a finance-led growth regime a viable alternative to Fordism? A preliminary analysis. *Econ. Soc.* **2000**, *29*, 111–145. [CrossRef]
2. Fernández, R.; Aalbers, M. Financialization and housing: Between globalization and Varieties of Capitalism. *Compet. Chang.* **2016**, *20*, 71–88. [CrossRef]
3. Cano Fuentes, G.; Etxezarreta Etxarri, A.J. La Crisis de los Desahucios en España: Respuestas Institucionales y Ciudadanas. *REC* **2014**, *17*, 44–57.
4. Abellán, J. La Vivienda, los Fondos de Inversión y la Reestructuración del Capitalismo Español. Contested Cities Madrid 2015. Available online: http://contested-cities.net/CCmadrid/la-vivienda-los-fondos-de-inversion-y-la-reestructuracion-del-capitalismo-espanol/ (accessed on 12 October 2018).
5. Midnight Notes Collective. Introduction to the New Enclosures. *Commoner* **2001**, *2*, 1–15.
6. Harvey, D. The 'New' Imperialism: Accumulation by dispossession. In *The New Imperialism*; Oxford University Press: Oxford, UK, 2003; pp. 63–87, ISBN 9780199264315.
7. López, I.; Rodríguez, E. *Fin de Ciclo. Financiarización, Territorio y Sociedad de Propietarios en la Onda Larga del Capitalismo Hispano (1959–2010)*, 1st ed.; Traficantes de Sueños: Madrid, Spain, 2010; p. 503, ISBN 978-84-96453-47-0.
8. Hodkinson, S. The new urban enclosures. *City* **2013**, *16*, 500–518. [CrossRef]
9. Gotham, K.F. Creating liquidity out of spatial fixity: The secondary circuit of capital and the subprime mortgage crisis. *Int. J. Urban Reg. Res.* **2009**, *33*, 355–371. [CrossRef]
10. Christophers, B. Revisiting the Urbanization of Capital. *Ann. Assoc. Am. Geogr.* **2011**, *101*, 1347–1364. [CrossRef]
11. Vives-Miró, S.; Rullan, O. La vivienda en el tránsito de la reproducción ampliada del capital a la acumulación por desposesión en España. In *Territorios Inconclusos y Sociedades Rotas, Proceedings of the XII Coloquio y Trabajos de Campo del Grupo de Geografía Urbana, Madrid & Castilla La Mancha, Spain, 11–14 June 2014*; AGE: Madrid, Spain, 2014; pp. 1–10.
12. Aalbers, M. The Financialization of Home and the Mortgage Market Crisis. *Compet. Chang.* **2008**, *12*, 148–166. [CrossRef]
13. Kaika, M.; Ruggiero, L. Land Financialization as a "lived" process: The transformation of Milan's Bicocca by Pirelli. *Eur. Urban Reg. Stud.* **2013**, *23*, 1–20. [CrossRef]
14. Wainwright, T. Laying the Foundations for a Crisis: Mapping the Historico-Geographical Construction of Residential Mortgage Backed Securitization in the UK. *Int. J. Urban Reg. Res.* **2009**, *33*, 372–388. [CrossRef]
15. Crump, J.; Newman, K.; Belsky, E.S.; Ashton, P.; Kaplan, D.H.; Hammel, D.J.; Wyly, E. Cities Destroyed (Again) For Cash: Forum on the U.S. Foreclosure Crisis. *Urban Geogr.* **2008**, *29*, 745–784. [CrossRef]
16. Fields, D. Contesting the financialization of urban space: Community organizations and the struggle to preserve affordable rental housing in New York city. *J. Urban Aff.* **2015**, *37*, 144–165. [CrossRef]
17. Walks, A. Mapping the Urban Debtscape: The Geography of Household Debt in Canadian Cities. *Urban Geogr.* **2013**, *34*, 153–187. [CrossRef]
18. Vives-Miró, S.; Rullan, O. Desposesión de Vivienda por Turistización? Revalorización y Desplazamientos en el Centro Histórico de Palma (Mallorca). *Rev. Geogr. Norte Gd.* **2017**, *67*, 53–71. [CrossRef]
19. Méndez, R.; Abad, L.D.; Plaza, J. Geografía de las ejecuciones hipotecarias en España. *Colección Estudios de la Fundación Primero de Mayo* **2014**, *84*, 1–40.
20. Obeso Muñiz, I. Análisis geográfico de los desahucios en España. *Ería* **2014**, *95*, 327–342. [CrossRef]
21. Méndez, R.; Abad, L.D.; Echaves, C. *Atlas de la Crisis. Impactos Socioeconómicos y Territorios Vulnerables en España*; Tirant lo Blanch: Valencia, Spain, 2015; p. 301, ISBN 978-84-16062-87-4.
22. Méndez, R.; Plaza, J. Crisis inmobiliaria y desahucios hipotecarios in España: Una perspectiva geográfica. *BAGE* **2016**, *71*, 99–127. [CrossRef]
23. Méndez, R. De la Hipoteca al Desahucio: Ejecuciones Hipotecarias y Vulnerabilidad Territorial en España. *Rev. Geogr. Norte Gd.* **2017**, *67*, 9–31. [CrossRef]
24. García-Hernández, J.S.; Díaz-Rodríguez, M.C.; García-Herrera, L.M. Auge y crisis inmobiliaria en Canarias: Desposesión de vivienda y resurgimiento inmobiliario. *Investig. Geogr.* **2018**, *69*, 23–39. [CrossRef]
25. Vives-Miró, S.; González-Pérez, J.M.; Rullan, O. Home dispossession: The uneven geography of evictions in Palma (Majorca). *DIE ERDE* **2015**, *146*, 113–126. [CrossRef]

26. Vives-Miró, S.; Rullan, O.; González Pérez, J.M. Consecuencias sociales del modelo económico basado en el crédito. Geografía de las ejecuciones hopotecarias en Menorca. *Scr. Nova* **2017**, *XXI*, 553. [CrossRef]

27. Parreño-Castellano, J.M.; Domínguez-Mujica, J.; Armengol Martín, M.T.; Pérez García, T.; Boldú García, J. Descapitalización inmobiliaria y desahucio en Las Palmas de Gran Canaria: Una aproximación desde fuentes judiciales. In *Ciudades Medias y Áreas Metropolitanas. De la Dispersion a la Regeneración, Proceedings of the XIV Coloquio de Geografía Urbana, Albacete and Valencia, Spain, 27–30 June 2018*; Cebrián Abellán, F., Ed.; Ediciones de la Universidad de Castilla-La Mancha: Cuenca, Spain, 2018; pp. 719–732, ISBN 978-84-9044-315-6.

28. Gutiérrez, A.; Domènech, A. The Spanish mortgage crisis: Evidence of the concentration of foreclosures in the most deprived neighbourhoods. *DIE ERDE* **2017**, *148*, 39–57. [CrossRef]

29. Gutiérrez, A.; Delclòs, X. The uneven distribution of evictions as new evidence of urban inequality: A spatial analysis approach in two Catalan cities. *Cities* **2016**, *56*, 101–108. [CrossRef]

30. Gutiérrez, A.; Declòs, X. Geografía de la crisis inmobiliaria en Cataluña: Una lectura a partir de los desahucios por ejecución hipotecaria. *Scr. Nova* **2017**, *XXI*, 55. [CrossRef]

31. Gutiérrez, A.; Arauzo-Carod, J.M. Spatial Analysis of Clustering of Foreclosures in the Poorest-Quality Housing Urban Areas: Evidence from Catalan Cities. *ISPRS Int. J. Geo-Inf.* **2018**, *7*, 23. [CrossRef]

32. Gutiérrez, A.; Domènech, A. Geografía de los desahucios por ejecución hipotecaria en las ciudades españolas: Evidencias a partir de las viviendas propiedad de la SAREB. *Rev. Geogr. Norte Gd.* **2017**, *67*, 33–52. [CrossRef]

33. Jiménez Barrado, V.; Sánchez Martín, J.M. Banca privada y vivienda usada en la ciudad de Madrid. *Investig. Geogr.* **2016**, *66*, 43–58. [CrossRef]

34. Gutiérrez, A.; Domènech, A. Spanish mortgage crisis and accumulation of foreclosed housing by SAREB: A geographical approach. *J. Maps* **2017**, *13*, 130–137. [CrossRef]

35. Raya, J.M. The determinants of foreclosures: Evidence from the Spanish case. *Pap. Reg. Sci.* **2018**, *97*, 957–970. [CrossRef]

36. Vives-Miró, S.; Gutiérrez, A. Extracting rents through foreclosures: The rescue of Catalunya Banc as a new urban strategy following the burst of the Spanish bubble. *MGRSD* **2017**, *21*, 151–159. [CrossRef]

37. Gutiérrez, A.; Vives-Miró, S. Acumulación de viviendas por parte de los bancos a través de los desahucios: Geografía de la desposesión de vivienda en Cataluña. *EURE* **2018**, *44*, 5–26. [CrossRef]

38. Parreño-Castellano, J.M.; Domínguez-Mujica, J.; Armengol Martín, M.T.; Boldú García, J.; Pérez García, T. Real Estate dispossession and evictions in Spain: A theoretical geographical approach. *BAGE* **2019**, in press.

39. Padrón, D.; Martínez, J.S. *Desigualdad, Pobreza y Cohesión Social en Canarias. Análisis de su Incidencia y Distribución Entre la Población Canaria. Informe Realizado Para el Comisionado de Inclusión Social y Lucha Contra la Pobreza del Gobierno de Canarias*; Universidad de La Laguna: Santa Cruz de Tenerife, Spain, 2016; p. 299.

40. Janoschka, M. Politics, citizenship and disobedience in the city of crisis: A critical analysis of contemporary housing struggles in Madrid. *Die Erde* **2015**, *146*, 100–112. [CrossRef]

© 2018 by the authors. Licensee MDPI, Basel, Switzerland. This article is an open access article distributed under the terms and conditions of the Creative Commons Attribution (CC BY) license (http://creativecommons.org/licenses/by/4.0/).

urban science

MDPI

Article

Qualitative Methodologies for the Analysis of Intra-Urban Socio-Environmental Vulnerability in Barcelona (Spain): Case Studies

Antonio Palacios [1,*], Ana Mellado [1] and Yazmín León [2]

[1] Geography Department, Universidad Autónoma de Madrid, Cantoblanco Campus, 28049 Madrid, Spain; ana.mellado.sangabino@gmail.com

[2] Geography Department, Universidad de Costa Rica, San José 2060, Costa Rica; yazmin.leonalfaro@ucr.ac.cr

* Correspondence: antonio.palacios@uam.es; Tel.: +34-606-846-093

Received: 19 October 2018; Accepted: 30 November 2018; Published: 3 December 2018

Abstract: The city of Barcelona, like other cities in the world, suffers strong internal socio-economic inequalities in its neighborhoods. Numerous works have sought to detect, quantify, characterize, and/or map existing intra-urban differences, almost always based on quantitative methodologies. With this contribution, we intend to show the importance that qualitative methodologies can play in studies on urban socio-environmental vulnerability. We consider aspects that are not quantifiable but that may be inherent to many such vulnerable spaces, both in the constructed environment and in the social ambit. These questions are considered through selected neighborhoods of Barcelona which have been shown (in prior works, mainly studies of quantitative manufacturing) to possess elements of vulnerability including a high presence of immigrants from less-developed countries, low per capita income, aging populations, or low educational levels. The results reveal the multidimensionality of vulnerability in the neighborhoods analyzed, as well as the essential complementarity among methodologies that detect and support possible public actions aimed at reducing or eliminating intra-urban inequalities.

Keywords: socio-environmental vulnerability; Barcelona; spatial analysis; qualitative methodology; vulnerable neighborhoods

1. Introduction

Urban socio-environmental vulnerability is a social phenomenon currently arousing much interest in the scientific community. The concept refers to the existence of intra-urban inequalities, established by differences in the social composition of a population through spatial distribution, as well as how this issue affects uneven behavior in the face of social, urban, economic, demographic, and/or environmental problems. From this perspective, it is important to investigate the factors, causes, and consequences being generated, as well as possible solutions, in order to improve the situation of those groups deemed most vulnerable to diverse threats.

In the orbit of vulnerability are found concepts such as exclusion, marginality, and poverty, which though not synonymous may be mutually reinforcing. Socio-environmental vulnerability is a broader concept that affects a potentially larger part of the population [1]. It is evident that the poor are by their very nature vulnerable in economic terms. However, here we are dealing in dynamic concepts, which are not necessarily always related. The present contribution is focused on the social approach to vulnerability: to show how socio-spatial structures and processes are indeed dynamic and may determine the daily lives of disadvantaged people and groups [2].

This contribution might be inserted in an even broader line concerned with the measurement of environmental injustices at the local level, focused on the unequal behavior of diverse externalities vis-à-vis sensitive or vulnerable groups such as children or the elderly, or populations with lower educational levels or income. The multifaceted character of the conditions impacting the phenomena in question must always be taken into account.

This paper is a continuation of a series of prior works [3,4], fundamentally quantitative in nature. From these emerged a synthetic indicator of relative socio-spatial vulnerability, which was then applied to all neighborhoods in the city of Barcelona. In this particular contribution, we apply a qualitative methodology to that city's four most vulnerable neighborhoods, in order to detect non-quantifiable urban and social deficiencies.

The following section briefly addresses the question of urban socio-environmental vulnerability in the scientific literature, also highlighting sources of information and methodological issues. Next the qualitative analysis is presented, and finally some concise conclusions are offered.

Vulnerability in the Scientific Literature

Socio-environmental vulnerability is in itself a multidimensional and multifaceted concept [5,6], with its own long and complex history [7], and there is no consensus regarding its definition or measurement [2]. From a strictly etymological conception, it usually implies physical, economic, political, or social susceptibility; that is, the potential of a population to be affected by an external issue or destabilizing phenomenon, whether of natural or anthropic origin [8], and which, if not resolved, could lead to more critical levels of disadvantage, poverty, and exclusion [9].

However, it must be borne in mind that when social inequalities are analyzed in any area, reference is inescapably made to personal issues having to do with the individuals who live there. That is to say that vulnerability, like any similar phenomenon under study, has a clear social component. It does not affect all populations (individual, household, group, society) equally, but represents a factor of internal risk corresponding to the susceptibility or predisposition of each to suffer harm [8]. It is this incapacity or difficulty of certain people or groups in the face of threat (risk) and/or propensity for later recovery that we understand as socio-environmental vulnerability. As noted by Mateos [6], based on prior studies and from a social and economic perspective, vulnerability is not a supervening condition, but rather a dynamic state. It influences diverse factors such as the unequal distribution of resources, the action or inaction of individuals, and historical patterns of domination and social marginalization. In fact, the most persistent cases of vulnerability reveal profound deficiencies in public policies and institutions, historical exclusions, and cultural practices, and long-established social norms.

Although anyone may be vulnerable at some point in their lives, some groups are more sensitive than others. The United Nations establishes three large groups: (1) the poor and informal workers; (2) women, migrants, minorities, young people, the elderly, and persons with disabilities; and (3) entire communities or regions.

The absence of a single definition demonstrates the variety of causes that may motivate or encourage vulnerability. Its relationship with risks and threats is evident, and this in turn may be the cause of its origin. The literature reveals two categories of hazards: those of natural origin (environmental hazards) and those of human origin (social hazards). The latter are of greater interest to the social sciences but are less defined or consolidated. In addition, they are precisely the hazards that appear in urban areas, linked to those groups most sensitive to the impacts mentioned above. The diversity of causes that motivate human vulnerability would also explain why it has been studied from many perspectives, with different approaches, definitions, and methodologies that depend on the particular risk being considered [1]. From this plenitude, various types of vulnerability (socio-demographic, socio-economic, environmental, residential, subjective) have been discerned. However, the unfixed definition of the term has led authors like Alexander [10] to distinguish more types of vulnerability (technological, residual, delinquent, new, and total). Subirats and Martí-Costa [11] have added to these vulnerability in relation to governance, and to habitat (the latter measured through indicators such as population density of artificial area, the percentage of displacements on foot, and the volume of electricity consumption).

With regard to the measurement of vulnerability, the intra-urban scale has not been prioritized until relatively recently by urban studies scholars [12]. Nevertheless, numerous attempts have been made in recent years to create indicators and measures from different perspectives and methodologies (in Wisner, cited above, in-depth analysis is made of the concept, its bibliometric review, and distinct forms of measurement). In the academic literature, approaches are common that analyze inequalities through variables and dimensions of demographics (age, race, sex, country of birth, education, occupation, etc.), economics (social status, income, savings, etc.), or another type (housing, endowments, social networks, security, etc.), usually referenced at the individual or household level. The contributions of Cutter et al. [13] and Cardona and Carreño [14] may serve as examples. Many studies opt for analytical methodologies that transform and combine the variables used, building indices of socio-economic status or social vulnerability [15]. Some of the references cited thus far offer extremely valuable statements on the use of quantitative methodologies over time.

Less often, works that seek to measure vulnerability have been complemented by qualitative methodologies. In such publications as by Birckmann and Wisner [16], or Anderson and Woodrow [17], tools have been created for the qualitative assessment of vulnerability and capacity in communities, as a form of cooperation between local and external experts, and as an aid to local communities.

In Spain we would highlight, for example, the Catalog of Vulnerable Districts, included in the Observatory of Urban Vulnerability, developed jointly by the Ministry of Development and the Department of Urban Planning of the Polytechnic University of Madrid. Elsewhere, a working group at the University of Granada led by Carmen Egea has long experience in the use of mixed methodologies. More recently, geo-demographic analysis has been incorporated into urban social geography, which (beyond providing a general index) focuses on the formulation of a specific geo-demographic classification to typologies of hazard and place, more heavily weighting the most significant variables to a specific geo-historical context, and based on mixed methodologies.

2. Objective, Materials, and Methods

Starting from the above considerations, our objective here is to show the role that qualitative methodologies can play in studies on urban socio-environmental vulnerability when detecting deficiencies or non-quantifiable social and urban problems.

The information sources used in the quantitative analyses pre-dating this work [3,4] were the statistical data provided by the Statistics Department of the Barcelona City Council (Municipal Register) and, occasionally, data from regional organizations. The year of reference is 2015.

The digital geodata layers of the city, with their respective divisions, were likewise facilitated by the municipal administration. The selected scale of analysis was the neighborhood and the "populated urban area" (AUP). The latter indicates the residential or mixed-use urban space where the population has greater presence in their daily lives (see Figure 1).

The facets or components of vulnerability considered (eight in total) were diverse and varied, depending on incidence and the availability of data. Seventeen variables were combined related to: *education*, given that persons with low or no training show limited capacities for self-protection and personal care, or limited recourse to existing defense facilities; *age*, which makes some people more fragile than others in the face of external factors; demographic *mortality* indicators that reflect living conditions and are an expression of extreme vulnerability; *income and professional status*, key to assuaging the vulnerability of individuals and certain groups; *immigration status*, supposing the individual has moved geographically; and *size of household*, in the number of members that compose it, reflective of housing shortages. All these facets can greatly impact on the intensity with which socio-environmental vulnerability is manifested. More information can be found relative to the quantitative information used in the publication by Moreno et al. [3].

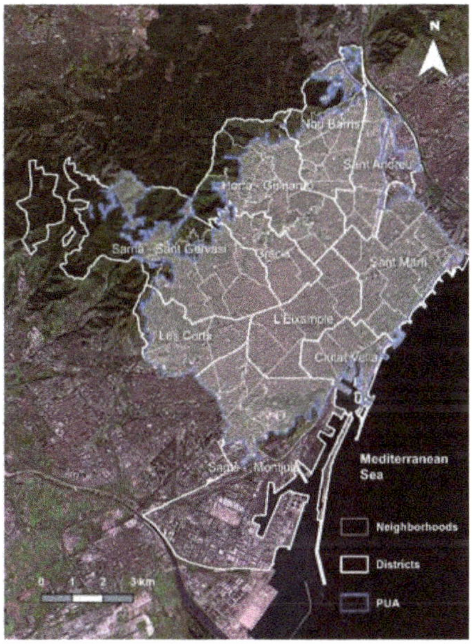

Figure 1. Territorial delimitations in Barcelona. Source: [3].

The research crystallized in a synthetic index of relative socio-spatial vulnerability (ISVuSAR), resulting from a principal component analysis (PCA) with a Varimax rotation, and in normalization of the variables linked to each of the above facets by matching amplitude and eventual transposition. This allowed for classification of the neighborhoods of the city (see Figure 2).

Taking this index as a starting point, the main contribution of the work here is essentially to show the results obtained in the qualitative analysis of the four most vulnerable neighborhoods of Barcelona to confirm, support, and verify that actually, these areas accumulate deficiencies and problems of a diverse nature.

The underlying idea, already raised by other authors [18], is to overcome the statistical vacuum that limits the information necessary to perform in-depth studies of this nature. Thus, intensive fieldwork was carried out by the authors during October 2017 in the selected case studies (the four most vulnerable neighborhoods of the city). This fieldwork consisted mainly in visual analysis of deficiencies, by numerous routes throughout the targeted urban spaces.

The results obtained were supplemented with relevant information from scientific publications, reports, press releases, and relevant websites. Alongside all this, interviews were conducted with the neighborhood associations involved (Trinitat Nova, El Raval, and Barceloneta) in order to verify the information collected, or to expand it based on the opinion of persons best acquainted with the spaces studied—the inhabitants.

Based on this information, detailed files were assembled by theme and by neighborhood, collecting certain non-quantifiable aspects which nonetheless represent facets or components of socio-environmental vulnerability. The aspects can be presented as belonging to one of two categories: the built environment and the social environment. The first includes issues such as deficiencies in infrastructures, in green spaces, in public spaces, in public transport, or in housing, whether in terms of status, age, or degree of deterioration, among others. To this should be added possible deficiencies derived from the difficulty of physical mobility in the neighborhood, or from environmental problems (air or noise pollution, for example). The social aspect, on the other hand, would refer to problems linked to endowments and equipment, to levels of association, to the presence of ethnic groups with integration difficulties, to the physical exclusion of the environment, to the presence of marginal activities, to the lack or closure of economic activities, to physical and/or social uprooting, or to latent or explicit insecurity, among other issues.

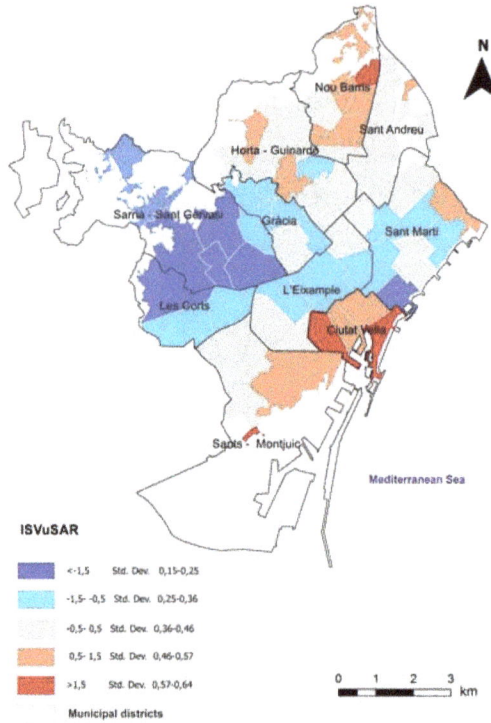

Figure 2. Map of the ISVuSAR results by neighborhood (AUP) of Barcelona. Source: [3].

3. Results and Discussion—The Most Acute Dimension of Vulnerability: Case Studies

Socio-environmental vulnerability manifests in different intensities, as we have seen. It would be impossible here to rigorously detail the many investigations into vulnerability in Barcelona carried out in recent decades. An article by Sargatal [19] gives a very complete review of the main contributions focused on the historical center, and the methodologies used. There is noticeable and increasing interest from diverse disciplines in the approach to, and knowledge around, socio-spatial reality. Similarity to our topic moves us to highlight works by Martori and Hoberg [20,21], Martínez et al. [22], Domingo and Bayona [23], and Subirats and Rius [24], which by using diverse methodological approaches have deepened knowledge on the reality of the city.

In this work, we focus on four neighborhoods to which the ISVuSAR has ascribed higher values (1.5 times the deviation). These are the Trinitat Nova, Raval, Marina del Prat Vermell, and Barceloneta neighborhoods. For these areas, aspects or qualitative problems stemming from both the constructed environment and the social sphere have been analyzed using the proposed methodology.

Trinitat Nova is a neighborhood of the Nou Barris district, located on the northeastern periphery of the city, on the mountain slopes of Collserola and on the left bank of the Besós (Figure 3). The neighborhood occupies an area of 0.80 km^2 and numbered 7257 inhabitants in 2016 (down from 8110 in 2008). Its physical boundaries coincide with the streets Aiguablava, Via Favéncia and Garbí, and Avenida Meridiana.

This dormitory quarter (monofunctional) is a clear example of massive collective social housing from the Franco regime. Its poor construction quality (aluminosis and carbonatosis), together with the gradual socio-economic and environmental deterioration of the site (Figure 4a), were the bases for two major urban interventions carried out in recent decades (Figure 4b). The first, in 1997, followed the city's Urban Plan and involved area remodeling through special planning (PERI), improvement of accessibility via the metro, and integration into the ECO-City Project (financed by the European Community within its Fifth Framework Program for Research and Development). The second intervention, the Trinitat Nova Urban Initiative of 2007–2013 (20 million euros) continued the process of integral urban regeneration supported by European and municipal funds. Currently, the Barrios Plan of 2016–2020 (http://pladebarris.barcelona/es), promoted by the Barcelona City Council, consists of ten plans involving 16 city neighborhoods in the city, targeting integrated actions in education, social rights, economic activity, and urban ecology, with a planned investment of more than 150 million euros. Of the four cases analyzed here, three (Trinitat Nova, Raval, and La Marina del Prat) are featured in some of these plans. Trinitat Nova will, without a doubt, see the reduction or elimination of a good many existing problems.

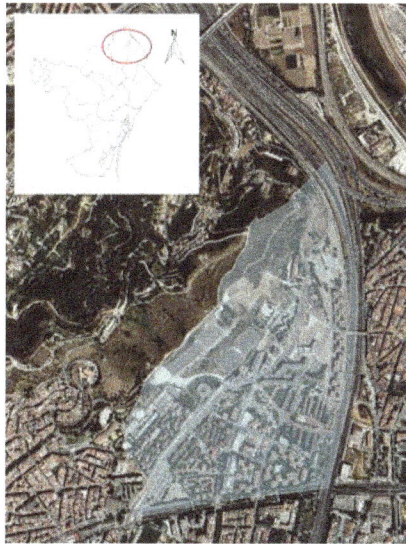

Figure 3. Location of the Trinitat Nova neighborhood. Source: own elaboration.

(a)   (b)

Figure 4. Trinitat Nova: (**a**) housing pending demolition, and (**b**) new homes.

The Trinitat Nova neighborhood, largely populated by the working class and immigrants, exhibits socio-demographic characteristics that could clearly be improved, as repeatedly demonstrated by historical and current association and protest movements. The Community Plan of Trinitat Nova (and its corresponding diagnoses), launched in 1996 on the initiative of the Neighborhood Association, has led to development of an innovative instrument and integrator of concerned social agents. Blanco [25] offers an interesting comparative analysis of the urban regeneration policies developed in the Raval and Trinitat Nova neighborhoods, two areas of Barcelona where family income is the lowest. Trinitat Nova presents a very high percentage of population without education (8.6%), a low rate of population with higher education (5.7%), a high percentage of foreign residents (around 24%), an unemployment rate around 18%, and the highest rate of teen pregnancy in the city.

Qualitative analysis reveals problems linked to the urban environment, including: the presence of architectural barriers; noise and pollution from road transport infrastructures; deterioration of public spaces, especially in the vicinity of the Les Freixes urban gardens; and problems (currently being addressed) related to the antiquity, the poor state of conservation, and lack of basic facilities within residential buildings. Special attention is needed to resolve issues deriving from a substantial increase in the property tax (IBI) borne by tenants of new officially protected housing (three or four times the prior rates).

The social environment is further defined by the physical exclusion of the neighborhood with respect to the city as a whole (barrier effect), derived from its geographical position and the layout of large transport infrastructures (Meridiana and Dalt Avenues). The lack of youth-oriented, sports facilities, and economic activities is also significant. The latter are present only in the commercial spaces of new buildings constructed during regeneration, or in the traditional market. According to *El Diario*, "While Barcelona averages one commercial establishment for every 28 inhabitants, in Trinitat Nova there is one for every 180 inhabitants" (eldiario.es, January 21, 2016). Added to this is the persistence of marginal activities, and latent insecurity near the housing blocks to which relocation of inhabitants affected by demolition of old structures is pending, as well as the difficulties of integration of certain groups (Gypsies from outside Barcelona and mainly Pakistanis).

For its part, the Raval neighborhood, long regarded as the Chinese neighborhood (denomination coined by journalist Paco Madrid in an article published in the weekly *El Escándalo* newspaper, in reference to the "chinar" technique employed by many pickpockets of that time) or a rogue area, is located in the Ciutat Vella district (Figure 5). Its defined boundaries are Parallel Avenue to the south (dividing it from the Poble Sec neighborhood); Sant Pau and Sant Antoni Avenues (separating Raval from the Sant Antoni district); and Pelayo Street and La Rambla, marking the division from the adjacent Gothic Quarter. Two large urban projects, Rambla del Raval and Illa Robadors, are located within the zone.

Figure 5. Location of the Raval neighborhood. Source: own elaboration.

The Raval presents two significant demographic features. On the one hand, it has a very high population density (around 44,000 inhabitants per km^2, or 47,000 inhabitants within an area of 1.07 km^2). On the other hand, almost half of the population (47%) is of immigrant origin, coming from less-developed countries. Furthermore, analysis shows that more than half of the houses are of small size (56.5%) and that around 40% of persons over 75 years of age live in one-person homes.

From the social perspective, this complex neighborhood is an authentic laboratory for urban studies [22], characterized by its curious socio-economic mix, with more-or-less differentiated areas tending to correspond to the country of origin of the inhabitants. Thus, areas of higher income tend to coincide with inhabitants of national origin, along with a significant number of European immigrants of fairly recent arrival. On the other side, the percentage of extra-European immigrants is extremely high, with a clear predominance of Filipinos, Pakistanis, and Moroccans.

This neighborhood first emerged as a suburb beyond the medieval wall, and it is rich in cultural and architectural heritage (Mercado de la Boquería, Contemporary Art Museum, Contemporary Culture Center, Güell Palace, etc.); however, this is currently marred by marginal activities linked to drugs and prostitution (traditional, perhaps), as well as notorious "narco-flats." Furthermore, given its central location, it is undergoing gentrification at high magnitude, served by intense tourist activity (festivals, fairs, congresses, cruises, etc.). This has led to the dispersal of longtime residents to the city's peripheral zones, and to a gradual denaturalization of the neighborhood's traditional character [26].

Our qualitative analysis reveals multiple problems linked to the urban environment such as: the lack of green spaces (the Jardins de Sant Pau del Camp and Rubió i Lluch being exceptions, in addition to the Plaza de Josep Folch); noise pollution and garbage (Figure 6a); difficulty in physical mobility due to the layout and narrowness of streets, and to problems derived from the scarcity of parking; and housing issues including superannuation, poor maintenance or reform, overcrowding, lack of basic facilities and, more recently, tourism outsourcing. Regarding the social environment, the main problems detected here include: difficulty of immigrants to integrate, with clear spatial differentiation by group; the gradual orientation of economic activities towards tourism, with the consequent loss of traditional trade; explicit insecurity, evidenced by robberies of tourists; the marginal activities described above; and the increase in real-estate pressures driven by gentrification (Figure 6b).

(a)   (b)

Figure 6. El Raval: (**a**) rubbish and deterioration, and (**b**) neighborhood demands.

The third neighborhood under analysis, La Marina del Prat Vermell, is located in the Sants-Montjuïc district (Figure 7) and presents certain singularities. It is currently inhabited by only a thousand people (1143 in 2016), of whom approximately one fifth are immigrants, and with much lower density (around 80 inhabitants per km^2). It is among the neighborhoods with the highest percentage of residents without education (7.8%), and of the four most vulnerable neighborhoods discussed here, it suffers the highest rate of unemployment (19.4%). Also high is the proportion of undersized houses (77.1%), mitigated by the city's lowest rental and sales prices, per square meter (396 euros and 684 euros, respectively).

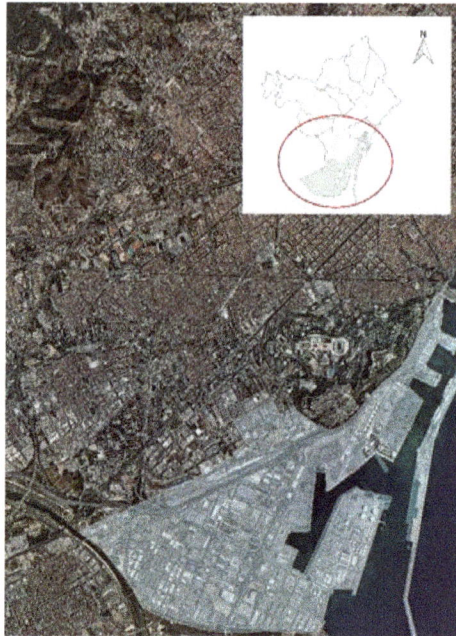

Figure 7. Location of the La Marina del Prat Vermell neighborhood.

This small neighborhood's origins were oriented to agriculture and livestock, and it is located between Montjuïc mountain and the Zona Franca industrial sector. The stamp of the Primo de Rivera regime was visible in the promotion of cheap "Eduardo Aunós" houses of 1929, the demolition/relocation of which in the 1990s made room for today's constructions. Some historic industrial (often obsolete) buildings survive, along with scattered residential nuclei (Figure 8a).

With other nearby neighborhoods (Polvorín, Can Clos, Can Tunis), La Marina del Prat Vermell represents a fragment of Barcelona's urban history, about which an interesting urban transformation project is under consideration by Barcelona Urban Planning Management (BAGURSA). The project was initially proposed in 2004 as part of a major urban renewal drive that included 22@ (Innovation District), La Sagrera, Plaça de les Glòries, and Can Batlló [27]. The new resultant neighborhood will cover 80 hectares and feature 11,000 homes (slightly less than half of them public) to accommodate 30,000 potential residents (http://www.bagursa.com/lamarina/proj.html). This process has been made possible thanks to modifications to the Metropolitan General Plan of 1976, through requalification of the land from industrial to mixed-use. The urban renewal project will mean development of the area around the inhabited nucleus, favoring the location of economic activities, along with significant additions of public facilities and spaces to help unite the old Free Trade Zone socially and urbanistically. This project's the lack of sensitivity to architectural and industrial heritage is perhaps its most controversial aspect, with the Bausili and Santiveri colonies and the Bertrand and Serra factories [28] slated for removal.

Today, problems linked to the urban environment are mainly to do with the scarcity and poor accessibility of urban transport (currently accessible only by bus, with plans for metro extension), and to the lack of parking and poor quality of certain buildings, despite their fairly recent construction (Figure 8b).

In terms of the social perspective, the neighborhood's problems are expressed in: a lack of endowments and facilities (there are no schools or nurseries); the physical exclusion of the area, given its distance from the core city; the social uprooting of inhabitants, many of whom had been relocated from other areas; and latent insecurity and the presence of marginal activities linked to drugs, despite the adjacent Mossos de Esquadra Police Station.

Finally, the neighborhood known as La Barceloneta is also located in the Ciutat Vella district (Figure 9), but its population volume and density, although quite high (16,000 inhabitants in 1.24 km^2, or 12,900 inhabitants per km^2), are lower than in nearby Raval. The percentage of foreign residents (31.3%) is the second highest among the neighborhoods analyzed.

(a)   (b)

Figure 8. La Marina del Prat Vermell: (**a**) homes of the Bausili Colony, and (**b**) deterioration of modern buildings.

Figure 9. Location of the Barceloneta neighborhood.

This old seaside district (the beach neighborhood), traditionally popular and working class, is strong in character. Urban contrasts exist between the maritime front (the promenade and beaches of San Miguel, San Sebastián, and Barceloneta-Somorostro), and the western border (Moll), and between large corporate headquarters buildings (Gas Natural or Mapfre), casinos, and hotels (Arts) and the residential nucleus, where traditional housing coexists with novel social housing (the MTM (Maquinista Terrestre y Marítima) project, Figure 10a). All of this shares an area limited by the sea and by urban pressures to densify the use of space. Notable are successful drives by local associations (the Ostia and the Platform in Defense of Barceloneta, now united as "La Barceloneta diu prou") to halt projects deemed harmful to the neighborhood [29].

Worthy of further note is recognition of the important role of the public space as useful and consistent, and the existence of facilities including schools, sports centers, and hospitals, all of which condition the urban impact or more traditional buildings of lower height, whose progressive growth contrasts with the narrowness of the streets.

Within the neighborhood, problems related to the urban environment include: the lack of green spaces (only Barceloneta Park, located at one extreme, is significant); difficulty in physical mobility, both for vehicles and pedestrians, given the narrowness of streets in the residential nucleus; the small number of surface parking spaces; housing concerns related to antiquity, poor maintenance, lack of facilities, and sometimes over-occupation (infamous "houses of rooms," Figure 10b). The excessive supply of tourist homes in the core neighborhood is also a current concern, driving out traditional residents and prompting fierce neighborhood protests (2014 saw many mobilizations under the slogan "La Barceloneta is not sold," seeking to publicize the proliferation of tourist apartments derived from transformation of older housing into modern flats destined exclusively for rental by tourists). Finally, as elsewhere, the neighborhood has experienced a significant increase in housing prices (a more detailed analysis of the evolution of this market in La Barceloneta can be found in Pareja and Simó [30].

(a)   (b)

Figure 10. La Barceloneta: (**a**) social housing in MTM, and (**b**) small houses.

Problems linked to the social environment are here fundamentally due to intensive tourism, which the neighborhood supports, also reflected in the commercial tertiarization towards this sector (hospitality) and in the lack (or expulsion) of local commerce. As a consequence, the (latent, at least) social uprooting of the residents is another growing concern.

In line with the above, Alamilla [31] offers an interesting analysis of the costs and benefits derived from tourism among a residential population. Chief among the costs would be a rise in consumption of alcohol, increased noise and crowding in public spaces, increases in the prices of goods and services, and mounting crime. Among the benefits would be the growth of commercial activity and employment and the conservation of typical local cuisine.

Summarizing, Table 1 shows the existence of urban and social problems more or less common to all the neighborhoods analyzed. Among them are those related to housing (low maintenance, age or lack of basic equipment), the existence of architectural barriers, the lack or "touristification" of economic activities, as well as those related to insecurity and the presence of marginal activities. On the other hand, there have been no problems or shortcomings related to infrastructures, spaces between buildings or the low degree of associationism.

Table 1. Indicators used in qualitative research (X means that the problem exists). (1: Trinitat Nova; 2: El Raval; 3: La Marina del Prat Vermell; 4: La Barceloneta).

Problems Linked to the Urban Environment									
	1	2	3	4		1	2	3	4
Infrastructures					**Public spaces**	X			
Obsolete					Low conservation				
Low general condition					Lack of cleanliness				
Inadequate					Deterioration	X			
Problematic					**Public transport**			X	
Green spaces		X		X	Scarce			X	
Absence and/or lack		X		X	Bad accessibility			X	
Low conservation					**Environmental**	X	X		
Lack of cleanliness					**Difficulty of physical mobility**	X	X		X
Deterioration					**Spaces between buildings**				
Housing	X	X	X	X	Difficulty of access				
Self-construction					Deterioration				
Age	X	X		X	**Others**	X	X	X	X
Low maintenance and/or reform	X	X	X	X					
Overcrowding		X		X					
Lack of basic equipment	X	X		X					
Problems Linked to the Social Environment									
Endowments and equipment	X		X		**Low degree of associationism**				
Insufficient					**Difficulty of group integration**	X	X		
Lack	X		X		**Economic activities**	X	X		X
Unsuitability to the demand					Lack of activities	X			
Deterioration					Closure and/or expulsion		X		X
Physical and/or social uprooting			X	X	**Latent or explicit insecurity**	X	X	X	
Physical exclusion	X		X		**Presence of marginal activities**	X	X	X	

4. Conclusions

Urban socio-environmental vulnerability is a problem that must be addressed by public stakeholders, supported by logical and operational methodologies [32]. The scientific community has undertaken the important challenge of detection, measurement, and analysis and there are already abundant works in this regard, especially from quantitative perspectives, and not so much qualitative. The use of these last ones has been object of our main interest, and for this we have resorted to the use of certain simple but decisive techniques for the detection of urban and social problems, difficult to demonstrate in another way. From the empirical point of view, the qualitative analysis developed allows us to propose the following reflections. In the Trinitat Nova neighborhood, time will tell whether the integral regeneration plan being undertaken is effective or not. The most colorful and evident urban transformation are already clearly visible. However, these sorts of urban operations have been practiced time and again in many other cities, without managing to significantly improve the living conditions of inhabitants in terms of employment, education, ecology, economy, etc. We hope that this will not be the case in Trinitat Nova, and that European and municipal resources will serve to reverse current imbalances vis-à-vis other neighborhoods of the city, as the slogan of the Neighborhood Plan promises.

In Marina del Prat Vernell, interventions have tended toward urban renewal, ignoring the neighborhood's past and seeking to bring it in closer alliance with the city center. It remains to be seen whether the zone's geographical location makes it a target location for hotels and offices, which could serve as an economic boost and help diminish its traditional isolation.

Raval, an archetypal space characterized by a mixed uses and social collectives, is among the most studied of Barcelona's neighborhoods, from various perspectives. The diversity and multidimensionality of the socio-spatial phenomena in this neighborhood presents the main obstacle to the adequate and consensual implementation of urban policies. Here, more than anywhere in

Barcelona, the participation of all relevant agents is necessary. This is no small challenge, but it must be confronted to alleviate the neighborhood's persistent vulnerabilities.

Like Raval, La Barceloneta is today characterized by a confluence of well-differentiated social groups, including immigrants, tourists, new urban tribes, and traditional residents. This is an example where urban processes and interventions have driven changes to the neighborhood's traditional residential function, mostly due to the increase in its tourist attraction. As recognized by Pareja and Simó [21], its potential as a gentrificable space is very high, and this is seen clearly in the protests and demonstrations of residents carrying banners.

In this work, we wanted to carry out an analysis of the multidimensionality and growing vulnerability of these neighborhoods, from a geographic/territorial perspective rather than a quantitative one. This seems to infer a further need to undertake (or to continue, in some cases) actions aimed at improving both the constructed environment and the social ambit, to ensure the right of people to the city itself, and a better quality of life to those who live there.

Author Contributions: All the authors have contributed in similar proportion to the development of this work. The sections have been developed jointly and coordinated among all authors. The supervisory task corresponded to the first signatory author.

Funding: This research has been funded by the Ministry of Economy and Competitiveness of Spain, within the framework of the Research Project "Air pollution, vulnerable populations and health: analysis of environmental injustices based on geotechnologies" (Ref CSO2014-55535-R).

Conflicts of Interest: The authors declare no conflict of interest. The funding organisation had no role in the design of the study; in the collection, analysis, or interpretation of data; in the writing of the manuscript; or in the decision to publish the results.

References

1. Morrone, A.; Scrivens, K.; Smith, C.; Balestra, C. Measuring vulnerability and resilience in OECD countries. In Proceedings of the IARW-OECD Conference on Economic Insecurity, Paris, France, 22–23 November 2011.

2. Sánchez, D.; Egea, C. Enfoque de vulnerabilidad social para investigar las desventajas socioambientales. Su aplicación en el estudio de los adultos mayores. *Papeles de Población* **2011**, *17*, 151–185.

3. Moreno, A.; Palacios, A.; Suárez, P. Elaboración de un índice de vulnerabilidad socio-ambiental intraurbana apoyado en sistemas de información geográfica. In *Naturaleza, Territorio y Ciudad en un Mundo Global*; Ediciones de la Universidad Autónoma de Madrid and AGE: Madrid, Spain, 2018; pp. 2629–2638.

4. Moreno, A.; Palacios, A.; Suárez, P. Medición de la vulnerabilidad socio-ambiental intraurbana: Un ensayo exploratorio basado en SIG. In *Aplicaciones Geotecnológicas para el Desarrollo Económico Sostenible*; XVII Congreso Nacional de Tecnologías de la Información Geográfica; Asociación de Geógrafos Españoles: Madrid, Spain, 2016; pp. 214–223.

5. Alguacil, J.; Camacho, J.; Hernández, A. La vulnerabilidad urbana en España. Identificación y evolución de los barrios vulnerables. *EMPIRIA Rev. de Metodología de Ciencias Sociales* **2014**, *27*, 73–94. [CrossRef]

6. Mateos, P. La doble segregación urbana: Desigualdades socio-espaciales y justicia ambiental. In *Actas del III Congreso Internacional de Desarrollo Local*; Universidad de La Habana: Havana, Cuba, 2013; pp. 3488–3510.

7. Wisner, B. Vulnerability as Concept, Model, Metric, and Tools. In *Oxford Research Encyclopedia of Natural Hazard Science*; Oxford University Press: New York, NY, USA, 2016.

8. Cardona, O. *La necesidad de repensar de manera holística los conceptos de vulnerabilidad y riesgo: Una crítica y una revisión necesaria para la gestión*; Centro de Estudios sobre Desastres y Riesgos de la Universidad de los Andes: Bogotá, Colombia, 2003.

9. Brooks, N. *Vulnerability, Risk and Adaptation: A Conceptual Framework*; Working Paper 38; Tyndall Centre for Climate Change Research, University of East Anglia: Norwich, UK, 2003.

10. Alexander, D. Vulnerability. In *Encyclopedia of Crisis Management*; SAGE: Thousand Oaks, CA, USA, 2013; pp. 980–983.

11. Subirats, J.; Martí-Costa, M. *Ciudades Vulnerables y Crisis en España*; Centro de Estudios Andaluces: Seville, Spain, 2014.

12. González Pérez, J.; Lois González, R.C.; Piñeira Mantiñán, M.J. The Economic Crisis and Vulnerability in the Spanish Cities: Urban Governance Challenges. *Soc. Behav. Sci.* **2016**, *223*, 160–166. [CrossRef]

13. Cutter, S.; Boruff, B.; Shirley, W. Social vulnerability to environmental hazards. *Soc. Sci. Q.* **2003**, *84*, 242–261. [CrossRef]

14. Cardona, O.; Carreño, M. System of indicators of disaster risk and risk management for the Americas: Recent updating and application of the IDB-IDEA approach. In *Measuring Vulnerability to Natural Hazards*, 2nd ed.; Birkmann, J., Ed.; United Nations University Press: Tokyo, Japan, 2013; pp. 251–276.

15. Holand, I.; Lujala, P. Replicating and adapting an index of social vulnerability to a new context: A comparison study for Norway. *Ann. Assoc. Am. Geogr.* **2013**, *65*, 312–328. [CrossRef]

16. Birkmann, J.; Wisner, B. *Measuring the Un-Measurable: The Challenge of Vulnerability*; United Nations University Institute for Environment and Human Security: Bonn, Germany, 2006.

17. Anderson, M.; Woodrow, P. *Rising from the Ashes: Development Strategies in Times of Disaster*; Lynne Rienner: Boulder, CO, USA, 1998.

18. Piñeira-Mantiñán, M.; Durán-Villa, F.; Taboada-Failde, J. Urban vulnerability in spanish médium-sized cities during the post-crisis period (2009–2016). The cases of A Coruña and Vigo (Spain). *Urban Sci.* **2018**, *2*, 37. [CrossRef]

19. Sargatal, M. El barrio del Raval de Barcelona (1999–2008). Transformaciones urbanas y nuevos enfoques metodológicos para el estudio del centro histórico. *Biblio 3W Rev. Bibliográfica de Geografía y Ciencias Sociales* **2009**, *XIV*, 824.

20. Martori, J.; Hoberg, K. Indicadores cuantitativos de segregación residencial. El caso de la población inmigrante en Barcelona. *Scripta Nova. Rev. Electrónica de Geografía y Ciencias Sociales* **2004**, *VIII*, 169.

21. Martori, J.; Hoberg, K. Nuevas técnicas de estadística espacial para la detección de clusters residenciales de población inmigrante. *Scripta Nova. Rev. Electrónica de Geografía y Ciencias Sociales* **2008**, *XII*, 261.

22. Martínez, S.; Carreras, C.; Frago, L. El Raval de Barcelona, un laboratori d'estudis urbans. *Treballs de la Societat Catalana de Geografia* **2015**, *79*, 125–150.

23. Domingo, A.; Bayona, J. Movilidad, vivienda y distribución territorial de la población marroquí en Cataluña. *Estudios Geográficos* **2007**, *68*, 465–496.

24. Subirats, J.; Rius, J. *Del Xino al Raval*; Editorial Hacer: Barcelona, España, 2008.

25. Blanco, I. Gobernanza urbana y políticas de regeneración: El caso de Barcelona. *Rev. Española de Ciencia Política* **2009**, *20*, 125–146.

26. Fernández, M. Asaltar el Raval. Control de población y producción de plusvalías en el barrio barcelonés. *URBS Rev. de Estudios Urbanos y Ciencias Sociales* **2012**, *2*, 51–68.

27. Badia, J. La Marina del Prat Vermell: ¿Nueva Centralidad Urbana? Master's Thesis, Polytechnic University of Catalonia, Barcelona, Spain, 2015.

28. Granados, J.O. Els grans projectes d'actuació a la Marina del Prat Vermell i al Morrot de Montjuïc. *Biblio 3W Rev. Bibliográfica de Geografía y Ciencias Sociales* **2013**, *XVIII*, 1049.

29. Makhlouf, M. Transformaciones Urbanas Desde la Resistencia. Aproximaciones a un Movimiento Vecinal en la Barceloneta. Ph.D. Thesis, Universitat de Barcelona, Barcelona, Spain, 2016.

30. Pareja, M.; Simó, M. Dinámicas en el entorno construido: Renovación, gentrificación y turismo. El caso de la Barceloneta. *ACE Arch. City Environ.* **2014**, *9*, 201–222.

31. Alamilla, C. Análisis de los impactos socioculturales desde la perspectiva del residente que el turismo genera en el barrio de La Barceloneta, España. *ROTUR Rev. de Ocio y Turismo* **2016**, *11*, 1–11.

32. Nesticò, A.; Sica, F. The sustainability of urban renewal projects: A model for economic multi-criteria analysis. *J. Prop. Invest. Financ.* **2017**, *35*, 397–409. [CrossRef]

urban science

MDPI

Article

Segregated in the City, Separated in the School. The Reproduction of Social Inequality through the School System

Aina Gomà Garcia * and Joel Muñoz Aranda *

Research Group on Energy, Territory and Society, Department of Geography, Autonomous University of Barcelona, 08193 Bellaterra (Cerdanyola del Vallès), Spain
* Correspondence: aina.goma@uab.cat (A.G.); joel.munoz@e-campus.uab.cat (J.M.)

Received: 20 October 2018; Accepted: 21 November 2018; Published: 27 November 2018

Abstract: This paper explores the relationship between urban segregation and the educational level of the population. In the first place, the impacts of segregation in educational careers are analysed. Secondly, the contribution explores the interrelationship between urban segregation and schooling in Barcelona. For this aim, different sources have been used: The map of urban segregation in Catalonia at the census tract level; data about the formal educational levels of the population, aged between 15 and 34 years, from the Catalan Youth Survey (*Enquesta de Joventut de Catalunya*); and schooling data in Barcelona's schools and neighbourhoods. The research shows how urban segregation effects the educational level and fosters social inequalities amongst neighbourhoods. It also points out how choosing school and enrolment strategies could act by increasing school segregation in Barcelona. Therefore, the role of segregation in the reproduction and perpetuation of inequalities in the living conditions of the population is exposed.

Keywords: urban segregation; school choice; educational level; social inequalities; neighbourhood effect

1. Introduction

Studies about social inequalities and differences in living conditions have often paid little attention to spatial issues. The available literature shows that, when territorial factors have been taken into account, they have been mainly focused on the classic categories of countryside and city or urban and rural. Conversely, differences inside the main urban areas, which require an approach at a highly detailed scale, have often been overlooked.

In the current stage of the urbanisation process—when the social, infrastructural, and territorial transformations of recent decades have brought about increasing territorial integration and an extension of the urban areas and urban conditions [1]—this detailed perspective takes on even greater importance. As is widely known, territorial integration has implied that the differences between the former urban and rural areas have declined and have lost explanatory power [2,3]. In contrast, spatial inequalities associated with the phenomena of spatial segregation have gained importance [4]. Spatial segregation is defined as the trend of social groups to split in the urban space according to their socio-economic profiles. This is then one of the most relevant and worrying aspects in the process of capitalist urbanisation and touches on the international debate about the significance of space in the (re)production of social inequality [3,5].

Residential segregation is the result of the differentiated capacity of social groups to choose their place of residence depending on the price of land and housing. As is clearly evident, for persons and families with the highest income levels the widest scope of choice is available. In the opposite sense, the most socially vulnerable groups are confined to those neighbourhoods in which housing prices are lowest, these often being the ones that accumulate the greatest urban planning deficits, the worst conditions in terms of habitability, reduced accessibility, and a downscaled service offer.

The existence of segregation has given rise to a significant debate and wide-ranging literature regarding its effects on living conditions and the opportunities offered to the population, something which has become known as the "neighbourhood effect" [6–9]. In this debate, the issue of reproduction of inequalities through the school system plays a significant role. The issues coming to the fore cannot, certainly, be belittled: Are the scholarly performances of schools in vulnerable neighbourhoods worse than those in other areas? Are equal opportunities affected by having been schooled in one of these schools? Do the relatively well-off families residing in vulnerable neighbourhoods tend to send their offspring to schools in other neighbourhoods? Does this set of factors contribute to the settling, increase, and perpetuation of social inequalities in the city?

To respond to these issues, the analysis of the relationship between urban segregation, on the one hand, and school segregation, on the other, is essential. The latter may be defined as the unequal distribution of students amongst schools located in the same region in accordance with a certain individual- or family-based characteristic [10]. It refers to a situation in which the schools in the same region enrol markedly different student profiles, depending on, firstly, the socio-economic status of their families. Many authors have studied the scope, causes, and impact of this phenomenon, largely from the seventies onwards, especially on the United States exploring racial segregation in schools [11]. Although there is no clear agreement on this matter, certain writers have signalled educational systems with quasi-market operative systems as a fundamental reason for school segregation. Increased possibility of choice tends to nurture dynamics such as the fleeing of the middle-class population from schools with greater concentrations of ethnic minorities in a similar way to the so-called "white flight" [10,12]. This phrase became common in the middle of the 20th century in the United States and refers to the migration of the white population away from heterogeneous urban areas to settle in socially homogenous ones. The social composition of schools tends to sharpen segregation creating a spiral that would lead the most vulnerable centres and students into decline [13–15]. Recent reports have suggested that school segregation is a genuine issue in Barcelona and Catalonia, as it is in all the major Spanish and European metropolitan areas [10,16].

Our contribution tackles this general debate and aims to provide reflections based on the combination of a triple line of analysis: Knowledge of the dynamics of urban segregation; educational levels achieved by the population aged between 15 and 34; and enrolment strategies and scholar performance according to place of residence. The scope of the study is Catalonia as a whole, even though special attention is paid to the city of Barcelona. The paper, from here onwards, is divided into the following sections: Firstly, a brief outline will be given as to the issue of residential and school segregation in Catalonia; after this, the hypotheses and methodology followed are detailed; in the third section, emphasis will be placed on the analysis of the impact of residential and school segregation along educational and training trajectories for Catalan youths; and finally, schooling demand and enrolment in Barcelona's neighbourhoods will be studied as an example of the mechanisms of school segregation. The work will conclude with some overall findings.

2. Residential Segregation and School Segregation in Catalonia

The economic recession in Spain, as a result of the real estate bubble and the austerity policies, have brought an increase in poverty, social exclusion, and inequality. Different studies have proven that, since 2008, the recession's impact on the socio-spatial configuration of Spanish cities is extremely relevant [17,18]. Similarly noteworthy has been its repercussion in the Barcelona metropolitan area, along with the rest of Catalonia [18,19]. Recent studies have shown that the increase in inequalities has led to an increase in urban residential segregation [20], which has been exacerbated over the period 2001–2012. Thus, in Catalonia, throughout the years indicated, the number of census tracts with extreme segregation (vulnerable or well-off) has shifted from 7.7% to 19.7% of the total. In demographic terms, the people who live in census tracts with extreme segregation have gone from 6.8% to 17.1% of the population. Specifically, in 2012, Catalonia had, on the one hand, 676,459 of its inhabitants living in vulnerable neighbourhoods, whereas 620,259 resided in comfortable neighbourhoods. The relationship of this dynamic with living conditions of the population has been studied by, amongst others, Nel·lo (2016) [21].

In turn, over recent years, several studies have analysed the shortfalls in equity in the Catalan educational system, warning of the growing threat of school segregation [10,22–27]. This process has led to increasing differentiation in the social composition of the schools, with a higher concentration of socially homogenous groups (both students from well-off families and also those in the vulnerable ones). Recent publications of the Jaume Bofill Foundation, specialised in studies about education and its social context in Catalonia, sustain the idea that school segregation is a reality and an unsolved issue in Catalonia [28].

The contextual causes to which the aforesaid studies attribute this situation in Catalonia are widespread: The increase in social inequalities and the deepening residential segregation; the arrival of immigrant students and the outflow of other families; the stigmatisation of certain schools as a result of their social outlook; the worsening of living conditions associated with the economic downturn; along with austerity measures and current educational policies [29], amongst others. It must be mentioned; however, that these contingent causes act in the context of a quasi-market-based educational system, defined by a certain freedom of choice, in a similar manner to the one that leads to residential segregation. That means that the families with the greatest levels of social, cultural, and economic capital are endowed with increased possibilities to choose the school and the type of educational project they want for their children. Within this framework, boosted furthermore through mechanisms and regulations imposed by the schools (such as quotas, fees, or access criteria) and the unequal ability to meet transportation costs, the real power of choice for vulnerable families becomes restricted. As a consequence of the foregoing, certain schools feature a much greater concentration of pupils with greater educational needs. Not surprisingly these are the schools often equipped with fewer teaching staff, materials, and installations. As can be seen, once again, there is a clear parallelism between this phenomenon and that of residential segregation.

School segregation is in line with the stigmatisation of certain neighbourhoods and schools, with this conditioning demand, as it will be seen in the second part of our study. This is a phenomenon that is by no means exclusive to Barcelona or Catalonia, moreover it has been studied and observed by different authors in a number of cities [22,26,30].

The negative impacts of segregation on the school performance of the most vulnerable groups, on the system as a whole, and on social cohesion in our region have been widely contrasted [10,21,25]. Many authors state that school segregation reduces educational opportunities for the most vulnerable population though the so-called "peer effect". Published work often states that students coming from socially vulnerable families obtain worse grades if they are enrolled in socially homogenous schools than if they attend schools with a greater social mix. Even though there is no common agreement, some authors find that this cultural and social mix does not bring, with it, negative effects on the children from higher income families, meaning; therefore, that the effect is asymmetric [22,25,28]. In a report issued by Síndic de Greuges de Catalunya [26], the spiral of reproduction of school segregation has been denounced; enrolment and schooling conditions affect the social structure of the schools and these, in turn, influences future enrolment strategies. According to certain authors, this reality becomes a determining factor to call into question equity, educational quality, and social cohesion in the Catalan educational system [10], thereby compromising its role in the equal distribution of opportunities amongst the population [28].

3. Hypothesis, Materials, and Methods

The starting point of this paper is the hypothesis that residential and school segregation does not just reflect social inequalities but; moreover, they reproduce and perpetuate them. Specifically, school segregation compromises both the educational system's capacity with regard to ensuring equality of opportunities, as well as its role in reducing social inequality. Thus, residential and educational segregation are deemed to be closely interlinked and mutually feed off each other. School segregation largely explains unequal educational paths amongst different social groups. Furthermore, the dynamics of school choice may be a mechanism that heightens segregation at schools, due to the unequal capacity of choice by families in a system where schools compete under unfair conditions.

These hypotheses will be debated through two approaches: On the one hand, the consequences of residential segregation in education; and on the other, the processes of segregation and stigmatisation in certain areas and their schools. Three main sources of data were used: The map of urban segregation in Catalonia; the Enquesta de Joventut de Catalunya (Catalan Youth Survey) 2017; and school enrolment data from Barcelona districts.

As base information on residential segregation, data on urban segregation in Catalonia at a census tract scale from the research *Barris i Crisi* was taken as a starting point [20]. In that study, a classification of the census tracts in Catalonia was established according to the values of four variables related to income: Percentage of foreign residents, percentage of unemployment, average built-up surface area of the residential property, and its cadastral value. The results of the research established three categories which, in 2012's values, could be specified in the following magnitudes for Catalonia: Inferior extreme segregation (vulnerable neighbourhoods), with 484 census tracts and 676,459 people; extreme superior urban segregation (well-off neighbourhoods), with 586 census tracts and 620,259 people; and areas without extreme segregation (intermediate districts), with 4359 census tracts and 6,386,428 residents [20].

The second source of information used was the 2017 Catalan Youth Survey, in the analysis of which the variable of residential segregation explained in the foregoing paragraph was included [31]. For this contribution, the data referring to educational paths and levels in the Catalan population aged between 15 and 34 was used.

Finally, a set of statistical information on enrolments in the second cycle of pre-school (P3–P5) and primary education (first to sixth grade) was gathered at a neighbourhood and district level in Barcelona. Specifically, the following data was considered: Population enrolled in pre-school and primary education per neighbourhood, as of 1 January 2017 [32]; location of 364 pre-school and primary schools in Barcelona [33]; enrolments and vacancies in Barcelona's schools for the 2017–2018 academic year [34]; school's characteristics in terms of ownership and complexity [33]; and school performance by districts in the percentage of failure in basic competences—common grades that all students take every two years—by the sixth grade of primary school in 2014 [34].

This data was georeferenced with the aim of carrying out a spatial analysis using geographical information systems (GIS). These tools enabled the mapping and cross-referencing of data and variables, exploring their distribution through neighbourhoods in Barcelona.

4. Analysis and Results: Segregation and Educational Paths

As has been indicated, the analysis of the data embraced three aspects: Firstly, the existing relationship between residential segregation and educational paths in the Catalan youth population; secondly, a detailed study of Barcelona in order to study inequality in terms of demands for enrolment in the city's neighbourhoods, and lastly, an analysis of data relating to school performance broken down by districts and related to income.

4.1. Residential Segregation and Educational Paths in Catalonia

The analysis of the relationship between residential segregation and the educational paths of the population is a key point of the debate on the neighbourhood effect, in terms of standards of living for the population. When analysing spatial inequalities amongst the youth population the approach taken in this paper paid special attention to urban segregation. This perspective holds particular interest amongst this group because in early ages socialisation mostly takes place in the immediate surroundings and in the neighbourhood of residence.

The results of the analysis on a wide-ranging sample of the Catalan population, aged between 15 and 34, has led us to conclude that, currently, the differences and inequalities in the habits and living conditions of the youth population in Catalonia can be better explained by residential segregation than by other spatial features [31]. This means that educational paths, professional activity, participation, etc. amongst the youth population depended more on socio-spatial conditions of the neighbourhood in which they live in than other more traditional classifications, such as the geographical area, the size of the municipality, or the intensity of urban development.

The variables referring to the formal educational system clearly confirmed this point. In 2017, 42.5% of the Catalan population aged between 15 and 34 were registered as students. This percentage varied in the diverse age groups, being higher with the younger members and lower with the older ones, as they were already entering the labour market. Along general lines, the most prolonged training paths over time corresponded to the highest levels of formal education, such as higher education and even postgraduate studies. Now, it is significant to note that, in all ages, the percentage of the population currently undertaking studies was lower in vulnerable areas than in well-off ones. The difference could be as much as 10 percentage points for the group aged between 25 and 29 years. People in this age range in vulnerable neighbourhoods displayed a lower rate of school enrolment (16.6%) than in any other spatial category of analysis. This was a clear sign of the shorter educational paths of the population in these neighbourhoods.

The briefest educational trajectories also coincided with the lower levels of formation. In the vulnerable neighbourhoods, the percentage of the youth population that had not completed compulsory education stood at 16.6% (amongst those who declare that they had finished studying), almost twice that of the non-vulnerable neighbourhoods (8.8%), and significantly above the Catalan average (9.9%).

In this sense, whilst 91.2% of the youth population in non-vulnerable areas successfully completed compulsory education, in vulnerable areas this was the case for only 83.4%. As Figure 1 shows, the difference grew at the higher levels of education. In the most vulnerable neighbourhoods, only 45.3% of the young population had completed post-compulsory secondary education, compared to 65.4% in the rest of the areas.

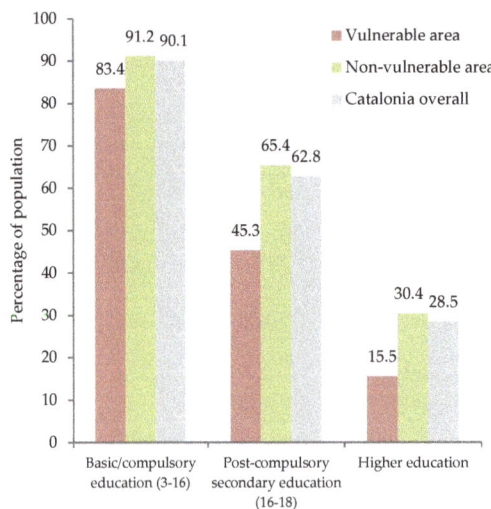

Figure 1. Rates for different educational levels. Population aged 15–34 years who had completed their educational path. Catalan Youth Survey 2017.

With regard to higher studies, merely 15.5% of young people in inferior segregation neighbourhoods held university degrees, compared to 30.4% in the rest. This behaviour was related to future expectations, the peers with whom the youth socialises, and also the economic possibilities of people in vulnerable areas; 23.8% of young people in vulnerable areas stated that they had to leave their studies in the last two years, or that they have not been able to enrol in those studies they would wish to owing to financial difficulties.

The results of the variables analysed showed that the neighbourhood's level of segregation influenced youths' educational paths more than any other territorial variable.

4.2. Choosing Schools in Barcelona

Another dimension of the relationship between segregation and educational training can be perceived through the study of spatially differentiated school enrolment patterns and strategies. This could be studied specifically through school enrolment data from the city of Barcelona. It is worthwhile noting that the city had, in its 73 neighbourhoods (Figure 2), a total of 364 schools offering the second cycle of pre-school (ages three to five) and primary (ages six to 12), of which 172 were state-run and 192 were private or part-financed schools. In total, these schools had approximately 130,300 places. With regard to the population, Barcelona's city census in 2017 recorded 124,504 children in ages of pre-school and primary school. On the other hand, it was found that a total of 127,153 pupils were enrolled in schools in the city, which gives a positive balance of 2649 enrolments and implies that some children travelled into schools from outside the city.

As has been mentioned beforehand, literature reveals the trend of families to enrol their offspring in neighbourhoods with greater economic power and a more positive social image than their own. In this way, well-off neighbourhoods tend to welcome students from other parts of the city and, conversely, vulnerable neighbourhoods end up relinquishing part of their school population to other neighbourhoods. A way to verify the existence of such a dynamic is through the differential values of students enrolled and the population with school age in each neighbourhood. With this method, the value obtained indicates whether the neighbourhood has more students enrolled in its schools than its corresponding school age population (positive balance), or, oppositely, fewer students enrolled in its schools than its school age population (negative balance). The former receives students from other parts of the city and, in the opposite sense, the latter send school age students outside of the neighbourhood. It is worthwhile mentioning that the data available allowed for the obtainment of the general balance for each neighbourhood, but not the determination of which neighbourhood students come from or to where they travel.

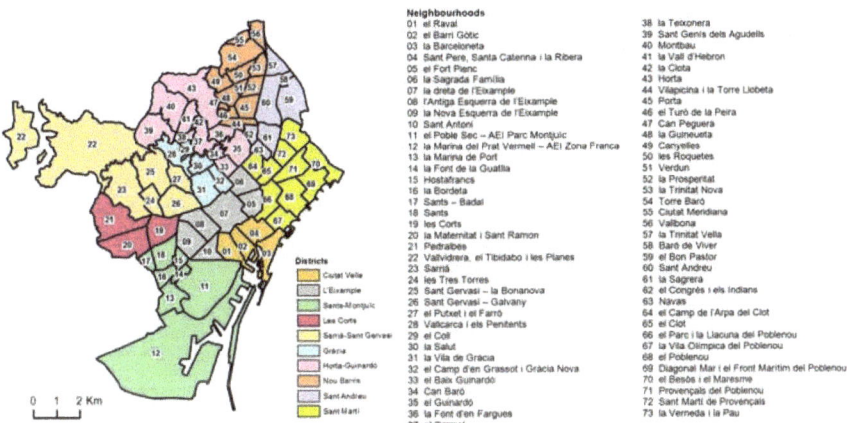

Figure 2. Districts and neighbourhoods of Barcelona.

As can be seen in the map given in Figure 3, there were notable differences amongst neighbourhoods with regard to the balance between enrolments and the school age population. These have been represented on the map in diverse tones of red, showing the neighbourhoods with less enrolments than school age population (low retention) and, in green, those which, in the opposite sense, had more students enrolled in their schools than residents with school age. On the other hand, the number represented on the map for each neighbourhood corresponds to the balance between enrolments and the school age population in absolute values.

Amongst the districts with the highest positive balance, we found, running from East to West, the neighbourhoods of Font d'en Fargues, Vall d'Hebrón, Sant Gervasi-Bonanova, Sarrià, and Pedralbes, which exceed 100% (dark green on the map), meaning that in these areas the number of enrolments doubled, and at times tripled, their school age population. Paying attention to absolute values, the neighbourhood of Sarrià was where the difference between its enrolled students and its school age population was greatest, with a positive balance of 7089 enrolled students. In general terms, the neighbourhoods with the greatest powers of attraction coincided with those that had the highest average incomes in the city (Sant Gervasi-Bonanova, Sarrià, and Pedralbes), yet also with those in a relatively comfortable situation with respect to those in their surroundings, as would be the case of Sant Andreu, la Prosperitat, and la Dreta del Eixample.

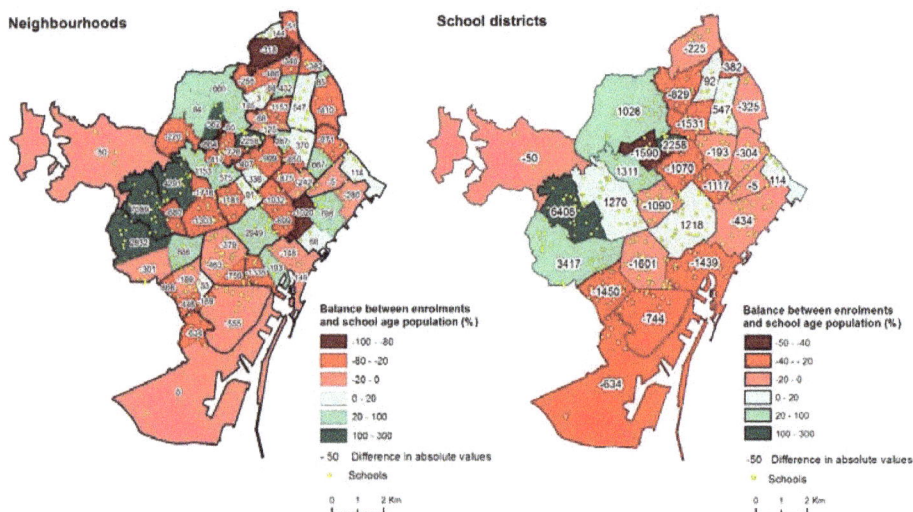

Figure 3. Attraction and discharge of the school age population by neighbourhoods and school districts in Barcelona, 2017.

At the opposite end of the scale (maroon on the map), we found Torre Baró, la Clota, la Teixonera, and el Parc i la Llacuna del Poblenou, whose school age population tended to be enrolled outside the neighbourhood where they live. This trend could be explained as a result of the paucity of school places in these neighbourhoods. However, it was also observed that an important number of neighbourhoods that boasted a well-served educational network sent students to other areas, namely la Trinitat Nova, Bon Pastor, el Raval, Sant Antoni, La Bordeta, etc. These were, largely, neighbourhoods with lower average incomes than other neighbourhoods in their surroundings.

This behaviour also explains the presence of certain neighbourhoods with relatively low-income levels, which, conversely, had more enrolments than the school age population. This was the case, for example, of Besòs-Maresme, Baró de Viver, Ciutat Meridiana, and la Prosperitat. As has been mentioned beforehand, data about the neighbourhood where each student lives was not available, but it seemed that Baró de Viver and Besós-Maresme attracted, respectively, students living in Bon Pastor and in Sant Adrià de Besòs (specifically from la Mina neighbourhood). Ciutat Meridiana probably attracted the school age population from Torre Baró and Can Cuiàs, which belongs to the adjacent city of Montcada i Reixac. Finally, la Prosperitat, the centre of Sant Andreu, and la Font d'en Fargues were relatively wealthier neighbourhoods than those surrounding them. Thus, it could be observed that, in general terms, neighbourhoods with the highest income levels and best reputations were those that had more enrolments than they should in relation to their number of school age residents. Certain exceptions to this rationale have been observed, such as, for example, the neighbourhoods of Tres Torres, Sant Gervasi-Galvany, and el Putxet i el Farró, which were comfortable neighbourhoods though they displayed a low level of self-containment in terms of school age population. According to the proximity and the school district map (second map in Figure 3), it seemed that their students travelled to bordering neighbourhoods that also had a high income.

In the second map in Figure 3, the difference between the number of enrolments and the school age population of the 29 school districts is represented. School districts are integrated by sets of proximity centres. Residence in one of these areas constitutes one of the prioritisation criteria to obtain a place in the school of choice, whether this is a state school or a part-financed school. Data displayed wholly confirmed the main features unearthed through the analysis undertaken in relation to the neighbourhoods. The fact that, despite the existence of school districts—intended, in theory, to ensure school enrolment under terms of equality for the school age population near its place of residence—there was an outflow of the population, shows a shortfall in the system's effectiveness.

With the aim of complementing this analysis, vacancies in each school were studied for each neighbourhood and school district. As can been seen in the map in Figure 4, the number of school vacancies was not homogenous in all Barcelona. On the one hand, there were 15 neighbourhoods that had a deficit in absolute terms of school places (shades of green), to which those with zero vacancies must be added. These were neighbourhoods with a high demand in terms of school enrolment, with more demand than availability. Worthy of special mention in terms of schooling demand was Sant Andreu, which as has already been mentioned, was one of the most well-off neighbourhoods in the northeast area of the city.

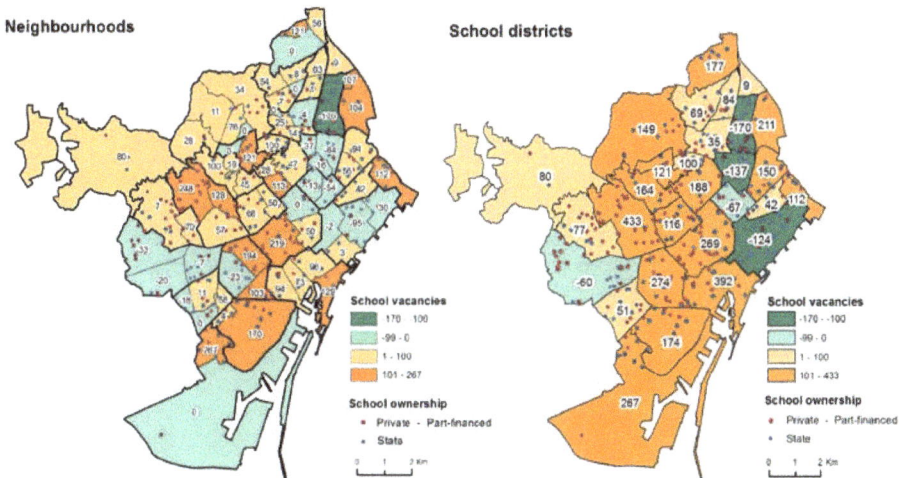

Figure 4. School vacancies (P3–P6) by neighbourhoods and school districts in Barcelona, in the 2017–2018 academic year.

On the other hand, as can be observed in the same map in orange tones, there were 50 neighbourhoods in Barcelona that had a significant number of school vacancies. If we compared this map with the one on income by neighbourhood (2016), it could be seen that the areas that had school vacancies were, firstly, those which had lower income levels, namely Bon Pastor, Baró de Viver, Ciutat Meridiana, and la Barceloneta. Alongside these, we could also find neighbourhoods with higher income levels, such as Dreta de l'Eixample or all of those that comprise the district of Sarrià-San Gervasi. This situation had a dual explanation: In the case of the vulnerable neighbourhoods, this was due to weak demand levels and the failure to retain own school age population in the neighbourhood; however, in the well-off neighbourhoods, this was explained by the predominance of private or part-financed schools. These schools, unlike those which were wholly state run, offered many places without overly careful adjustment to demand.

By focusing on neighbourhoods with school vacancies and with low income, worthy of further attention were the cases of Vallbona, Trinitat Nova, and les Roquetes, which had a highly elevated number of unfilled places despite only having one school, which was, furthermore, state run. The figures of the 54 unfilled school spaces in Roquetes, 56 in Vallbona, and 83 in Trinitat Nova indicated clearly that families in these neighbourhoods, despite having vacant places nearby, preferred to enrol their children in pre-school and primary centres in neighbouring areas.

If we observe the second map in Figure 4, with the school vacancies by school districts, it can be seen how Sant Andreu, Navas–la Sagrera–el Congés i els Indians, and el Parc i la Llacuna–la Vila Olímpica del Poblenou–Diagonal Mar i el Front Marítim del Poblenou–Poblenou, were areas that had more demand than the number of places on offer. In the opposite sense, two axes that show school vacancies were clearly detected: Running from North to South, from Horta-Guinardó to Sants-Montjuïc; and the section in the Besós River area. This could also be explained by the duality already mentioned; some of the areas having a surplus of vacancies were neighbourhoods with a low income (such as Ciudad Meridiana- Torre Baró—Vallbona), whilst others comprised well-off neighbourhoods that displayed a high number of unfilled school places due to the predominance of privately-owned or part-financed schools (as is the case of Putxet i Farró—San Gervasi-Bonanova—Sant Gervasi-Galvany).

4.3. Inequalities in School Performance

The final part of this paper analyses the relationship between the socio-economic variables, the complexity of the schools' situation, and the academic results of the students. The available data on school performance refers to the percentage of students in the sixth grade of primary school that did not achieve the basic competence in the 2013–2014 academic year [34]. In this case, no data detailed by neighbourhoods was available and, for this reason, work was undertaken with the 10 districts of Barcelona.

As can be seen in Figure 5, the districts with a higher percentage of students that failed basic competences at sixth grade were those of Ciutat Vella and Nou Barris, with the percentage standing at around 20%. Following these, with fail rates at around 12%, we found Sant Martí, Horta-Guinardó, and Sant Andreu. The district of Gracia showed a 10% fail rate and Eixample an 8.5% fail rate. Finally, the districts showing the best results were Les Corts and Sarrià-Sant Gervasi, with merely 5% of the students failing these tests. It is worthwhile highlighting that the differences were highly remarkable, reaching up to 15 percentage points between districts.

Complementary information refers to school complexity. Maximum complexity schools were defined by the Departamanet d'Ensenyament (Teaching Department) based on the following context variables: Low parental level of instruction, parental employment on low professional qualification posts, significant number of parents of students receiving guaranteed minimum income, high percentage of parents unemployed, high percentage of students with specific educational needs, and high percentage of immigrants. The results clearly showed a direct relationship between the number of schools defined with the category of maximum complexity and the percentage of sixth grade primary students that did not achieve the basic competences, with an adjustment rate of $R^2 = 0.7464$. In this sense, the districts with the most schools deemed to be in complex situations (Ciutat Vella, Nou Barris, Sants-Montjuïc, and Sant Martí) were the ones with the most deficient results on the basic competences. These results may be the expression of the spiral of reproduction of school segregation, specifically of the conditions of vulnerability experienced by some areas and schools.

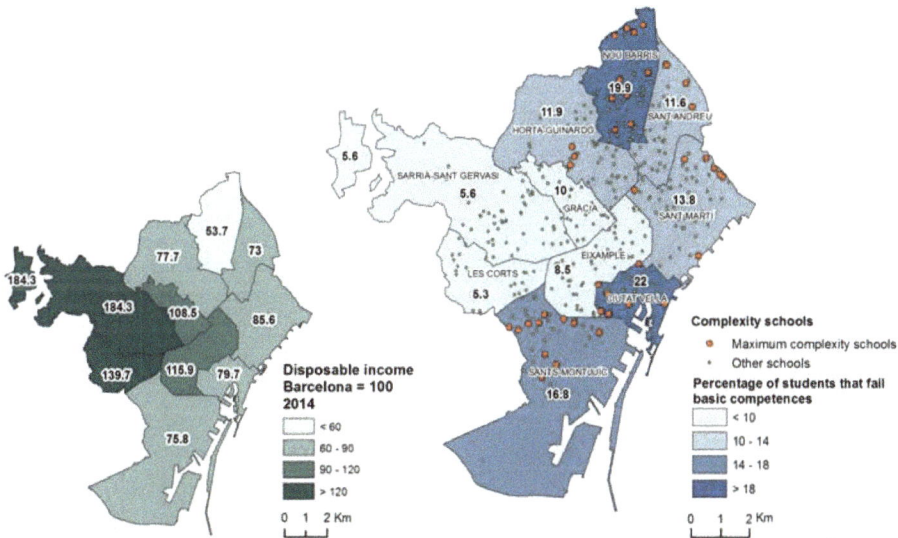

Figure 5. Disposable income per capita (Barcelona = 100) and percentage of students that failed basic competences tests (%) by districts in Barcelona, 2014.

The relationship between academic performances and the average disposable income was even more revealing. As can be seen from Table 1 and Figures 5 and 6, the relationship was of an inverse nature: the lowest percentages of students failing basic competences corresponded to the higher income districts (that is, the districts of Sarrià-Sant Gervasi and Les Corts, as well as those of Eixample and Gràcia). In the opposite sense, where the average income was lower, the percentage of students that failed basic competences was higher (as can be seen in Nou Barris, Ciutat Vella, and Sants-Montjuïc). Literature dealing with the "neighbourhood effect" as a generator and perpetuator of social inequalities would undoubtedly find food for thought in this data.

Table 1. Disposable income, percentage of students that failed in basic competences tests (%), and the number of maximum complexity schools in Barcelona by district.

District	Disposable Income per Capita 2014 (Barcelona = 100)	Failed on Basic Competences in 6th Grade, 2014 (%)	No. Maximum Complexity Schools
1. Ciutat Vella	79.7	22	7
2. Eixample	115.9	8.5	0
3. Sants-Montjuïc	75.8	16.8	11
4. Les Corts	139.7	5.3	0
5. Sarrià-St Gervasi	184.3	5.6	0
6. Gràcia	108.5	10	0
7. Horta-Guinardó	77.7	11.9	3
8. Nou Barris	53.7	19.9	10
9. Sant Andreu	73	11.6	4
10. Sant Martí	85.6	13.8	7

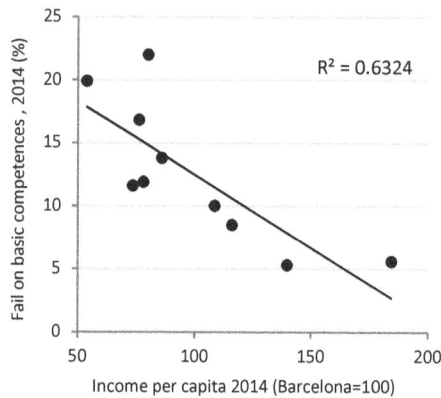

Figure 6. Relationship between disposable income and scholar performance.

5. Conclusions

This article has explored the relationship between urban segregation, on the one hand, and the education levels obtained by the population, on the other. Specifically, the spatial distribution of social groups has been studied in relation to two types of variables: (a) Educational levels amongst the Catalan youth population; and (b) the differences in terms of enrolment and educational performance in the neighbourhoods and districts of Barcelona. In this way, this paper examined the relationship between urban segregation and inequality from one of the aspects with, undoubtedly, the most weighting in the (re)production of social inequality—education.

Based on the analysis carried out, it would seem feasible to state that the place of residence, specifically the neighbourhood, and its conditions (amenities, social conditions, accessibility, services) are related to educational trajectories and expectations of the youth population, acting, thus, as a mechanism for the (re)production of social inequality. It has been verified, for example, in 2017, that the proportion of the youth population living in non-vulnerable neighbourhoods obtained double the number of university titles than compared to those living in vulnerable neighbourhoods.

On the other hand, spatial differences in schools' conditions act as enhancer elements for school segregation, due to, above all, the stigmatisation of schools in vulnerable neighbourhoods and the enrolment procedure. It can be highlighted that families who have a greater capacity of choice tend to send their children to schools outside the most vulnerable neighbourhoods. In most of the vulnerable neighbourhoods we find less school enrolments than the current population aged between three and 12 living there, even in the cases when there are state schools with vacancies. This process may act as a spiral of reproduction of school segregation (and as a result, residential segregation), confining students with greatest educational needs in the schools in vulnerable neighbourhoods, a process that bears a relation with the "white flight" phenomena mentioned at the start of the article.

To ensure equal opportunities all schools should have the same educational conditions. This would surely require a greater investment in terms of human, educational, and material resources in the most vulnerable areas, with the aim of meeting the greater needs of the students largely coming from families with socially vulnerable backgrounds, lower incomes, and migrant origins. These actions, aside from guaranteeing the equality of conditions and opportunities, would increase the appeal of schools suffering stigmatisation, and would contribute to stop or revert the spiral that leads to growing segregation. School segregation and residential segregation, thus, appear to be inextricably linked. Any policy addressing these dynamics will have to deal with them together.

Author Contributions: Data curation, A.G.G. and J.M.A.; formal analysis, J.M.A.; methodology, A.G.G. and J.M.A.; visualization, J.M.A.; writing—original draft, A.G.G. and J.M.A.; writing—review and editing, A.G.G.

Funding: This research has been funded with contributions of the following institutions: Ministerio de Economia, Industria y Competitividad. Programa Retos—Project: *Efecto Barrio. Los impactos sociales de las desigualdades territoriales y las políticas urbanas redistributivas en las grandes ciudades Españolas*; Agència Catalana de Joventut – Projecte: *Enquesta de Joventut de Catalunya, 2017.* Cooperation agreement with Universitat Autònoma de Barcelona; Ministerio de Educación, Cultura y Deporte—Beca de colaboración.

Conflicts of Interest: The authors declare no conflicts of interest.

References

1. Nel·lo, O.; López, J. El procés d'urbanització. In *Raó de Catalunya. La Societat Catalana al Segle XXI*; Giner, S., Homs, O., Eds.; Institut d'Estudis Catalans i Enciclopèdia Catalana: Barcelona, Spain, 2016; pp. 119–148.

2. Indovina, F. *La Ciudad de Baja Densidad: Lógicas, Gestión y Contención*; Diputació de Barcelona: Barcelona, Spain, 2007.

3. Soja, E.W. *Seeking Spatial Justice*; Univeristy of Minnesota Press: Minneapolis, MN, USA, 2010.

4. Tammaru, T.; Marcinczak, S.; Van Ham, M.; Musterd, S. *Socio-Economic Segregation in European Capital Citites. East Meets West*; Routledge: London, UK, 2016.

5. Secchi, B. *La Città dei Ricchi e la Città dei Poveri*; Laterza: Bari, Italy, 2013.

6. Atkinson, R.; Kintrea, K. Disentangling Area Effects: Evidence from Deprived and Non-deprived Neighbourhoods. *Urban Stud.* **2001**, *38*, 2277–2298. [CrossRef]

7. Galster, G.; Anderson, R.; Mustered, S. Who is affected by neighbourhood income mix? Gender, age, family, employment and income differences. *Urban Stud.* **2010**, *47*, 2915–2944. [CrossRef]

8. Slatter, T. Your Life Chances Affect Where You Live: A critique of the 'Cottage Industry' of Neighbourhood Effects Research. *Int. J. Urban Reg. Res.* **2013**, *37*, 367–387. [CrossRef]

9. Cheshire, P. *Segregated Neighbourhoods and Mixed Communities. A Critical Analisys*; Joseph Rowntree Foundation: York, UK, 2007.

10. Bonal, X. La política educativa ante el reto de la segregación escolar en Cataluña. *Int. Inst. Educ. Plan.* **2018**, 7–17. Available online: http://unesdoc.unesco.org/images/0026/002614/261471s.pdf (accessed on 4 April 2018).

11. Sikkink, D.; Emerson, M.O. School schoice and racial segregation in US schools: The role of parents' education. *Ethnic Racial Stud.* **2008**, *31*, 267–293. [CrossRef]

12. Bagley, C. Black and white unite or flight? The racialised dimension of schooling and parental choice. *Br. Educ. Res. J.* **1996**, *22*, 569–580. [CrossRef]

13. Burgess, S.; McConnell, B.; Propper, C.; Wilson, D. The impact of school choice on shorting by ability and socioeconomic factors in English secondary education. In *Schools and the Equal Opportunity Problem*; Wössmann, L., Peterson, P.E., Eds.; MIT Press: Cambridge, UK, 2007.

14. Cullen, J.B.; Jacob, B.A.; Levitt, S.D. The impact of school choice on studemt outcomes: An analysis of the Chicago public schools. *J. Public Econ.* **2005**, *85*, 729–760. [CrossRef]

15. Gewirtz, S.; Ball, S.; Bowe, R. *Markets, Choice and Equity in Education*; Univerisity Press: Buckingham, UK, 1995.

16. Bonal, X.; Zancajo, A. Educació, pobresa i desigualtats en un context de crisi. *Nota d'economia* **2016**, *103*, 91–103.

17. Méndez, R.; Abad, L.D.; Echaves, C. Atlas de la crisis. In *Impactos Socioeconómicos y Territorios Vulnerables en España*; Tirant lo Blanch: Valencia, Spain, 2014.

18. Nel·lo, O.; Donat, C. Los efectos territoriales de la crisis en la región metropolitana de Barcelona. In *Geografía de la Crisis Económica en España*; Albertos, J.M., Sánchez, J.L., Eds.; Publicaciones de la Universitat de València: Valencia, Spain, 2014; pp. 565–608.

19. Sarasa, S.; Porcel, S.; Navarro-Varas, L. L'impacte social de la crisi a l'Àrea Metropolitana de Barcelona i a Catalunya. *Papers* **2013**, *56*, 10–87.

20. Blanco, I.; Nello, O. *Barrios y Crisis. Crisis Económica, Segregación Urbana e Innovación Social en Catalunya*; Tirant lo Blanch: Valencia, Spain, 2018.

21. Nel·lo, O. Desigualdad social y segregación urbana en la región urbana de Barcelona. In *Estudios de Geografía Urbana en Tiempos de Crisis. Territorios Inconclusos y Sociedades Rotas en España*; Brandis, D., del Río, I., Morales, G., Eds.; Biblioteca Nueva: Madrid, Spain, 2016.

22. Benito, R.; Gonález, I. Processos de segregació escolar a Catalunya. *Fundació Jaume Bofill* **2007**, *59*, 11–155. Available online: http://www.fbofill.cat/sites/default/files/464.pdf (accessed on 6 April 2018).

23. Síndic de Greuges. La segregació escolar a Catalunya. Informe Extraordinari. *Síndic de Greuges* **2008**, 5–131. Available online: https://www.sindic.cat/site/files/docs/60_INFORME%20SEGREGACIO%20ESCOLAR. pdf (accessed on 6 April 2018).

24. García-Castaño, F.J.; Olmos alcaraz, A. *Segregaciones y Construcción de la Diferencia en la Escuela*; Trotta: Madrid, Spain, 2012.

25. Martínez, M.; Albaigés, B. L'estat de l'educació a Catalunya. Anuari 2013. *Fundació Jaume Bofill* **2013**, *80*, 13–563. Available online: http://www.fbofill.cat/sites/default/files/582.pdf (accessed on 6 April 2018).

26. Síndic de Greuges. La segregación escolar en Cataluña (I): La gestión del proceso de admisión del alumnado. *Síndic de Greuges* **2016**. Available online: http://www.sindic.cat/site/unitFiles/4155/Informe% 20segregacion%20escolar_I_gestionprocesoadmision_castellano_def.pdf (accessed on 7 April 2018).

27. Síndic de Greuges. La segregación escolar en Cataluña (II): Condiciones de escolarización. *Síndic de Greuges* **2016**. Available online: http://www.sindic.cat/site/unitFiles/4227/Informe%20segregacio%20escolar_II_ condicions_escolaritzacio_cast_ok.pdf (accessed on 7 April 2018).

28. Alegre, M.A. Polítiques de tria i assignació d'escola: Quins efectes tenen sobre la segregació escolar? *Què Funciona en Educació* **2017**, 1–41. Available online: http://www.fbofill.cat/sites/default/files/Que_funciona_ 07_segregracioescolar_301017.pdf (accessed on 7 April 2018).

29. Bonal, X.; Tarabini-Castellani, A.; Verger, A. La nova política educativa i les desigualtats. *Nous Horitzons* **2015**, *209*, 16–21. Available online: http://www.noushoritzons.cat/sites/default/files/la_nova_politica_ educativa_i_les_desigualtats.pdf (accessed on 7 April 2018).

30. Alegre, M.A.; Benito, R.; Chela, X.; Gonález, S. Les famílies davant l'elecció escolar. Dilemes i desigualtats en la tria de centres a la ciutat de Barcelona. *Fundació Jaume Bofill* **2010**, *72*, 11–304. Available online: http://www.fbofill.cat/sites/default/files/528.pdf (accessed on 7 April 2018).

31. Nel·lo, O.; Gomà, A. Territori. Diversitat espacial en els hàbits i condicions de vida juvenils: El paper clau de la segregació residencial. In *Enquesta de Joventut de Catalunya*; Serracant, P., Ed.; Generalitat de Catalunya: Barcelona, Spain, 2018.

32. Departament d'Estadística, Ajuntament de Barcelona. Available online: http://www.bcn.cat/estadistica/ catala/index.htm (accessed on 5 December 2017).

33. Departament d'Ensenyament, Generalitat de Catalunya. Available online: http://ensenyament.gencat.cat/ ca/inici (accessed on 31 January 2018).

34. Consorci d'Educació de Barcelona, CEB. Available online: http://edubcn.cat/ca/ (accessed on 11 December 2017).

urban science

MDPI

Article
Touristification, Sharing Economies and the New Geography of Urban Conflicts

Luis del Romero Renau

Department of Geography, University of Valencia, 46010 Valencia, Spain; Luis.romero@uv.es

Received: 10 September 2018; Accepted: 8 October 2018; Published: 15 October 2018

Abstract: The aim of this study was to address the highly controversial problem of the increasing touristification of urban centers, analyzing the case of Valencia. The paper begins with a theoretical reflection to disambiguate the term "sharing economy", the emergence of all kinds of digital service platforms that are revolutionizing traditional economic sectors of services, such as transport, tourist accommodation, or personal services. The new geography of urban conflicts that has arisen in recent years in this city, largely as a consequence of the paradigm of the collaborative economy in the tourism sector, was analyzed. This situation contrasts sharply with the panorama of conflicts that existed before and during the international financial crisis. Finally, the main social, economic and environmental impacts of collaborative economies are discussed, from the approach of a new phase in neoliberal capitalism.

Keywords: sharing economies; urban conflicts; Valencia; Airbnb; Uber

1. Introduction, Materials, and Methods

The digital revolution has profoundly transformed not only the way of working, or mobility in cities, but also the way of conceiving leisure, tourism, and culture. New digital technologies are turning everything into an available resource: services, products, spaces, connections, and knowledge [1] This revolution came along with the development of Internet 3.0, and has been called "the sharing economy" [2], "the peer-to-peer economy" (P-2-P), [3] "the gig economy" [4], or more broadly "sharing consumption" [5]. Each of these terms represents an aspect of the digital platform revolution, but none completely captures the entire scope of the paradigmatic shift in the ways we produce, consume, work, finance, and learn [1]

This paper focuses on the for-profit sharing economy in the tourism sector, through the study of different digital platform examples and their implications for urban planning, and specifically to one of the most recurrent problems: the touristification of urban areas. Touristification could be defined as a process, and the resulting state in a definite space, of relatively spontaneous, unplanned massive development of tourism, which leads to the transformation of this space into a tourism commodity itself. Tourism has been identified as one of the four production-consumption regimes affected by platform economies, along with waste, mobility, and employment [6]. These platforms are transforming not only the way we travel but also the way we live in general, with a wide range of services available through different apps. In the tourism sector, the expansion of the platform economy, such as Airbnb, Uber or Just Eat, are notably affecting traditional transportation, tourism, and restaurant businesses, and this is rescaling the landscape of urban conflicts existing in many cities, around issues such as gentrification or social and economic segregation. This contribution aims to illustrate how platform economies in the tourism sector are changing the geography of urban conflicts. The case study is located in Valencia (Spain), a Mediterranean city in which urban tourism is a key driving force. Academic literature tends to focus research of new social phenomena, e.g., digital platforms, in big cities such as London, Paris, New York or Shanghai, whereas the literature gap in middle-sized or smaller cities around these issues is considerable. In the case of Spain, dozens of academic articles have been recently published on the topic of sharing economy and tourism industry for the cases of Madrid and Barcelona [7–9] (Gutiérrez et al., 2017; Artigot-Golobares, 2017, Sequera, 2018), but there are almost no contributions on other territorial scales, such as Valencia, Palma de Mallorca, Málaga or Tenerife, smaller touristic cities that might also be deeply affected by these new digital platforms

To carry out these objectives, a three-step methodology was performed. Firstly, the data on urban conflicts were collected through the content analysis of regional print media. All the issues of the daily newspaper El Levante and El País published between 2014 and March 2018, were examined, in total 114 articles concerning urban conflicts with sharing economy platforms. The reason to choose this period relies on the fact that 2014 is an important turning point. In October 2014, Uber arrived in the city, and Airbnb, active in Valencia since 2010, began an important rise in the number of tourist apartments. Although there are plenty digital platforms, this contribution focuses mainly on these two, since they are the most relevant and have more implications in the tourism sector [10]. After completing the database, a map showing the location of different conflicts arisen linked to digital platforms and urban tourism was made. Such conflicts include neighbor protests against the touristification or gentrification of urban suburbs, Uber conflicts with local taxi companies for the tourism market, and other conflicts with local hotels and accommodation chains due to Airbnb and tourist apartments in Valencia. The methodology followed to develop the database with news and the GIS treatment was inspired by Trudelle and Pelletier's conflict research [11]. Since the same methodology was used to build a larger database on urban conflicts in Valencia from 2002 to 2014, the analysis could include a temporal dimension to contrast urban conflicts before 2014 and the arrival of digital platforms, and from that year to the present. This analysis was also complemented with other data about digital platforms use in Valencia (namely, Airbnb and Uber), linked with the tourism sector.

2. The Emergence of a for-Profit Sharing Economy: Neoliberalizing Domesticity

According to [2], it is possible to distinguish four main driving forces that supported the emergence of the sharing economy. The first would be undoubtedly the digital revolution with new technologies, such as web and mobile technologies, which play a critical role in building large-scale sharing communities, since they offer speed of contact and of the supply–demand cycle. Practices of sharing, renting and bartering already existed before the Internet, but it is evident that the emergence of new web and mobile technologies has accelerated and facilitated the rise of the sharing economy, enabling, upscaling and enhancing economic impact [12]. The second driving force would be sustainability and environment defense. Both concepts are narrowly linked and people who adopt sharing practices claim to be "greener" than conventional ones, and it is an increasing demand in the tourism industry. There is a considerable interest in the sharing economy as a means of promoting sustainable consumption practices [6].) heralded the sharing economy as a "potential new pathway to sustainability". In times of scarcity, to share resources and assets means to collaborate for more sustainable ways of living. One of the examples given to defend sharing economy as a sustainable practice in contrast to unsustainable, wasteful and consumer capitalist economies would be the great garbage patch of plastic discovered years ago in the Pacific Ocean [2]). Another important driving force would be the role played in recent years by the great recession. Although environmental narratives are present in sharing economy discourses, one of the key factors that explain the success of sharing economies is the possibility to save money. This is particularly crucial in times of austerity, loss of purchasing power and therefore more awareness about purchasing decisions, especially in a sector such as tourism, which is not a vital necessity. According to [13], the success of digital platforms in the tourism sector, such as Airbnb, is due to the possibility to access to affordable tourist accommodation for middle classes that lose purchasing power during the crisis, in contrast with average higher prices in conventional hostel or hotels. This digital platform permitted the continuity of a high level of consumerism in tourism and travel sectors, despite the economic crisis. Some studies find that consumers who use Airbnb stay on vacation longer than they would if they stayed at a hotel, and some guests would not have gone on a vacation at all without access to the lodging platform [1]. Finally, the fourth driving force would be the community. According to [12], the network paradigm can be seen as a re-enactment of the ancient concept of community. Online connectivity facilitates offline sharing and social activities, allowing direct contact among people who live in the same area but do not interact. Many authors celebrated the arrival of the sharing economy as a claim for creation and restoration of the commons, following Ostrom's ideas on assets and resource management beyond public or private models [14,15]. The sharing economy would enable people to manage assets and resources organized in communities. In the tourism sector, there is a wide range of digital social networks that promote finding travel partners, getting more informed about every single detail of a tourist destination, and find even a local restaurant. All these webs are based on the creation of different digital communities that focus in a definite aspect of the tourism experience: a destination, accommodations, best restaurants, sightseeing, local culture, etc.

A critical point in the sharing economy is the shift from ownership to access to services and goods, such as cohousing, car-pooling or crowdfunding. This shift characterizes a new era or age in which "you are what you can access" [16]. The age of access [17] describes how markets are making ways for networks, and ownership is steadily being replaced by access [17]. According to this author, in the rise of the age of access, suppliers hold on to property in the new economy and lease, rent or charge an admission fee, subscription or membership dues for its short-term use [17]. The emergence of the digital platform offering a wide range of access to different services is a good example. While cheap, durable goods will continue to be sold and bought in the market, more costly items such as appliances, automobiles, and homes increasingly will be held by suppliers and accessed by consumers in the form of short-term leases, rentals, memberships and other service arrangements [17], in which the tourism sector is already being one of the most affected. It is not a coincidence that today the most powerful digital platform businesses, such as Uber, Cabify, Airbnb or Blablacar are just focused on housing and transportation, two critical aspects for the development of tourism industry. For other authors instead, this shift is a broader cultural change "from generation me to generation we" [2]. They conceive sharing economy as a new and more sustainable way to meet needs and wants [14] (Buczynski, 2013) with a strong belief in the commons, giving the example of the copyleft creative commons permissions for publishing, as an alternative to traditional copyright permissions [2,14] considered sharing economy even revolutionary, a new vision that turns consumption-obsessed society into an economic democracy, a total paradigm shift in how we produce, consume and govern [14].

Some other authors notice some problematic issues concerning sharing economy, especially considering whether a sharing economy community works for profit or for solidarity reasons [1,13,16–18]. According to Alonso [13], many cases of the so-called sharing economy began with altruist purposes, but are really examples of ruthless egoism. Tom Slee's book "Whats yours is mine", an acid criticism on Botsman and Rogers [2] (2010), stated that the most significant examples of what used to be called the "sharing economy" are really giant corporations pursuing monopoly power and the "sharing" in the Sharing Economy has been reduced to simple market exchange [18]. According to this author, the appeal of a bottom-up, personal, community-driven alternative to traditional corporations have fizzled: we are left with Uber, a company financed by high-net-worth investors via Morgan Stanley and by Saudi Arabia's Public Investment Fund, and Airbnb, by some measures the largest hotel company in the world [18]. It is clear that the sharing economy concept has become an umbrella for different practices that include for profit and not-for-profit economic practices, in which a variety of digital platforms, associations, social movements, and Internet activists play a role. Figure 1 summarizes this variety.

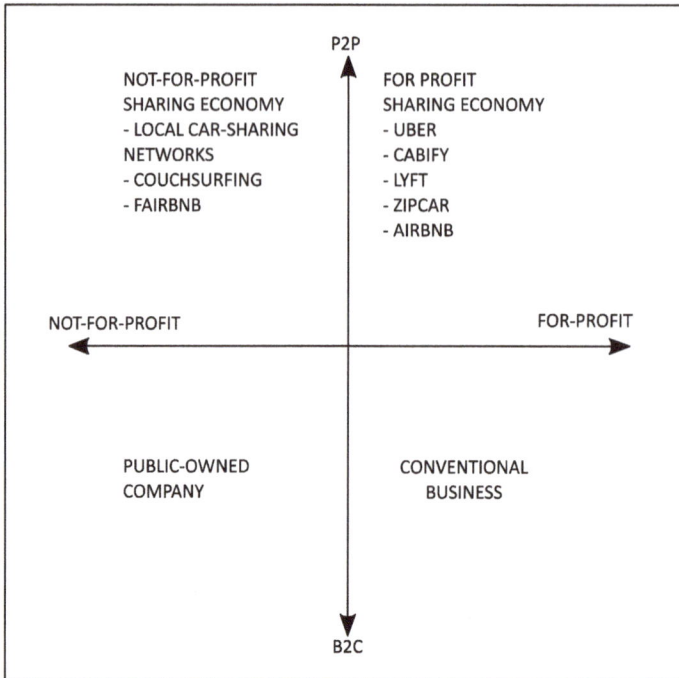

Figure 1. Sharing and conventional economy. Source: Own source adapted from Alonso (2017).

A clear distinction can be made, according to [13], between sharing economy (peer-to-peer) and conventional economy (B2C, business-to-consumer). Apart from that, the "for-profit" line divides those organizations that are contributing to the commodification of sharing or collaborative economies, to others that operate under a clear altruist, or sharing cost purposes. In the tourism sector, some alternatives are local car-pooling networks for mobility and Couchsurfing the "Fairbnb" project for accommodation. The space between not-for-profit top-down oriented practices following classical business-to-consumer, or rather an institution-to citizen classical model, is the "ruins of the welfare state" [13] that still today offer some services based in public-owned companies. According to Srnicek [19] for-profit sharing economies through digital platforms are just another phase in the long history of the capitalist mode of production after the 2008 crisis restructuration. The platform has emerged as a new business model, capable of extracting and controlling immense amounts of data, and with this shift, we have seen the rise of large monopolistic firms [19] This new model business is just a new form of capitalism, a crowd-based capitalism, a sharing economy based on the peer-to-peer commercial exchange that may supplant the traditional corporate-centered model [20] Rather than sharing economies, digital for-profit platforms should be labeled just platform capitalism or platform economies.

The distinguishing characteristic of modern capitalism is the expropriation of various facets of life into commercial relationships [17]. Today, with the expansion of digital platforms, every aspect of the daily routine, a tourism experience included, has become a purchased affair and an increasing commodification of all human experience. Few industries are exempt from potential disruptive change within the sharing economy [16]. A huge range of different digital platforms offers convenience services, as Figure 2 shows. Activities traditionally embedded in the family sphere, such as childcare, food or even pet care, are today possible to cover by different platforms, such as *Bubble* or *Bambino* that offer babysitters by the hour, *Just eat* or *Deliveroo* that permit ordering food to be delivered in less than 40 min, or *Dogbuddy*, offering different services of accommodation and care for pets.

Even personal relationships appear today a lucrative business for digital platforms, such as *Meetic* or *Tinder*, that facilitate the possibility of flirting or finding new friendships without leaving home, or even meeting new people in a tourist destination when traveling. Finally, second-hand economy platforms have developed a new on-line market of shareable items. A majority of consumer goods can be understood as having excess capacity, including houses, cars, boats, houses, clothing, books, toys, appliances, tools, furniture, computers, etc.; all these items provide the consumer with an opportunity to lend out or rent out their goods to other consumers [21]. Over 10,000 new platform companies have sprouted and mushroomed in less than a decade [1].

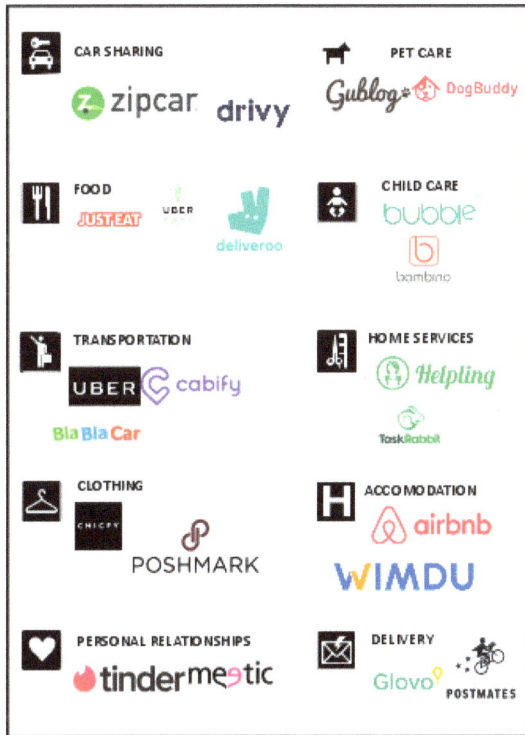

Figure 2. Some examples of digital platforms offering a wide range of services.

Tourism is obviously not an exception and today, all the aspects surrounding travel, including accommodation, transportation, and cultural, sport or leisure activities as well as meeting local people to make the journey more "authentic", are services provided by different for-profit digital platforms. Even potential services needed during the journey, such as cleaning the home, watering the plants, looking for the pets, walking the dogs, taking care of children or relatives, can be provided by different specialized digital platforms. Apps such as Airbnb permitted the expansion of tourism apartments but through a short-term rental model, instead of the traditional model of property-owning, the same case as Uber with urban mobility. However, the emergence of digital platforms has led to different conflicts.

3. Results: Tourism and Digital Platform Conflicts in Valencia

Valencia is today the third most important city in the country, with over 800,000 inhabitants, and a metropolitan area with more than 1.5 million. Tourism and real estate sector were for years some of the most important economic activities. Thus, the financial crisis heavily affected the city and was one of the causes why in 2015 local elections, for the first time since 1979, a coalition of left-wing parties won these elections. This coalition presented a wide range of new policy projects to manage social problems, such as house evictions, urban poverty, unemployment and other consequences of the economic crisis. Nevertheless, new challenges emerged from 2015, especially important the touristification of the urban space and the arrival platforms in the tourism sector [22]. These new challenges led to a completely new scenario in a city in which there were not local regulations for platforms, such as Airbnb, Uber, Cabify or similar [23].

This is one of the reasons that, despite the crisis, tourism marked historic records in Valencia in terms of tourism arrivals in Spain. According to Figure 3, short-term rentals in tourism apartments had an increase of more than 30% some months compared to the same period the previous years, whereas accommodation in hotels less than 7% [24]. Figure 4 shows the evolution of tourist demand in hotels and apartments in the last years in Valencia. Hotels continue to be the preferred accommodation option by the vast majority of tourists and concentrate today 71% of beds. Nevertheless, the growth in the number of apartments listed in Airbnb is spectacular, with an average annual increase of 200% and, in some central districts, such as Ciutat Vella or Extramurs, Airbnb offer is bigger than traditional hotel and hostels, as well as in the beach district of Poblats Marítims (Figure 5). These are the tourist hotspots in Valencia, where Airbnb is beginning to win the war against traditional accommodation options, but, even in less tourist areas such as Saïdia or Poblats del Nord, Airbnb is the only tourist accommodation possibility today. It is important to note precisely the change of trend in the years of the crisis: Hotel accommodation dropped between 2011 and 2013, but Airbnb offer increased notably those years (Figure 6).

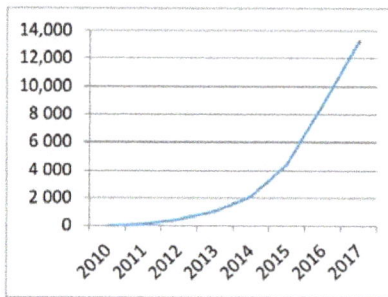

Figure 3. Tourist apartments listed in Airbnb in Valencia. Source: Airdna (2018).

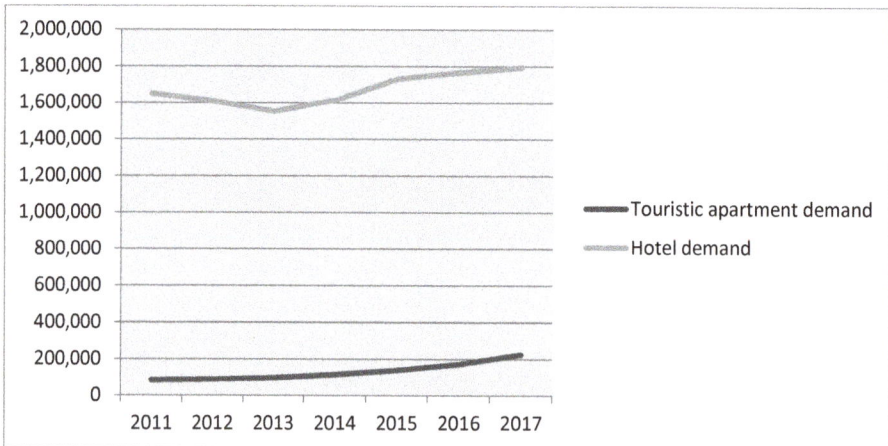

Figure 4. Evolution in tourist demand in Valencia in hotels and tourist apartments. Source: [24].

Transportation follows a similar trend to the popularization of the Internet and digital platforms: in the last two years, the arrival of tourists by flight represented more than 80% of the total, while car and train only represented 15.7% and 0.4%, respectively. There is a clear trend towards the increase of arrivals by flight and the decrease of arrivals by private car [24]. The traditional mobility model of sun and beach tourist coming by car to Spanish beaches from their origin, mostly Britain, France, and Germany, is being replaced by a new one which combines low-cost airlines with short-term car rentals. Traditional urban transportation means such as taxi is in crisis since the arrival of Uber. Uber and Cabify driving permissions are rising dramatically (Figure 4). Only in 2017, Uber licenses boosted from 600 to 2000, a 333% increase in only one year [25], whereas almost 100 taxi licenses disappeared [24]. Today, there are in Spain 5890 driving licenses for digital platforms and 67,089 taxi licenses, 1% less than in 2012 [24] but in some touristic cities such as Málaga, driving licenses linked to Cabify and Uber represent already 20% of the overall, 14.2% in Madrid [25].

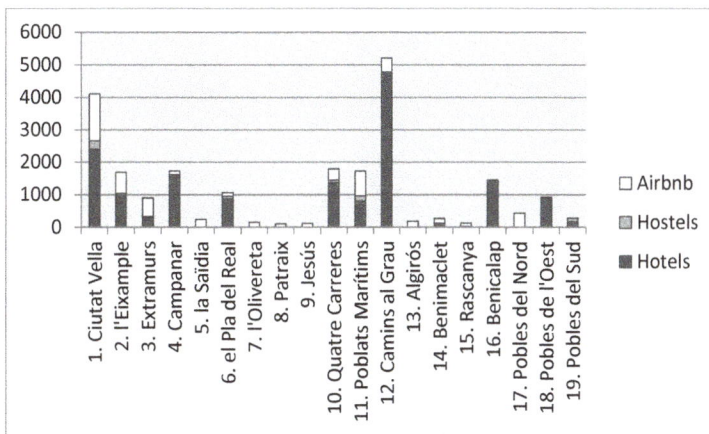

Figure 5. Evolution of Uber and Cabify drivers in Spain. Source: [26].

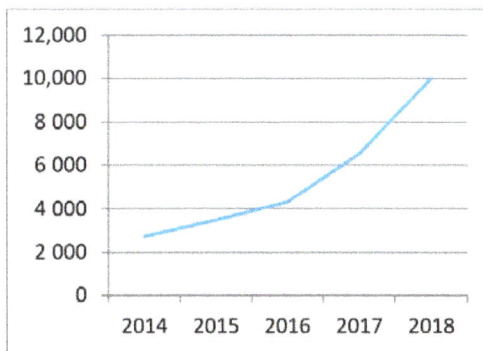

Figure 6. Accommodation options per district in Valencia. Source: [27].

This shift towards digital platforms has already had an impact on the geography of conflicts in cities like Valencia. Figures 7 and 8 show the main results of the carried out research on conflicts linked to tourism. Figure 7 show conflicts between 2002 and 2014, based on a conflict database from which tourism-related conflicts were extracted [28]. Figure 8 covers the 2014–2018 period as a result of the database on conflicts linked to tourism issues in the city of Valencia.

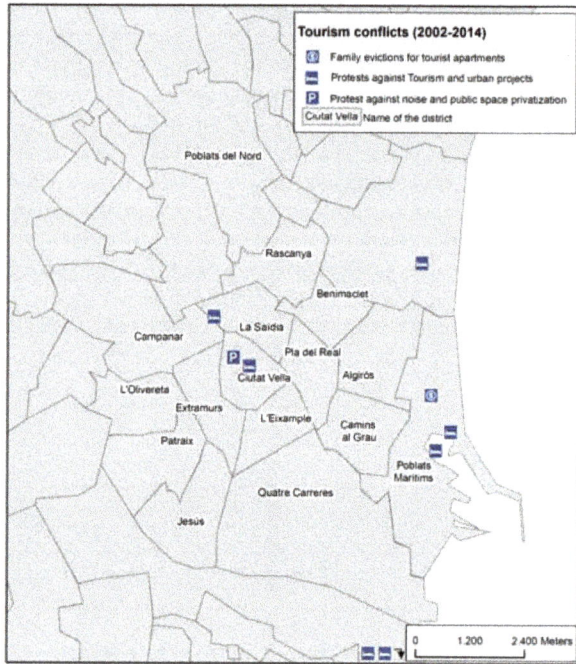

Figure 7. Tourism conflicts, 2002–2014. Source: [28].

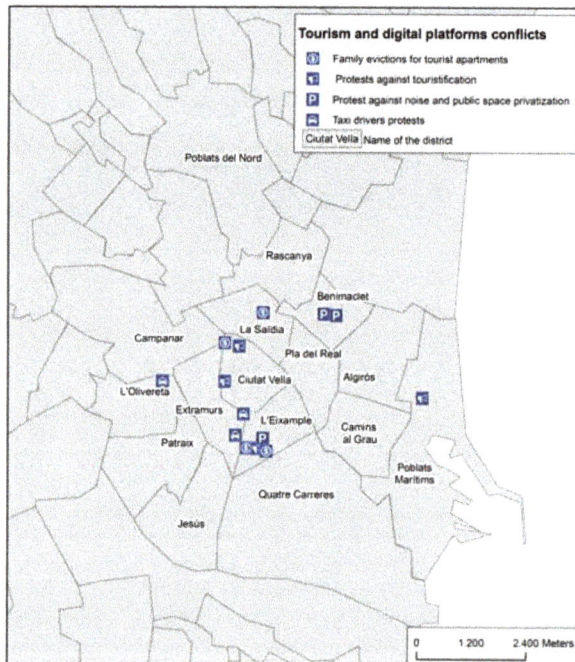

Figure 8. Tourism and digital platform conflicts, 2014–2018. Source: News database from El País, Levante, and Las Provincias.

Despite the variety of digital platforms with public contestation, only conflicts related to tourism are included in Figure 8. Figure 7 shows conflicts emerged in a historic period subdivided into the economic boom until 2007, and the financial crisis from 2007 to 2014. The majority of conflicts represented here began as a result of tourism and urban development projects, such as hotel, restaurants or tourism apartment projects. Indeed, the most intense conflict in this period was the Blasco Ibáñez Avenue project, an urban mega-project that implied the eviction of more than 1600 families from the poor neighborhood of El Cabanyal, to construct more than one thousand apartments and tourism apartments and hotels. The only conflict linked to noise and tourism emerged in the central district of Ciutat Vella, which is one of the most long-lasting conflicts in the city. Although the whole period was intense in protests and conflicts, with more than 80 [28], only nine, less than 10%, were tourism-related.

Figure 8 shows in total, 14 tourism-related conflicts reported through local media, all of them linked to Airbnb or transportation digital platforms, such as Uber or Cabify. Some examples of conflicts mapped here include the confrontation between the Entrebarris neighbor association in Russafa and a private company that bought an entire building and evicted seven families in the Russafa suburb, a very similar case in the Saïdia suburb, or the confrontation, even with physical violence, between taxi drives and Cabify and Uber drivers in tourism hotspots such as the main train station, or the High Speed train station. The other two types of conflicts represented in the map consist of a series of neighbor protests and actions against the touristification of some suburbs, and its consequences, namely more noise and widespread increase in tourism land-uses (hotels, restaurants, pubs, hostels, and of course, tourist apartments). Obviously, the stakes at conflict are not only tourism-related digital platforms such as Airbnb or Homelidays that threaten traditional tourist accommodation markets as well as the management and growth of the tourism sector in the city, but undoubtedly digital platforms are a key issue in this type of conflicts.

The ensemble of conflicts represented here could be divided into three categories, according to the source or interest at stake: land-use conflicts, land revenue conflicts, and mobility conflicts. In the first type of conflicts, the use of land and public space is the main ground for social mobilization. These conflicts are linked to urban projects in the 2002–2014 period, and later to the noise generated by tourism, as well as the privatization of public spaces, such as squares or streets. Neighbors in some suburbs feel invaded by tourists and even routine activities such as shopping or moving by public transportation become sometimes a difficult task. The second type of conflicts relate to revenue prospects generated by tourism activities, basically accommodation, against the right or will of the local population, to remain in their rented houses and to live in a suburb with facilities for their inhabitants and not only tourists. This type of conflicts is dominant in the 2014–2018 period. Figure 9 shows Airbnb average monthly revenue per district, according to real data [27]. Tourist districts have a high monthly revenue of more than 700 Euros and L'Eixample even more than 800 euros. These data are relevant, since they show the average revenue, taking into account the days in which tourist apartments or rooms remain empty, or low season months. In contrast, Figure 10 compares Airbnb potential monthly revenue (a full-booked month in a tourist apartment), with average rent prices in each suburb. Today, an owner can obtain between 200% and 500% higher potential revenue in Airbnb compared to rent in the conventional housing market. This potential revenue is quite real during the high season, in which the housing and hotel occupation rate is 100%. This is one of the main reasons local owners, but especially international investment funds, are interested in housing markets in cities such as Valencia, and why entire buildings are being evicted to be transformed as tourist apartments to be booked via an app. A proof of how Airbnb is becoming a very profitable professional business, rather than a sharing economy example, is that today in Valencia 61% of hosts are multi-listing, some with more than 10 apartments under the same profile and 65% offer entire apartments, and only 35% private rooms in shared flats [27]. These data show how for-profit platforms have co-opted what began as a progressive, socially transformative idea, e.g., home-sharing. According to Slee, this shows the great shift in sharing economy: what started as an appeal to the community, person-to-person connections, sustainability, and sharing has become a Wall Street and venture capitalists extending their free-market values into our personal lives [18]. The tourism sector in Valencia is a good example of digital platforms as new businesses with considerable revenue. Today, Valencia multi-listing hosts possess 4590 properties in Valencia, 58% of the total [27]. The majority of these multi-listing hosts are big corporations, such as Friendly Rentals an international rental company with properties in 20 different cities in Europe, and, in the case of Valencia, this corporation has already over 30 apartments in Airbnb [29–31].

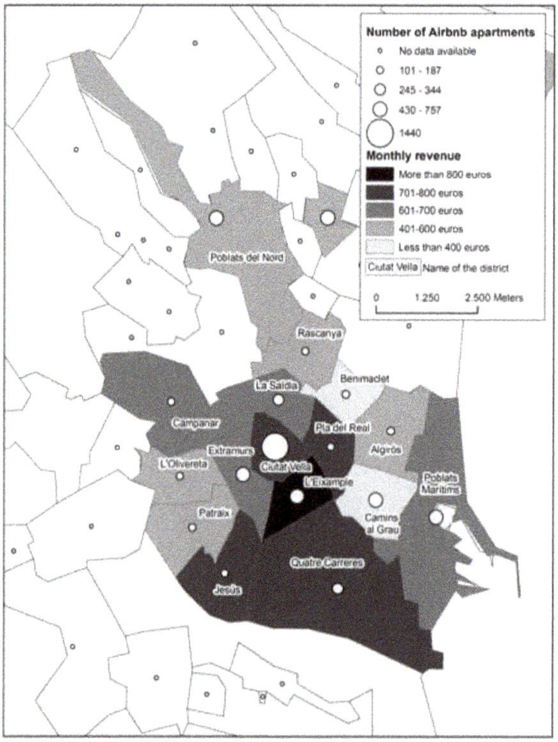

Figure 9. Number of Airbnb apartments per district in Valencia. Source: Own source from [27].

Finally, mobility conflicts relate to disputes against traditional transportation operators, basically taxi drivers. Cabify and Uber retain up to 25% revenue for each service and their tariffs are between 10% and 60% higher than average taxi tariffs in cities such as Madrid [31]. However, the potential revenue for Cabify or Uber drivers is higher than conventional taxis, since they have a potential demand that covers the whole city through the app, whereas taxis work mostly looking for potential customers while driving, which is much more limited in terms of potential demand. According to [32], Uber drivers work fewer hours and earn more per hour than traditional taxi drivers, even after accounting for their expenses. Apart from that, the difficulty that entails obtaining a taxi license, discourages many young professionals that find in Uber and Cabify interesting alternatives.

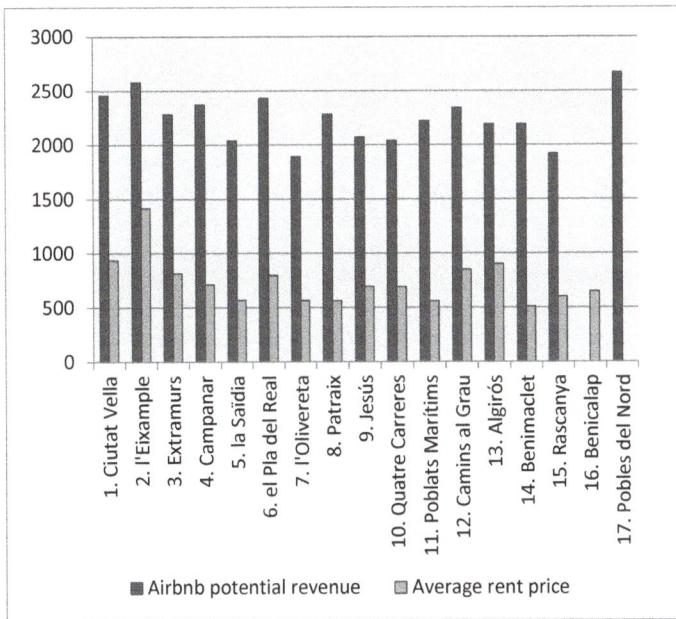

Figure 10. Airbnb potential revenue versus average rent price per district in Valencia, Source: [27,33].

4. Discussion. Touristification and the New Geography of Conflicts: The Case of Valencia

The digital economy is becoming a hegemonic model: cities are to become smart, businesses must be disruptive, workers are to become flexible, and governments must be lean and intelligent [19]: 8). Within the tourism sector, the emergence of digital platforms offering different services for traveling, such as Airbnb or Uber, is reinforcing the already active landscape of conflicts around tourism and the city [34], and is a step forward to the total commodification of every aspect and minute of a travel experience [1]: 147). Cities such as Berlin, Venice, Florence, Paris or New Orleans already had important conflicts around the touristification of urban centers since at least the 1990s [34]), so the digital revolution only intensified an already vivid landscape of urban conflicts, mostly between tourism widespread increase and the local population. In countries such as Spain, tourism sector was completely liberalized long before the arrival of Airbnb or Uber [35].

Madrid, Barcelona or Valencia had before the financial crisis a vivid landscape of urban conflicts, in many cases, linked to the economic boom, urban speculation and the construction of urban mega-projects and mega-events [28], as can be seen in Figure 7. A protest cycle ended in 2011 with the financial crisis and the important social mobilizations of the indignados and 15M movements [28], leading to a new political cycle in which new political parties such as Podemos (We can) or Ciudadanos entered the political arena. In this period, from the 1990s to 2011, many conflicts linked to the construction of urban mega-projects to attract tourism were an important source of conflicts, such as the Formula 1 project in Valencia, the failed Eurovegas project in Madrid, or the High-speed train to the airport in Barcelona [36]. Nevertheless, conflicts arisen in the post-crisis period from 2014 show a very distinctive landscape: more conflicts, often located in the city center, and linked to the use of the urban space (public space, housing, and mobility), rather than the construction of the urban space, as in the previous period. Whereas the grounds for protesting in this period were linked to heritage, environment protection and housing rights [28], with the emergence of digital platforms linked to tourism, the situation has dramatically changed.

Academic literature and media have focused their attention on the possible negative impacts and hence the main possible causes for conflict because of the irruption of for-profit digital platforms. These impacts can be summarized in four different areas: labor conditions; lack of legal and fiscal regulations; gentrification and touristification; and environmental impacts.

Labor conditions and deregulation in digital platforms is one of the most intense discussions in media and academic literature [37]. The main worry is that absent regulatory controls, the platform will lead work to be so app-driven that the internal logic of full-time employment, job security, and worker rights will collapse [1]. Some critics consider for-profit platforms as architects of a growing "precariat", a class on the precarious edge of economic security, and argue that the impetus for sharing is not trust, but desperation [37]. The employment status of the providers on these digital platforms remains uncertain because they are not considered employees of a definite corporation. Beyond these problematic issues, for [1], the rise of the platform is partly due to the decline of full-time, long-term jobs and cycles of high rates in unemployment and also represents a shift in preference, as many people entering the labor market today prefer flexibility and control over their work-time [1]. In the case of Valencia, this is a very important discussion in the legal and political arena, since workers for digital platforms do not have a definite status within the labor regulations.

Concerning the lack of legal and fiscal regulation, the legal battles often turn on how to define the platform business: the still unclear big question is whether digital companies are just service providers or brokers of individualized exchanges that have been running against existing regulations [18]. For some authors, digital platforms are presenting a great challenge for consumer protection laws, safety, and health regulations, business permits and licenses, property and zoning laws, and financial services regulations [18]. Sharing economy platforms, in particular, Airbnb and Uber, are critiqued for transferring risk to consumers; creating unfair competition; establishing illegal, black or grey markets; and promoting tax avoidance [6]. In contrast, digital platforms claim to be operating in outdated legal frameworks that are really guild protectionists, unable to capture its new business model or even fit the new economy. They add, in cases such as Uber, that they are merely an app and network not owing assets [38]. Digital platforms are introducing new forms of private regulation: reviews, ratings, and social network recommendations. These features can combine to provide alternatives to traditional regulation, as for example quality standards assigned to a hotel in terms of stars is today less trusted than Booking.com ratings and reviews [13]. Fiscal regulation is another unsolved issue in Spain, which is in the center of the conflict between digital platform and corporations. A primary concern of local regulators involves whether the platform economy should be taxed at the same levels as competing industries. Digital platforms consider taxation as another regulatory challenge: "there were laws created for businesses, and there were laws for people. What the sharing economy did was creating a third category: people as businesses" [39].

The environmental effects associated with the sharing sector are also complex. Sharing is thought to be eco-friendly and a more sustainable form of consumption [6] because it is assumed to reduce the demand for new goods or the construction of new facilities (in the case of hotels or shared spaces). Despite these widespread beliefs, there is not yet empirical evidence on these claims [21]. To determine full carbon and eco-impacts, it is also necessary to analyze all the changes that are set in motion in the system as a result of a new sharing practice [37]. For example, if the sale of a household's used items creates earnings that are then used to buy new goods ("rebound effect"), the original sale may not reduce carbon emissions or other environmental impacts [21]. Furthermore, according to the evolution of Uber and Cabify in the transportation sector, some cities such as Barcelona could be facing a situation of heavy pollution and traffic saturation [40]. Only in this city the number of Uber and Cabify vehicles could increase to more than 3000 units in the next years, in a city already with important traffic, parking and pollution problems [40].

These three issues are indeed present in the discourses of actors in the different conflicts represented in Valencia. Obviously, taxi associations attack Uber on Cabify because of their lack of a clear and fair labor and fiscal regulation, but the rest of the conflicts sees in the arrival of digital platforms offering lodging and transportation services to tourists, rather than these problems an old one: gentrification. Gentrification and touristification is the main negative aspect highlighted by neighbors in Valencia, who claim new zoning laws to keep residential areas quiet, clean and safe, and public housing policies to avoid family evictions for tourist apartments. An example of zoning law is the noise-free areas, which is a legal concept already present in two suburbs in the city, that had conflicts due to the noise from bars and pubs. Gentrification and touristification often come together, since tourism often follows urban gentrifiers [41]. Touristification or tourism gentrification can be defined as the transformation of a working-class or middle-class neighborhood into a relatively affluent and exclusive enclave marked by a proliferation of corporate entertainment and tourism venues [42]. This concept brings out the dual processes of globalization and localization embedded in urban redevelopment, since tourism is characterized by international global actors (digital platforms included), while at the same time investing at the local level by developing local culture, products and places for consumption that will appeal to visitors [41].

Tourist behaviors and markets have considerably changed during recent years. Boundaries between tourism and locals have become increasingly blurred [43]. International tourists seek authentic local experiences, "exploring" ordinary but lively and diverse neighborhoods and visiting cafés, bars, and markets that were previously almost exclusively frequented by locals [43]. This quest for "authenticity" of local life, as opposed to the tourist hot-spots and designated attractions, combined with the ability of transnational elites to technically, socially and economically live their life in selected places around the world and an "elective affinity" between tourists and the upper class, have considerably impacted not only the city centers but also on the peripheries [41]. This shift has impacted profoundly in the geography of urban conflicts. As explained above, the 2002–2014 period is marked by conflicts around urban mega-projects willing to attract tourism to definite spots that are conceived and designed as a tourism product (Formula 1 circuit, luxury hotel projects, and port redevelopment plans). However, after the crisis, this new pattern is consolidated: the local lifestyle is turned itself into a tourist commodity. The quest for authenticity, "exploring" genuine bars and suburbs rather than "visiting" typical tourist places, is the new motivation for traveling. In parallel, another growing trend is the second home ownership for leisure and leisure-related investment purposes and the rise of a transnational class able to be "at home" and to live "like a local" in different contexts around the world [41].

Digital platforms and their ability to offer (share) private accommodation, beyond traditional commercial and impersonal accommodations, and a wide range of services by locals, have the great potential to fulfill the demand of the new profile of the "explorer tourist", leading to a touristification or everyday life, andl consequently, to a tourism gentrification that displaces not only people, but also commercial activities. Whereas mass tourism used to invade in guided tours some central areas of Valencia years ago, now the "explorer tourist" rents a bike or a motorbike to stroll about. The problem of Airbnb and Uber is that they are exacerbating an on-going problem, especially in central neighborhoods. They target the most attractive tourist-oriented areas of the city, in the case of Valencia, Ciutat Vella or Russafa. This latter case already had a very deep commercial gentrification process before the arrival of Airbnb [44]. The new wave of gentrification led by Airbnb is reinforcing this gentrification process. With more than 450 apartments (1200 beds approximately) in a neighborhood of 23,000 inhabitants, the possibility of intensification is real. Today, Russafa has an occupancy rate of 40% in [27], but a monthly revenue of 832 euros per apartment on average. A similar situation presents the historic district of Ciutat Vella, only 34% occupancy rate but 738 euros of monthly revenue. The potential for growth and occupation of tourist apartment is considerable, but the risk to transform these already gentrified districts, into what Lees called a "super-gentrification" or second-wave gentrification process is real [45]. Another important consequence already visible is a complete shift of the geography of conflicts, now marked by a new centralization of protests in the city center, whereas in previous years were especially intensive in the peripheries, due to the proliferation of urban and tourist-oriented megaprojects.

The new geography of conflicts is reframing completely the landscape of social movements in the city. Social networks are not only promoting digital platforms but also social resistances. New urban-based movements, such as Entrebarris (between neighborhoods), Russafa descansa (Russafa rests), or Escoltem Velluters (listen to Velluters neighborhood), are some examples of grass-roots movements recently organized to face tourism negative impacts of digital platforms such as Airbnb. Political parties, traditional urban-based movements such as neighborhood associations and above all the local administration are in a situation of paralysis by analysis. The current local administration of Valencia is a constellation of left-wing political parties and grass-roots movements that were fueled by the protest cycle ended in 2011 with the economic and political crisis of those days. As explained above, the challenges they included in their political agenda, namely fight unemployment, privatization of public services, housing evictions or public participation methods, are still important but have been completely overtaken by the digital platform paradigm, which is precisely affecting housing, employment, and public services. Even more, touristified Spanish cities such as Barcelona are just beginning to design new policies to face platforms such as Airbnb, the same case as Valencia. Today, touristification and gentrification-led processes by digital platforms is an issue more discussed in legal, rather than in political arenas. A new political agenda for digital platforms, civil and labor rights is urgently needed in cities like Valencia, but as well in the amount of worldwide tourist urban destinations in which Uber, Airbnb or Deliveroo are starting to change housing, labor and mobility conditions. This political agenda should start distinguishing clearly for-profit "business-as-usual" digital platforms from other forms of sharing economies really desirable to improve social cohesion and environmentally friendly. Then, it would be useful to go beyond the legal conflict in which the majority of conflicts is embedded (taxi drivers claiming for Uber prohibition, Deliveroo rides claiming for labor rights, and neighbors defending a total prohibition of Airbnb apartments) to enter the political arena. It is in this arena in which a public policy for social housing, labor rights and inclusive mobility must be designed to face this new wave of neo-liberalization after the financial crisis, which digital platforms represent.

5. Conclusions

Digital platforms are the protagonist of a new chapter in the long history of capitalism and digital technology. Sharing economies appeared to be radical novelties as a response to the 2008 crisis. Airbnb, Uber, Deliveroo or Task Rabbit were born as a real possibility of sharing and were defended by some authors as a real environmentally friendly, socially fair and economic viable alternative to the conventional world of corporations. They were even announced as the new revolution of the commons. Nevertheless, capitalism, when a crisis hits, tends to be restructured with new technologies, new organizational forms, new forms of exploitation and new markets [19] for the sake of capitalist accumulation. Digital platforms represent the new paradigm after the crisis. The "uberization" of the economy and the arrival of digital platforms seem to have more of simple continuity, than of an alternative or anti-capitalist social or economic paradigm, showing how capitalism is an incredibly flexible system.

This contribution has focused on a very definite aspect of the emergence of digital platforms: their complex and contested link with urban tourism. The main features of this for-profit sharing economy are visible in urban tourism: access through an app over ownership, "collaborators" instead of employees and the commodification of everything: from housing to the lifestyle of a city. Rather than a city with spatially and temporally limited tourist spots, the city landscape is itself a commodity. The development of digital platforms in cities such as Valencia, a consolidated tourist hotspot, as it has been shown, is simply spectacular in terms of rise of Uber or Airbnb users, and of course, in potential revenues. Traditional economic lobbies such as hotel chains, rent-a-car companies or real estate or transportation companies have invisible new competitors, with no face, head office or infrastructure in the city: the digital platforms. They are moving from the confrontation to the imitation of these new market models, for example, rent-a-car companies with app transportation services very similar to

Urban Sci. **2018**, *2*, 104

Uber, or international investment funds looking for apartments to boost the tourist apartment market available through the Internet.

Nevertheless, these new features have reinforced old social problems narrowly linked to capitalism contradictions, such as gentrification, touristification of urban centers, labor exploitation, and environmental impacts. Neighbors in central areas of cities such as Valencia are beginning a new wave of protests, in this case not against the administration or local construction lobbies and some ambitious urban mega-projects to attract tourism and investments, but to face California-based digital platforms and global investors that are in a more subtle way contributing to the touristification, gentrification and the commodification of urban areas. Meanwhile, local administrations, political parties and trade unions (especially defending taxi drivers) offer more reactive, violent or even NIMBY attitudes toward digital platforms than proactive alternatives. A combination of a brand new and necessary legal framework for digital platforms would be desirable, with a new comprehensive tourism strategy for the city, with land-use clear regulations, sustainable mobility measures, and a better distribution of the tourist offer to allow living in the center or in tourist areas.

Funding: This research was funded by the Spanish Ministry of Economy, the CRETLIT project with reference: CSO2015-64468-P.

Conflicts of Interest: The author declares no conflict of interest.

References

1. Lobel, O. The law of the platform. *Minn. Law Rev.* **2016**, *101*, 87.
2. Botsman, R.; Rogers, R. *What's Mine is Yours: The rise of Collaborative Consumption*; Harper: New York, NY, USA, 2010.
3. Hamari, J.; Sjöklint, M.; Ukkonen, A. The sharing economy: Why people participate in collaborative consumption. *J. Assoc. Inf. Sci. Technol.* **2016**, *67*, 2047–2059. [CrossRef]
4. Rauch, D.E.; Schleicher, D. *Like Uber, but for Local Government Law: The Future of Local Regulation of the Sharing Economy*; Elsevier: Amsterdam, The Netherlands, 2015; Volume 76.
5. Felson, M.; Spaeth, J.L. Community structure and collaborative consumption: A routine activity approach. *Am. Behav. Sci.* **1978**, *21*, 614–624. [CrossRef]
6. Martin, C.J. The sharing economy: A pathway to sustainability or a nightmarish form of neoliberal capitalism? *Ecol. Econ.* **2016**, *121*, 149–159. [CrossRef]
7. Artigot-Golobardes, M. Challenges of Tourist Apartments in Barcelona: Between the Market and Regulation. *Pap. Econ. Esp.* **2017**, *151*, 189–206.
8. Gutiérrez, J.; García-Palomares, J.C.; Romanillos, G.; Salas-Olmedo, M.H. The eruption of Airbnb in tourist cities: Comparing spatial patterns of hotels and peer-to-peer accommodation in Barcelona. *Tour. Manag.* **2017**, *62*, 278–291. [CrossRef]
9. Sequera, J.A. Expansión de la Ciudad Turística y Nuevas Resistencias. El caso de Airbnb en Madrid. *Empiria* **2018**, *41*, 15–32.
10. Zafra, I. La Aplicación Uber Irrumpe en Valencia y Desafía al Taxi. *El País*, 2014. Available online: https://elpais.com/ccaa/2014/10/29/valencia/1414576992_162968.html (accessed on 29 October 2014).
11. Trudelle, C.; Pelletier, M. Analysis of urban conflict networks: Theoretical and methodological perspectives. In *Conflicts in the City. Reflections on Urban Unrest*; Del Romero, L., Ed.; Nova Publishers: New York, NY, USA, 2016.
12. Selloni, D. *CoDesign for Public-Interest Services*; Springer International Publishing: New York, NY, USA, 2017.
13. Alonso, L.E. Consumo colaborativo: Un análisis sociológico. In Proceedings of the Society for the Advancement of Socioeconomics Congress, Lyon, France, 29 June–1 July 2017.
14. Buczynski, B. *Sharing is Good: How to Save Money, Time and Resources through Collaborative Consumption*; New Society Publishers: Gabriola Island, BC, Canada, 2003.
15. Walljasper, J. *All That We Share*; The New Press: New York, NY, USA, 2010.

16. Belk, R. You are what you can access: Sharing and collaborative consumption online. *J. Bus. Res.* **2014**, *67*, 1595–1600. [CrossRef]

17. Rifkin, J. *The Age of Access: The New Culture of Hypercapitalism, Where All of Life is a Paid for Experience;* Penguin: New York, NY, USA, 2000.

18. Slee, T. *What's Yours is Mine. Against the Sharing Economy;* OR Books: London, UK, 2017.

19. Srnicek, N. *Platform Capitalism;* Polity Press: Cambridge, UK, 2017.

20. Sundararajan, A. *The Sharing Economy. The End of Employment and the Rise of Crowd-Based Capitalism;* MIT Press: Cambridge, UK, 2016.

21. Frenken, K.; Schor, J. Putting the sharing economy into perspective. *Environ. Innov. Soc. Transit.* **2017**, *23*, 3–10. [CrossRef]

22. Del Romero, L.; Campos, A. Diagnóstico de cambio en Valencia: Análisis de las políticas de gobierno en la ciudad de Valencia (1991–2015). Available online: http://contested-cities.net/working-papers/ (accessed on 28 September 2018).

23. Rejón, R. Las Empresas Aprovechan la Falta de Regulación Para Convertir la Movilidad Verde en un Negocio Privado. *Eldiario.es* 2018. Available online: https://www.eldiario.es/sociedad/empresas-aprovechan-regulacion-convertir-movilidad_0_818569003.html (accessed on 27 September 2018).

24. INE. Frontur. Estadística de Movimientos Turísticos en Frontera. Available online: http://www.ine.es/dyngs/INEbase/es/operacion.htm?c=Estadistica_C&cid=1254736176996&menu=resultados&idp=1254735576863 (accessed on 24 February 2018).

25. Gutiérrez, H. La Batalla de las Licencias: 67.089 Taxis y 5.890 VTC. *El País*, 2017. Available online: https://elpais.com/economia/2017/04/28/actualidad/1493390941_523371.html (accessed on 30 May 2017).

26. Semprún, A. Las Licencias VTC se Duplican en Tres Años por el Vacío Legal que Irrita al Taxi. *elEconomista.es* 2017. Available online: http://www.eleconomista.es/transportes/noticias/8797300/12/17/Las-licencias-VTC-se-duplican-en-tres-anos-por-el-vacio-legal-que-irrita-al-taxi.html# (accessed on 20 February 2018).

27. Airdna. *Airbnb Market Minder;* Airdna: Valencia, Spain; Available online: https://www.airdna.co/market-data/app/es/default/valencia/overview (accessed on 22 February 2018).

28. Del Romero, L. (Ed.) *Conflicts in the City. Reflections on Urban Unrest;* Nova Publishers: New York, NY, USA, 2016.

29. Friendly Rentals. Apartments in Valencia. 2018. Available online: https://www.friendlyrentals.com/en/ (accessed on 27 September 2018).

30. Garijo, M. Esto es lo que te Cobran Uber, Cabify y MyTaxi por Sus Servicios. *El diario.es* 2017. Available online: http://www.eldiario.es/economia/tarifas-cobran-Uber-Cabify-MyTaxi_0_651285521.html (accessed on 15 June 2017).

31. Garijo, M. Estas Son las Empresas Que Explotan el Negocio del Alquiler Turístico al Calor de Airbnb. *Eldiario.es* 2017. Available online: https://www.eldiario.es/economia/negocio-alrededor-alquiler-turistico-Airbnb_0_610339359.html (accessed on 27 September 2018).

32. Hall, J.V.; Krueger, A.B. *An Analysis of the Labor Market for Uber's Driver-Partners in the United States;* Princeton Univ. Indust. Relations Section, Working Paper No. 587; National Bureau of Economic Research: Cambridge, MA, USA, 2015.

33. Mohorte, A. Lo que Cuesta un Alquiler en Valencia: Pisos Entre 1.400 y 400 Euros al Mes. *Las Provincias* 2018. Available online: http://www.lasprovincias.es/economia/vivienda/alquiler-viviendas-valencia-20180202011622-ntvo.html (accessed on 7 February 2018).

34. Colomb, C.; Novy, J. *Protest and Resistance in the Tourist City;* Routledge: Abingdon, UK, 2017.

35. Blanco-Romero, A.; Blázquez-Salom, M.; Mínguez, C. Claves de la reestructuración turística de la ciudad. In Proceedings of the XXV Congress of the Spanish Geographers Association, Madrid, Spain, 25–27th October 2017.

36. Del Romero, L. Análisis comparativo de conflictos territoriales: El caso de Poblats Marítims (Valencia, España) y el distrito Sud-Ouest (Montreal, Canadá). *Bol. Asoc. Geógr. Esp.* **2014**, *66*, 83–104.

37. Schor, J. Debating the Sharing Economy. Available online: http://www.greattransition.org/publication/debating-the-sharing-economy (accessed on 21 February 2018).

38. Ward, S.F. 'App' Me a Ride: Internet Car Companies Offer Convenience, but Lawyers See Caution Signs. Available online: http://www.abajournal.com/magazine/article/internet_car_companies_offer_convenience_but_lawyers_see_caution_signs/ (accessed on 21 June 2018).

39. Kaplan, R.A.; Nadler, M.L. Airbnb: A Case Study in Occupancy Regulation and Taxation. *Univ. Chic. Law Rev. Dialogue* **2016**, *82*, 103–116.

40. Jorro, I. Barcelona Prevé Más Tráfico, Parquin y Polución con las 3.000 Nuevas VTC. *Crón. Glob.* **2017**. Available online: https://cronicaglobal.elespanol.com/business/amb-alerta-saturacion-trafico-parquin-polucion-3-000-vtc_108929_102.html (accessed on 22 December 2017).
41. Gravari-Barbas, M.; Guinand, S. (Eds.) *Tourism and Gentrification in Contemporary Metropolises*; Routledge: Abingdon, UK, 2017.
42. Gotham, K.F. Tourism Gentrification: The Case of New Orleans' Vieux Carre (French Quarter). *Urban Stud.* **2005**, *42*, 1099–1121. [CrossRef]
43. Bock, K. The changing nature of city tourism and its possible implications for the future of the cities. *Eur. J. Futures Res.* **2015**, *3*, 20. [CrossRef]
44. Del Romero, L.; Lara, L. De barrio problema a barrio de moda. Gentrificación comercial en Russafa, el Soho valenciano. *An. Geogr. Univ. Complut.* **2015**, *34*. [CrossRef]
45. Lees, L. Super-gentrification: The Case of Brooklyn Heights, New York City. *Urban Stud.* **2003**, *40*, 2487–2509. [CrossRef]

urban science

MDPI

Article

The Clandestine Transition towards an Unsustainable Urban Model in Extremadura, Spain

Víctor Jiménez * and **Antonio-José Campesino**

Departamento de Arte y Ciencias del Territorio, Universidad de Extremadura, 10071 Cáceres, Spain;
acampesi@unex.es
* Correspondence: victorjb@unex.es; Tel.: +34-629-309-047

Received: 17 September 2018; Accepted: 8 October 2018; Published: 12 October 2018

Abstract: Given the incessant and clandestine proliferation of housing on the Undevelopable Land of Extremadura, Spain, and that administrative attention to this problem has been scarce, it is inevitable that urban geographers will turn away from the main focus of their study: cities. Thus, a methodology has been designed to discover housing irregularities in the countryside, and to quantify, locate, and date them. To do this, we have digitalized all urban planning in the region and performed sweeps on orthophotos at a maximum scale of 1:1500. Every single dwelling in the region has been detected using this method. The rurbanization in this region means that there has been a change in the urban model that has not been gradual. The fragile and weakened urban network of Extremadura has agglutinated a large part of the population, which has resulted in territorial emptying, but not in a stagnation of artificialization. In fact, the urban network has become increasingly dispersed and isolated because of residential growth outside the limits of Urban and Developable Land. In addition, this growth is eminently clandestine. The worrying results show us that there is an urgent need for the Administration to create and apply a Regional Plan for the Management and Control of Rurban Development.

Keywords: counter-urbanization; Extremadura; urban expansion; periurbanization; rurbanization; suburbanization; illegal urbanization

1. Introduction

The adoption of the radical geography paradigm [1] pushes us to the practice of urban geography that takes into account the context in which we live and the problems that take place in it. Consistent with the above, urban geographers in Extremadura, Spain, should be concerned primarily with the particular evolution of the urban phenomena in their region. The Autonomous Community of Extremadura (Figure 1), which is socially and economically burdened by the absence of transformation and productive artificialization in its territory (negligible industrialization), currently has the lowest (49.07%) Average Urbanization Rate (AUR) in the country.

In Extremadura, the number of population centers that exceed the threshold of 10,000 inhabitants, which was set by the National Institute of Statistics to separate the urban from the rural, is only 13 out of the 388 municipalities that make up the region. In addition, the size of these municipalities is only relevant in the population centers of Badajoz, Cáceres, and Mérida, which, in any case, do not exceed the level of small cities. The physical and demographic evolution of this urban triad depends specifically on its administrative functionality, such as provincial and autonomous capital, from which its area of influence derives. As can be observed from the latest population trends, Extremadura's urban centers must compete under conditions of inequality with other national and international urban nodes. For this reason, the real estate dynamism of these cities depends on the flow of demographic attraction that they can retain.

Given the current characteristics of the region, in which the growth of cities is stagnant, rurbanization must take a leading role as the main object of study in territorial and urban issues.

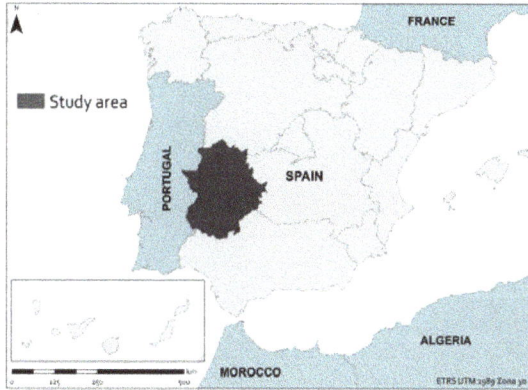

Figure 1. Autonomous Community of Extremadura, Spain (study area).

This influence of cities and urban areas on rural areas, which was first noticed by Galpin in 1918 [2], and later defined by Bauer and Roux in 1976 [3], has particularly benefited from the neoliberal economic model. Under a system that aims at economic and urban deregulation [4], the Administration has clearly contributed to making Undevelopable Land (UL) more flexible, which is a predisposition that can be found at both the national level [5] and the international level [6].

Within this deregulatory transition, the rurban expansion has expanded thanks to the factual imposition of the law on what was built. However, in this implementation of an imported and improper urban model, there have been several imbalances. Firstly, the negative consequences of social conquests (higher purchasing power and leisure time) have materialized in the capitalization of income through secondary housing, which acts as an instrument of dissemination and dispersion of the city to the countryside [7]. Secondly, the colonization of certain places, such as Protected Natural Spaces, has its own real estate appeal. This spatial suggestion, which has been synthesized under the term naturbanization [8], has propitiated the transformation of the most vulnerable territories. Third and finally, human beings who occupy lands that are threatened by extreme natural conditions (floods and fires) are vulnerable to life-threatening situations. The result has been the consolidation of an unsustainable model, presumably uncontrollable, which society has progressively tolerated.

The consequences of this change in the urban model will have greater repercussions in the near future. This is because this new scenario inhibits the productive transformation of the territory by introducing a substitute seasonal residential land use for the traditional agricultural land uses due to the implementation of new unproductive activities. These changes have become a trend, and a new pattern of urban expansion, that has given a new role to the rural environment not only in Spain, but also in other Central European [9], North European [10], and Mediterranean [11] areas. Thus, this diffuse pattern of urbanization will strongly influence Extremadura, which remains at the bottom of the socioeconomic indexes of the country, and which has been particularly affected by a demographic depletion. The transition, in which in one way or another the Administration (inaction) and society (protagonists of urban transformation) have both participated, threatens not only the traditional model of settlement but also the sustainability of the system as a whole. The legal solutions that have been practiced in other spaces, such as housing amnesties [12], will not solve the unsustainability of the new system.

Initial Conditions. The Urban Network of Extremadura

Extremadura lacks an urban system due to its geographical, historical, social, economic, and political conditions. Its AUR (measured on a threshold of settlements with a population of more than 20,000 inhabitants) is 40%, thirty points lower than the Spanish average (70%), which places it second last among the Spanish autonomous regions. It is, and continues to be, a rural and ruralized region, with an extensive territory of 41,634.4 km^2 and a minimal and embryonic urban network of urban centers, urban sub-centers, and "agrovillas" (population centers that are halfway between urban and rural). These, far from being consolidated, have been deconstructed in the last six decades. Nowadays, the few urban centers that remain form artificial oases in the middle of the demographic desert of the declining rural areas. The political opposition to the development of the Functional Districts Project [13] largely explains the regressive effects on sub-centers and agrovillas.

As can be seen from Table 1, the 1950 census marked the ceiling of demographic growth in Extremadura with 1,364,857 de facto inhabitants. As of 1 January 2017, the population stood at 1,079,022 de jure inhabitants, with a regression of −20.94% and annual losses that were derived from an already irrepressible bleeding due to depopulation, aging, and uncontrolled internal immigration from the countryside to the capital cities.

Table 1. The urban network of Extremadura (1950–2017).

Urban Network	Population Centers 1950	Inhabitants 1950	Population Centers 2017	Inhabitants 2017	Results (%) 1950–2017
Urban centers [1]	5	192.789	7	443.107	129.84
Sub-centers [2]	18	242.654	6	87.918	−63.76
Agrovillas [3]	47	308.552	24	158.927	−48.49
Group totals	70	743.995	37	689.952	−7.26
Regional total	386	1364.857	388	1079.022	−20.94

[1] >20,000 inhabitants; [2] 20,000–10,000 inhabitants; [3] 10,000–5000 inhabitants. Own elaboration.

In 1950, the five urban centers (with over 20,000 inhabitants) Badajoz (79,291), Cáceres (45,429), Mérida (23,835), Don Benito (22,840), and Almendralejo (21,394), which represented 1.29% of the 386 existing municipalities, formed a concentration of 192,789 inhabitants (14.1% of the total population). In 2017, the seven urban centers Badajoz (149,946), Cáceres (95,814), Mérida (59,174), Plasencia (40,663), Don Benito (36,975), Almendralejo (34,543), and Villanueva de la Serena (25,992), which represent 1.8% of the current 388 municipalities, form a concentration of 443,107 inhabitants (41% of the total population).

This group (called "G-7") has been, and will continue to be, the great beneficiary of the territorial and urban deregulation of Extremadura that occurred during the Franco dictatorship and that has continued throughout the democratic period. This is due to the absorption of people, goods, services, and central functions, and to the political decision to maintain, reinforce, and reproduce capital centralism during self-government, after the centralism of Madrid had been criticized for decades.

Intermediate centers (from 10,000 inhabitants to 20,000 inhabitants) occupy the second level in Extremadura's urban hierarchy. These centers underwent notable contractions until they were totally dismantled. In 1950, the 18 sub-centers Azuaga (19,326), Villanueva de la Serena (18,391), Plasencia (18,203), Villafranca de los Barros (16,395), Jerez de los Caballeros (15,966), Valencia de Alcántara (15,586), Trujillo (14,587), Olivenza (13,894), Oliva de la Frontera (12,710), Montijo (12,100), Fregenal de la Sierra (11,993), Cabeza del Buey (11,931), Zafra (11,500), Arroyo de la Luz (10,424), Fuente de Cantos (10,354), Castuera (10,169), Barcarrota (10,099), and San Vicente de Alcántara (10,026) represented 4.7% of the total number of municipalities and formed a concentration of 242,654 inhabitants (17.8% of the total population). In contrast, in 2017, the six sub-centers Navalmoral de la Mata (17,247), Zafra (16,855), Montijo (15,674), Villafranca de los Barros (13,244), Coria (12,886), and Olivenza (12,032) represent only 1.5% of the total number of municipalities and 87,918 inhabitants (8.1% of the total population).

Agrovillas (10,000–5000 inhabitants) occupy the third level of the urban hierarchy of Extremadura; however, their role has been reduced by half. In 1950, there were 47 agrovillas, which represented 12.2% of the total number of municipalities and 308,552 inhabitants (22.6% of the regional population). In 2017, there were 24 agrovillas, which represented only 6.1% of the total number of municipalities (14.7% of the total population of Extremadura). Throughout this difficult transition, services have been dismantled and people have been displaced, including heads of districts, such as Jerez de los Caballeros, Trujillo, Azuaga, Jaraíz de la Vera, Castuera, and Valencia de Alcántara, Alburquerque.

In synthesis, the 70 centers that in 1950 represented 18.1% of the municipality of Extremadura and brought together 54.5% of the inhabitants, have now descended to 37 centers, 9.5% of the total, but concentrating 64.0% of the population. An evident example of the destructuring of the territory is that Extremadura today maintains its status as rural as in 1950, but with a serious problem of land depopulation, then nonexistent. These demographic losses are motivated by massive emigration, aging, dependence, lack of qualification and, above all, the immutable maintenance of the obsolete administrative structure inherited from the first Division of the Spanish Territory in 1822–1833: provinces and deputations, which block regional cohesion, and unviable mini-municipalities, converted into nursing homes.

Sixty-two years after the promulgation of the land law of 1956, which opened the way to urban growth planned through today obsolete figures, the phenomenon of rurbanization in Extremadura during the last forty years is today a serious problem. We are witnessing the substitution involution of the order planned by the spontaneous urban disorder on UL, caused by irregular, illegal, and clandestine constructions that are unsustainable. This disorder is not justified by the corresponding economic and demographic expansion, is in flagrant regression and is politically consented.

Municipal planning does not work since dynamic urban centers physically and functionally overflow the rigid limits of municipal boundaries. It is not even useful given its inability to understand and solve the narrow causal interrelations of influence between city and surrounding centers.

It is incomprehensible that, by arranging the municipalities of Extremadura regulated, urban and developable land to meet the scarce demands of urban growth, clandestine and illegal constructive developments take place on UL, presumably non-constructible land. In fact, this land type is in practice the most attacked by contradictory constructive uses, which even affect protected natural spaces.

The obsolete urban planning of municipal scale is incapable of ordering the rurban peripheries that already surpass the municipal limits [14]. We must resort to supramunicipal planning to solve this problem of management, since the periphery is a fragmented and confused space [15].

2. Materials and Methods

2.1. Study the Hidden Side

Facing the study of an urban phenomenon traditionally ignored, when not hidden, concerns a series of difficulties added to those inherent in any scientific research work. The problems increase when the agencies responsible for giving up the necessary information are potentially responsible (sometimes at a criminal level) for the propagation of the phenomenon studied and its conversion into a problem. Administrative neglect in Extremadura is expressed in the real magnitude of the phenomenon, through the anecdotal publications of an informative manual on the constructions in UL (Figure 2) and a report of these publications, whose results, although barely approximating reality, were also destined to oblivion. This last document, entitled "Study on the subdivisions, urbanizations and buildings outside the urban and urbanized perimeters. Extremadura and Évora," is a basic and original dissertation published in the dawn of the validity of the current urban norm [16]. This work was partially funded by the Urban and Territorial Planning Department of the regional government, together with a Portuguese association of the same level, within the framework of cross-border relations of regional and local governments, Spanish and Portuguese.

The comparison between the results of the research carried out here and that carried out by the Public Administrations reinforces our position of maintaining uncertainty about the veracity of the data provided by official sources. The global computation performed (10,149 homes) does not represent even a third of those recorded by our research at that time.

The research objectives are the location, quantification, and dating of each residential building on UL, in addition to the control of possible constructive changes in terms of surface. Accordingly, there is an information gap on the part of the Local and Regional Administration; at the same time, there is a cadastral database full of errors and omissions. This database is currently being reviewed by the Department of Cadastre in the municipalities of Extremadura, within the framework of the cadastral regularization promoted by the Ministry of Finance. However, it is still an incomplete and useless process for the resolution of the problem by the Administrations, due to the lack of cooperation and exchange of data between them.

Once the availability of a reliable and accurate cartography was ruled out, the only viable alternative was the construction of an own database from scratch. To achieve the proposed goal, different methods and materials were used.

Figure 2. Cover of the informative manual on the constructions in Undevelopable Land (UL).

2.2. Sources and Processes to Reveal the Secrecy

The Territorial Information System of Extremadura (SITEX, Spanish acronym) is the regional and centralized repository of all current urban and territorial planning documents. Without the existence of this source, the collection of normative and planimetric information would have been chimerical since it would depend on an application for each municipality (388) and different response periods. Despite the advantage offered by this source, the status and characteristics of the documents make it difficult to transpose them into the Geographic Information Systems that will help us to practice spatial analysis. Because of the outdated state of planning, many documents are between 20 and 30 years old. The repository contains scans of originals and photocopies in PDF format, which means a necessary subsequent conversion to new formats to geo-reference and digitize them.

Once this process is completed, we have a vector layer with shapefile format and polygon topology on the urban classification and categorization of land throughout Extremadura. This means that we have precisely defined our study area: UL.

Along with this, analyses compared with other cartography, such as the sectorial one, allow us to notice discrepancies between the current classification of land and what should be by legal mandate. These examples are especially serious in the case of the existence of natural risks such as flood risks (Figure 3).

The essential and main source within the building section is the National Geographic Information Center (CNIG, Spanish acronym). This free container of spatial information provides the necessary cartographic base to locate and quantify the phenomenon. The material used is the Aerial Orthophotography Series of the National Aerial Orthophotography Plan (PNOA, Spanish acronym), particularly the most current available ones.

The detection was carried out by sweeps (a maximum scale of 1:1500) of the entire regional territory, which made it possible to discover all existing buildings on the UL of Extremadura. It is a vector layer in shapefile format, with topology of polygons, which allows the very approximate knowledge of the surface area of all buildings (mostly, the residential construction in UL is led by single-storey homes).

This methodological phase is followed by one in which buildings are distinguished by uses. Because the theme studied is related to the residential function, four possible categories have been included: housing, possible housing, auxiliary buildings for housing, and others. To achieve this, a triple path has been followed. First, the orthophoto contains a series of informants for residential use, among which is the image of the building roof but also the adjacent space (landscaped areas, road network, enclosures, swimming pools, sports courts, etc.). Secondly, Google Earth images have been used, which in certain contexts have higher resolution than those belonging to the PNOA Series. The Google Street View and 3D modeling tools, available in its Google Maps portal and Google Earth software, also allow for the determination of the elevation and facade of the buildings. This is, in many cases, defining to discriminate the use of construction. For third and last place, in those cases where uncertainties persisted, it has been decided to determine their use through fieldwork. Despite these various paths, the category "possible housing" denotes that there are some cases in which it is impossible to reliably determine its residential use (hiding behind vegetation, buildings on very large plots, distanced from boundaries and access denied, lack of clear informers, etc.). As a prudential measure, it has been decided to register these cases but exclude them from the subsequent analysis.

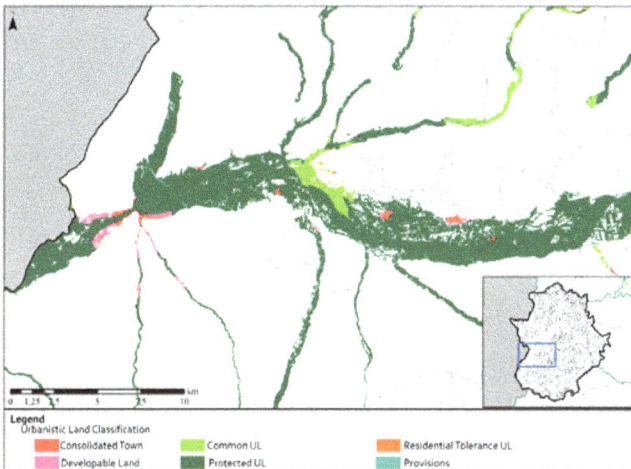

Figure 3. Urban classification of flood zones.

Once the number of houses and their location (cross-analysis with the cartography created on classification and urban categorization) were determined, their appearance and the characteristics of their persistence in the territory were dated. For this, Web Map Servers available in the Spatial Data Infrastructure of Extremadura (IDEEX, Spanish acronym) were used to determine control points, depending on the series of aerial photography and orthophotography available. Finally, 6 control points were established (Figure 4):

- Interministerial Sweep (1973–1986) [1° control point]: This helped to determine the starting situation, dated in Extremadura around the year 1981 (dawn of the democratic period).

- Ministerial Sweep (1980–1986): This is a register of the first urban growths in democracy and within a decentralized Spanish State.
- SIG "Oleícola" Sweep (1998): Initially, this flight was designed to quantify the number of olive trees and the extension of this type of crops. Its wide spatial coverage and date of taking the photographs served to discern what the urban growth was prior to the state land law of 1998.
- "SIGPAC" Sweep (2002): This was used to determine the urban growth before and after the regional planning law, although the main and general purpose of this flight is the identification of agricultural parcels that are beneficiaries of the Common Agricultural Policy (PAC, in Spanish acronym).
- PNOA Serie (2005–2006): This was used to determine urban growth until the end of the housing bubble in Spain.
- PNOA Serie (2012–2014) [6° control point]: This is an approach to the most current state of the residential expansion on the UL of Extremadura.

Figure 4. Mosaic of used sweeps.

This material was used to measure rurban phenomenon evolution. The buildings were dated by means of an encoding process that contemplated the non-existence of the building at each control point (corresponding to a value of 0) and its existence (a value of 1). In addition, when the building lost more than 50% of the area recorded in the last control point, PNOA Serie 2012–2013, the event was identified with another value (a value of 5 appeared in the data table). The assignment of figures is a simple coding process and does not imply a posteriori calculation on these numerical values.

After dating the residential buildings, we proceeded to define their legal status. For this, we used the Urban Qualification Records (UQRs) and the only possible source, the regional government. The UQRs are the previous and indispensable authorization for building on the UL of Extremadura. Luckily, these are in a vector and geo-referenced format, although with duplications and errors that have been fixed. A simple analysis of spatial concomitance between these and the database created allowed us to approach the legal status of the dwellings. However, all this information offered a finite level of detail. This is because the regional database only covers the years of validity of the regional law (2002–present), the previous years remaining under local competition and whose data is not covered by centralized databases. On the other hand, it is also necessary to point out that, although the files are typified by uses, it is impossible to contrast the building reality with what is specifically allowed (heights, materials, dimensions of the construction, etc.) since the content thereof is not accessible. Even when an UQR authorizes a home, this does not mean that the rest of the subsequent and necessary procedures have been fulfilled (such as the request and the fulfillment of the urban planning license, still in the hands of the municipal corporations).

Another source of fundamental information is the press, the pulse of the social relevance of the phenomenon, consolidating itself as an indicator. Analysis of the regional press in a region like Extremadura, far from the national media focuses, elucidates their daily life. For the particular monitoring of the rurbanization (only in the arena when it has an irregular status), it is necessary to consult the two most important newspapers, "Diario Hoy Extremadura" and "El Periódico Extremadura", both belonging to the written press, but with digital editions. The search process during the research period (2012–2017) has been daily, resulting in an uninterrupted media impact during all months recorded (72). This translates into about 700 news stories related specifically to illegal urban development developed on UL. This data reveals that this phenomenon within Extremadura is still very active.

The study through the press also allows us to position the media impact on a map, quantifying and locating not only the specific issues addressed (housing complaints, demolitions, political derivations, etc.) but also the media impact according to the affected municipalities. In addition to its function as a source, the press serves as a vehicle for the transfer of research results. In this sense, a symbiotic relationship that benefits the research is not only known by the scientific community but by the parts of society that are affected by the problem (Figure 5).

Figure 5. Public impact of the study on a newspaper cover.

Treating a problem that concerns laws and urban discipline inevitably leads to recourse to competent agencies in these matters. In this way, the Nature Protection service of the Spanish military police (called SEPRONA) can constitute another source of data. This information will help us not just to discover the phenomenon but also to determine the methodology used in the fight against crimes in territorial and urban planning. In response to the data received, the action of this agency, in spite of relatively effective agencies (Agents of the Natural Environment, National Police, municipal surveillance teams and rural guards, etc.), is very far from the true magnitude of the phenomenon. The spatial analysis of the denunciations reveals, moreover, that their productivity depends more on the close existence of dependencies of the Spanish military police than on the very magnitude of the rurban phenomenon. Last and most worrying is the fact that, within the methodology used for the detection of housing on UL, chance comes into play as a variable of great weight. This is because the localization procedures are carried out in situ, through physical patrols, and without an editable and centralized registry. This procedure makes repetitions, failures, and omissions feasible, reducing their effectiveness and triggering the costs of surveillance.

For a full knowledge of the problem, the methodological process requires in addition to the information provided by the Delegate Office of the Environment and Urbanism. Thus, interviews and personal encounters with those responsible for such an organization are essential to explore the criminal aspect of this urban and territorial phenomenon.

This same procedure has been used to determine municipal work and perceptions of the phenomenon. In the present case, almost a hundred online surveys were carried out on municipal officials, which means that almost a quarter of the localities responded. This value must be put in context, as the subject is considered by municipal officials to be taboo in light of the legal and criminal consequences, which makes the answers difficult.

3. Results

The application of the methodological process led to the detection of almost 40,000 houses on the UL of Extremadura, with a distribution very unbalanced in the quantitative level but very distributed in spatial terms. In fact, only two municipalities of the 388 that compound Extremadura are free of housing on the UL, according to the last control point used (Figure 6).

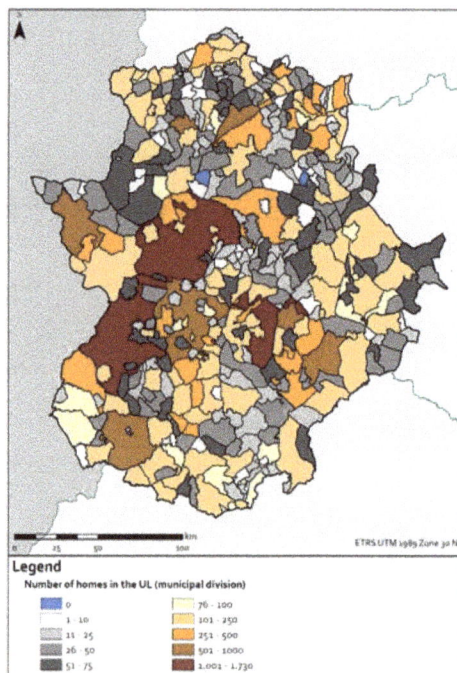

Figure 6. Number of homes on UL (municipal division).

The unequal distribution is due to the influence that certain factors have on the territory. The first and main factor is the urban irradiation that the urban centers of Extremadura generate. In a much lower magnitude, but with equally worrying results, the presence of population centers determines the near existence of scattered housing. The peripheral spaces of these nodes are colonized by residential construction, regardless of whether they belong to the rural environment.

In the same way, the communication routes are fundamental, since their close presence increases the enclaves' level of accessibility. This factor, combined with the previous one, determines a greater or lesser colonization of the urban peripheries.

The environmental and landscape aspect is very relevant when measuring the real estate attractiveness of the land. Setting only the analysis in the official delimitation of Protected Natural Spaces, the present investigation revealed the existence of more than 5300 houses within its limits. These houses represent a serious threat not only for the territorial organization but also for the environmental values of the region.

In a still more worrying stage are those homes at risk of suffering a natural catastrophe. If we use the risk cartography available to Public Administrations and combine it with the database created, we can assure that there are more than 1500 homes in the area at risk of being flooded (350 residences built in the areas of shorter recurrence time, 10 years) and more than 15,000 homes in fire risk zones (around 13,000 residential buildings in the High Risk Areas).

The relevance of the phenomenon has promoted actions aimed at regularizing housing, such as the integration of entire groups (made up of hundreds of residences) in isolated sectors of Developable Land.

Although the Extremadura law indicates that this simple demarcation operation is not enough (since it requires starting specific regularization processes), this serves to silence criticisms and hide, at least partially (Figure 7), the presence of housing for our methodology.

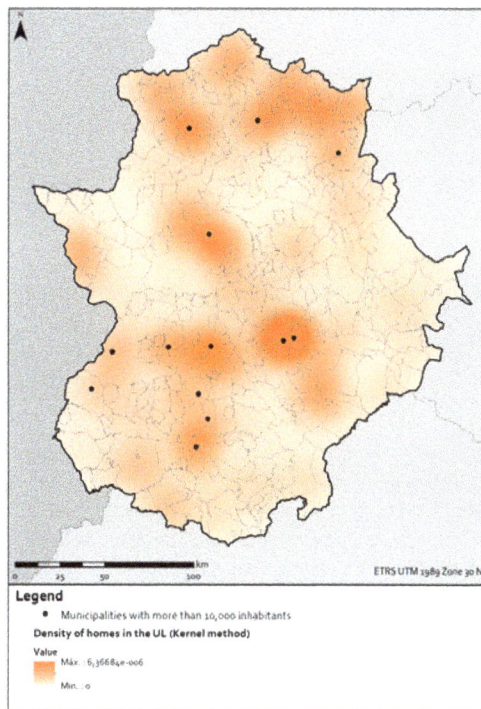

Figure 7. Density of homes on UL.

This is the case of Badajoz, which is the municipality that has the greatest and most prominent rurban development in the region, although it ranks third in terms of the number of homes on UL.

The dating of the houses (Figure 8) helps us to understand the proliferation of residences on UL as a progressive phenomenon, dependent on economic cycles. Although the construction of houses in the first control point represented almost a third of the existing ones, their formal and constructive characteristics ("cortijos" and large houses) indicate that they were residences linked to an agricultural use or, as recreational housing, belonged to middle-upper and upper classes.

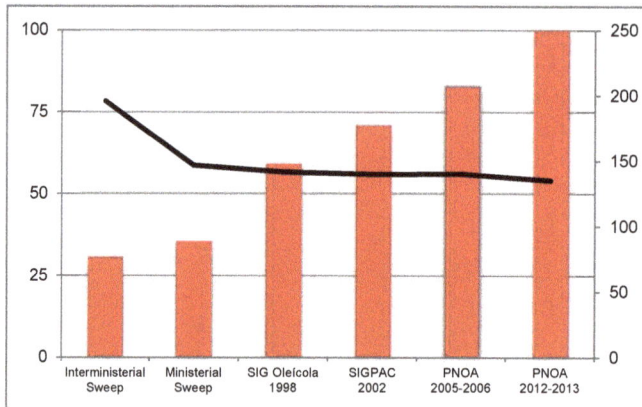

Figure 8. Evolution of rurban development in Extremadura. The percentage of the total number of homes built on UL (bars) and average area (m^2) of homes (lines).

Over time and socio-economic progress, the phenomenon became more transversal, which reduced the average size of the houses and densified certain spaces, such as the peripheries to settlements. In these environments, the rustic smallholding of atomized property was replaced by secondary homes.

The influence of certain flexibilizing legislation, such as the 1998 land law, led not only to the increase in real estate activity in Urban and Developable Land, but also to UL. In just four years, the number of homes on UL grew by around 4500. Consequently, the prodigious decade of Spanish urbanism reported to Extremadura an increase of 10,000 homes on UL.

Finally, looking exclusively at the legal aspect of the matter, data on UQRs place the maximum threshold of legally constructed homes since 2002 at 760. This figure is substantially below the total number of residences built in this class of land, which demonstrates the eminent irregular nature of the rurbanization, despite the continued flexibility of the regulations and urban planning.

4. Discussion

Given the important magnitude and actuality of the rurban phenomenon in Extremadura, the certainty of being able to practice urban geography outside the cities, and even its opportunity and usefulness, is reaffirmed. Having overcome the monopoly and prominence of architects and road engineers in urban planning [17], this work aims to reaffirm our role as geographers in the study of a process that concerns the territory and people. The importance of the study of urban expansion in rural areas, substantially the deepest and most peripheral, is dispelled by the inability or impossibility of finding concrete urban landmarks (already re-signified as icons), which provide research with attractiveness and remarkableness.

The particular legal aspect of the rurbanization in Extremadura (an antithetical example of the urban discipline) and the scarce administrative and academic attention confirm the need for an independent geographical study, not only in its approach and elaboration but also with respect to the sources that build the database.

The only attention comes from media (consequence of the possible criminal repercussions for the political class and very dependent on the potential repercussion in supramunicipal spheres), although this only has the function of alerting others of the phenomenon, without proposing solutions. In fact, the recurrent appearance of related news does not even encourage resolute action, since the published cases affect the municipal sphere, which prevents understanding of the situation in its true dimension, the regional one.

This last point is what triggers the study carried out from urban geography, since the knowledge and analysis of the event has no significance if it is not accompanied by urban and territorial reorganization.

In the face of a consensual clandestine development, it is only possible to carry out a scientific study that is separate from the collection of official information and focuses on the collection and production of own data, taking official data into account or potentially constituting a new point of reference.

5. Conclusions

The irregular rurban expansion is the main urban and territorial problem of the region. The almost 40,000 homes built on the UL of Extremadura, most of which are illegally implemented, are a tangible and living reality that will be maintained over time (at least in its current magnitude), by the prescription of a large part of the infractions and crimes.

In addition, this phenomenon affects the region as a whole vector (only two municipalities of the 388 that compound Extremadura do not have housing on UL) that should encourage decision making in this regard.

Extremadura needs a new territorial scheme that conditions urban regulation. This is only possible through the promulgation of a new regional land law and the implementation of a better control system of urban discipline.

This vigilance is fundamental to stop an illegal and clandestine urban development that expands by contagion and reaches highly relevant values in peripheral zones of the "big" cities in Extremadura. Urban irradiation of the cities generates these results in their UL and in the neighboring rural municipalities, which act as dormitory settlements.

Obviating this fact again implies allowing the validity of the norm and planning to be questioned. These are the mechanisms that will later serve to justify theoretically and politically the deregulation and flexibilization of UL, which for decades has been practiced in Spain and other countries.

The legal mandate to maintain urban discipline fails, in the first place, due to administrative inaction (caused by a combination of factors, including the Administration's lack of interest, the political yield of permissiveness, and the negative electoral consequences of the persecution of illegality and citizen pressure) and to the methodological deficiencies of the agencies responsible for ensuring this respect (SEPRONA, Local Police, Natural Environment Agents, etc.).

Due to this, Extremadura must face the creation and application of a Regional Plan for Management and Control of Rurban Development. This plan has to have a centralized technical management (not political), which contains both legalization and demolition programs. Only in this way will it be possible to erect a point of inflection that will redirect and reorganize the most important type of urban development in the regional present.

Author Contributions: V.J. and A.-J.C. developed the conceptualization and the topic; V.J. set up the methods; V.J. and A.-J.C. wrote the paper; A.-J.C. supervised the original draft and analyzed the data.

Funding: This research was funded by FPU pre-doctoral research grant of Ministry of Science, Innovation and Universities (Spanish Government), grant number FPU13/00990.

Acknowledgments: We want to thank the work of the Urban Geography Group of the Association of Spanish Geographers (AGE) for the dissemination and internationalization of this discipline.

Conflicts of Interest: The authors declare no conflict of interest. The funders had no role in the design of the study; in the collection, analyses, or interpretation of data; in the writing of the manuscript; or in the decision to publish the results.

References

1. Mattson, K. Una Introducción a la Geografía Radical. *GEOcrítica* **1978**, *13*. Available online: http://www.ub. edu/geocrit/geo13.htm (accessed on 21 February 2018).
2. Galpin, C.J. *Rural Life*, 1st ed.; The Century Co.: New York, NY, USA, 1918.
3. Bauer, G.; Roux, J.-M. *La Rurbanisation ou la Ville Éparpillée*, 1st ed.; Editions du Seuil: Paris, France, 1976; pp. 1–192.
4. Rullán, O. Economía y sostenibilidad de las ciudades: Entre la desregulación y la planificación. In *La Ciudad: Nuevos Procesos, Nuevas Respuestas*, 1st ed.; López, L., Relea, C.E., Somoza, J., Eds.; Biblioteca Virtual Miguel de Cervantes: Alicante, Spain, 2003; Volume 1, pp. 151–168.
5. Jiménez, V.; Delgado, C.; Campesino, A.J. Desregulación urbanística del suelo rústico en España. Cantabria y Extremadura como casos de estudio. *Revista Geografía Norte Grande* **2017**, *67*, 73–92. [CrossRef]
6. Jiménez, V.; Hidalgo, R.; Campesino, A.J.; Alvarado, V. Normalización del modelo neoliberal de expansión residencial más allá del límite urbano en Chile y España. *EURE* **2018**, *132*, 27–46. [CrossRef]
7. Delgado, C. Vivienda secundaria y turismo residencial como agentes de urbanización y segregación territorial en Cantabria. *Scr. Nova* **2008**, *269*, 256–280.
8. Prados, M.J. Naturbanización y patrones urbanos en los parques nacionales de Andalucía. *Boletín Asociación Geógrafos Españoles* **2012**, *60*, 19–44.
9. Biegańska, J.; Środa-Murawska, S.; Kruzmetra, Z.; Swiaczny, F. Peri-urban development as a significant rural development trend. *Quaest. Geogr.* **2018**, *37*, 125–140. [CrossRef]
10. Adamiak, C.; Pitkanen, K.; Lehtonen, O. Seasonal residence and counterurbanization: The role of second homes in population redistribution in Finland. *GeoJournal* **2017**, *82*, 1035–1050. [CrossRef]
11. Barbati, A.; Corona, P.; Salvati, L.; Gasparella, L. Natural forest expansion into suburban countryside: Gained ground for a green infrastructure? *Urban For. Urban Green.* **2013**, *12*, 36–43. [CrossRef]
12. De Biase, C.; Losco, S. Up-grading Illegal Building Settlements: An Urban-Planning Methodology. *Procedia Environ. Sci.* **2017**, *37*, 454–465. [CrossRef]
13. Junta de Extremadura. *Estudio Territorial de Extremadura I*; Junta de Extremadura: Mérida, Spain, 1992.
14. Campesino, A.J. Centros y periferias urbanas: Ordenación y desgobierno. In *Reflexiones Sobre las Ciudades y el Sistema Urbano en Tiempos de Crisis*, 1st ed.; Lois, R.C., Miramontes, Á., Eds.; Universidad de Santiago de Compostela, Grupo de Geografía Urbana (AGE): Santiago de Compostela, Spain, 2014; Volume 1, pp. 91–117.
15. Feria, J.M. Nuevas periferias urbanas y planificación pública. In *La Ciudad. Tamaño y Crecimiento*, 1st ed.; Domínguez, R., Ed.; Universidad de Málaga, Grupo de Geografía Urbana (AGE): Málaga, Spain, 1999; Volume 1, pp. 309–316.
16. Junta de Extremadura. *Estudio Sobre las Parcelaciones, Urbanizaciones y Edificaciones Exteriores a los Perímetros Urbanos y Urbanizables*; Junta de Extremadura: Mérida, Spain, 2004.
17. Campesino, A.J. El geógrafo en el planeamiento urbano: Avatares de una conquista profesional. *Boletín Asociación Geógrafos Españoles* **1985**, *2*, 24–35.

MDPI

St. Alban-Anlage 66

4052 Basel

Switzerland

Tel. +41 61 683 77 34

Fax +41 61 302 89 18

www.mdpi.com

Urban Science Editorial Office

E-mail: urbansci@mdpi.com

www.mdpi.com/journal/urbansci

www.ingramcontent.com/pod-product-compliance
Lightning Source LLC
Chambersburg PA
CBHW051314020426
42333CB00028B/3330